The System-Wide Approach to

Microeconomics

The System-Wide Approach to

Microeconomics

Henri Theil

The University of Chicago Press

The University of Chicago Press, Chicago 60637
Basil Blackwell, Oxford
© 1980 by The University of Chicago
All rights reserved. Published 1980
Printed in the United States of America
84 83 82 81 80   5 4 3 2 1

HENRI THEIL is university professor in the
Department of Economics and the Graduate
School of Business at the University of
Chicago, where he is also director of the
Center for Mathematical Studies in Business
and Economics. He has written ten other
books on economic theory and econometrics.
His work has been translated into Spanish,
German, Japanese, Italian, Russian, and
Dutch.

Library of Congress Cataloging in Publication Data

Theil, Henri.
   The system-wide approach to microeconomics.

   Bibliography: p.
   Includes index.
   1. Microeconomics. 2. Consumption (Economics)
I. Title.
HB171.5.T26   338.5   78-31999
ISBN 0-226-79437-7

Contents

Preface

Since the mid-1960s there has been considerable research activity in the area of systems of consumer demand equations. Two review articles have been published, the first by Britain's Alan Brown and Angus Deaton in the *Economic Journal* of 1972, the second by Anton Barten of the University of Louvain in *Econometrica* of 1977. The research has been truly international in scope. The first book-length publication was *Théorie des choix et fonctions de consommation semi-agrégées* by Luigi Solari of the University of Geneva, which came out in 1971. In 1974 Australia's Alan Powell published his *Empirical Analytics of Demand Systems*, and Louis Phlips of the University of Louvain his *Applied Consumption Analysis*. These books were followed in the next two years by *Models and Projections of Demand in Post-War Britain* by Angus Deaton, who is now at the University of Bristol, *Private and Enlarged Consumption* edited by L. Solari and J.-N. Du Pasquier, and the two volumes of my *Theory and Measurement of Consumer Demand*. A Spanish-Australian triumvirate consisting of Constantino Lluch, Alan Powell, and Ross Williams published *Patterns in Household Demand and Saving* in 1977.

This rapid development has at least three causes. First, there are now data for many more countries than used to be the case. This feature was particularly exploited by Lluch, Powell, and Williams in their book. Second, recent computational advances in nonlinear estimation have contributed substantially to the implementation of nonlinear demand systems. Third, the analysis of consumer demand is of great importance, which is summarized in the Brown-Deaton survey article in an admirably succinct way: "Consumer's expenditure is the largest item in the gross domestic product of most economies and thus the usefulness of disaggregated planning or prediction is likely to depend on its correct allocation. The changing structure of industry over time depends crucially on the evolution of the elements of consumer's expenditure in response to increasing income, while knowledge of price responses is an important element in the formulation of fiscal policy or any other type of economic control" (p. 1150).

The importance of the analysis of consumer households is further increased when the demand for consumer goods is extended so that it includes the demand for leisure. The reason is that a demand function for leisure is equivalent to a supply function of labor. This subject is pursued in the forthcoming book, *Consumer Demand and Labor Supply*, by William Barnett of the Federal Reserve Board in Washington, D.C. There have also been parallel developments in the theory of the firm. Although it has been known for a long time that the theories of the consumer and the firm have much in common, this parallelism has increased in recent years due to the increased importance of duality theory. One of the results is that systems of input demand equations and of output supply equations have joined the company of the systems of demand equations of the consumer.

It is true that many approaches in this general area are still in the experimental stage and require more pilot studies. But numerical evidence is accumulating fast. Being an optimist, I expect practical applications in a near future. For example, proposals have been made to give federal subsidies to students attending American colleges. How will this affect the attendance of high-tuition private colleges relative to that of low-tuition public colleges? A natural approach to this problem consists of the construction of conditional demand equations for private and public higher education under the assumption that higher education is separable from other goods and services in the consumer's utility function.

Such conditional demand equations are of particular importance. One of the misunderstandings with respect to consumer demand systems is that they can be used for broad aggregates only. This is not correct. Under appropriate separability assumptions it is possible to formulate such systems at two (or more) levels. One level consists of a system of composite demand equations for groups of goods; the next level consists of several subsystems, each of which is a conditional demand system for goods within a group. Of course, such a hierarchy of demand equations raises the question of whether the disturbances in these equations are correlated; this is one of the problems that are considered at some length in this book (see chapters 7 to 9). The last section of chapter 12 considers a detailed analysis of flows among narrowly defined goods and should be viewed as an attempt to dispel the idea that systems of demand equations are good for broad aggregates only.

The Organization of This Book

The objective of this book is to present an overview of certain recent developments in the theory of the consumer and the firm, and to illustrate this theory with applications to statistical data. In order to prevent the book from becoming too lengthy, several topics have been omitted or are discussed very briefly. Such topics are dynamic extensions, problems of general equilibrium, the theory and measurement of technical change, and computational problems. Proofs of several theorems are given in the text in outline form only and in the Appendix in more detail; this arrangement should serve to make this fast-growing area more accessible. I hope that this book will be useful for courses in microeconomic theory, applied economics, and econometrics.

The book is particularly addressed to the application-oriented reader. I want to advise him to skip chapter 5 on the multiproduct firm in a first reading. If he follows this advice, he should also skip chapter 6 as well as the last three sections of chapter 8 and the last two of chapter 9 (sections 8.5 to 8.7 and 9.6 and 9.7). Then, having read chapter 10 and section 11.1, he should move to chapter 13. This path will enable him to get much faster to the empirical results discussed in sections 8.3, 9.4, and 11.1, and several sections of chapter 13. The path emphasizes the consumer; its treatment of the firm is largely confined to the demand side of the single-product firm. Having completed chapter 13, the reader should return to chapter 5, followed by chapter 6 and the sections which he skipped in chapters 8, 9, and 11, after which he completes the book by reading chapters 12, 14, and 15. This second path will (I hope) provide him with considerable additional insight into the theory of the firm and its relationship to consumption theory.

Although the organization of the book allows the quick path to empirical results described in the previous paragraph, its fifteen successive chapters are in "logical" order. The only exceptions are chapters 7 and 8 on the decision distributions which result from the theory of rational random behavior. This theory is much more general because its decision-maker need not be a consumer or a firm. I have made a special effort to write chapter 7 and the first two sections of chapter 8 in such a way that they can be read independently by those who feel that their expertise in the theories of the consumer and the firm is limited or nonexistent. Such a reader may want to skip the application to the linear expenditure system in section 7.4; alternatively, he can read section 2.1 and the first two paragraphs of section 2.2, which is a very modest investment.

Several approaches are explained and illustrated in this book, but the exposition emphasizes the differential approach, which has considerable merit as a unifying tool in the theories of the consumer and the firm. This approach includes, as an early forerunner in the 1920s, Divisia's work on index numbers in differential form. Among later contributions prior to 1960 I should mention Gorman's work on separable utility and Ragnar Frisch's article in the 1959 issue of *Econometrica*. It is well known that Frisch introduced "want independence" in this article, but it is apparently less well known that he also considered weaker independence assumptions.

There is considerable confusion about the differential approach in the literature, particularly with respect to the issue of the constancy of coefficients. I have tried to resolve this problem by making a careful distinction between the differential approach as a general tool of economic analysis, which makes no assumptions about constancy of coefficients, and particular parametrizations which use the results of this approach. The so-called Rotterdam model is among these parametrizations. This model has been criticized because integrability conditions allegedly restrict its use, but recent results obtained by Barnett have shown that the application of this model to aggregate (per capita) data does not require conditions such as aggregate integrability. These and related issues are discussed in sections 14.3 and 14.4.

Acknowledgments

This book has gone through several drafts which I used in my classes. The reactions of my students resulted in many improvements, for which I am grateful. I also want to express my appreciation to six people who provided detailed comments on the penultimate draft: Kenneth Clements (now at the Reserve Bank of Australia, Sydney), Angus Deaton of the University of Bristol, Georg Hasenkamp of the University of Bonn, Leif Johansen of the University of Oslo, Kenneth Laitinen, and J. I. Vorst of the University of Manitoba. I followed many of their suggestions, but none should be held responsible for whatever imperfections remain.

Finally, it gives me pleasure to thank my secretary, Ms. Joanne Schlichter, for her careful checking of the proofs, and the National Science Foundation for a series of grants which facilitated my research.

Chicago, June 1979   Henri Theil

One

Introduction

The theory and measurement of demand are both more than one hundred years old. Measurement based on household data gave rise to Engel's laws [126], which were reviewed by Houthakker [193] about twenty years ago, a century after these laws were first formulated. The theory dates back, at least, to Cournot [92], Dupuit [122], and Gossen [163] in the period from the late 1830s to the early 1850s. However, the influence of these three authors was very modest at that time. This changed when Jevons [201], Menger [274], and Walras [426] published their work on utility theory in the 1870s. Since that time developments have continued; I should mention Edgeworth [124], Fisher [134], Marshall [267], Pareto [299], Slutsky [363], and—in the 1930s and 1940s—Hicks and Allen [184], Samuelson [341], and Wold [430]. Much of the theoretical work of these authors was directed toward weaker assumptions. In the last twenty years, however, there has been a move toward greater specificity rather than greater generality. This new development is largely the result of the emergence of the *system-wide approach* to demand analysis. My first objective is to explain what this approach involves.

1.1 Ordinal Utility Theory

A convenient starting point is the consensus (or near-consensus) on consumer demand theory which emerged in the mid-1930s with the work of Hicks and Allen. This theory assumes that the consumer has a fixed amount of income available for spending, and that he can buy n goods and services at fixed prices. Hence there is a budget constraint on the n quantities which the consumer can buy. To determine the quantities that are actually bought we assume that the consumer has certain preferences which can be represented by a utility function. The quantities bought are obtained by maximizing this function subject to the budget constraint, which yields (under appropriate conditions) a unique demand function for each good. Each such function describes the demand for a good in terms of the consumer's income and the prices of all goods. In particular, a price change has an effect on the demand for each good that can be divided into two parts: an income effect, which reflects the fact that a price increase reduces real income, and a substitution effect. One of the interesting results of this theory, known as Slutsky symmetry, is that the substitution effects are symmetric: the effect of a small increase in the price of good *A* on the demand for good *B* is the same as that of a numerically equal increase in the price of *B* on the demand for *A*, where it is to be understood that we confine ourselves to substitution effects by providing appropriate income compensations so as to eliminate the income effects of the two price changes.

An important consideration, which has been emphasized particularly since the 1930s, is that the utility function to be maximized represents only a preference ordering. This means that utility is viewed as an "ordinal" concept in the sense that the consumer is supposed to be able to *rank* different sets of quantities according to decreasing preference; it is not assumed that the consumer is able to state that one set of quantities is, say, twice as good as another set. The mathematical implication is that the demand equations which result from maximizing a utility function subject to a budget constraint are invariant under monotone increasing transformations of this function.

1.2   Theory of the Firm

There is a theory of the firm which is quite similar to that of the consumer. Let this firm make one product, for which it uses *n* inputs (or production factors) that are available at fixed prices. The firm's technology is described by a production function which expresses the maximum output that can be obtained from any given set of inputs. One important problem is that of minimizing the total expenditure on all inputs, given a certain output and certain input prices. This minimization yields the cost function which describes the smallest amount of input expenditure needed to produce a given rate of output at given input prices. The consumer also has a cost function; it describes the smallest amount of expenditure needed to attain a given utility level at given prices of all consumer goods. This similarity of the theories of the firm and the consumer has been given greater emphasis in more recent theoretical contributions because of the increased awareness of the applicability of duality theory to both areas. The consumer's cost function plays an important role in the formulation of cost-of-living indexes (see chapter 3).

Minimizing total input expenditure for given output and given input prices yields (under appropriate conditions) a demand equation for each input which describes this demand in terms of output and the input prices. As in the consumer's case, such equations are characterized by Slutsky symmetry: given fixed output, the effect of a small increase in the price of input A on the demand for input B is the same as that of a numerically equal increase in the price of B on the demand for A. The consumer's income compensations needed to keep real income constant correspond here to the assumption that the firm's output remains constant.

If the objective is extended from cost minimization to profit maximization for a given price of the product, we obtain under appropriate conditions a supply equation for the product. This equation expresses supply in terms of the output price and the input prices. When the firm makes several products, profit maximization yields a supply equation for each.

1.3   Critics of the Ordinal Approach

The ordinal approach to utility theory was mentioned at the end of section 1.1. This approach has not always been accepted. In fact, in earlier years this was probably not much of an issue at all. Samuelson writes [341, p. 206], "To a man like Edgeworth, steeped as he was in the Utilitarian tradition, individual utility—nay, social utility—was as real as his morning jam." The idea that utility was something mysterious came later.

An important development was the introduction of a cardinal utility concept by Von Neumann and Morgenstern [294]. They considered the problem of choice among *uncertain* prospects, and formulated axioms under which a person behaves as if he maximizes expected utility.[1] This utility function is well defined when a zero and a unit of measurement of utility have been selected. The invariance under monotone increasing transformations of the utility function is then reduced to invariance under increasing linear transformations. The expected-utility approach has been widely used in many areas ever since it was formulated in the mid-1940s.

Note that this approach involves problems of uncertainty. It is not difficult to argue that one type of utility measurement (that of the ordinal theory) may apply to certainty and another type (that of Von Neumann and Morgenstern) to uncertainty. However, there are those who are not satisfied with the purely ordinal approach even under conditions of certainty. Is it not plausible, such people might argue, that the marginal utility of a good declines when its consumption increases? But a declining marginal utility is a property which is not invariant under monotone increasing transformations of the utility function; hence, if we use this property, our utility concept ceases to be ordinal. The most prominent advocate of the nonordinal approach from the early 1930s onward was

1. For an alternative and more appealing set of axioms see Marschak [265].

Ragnar Frisch [142, 144], who argued that ordinal utility theory provides insufficient guidance for applied demand analysis. Similar ideas had been expressed by Irving Fisher (see Fellner [129]) and Pigou (see Deaton [100]), but these two authors were not as influential as Frisch.

1.4   The System-Wide Approach

The need for more guidance is particularly great when the number of goods is not very small. This problem is concealed in the usual elementary textbook treatment because indifference curves refer to only two dimensions. Also, the earlier empirical applications considered demand equations one by one, in which case Slutsky symmetry is not an issue. This symmetry does play a role when we consider two demand equations simultaneously. For example, if these two equations describe the demand for butter and for margarine in terms of real income and the prices of butter and margarine (and possibly other prices), Slutsky symmetry implies a constraint on the coefficient of the price of butter in the margarine equation and the coefficient of the margarine price in the butter equation. As we shall shortly see, the number of such constraints rises rapidly when there are more than two equations. This is bound to occur when we consider the demand for milk, cheese, and eggs in addition to that for butter and margarine.

The system-wide approach to microeconomics emphasizes equation systems rather than separate equations: a system of consumer demand equations (one for each consumer good), a system of input demand equations of a firm (one for each input), and a system of output supply equations of a multiproduct firm (one for each product). Considering demand equations in particular, one of the problems which we must face is that the number of Slutsky symmetry relations increases almost proportionately to the square of the number of goods. Testing for Slutsky symmetry is not a matter of testing each symmetry relation individually; all these relations must be considered simultaneously. In earlier years this presented almost insurmountable problems; we should have great respect for Henry Schultz's efforts [357] in this area, given the limited means available in the 1930s. Today we have greatly improved methods of statistical inference as well as fast computers, which provide an incentive to go much further. We also have more and (hopefully) better data, but progress in this respect is much less spectacular. The latter feature is one major limitation.

Another major limitation is this: Although the number of Slutsky symmetry relations increases quickly when we proceed to systems consisting of more demand equations, the number of unconstrained coefficients which remain when Slutsky symmetry is imposed increases even more quickly. This leads to a degrees-of-freedom problem, since these coefficients must all be estimated simultaneously. To solve this problem we need more restrictions than just Slutsky symmetry. It is therefore appropriate that we return to our starting point: that of maximizing a utility function subject to a budget constraint. Since the budget constraint provides no opportunity to structure the problem, we must impose special conditions on the utility function. One of the first versions (which is still rather popular) postulates that the utility function is the sum of n functions, one for each good, which implies that the marginal utility of each good is independent of the quantities consumed of all other goods (see eq. [2.3] in chap. 2).

Let me emphasize that this additive utility specification is the simplest approach that has been suggested, and that it does not appear to be realistic when confronted with statistical data. Nevertheless, it is interesting to note that this specification goes all the way back to Gossen, in the 1850s, who also postulated additivity and who was, of course, severely criticized for doing so by later generations of theoreticians. It is also interesting to compare this new development with the position chosen by Gustav Cassel [79], who was dissatisfied with the results of utility theory and proposed that demand equations be formulated directly, without utility considerations. This would eliminate Slutsky symmetry. The proponents of the system-wide approach are also dissatisfied, but they certainly do not want to eliminate Slutsky symmetry as a testable constraint; they want more such constraints, not fewer. Thus, the newer development is halfway toward Gossen and away from Cassel.

1.5 Advantages and Disadvantages of the System-Wide Approach

An obvious question is whether the restrictions accepted by the system-wide approach are in fact acceptable. The earlier developments were toward more rather than less generality. We may wonder whether the price paid by the system-wide approach is perhaps too high.

The proponents of this approach would argue that the increase in generality achieved by these earlier developments is only an increase in theoretical generality. We can make a theory more general by making it more empty. The traditional approach has not been very helpful in the specification of demand equations in numerical form. The proponents of the system-wide approach are people who tend to prefer numbers to derivatives. They do not object to the calculus of partial derivatives, but they view calculus as a tool suitable for the production of numerical results.

Regarding the theory of consumer demand in particular, the proponents of the system-wide approach tend to view this theory as a prototype of an allocation or a decomposition theory. Such a theory considers a given total (in the consumer's case, the amount available for spending), and asks how this total is subdivided into components (the amounts spent on the individual goods). Allocation problems occur on a large scale. For example, in international trade we can consider the total imports of some country and ask how this is distributed over the various exporting countries.[2] Another example is provided by the availability of various modes of transportation. What is the percentage of people who commute by train, bus, or their own car or bicycle? How is this distribution affected by the distance between home and work and by the prices of train and bus tickets, fuel, and so on? Note that such decomposition problems are not confined to problems in economics. The measurement of integration and segregation of students in schools and the analysis of proportions of votes cast for various candidates or parties are examples outside economics. Clearly, decomposition models are favorites among those who are interested in removing the barriers that separate the social sciences.[3]

Another consideration is that the construction of a *system* of demand equations offers new opportunities. Once such a system has been formulated, so that we have a view from the top of the mountain, we can ask whether useful summary measures can be designed. For example, we may be interested in measuring the change in the quality of consumption as a whole. Can this be done in a sensible manner and, if so, how? Another example is the degree of utility interaction among the consumer goods. I mentioned above that some versions of the system-wide approach imply marginal utilities that are all independent of the consumption of other goods, but most versions do not go so far. In the latter case we may ask whether we can measure the degree of utility interaction, and whether it is possible to transform the system so that this interaction is eliminated.

The previous paragraphs describe some of the advantages of the system-wide approach. It is a matter of honesty to admit that the approach has disadvantages also. If the analyst chooses his position at the top of the mountain, he concentrates his attention on the logical consistency and the strict symmetry in the treatment of individual components. He prefers to reduce ad hoc explanations to a minimum, but he may go too far in this respect. When the Korean War broke out in the early 1950s, housewives in many countries responded by hoarding nonperishable goods. The oil embargo some years ago had its effect on spending, at least temporarily. Proponents of the system-wide approach have only a limited inclination to take such special factors into account. Extending the system by including these elements is largely a task for the future.

2. Import allocation models were formulated by Barten [33] and Barten, d'Alcantara, and Carrin [36]. See also Armington [10], Clements [88], Hickman and Lau [180], Marwah [268], and the collection of essays edited by Ball [15].
3. I analyzed a variety of such models in my *Statistical Decomposition Analysis* [389]. For a more recent survey and an extensive bibliography see McFadden [272].

1.6   A Brief Overview of What Follows

The chapters which follow provide an overview of certain recent developments in the system-wide approach to microeconomics. The selection of these topics is partly motivated by the availability of recent survey articles by Brown and Deaton [69] and Barten [35].[4] The former article contains a rather extensive review of earlier empirical studies in consumer demand; hence there is no need to consider this topic here. Neither article considers the theory of the firm. The exposition of this book provides a unified approach to the theory of the consumer and the firm. Also, neither of these articles pays much attention to price and volume indexes (index numbers), whereas we shall find that such indexes provide valuable insight in both demand and supply equations.

The major topics of the following chapters are the formulation of the consumer's demand equations for goods and services, and of the firm's demand and supply equations for its inputs and outputs, respectively. These are among the prominent topics discussed in the classical Appendix of Hicks's *Value and Capital*. I will follow his example by using appropriately differentiable utility, production, and cost functions, which simplifies the mathematics.

Chapters 2 and 3 deal with the consumer, chapter 4 with the single-product firm, and chapter 5 with the multiproduct firm. This treatment is to a large extent a series of successive generalizations. The implied similarities of the firm and the consumer are further considered in chapter 6.

In chapters 7 and 8 we introduce random disturbances in the demand and supply equations, and we discuss the relation between the distribution of these disturbances and the coefficients in the equations. Chapter 9 deals with various separability conditions on the consumer's goods and services, the firm's inputs, and the outputs produced by the multiproduct firm. The strongest separability condition takes the form of preference independence for the consumer, input independence for the firm's inputs, and output independence for the supply side of the multiproduct firm. Chapters 10 and 11 describe how this condition can be imposed by means of an appropriate transformation. Once this transformation has been performed, we obtain the most elementary description of the consumer's behavior and that of the firm. Chapter 12 considers several features of this description.

Chapters 13 and 14 deal with the empirical implementation of the models discussed in earlier chapters. Chapter 15 provides a discussion of generalizations and possibilities for future research.

---

4. The earlier survey articles by Stigler [372, 373] are also still worth reading.

Two

Two Approaches to the Theory of the Consumer

2.1 Preliminaries

Let $\mathbf{p} = [p_1, \ldots, p_n]'$ and $\mathbf{q} = [q_1, \ldots, q_n]'$ be price and quantity vectors, respectively, and M the consumer's disposable income, where $M > 0$ and $p_i > 0$ for each i. Hence the budget constraint is $\sum_i p_i q_i = M$ or $\mathbf{p'q} = M$. We assume that the consumer's utility function $u(\mathbf{q})$ has positive first-order derivatives and continuous second-order derivatives; also, that when this function is maximized subject to $\mathbf{p'q} = M$ for relevant values of $\mathbf{p}$ and M, the resulting quantities are unique and positive. We write this solution in the form

$$(2.1) \qquad \mathbf{q} = \mathbf{q}^0(M, \mathbf{p}),$$

which is a system of n consumer demand equations, each describing the demand for a good as a function of income and all n prices.

To maximize $u(\mathbf{q})$ subject to the budget constraint, we introduce the Lagrangean function $u(\mathbf{q}) - \lambda(\mathbf{p'q} - M)$, where λ is a Lagrangean multiplier. We differentiate this function with respect to q_i and equate the derivative to zero,

$$(2.2) \qquad \frac{\partial u}{\partial q_i} = \lambda p_i \qquad i = 1, \ldots, n,$$

which is the familiar proportionality of the marginal utilities of the n goods to the corresponding prices. When (2.2) is combined with the budget constraint, we obtain as many $(n + 1)$ equations as there are unknowns: the n quantities and the Lagrangean multiplier λ. The value of this multiplier at the point of the budget-constrained utility maximum is known as the *marginal utility of income*. To clarify this term we divide both sides of

(2.2) by p_i, which yields $(\partial u/\partial q_i)/p_i = \lambda$ or $\partial u/\partial(p_i q_i) = \lambda$. The latter equation indicates that if the consumer receives a one-dollar income increase, he will raise his utility level by λ units when he spends this increase on any of the n goods. This agrees with the designation of λ as the marginal utility of income. A more formal analysis of the dependence of utility on income requires the introduction of the indirect utility function (see section 3.1).

Several approaches are available for the derivation of a system of demand equations from (2.2) and the budget constraint. One of these (described in section 2.2) specifies a particular algebraic form of the utility function. A second approach, described later in this chapter, formulates demand equations in terms of differentials. Other approaches will be considered in section 3.7.

2.2   Specifying the Algebraic Form of the Utility Function

Consider the additive utility specification [1]

$$(2.3) \qquad u(\mathbf{q}) = \sum_{i=1}^{n} a_i \log (q_i - b_i),$$

where the a's and the b's are constants which satisfy $a_i > 0$, $\sum_i a_i = 1$, and $b_i < q_i$. We shall obtain the same demand equations when we transform this utility function monotonically, i.e., when we generalize (2.3) to

$$(2.4) \qquad u^*(\mathbf{q}) = \Phi\left(\sum_{i=1}^{n} a_i \log (q_i - b_i)\right),$$

where $\Phi(\ )$ is any monotonically increasing function of its argument. However, we prefer to use (2.3) because of its greater simplicity.

When we apply (2.2) to (2.3) and use the budget constraint to eliminate λ, we obtain, after rearrangements,

$$(2.5) \qquad p_i q_i = p_i b_i + a_i\left(M - \sum_{j=1}^{n} p_j b_j\right) \qquad i = 1, \ldots, n,$$

which is known as the *linear expenditure system* (the expenditure on each good is described as a linear function of income and prices). If the b's are nonnegative, the model (2.5) can be described in words as follows. First, the consumer buys b_i units of the ith good, which requires an amount of

1. All logarithms in this book are natural logarithms.

$p_i b_i$ dollars. Having made these initial purchases for all goods, the consumer concludes that an amount equal to $M - \sum_j p_j b_j$ is still available; this amount is known as "supernumerary income." It thus follows from (2.5) that the consumer completes his purchases by spending a fraction a_i of supernumerary income on the ith good.

The linear expenditure system contains $2n - 1$ unconstrained parameters, which is a modest number (n parameters a_i subject to one constraint, $\sum_i a_i = 1$, and n parameters b_i). This system has been one of the most popular demand models since Stone [376] applied it to British data in 1954 (see Solari [364] and Lluch, Powell, and Williams [259]). The utility specification (2.3) goes back to Klein and Rubin [217], although Samuelson [342] was the first to make the form (2.3) explicit. It is sometimes referred to as the Klein-Rubin utility function, sometimes as the Stone-Geary utility function (see Geary [150]).

The additivity of (2.3) is obviously restrictive. Christensen, Jorgensen, and Lau [83] proposed a utility function which is quadratic in the logarithms of the quantities,

$$(2.6) \qquad u(\mathbf{q}) = \sum_{i=1}^{n} c_i \log q_i + \frac{1}{2} \sum_{i=1}^{n} \sum_{j=1}^{n} d_{ij} \log q_i \log q_j,$$

where the c's and d's are constants. This form, which is frequently referred to as the *translog utility function*, is more difficult to handle than (2.3). When we apply (2.2) to (2.6), we obtain a result that can be expressed in terms of budget shares,

$$(2.7) \qquad w_i = \frac{p_i q_i}{M} \qquad i = 1, \ldots, n.$$

If the utility function has the form (2.6), the ith budget share takes the following value:

$$(2.8) \qquad w_i = \frac{c_i + \sum_{j=1}^{n} d_{ij} \log q_j}{\sum_{k=1}^{n} c_k + \sum_{k=1}^{n} \sum_{j=1}^{n} d_{kj} \log q_j}.$$

Note that (2.8) cannot be considered a demand equation because it contains more than one quantity. Nevertheless, it is possible to use (2.8) for the estimation of the c's and d's under certain conditions (see section 13.3).

Several other forms of the utility function are described in Appendix A.

2.3 Differentials and the Divisia Indexes of Income

The approach taken by Hicks in the Appendix of *Value and Capital* consists of evaluating derivatives of demand functions. This line of attack has also proved useful for the formulation of demand systems. It requires no algebraic specification of the utility function such as (2.3) or (2.6), which are bound to be imperfect approximations anyway. Thus, one advantage of this alternative (differential) approach is that it postpones the parametrization decision until the stage at which differentials are replaced by finite differences. Another advantage is that it clearly distinguishes between first-order and second-order effects. For example, substitution effects of price changes are second-order effects; this will be clarified in section 6.5.

In the differential approach, the Divisia indexes [120] of the consumer's income play an important role. We write the differential of the budget constraint as $dM = \sum_i q_i dp_i + \sum_i p_i dq_i$, which is a decomposition of dM in terms of a price component and a volume component. When we divide both sides of this decomposition by M and use (2.7), we obtain

$$(2.9) \qquad d(\log M) = d(\log P) + d(\log Q),$$

where

$$(2.10) \qquad d(\log P) = \sum_{i=1}^{n} w_i d(\log p_i)$$

is the Divisia price index of the consumer's income in differential form, and

$$(2.11) \qquad d(\log Q) = \sum_{i=1}^{n} w_i d(\log q_i)$$

is the corresponding Divisia volume index. These indexes are weighted means of logarithmic price or quantity changes with weights equal to the corresponding budget shares.

Remarks

1. The word "changes" may suggest that we confine ourselves to changes over time. This is not true; it is simply convenient to talk about changes. The differentials on the right in (2.10) and (2.11) may refer to any kind of displacement. The differential approach is in the tradition of general comparative statics.

2. Note that (2.10) and (2.11) do not define P and Q or $\log P$ and $\log Q$. The expressions on the left in these two equations should be viewed as abbreviations of the corresponding expressions on the right. We shall use Divisia indexes only in the differential form shown in these equations. Problems of finite (rather than infinitesimal) changes will be considered in section 13.4.

3. It will be convenient to write (2.9) in the equivalent form,

$$(2.12) \qquad d\left(\log \frac{M}{P}\right) = d(\log Q),$$

with the expression on the left defined as $d(\log M) - d(\log P)$. We interpret (2.12) as stating that the logarithmic change in money income deflated by the Divisia price index is equal to the Divisia volume index.

2.4   The Case of Preference Independence

The differential approach yields the simplest result when the utility function is additive,

$$(2.13) \qquad u(\mathbf{q}) = u_1(q_1) + \cdots + u_n(q_n),$$

which contains (2.3) as a special case for $u_i(q_i) = a_i \log(q_i - b_i)$. Since (2.13) implies that the marginal utility of each good is independent of the consumption of all other goods, we shall refer to this case as that of *preference independence.*[2]

It can be shown (an outline of the proof is given in section 2.5) that under preference independence the demand equation for the ith good may be written in the form,

$$(2.14) \qquad w_i d(\log q_i) = \theta_i d\left(\log \frac{M}{P}\right) + \phi \theta_i d\left(\log \frac{p_i}{P'}\right),$$

where the differential on the far right is interpreted as $d(\log p_i) - d(\log P')$, with $d(\log P')$ defined in equation (2.20) below. This interpretation is similar to that of $d[\log(M/P)]$ in (2.12).

2. This case is frequently also referred to as strong separability, which is in contrast to weak separability. We will not use this terminology because we shall have to consider three cases rather than two: preference independence, block independence (see section 2.7), and blockwise dependence (see section 9.2).

We proceed to discuss (2.14) term by term. The expression on the left can be viewed as the contribution of the ith good to the Divisia volume index (2.11). A second interpretation is obtained by taking the differential of (2.7) in logarithmic form,

$$(2.15) \qquad dw_i = w_i d(\log p_i) + w_i d(\log q_i) - w_i d(\log M),$$

which shows that dw_i consists of three components and that the left-hand side of (2.14) is the quantity component of dw_i. This is the endogenous component from the consumer's point of view. The two other components are less plausible candidates for the left-hand variable of a demand equation because they involve price or income changes which the consumer takes as given.[3]

The right-hand side of (2.14) consists of a real-income component and a relative price component. Note that the deflators in these two components are different; we shall have more to say about this difference shortly. Also note that (2.12) implies that (2.14) can be equivalently written in the form

$$(2.16) \qquad w_i d(\log q_i) = \theta_i d(\log Q) + \phi \theta_i d\left(\log \frac{p_i}{P'}\right),$$

which shows that the real-income component is a multiple θ_i of the Divisia volume index. This θ_i is defined as

$$(2.17) \qquad \theta_i = \frac{\partial(p_i q_i)}{\partial M}, \qquad \sum_{i=1}^{n} \theta_i = 1,$$

which means that θ_i is the marginal share of the ith good, the additional amount spent on this good when income increases by one dollar.

The ratio of this marginal share to the corresponding budget share is equal to the income elasticity of the ith good:

$$(2.18) \qquad \frac{\theta_i}{w_i} = p_i \frac{\partial q_i}{\partial M} \frac{M}{p_i q_i} = \frac{\partial \log q_i}{\partial \log M}.$$

The weighted mean of the income elasticities, with weights equal to the budget shares, is equal to 1: $\sum_i w_i(\theta_i/w_i) = \sum_i \theta_i = 1$. Goods with income elasticities larger than 1 are usually called *luxuries*, and those with income elasticities smaller than 1 *necessities*. If a good has a negative income elasticity (and hence a negative marginal share), it is called *inferior*. We shall

3. Also, using a budget share (or the change in this share, or a component of this change) as the left-hand variable of a demand equation has the advantage that it emphasizes the role of consumption theory as an allocation theory. The translog approach similarly yields (2.8) with a budget share on the left, but note that (2.8) has quantities on the right.

find in section 2.7 that inferior goods cannot occur under preference independence, but they may occur under weaker conditions.

In the substitution component of (2.16) we find ϕ, the reciprocal of which is the income elasticity of the marginal utility of income,

$$(2.19) \qquad \frac{1}{\phi} = \frac{\partial \log \lambda}{\partial \log M},$$

and a price deflator of the form

$$(2.20) \qquad d(\log P') = \sum_{i=1}^{n} \theta_i d(\log p_i).$$

This deflator is the Frisch price index, which should be carefully distinguished from the Divisia price index (2.10).[4] The former uses marginal shares as weights and the latter uses budget shares instead. Therefore, luxuries (with $\theta_i/w_i > 1$) have a greater weight in the Frisch price index than in the Divisia price index, while the opposite is true for necessities. If a good is inferior, its weight in the Frisch index is negative so that an increase in the price of this good lowers the Frisch price index. We shall have more to say about these indexes in section 3.6. In what follows we shall refer to the differential on the far right in (2.16) as the logarithmic change in the Frisch-deflated price of the ith good.

The marginal share θ_i has the same interpretation as a_i in the linear expenditure system (2.5), which may be verified by differentiating equation (2.5) with respect to M. However, there is a difference in that a_i is a constant, whereas the differential approach allows its coefficients to be variable. Hence, the θ_i's and ϕ in equations (2.14) to (2.20) may depend on the levels of income and prices. In fact, Frisch [144, p. 189] stated explicitly that the income elasticity of the marginal utility of income (the reciprocal of ϕ) is a function of real income. He conjectured that this elasticity should be about -2 for "the median part" of the population, about -10 for the very poor, and about -0.1 for the very rich with ambitions toward "conspicuous consumption." In what follows we shall refer to ϕ as the *income flexibility* in order to avoid the awkward expression "the reciprocal of the income elasticity of the marginal utility of income."[5]

---

4. Note that the Frisch price index is not a "marginally weighted Divisia price index." Divisia indexes have the property that the sum of the price and volume indexes is equal to the logarithmic change in the corresponding dollar amount [see (2.9)]. Frisch indexes do not have this property; a volume index weighted similarly to the Frisch price index will be considered in section 12.2.

5. Note that ϕ is not invariant under monotonic transformations of the utility function. Hanoch [173] related ϕ to a measure of risk aversion; see also Deschamps [109].

2.5   A Generalization

The presence of only one deflated price in (2.16) results from the preference independence assumption (2.13). ·When this assumption is abandoned, n price terms appear. Below is a brief summary of the developments which yield this result, after which (2.16) will appear as a special case. Intermediate steps are given in Appendix B.

First, we differentiate (2.2) and the budget constraint with respect to income and all prices. The result can be written in the form of Barten's [24] fundamental matrix equation,

$$(2.21) \qquad \begin{bmatrix} \mathbf{U} & \mathbf{p} \\ \mathbf{p}' & 0 \end{bmatrix} \begin{bmatrix} \partial\mathbf{q}/\partial M & \partial\mathbf{q}/\partial\mathbf{p}' \\ -\partial\lambda/\partial M & -\partial\lambda/\partial\mathbf{p}' \end{bmatrix} = \begin{bmatrix} \mathbf{0} & \lambda\mathbf{I} \\ 1 & -\mathbf{q}' \end{bmatrix},$$

where $\mathbf{U} = [\partial^2 u/\partial q_i \partial q_j]$ is the Hessian matrix of the utility function, $\partial\mathbf{q}/\partial M$ and $\partial\mathbf{q}/\partial\mathbf{p}'$ are matrices of derivatives of the vector demand system (2.1), and $\partial\lambda/\partial M$ and $\partial\lambda/\partial\mathbf{p}'$ are analogous derivatives of the marginal utility of income. (These derivatives are all evaluated at the point of the budget-constrained utility maximum.) We assume that $\mathbf{U}$ is symmetric negative definite, which is a sufficient condition for the existence of a utility maximum.[6] This condition implies that the income flexibility (ϕ) is negative.

Next we solve (2.21) to obtain the price derivatives of the demand system. The result in scalar form is

$$(2.22) \quad \frac{\partial q_i}{\partial p_j} = \lambda u^{ij} - \frac{\lambda}{\partial\lambda/\partial M} \frac{\partial q_i}{\partial M} \frac{\partial q_j}{\partial M} - \frac{\partial q_i}{\partial M} q_j \qquad i,j = 1,\ldots,n,$$

where u^{ij} is the (i,j)th element of $\mathbf{U}^{-1}$. The last term in (2.22) represents the income effect of the change in p_j on the demand for the ith good. The first two right-hand terms jointly represent the substitution effect of this change. The first term (λu^{ij}) describes the *specific* substitution effect and the second the *general* substitution effect. The latter effect is concerned with the competition of all goods for an extra dollar of the consumer's income, whereas the former deals with the utility interaction of the ith and the jth goods.

Finally, we use (2.22) to obtain a demand equation for the ith good in differential form. The result is an extension of equation (2.16),

$$(2.23) \qquad w_i d(\log q_i) = \theta_i d(\log Q) + \phi \sum_{j=1}^{n} \theta_{ij} d\left(\log\frac{p_j}{P'}\right),$$

---

6. This assumption is slightly stronger than necessary, but very convenient because it ensures that $\mathbf{U}$ has an inverse. See also Barten, Kloek, and Lempers [38].

where

$$(2.24) \qquad \theta_{ij} = \frac{\lambda}{\phi M} \, p_i u^{ij} p_j \qquad i, j = 1, \ldots, n,$$

$$(2.25) \qquad \sum_{j=1}^{n} \theta_{ij} = \theta_i \qquad i = 1, \ldots, n,$$

$$(2.26) \qquad \sum_{i=1}^{n} \sum_{j=1}^{n} \theta_{ij} = \sum_{i=1}^{n} \theta_i = 1.$$

To interpret (2.23) we note that $d(\log Q)$ on the right can be written as $d(\log M) - \sum_j w_j d(\log p_j)$ (see eqs. [2.9] and [2.10]). The price component of this expression is the income effect of the n price changes on the demand for the ith good, so that this income effect serves as the deflator which transforms money income into real income. The other term on the right in (2.23) is the substitution term. This term can be written as the difference between $\phi \sum_j \theta_{ij} d(\log p_j)$, which is the specific substitution effect of the n price changes on the demand for the ith good, and

$$(2.27) \qquad \phi d(\log P') \sum_{j=1}^{n} \theta_{ij} = \phi \theta_i d(\log P'),$$

which is the general substitution effect. (The equal sign in eq. [2.27] follows from eq. [2.25].) Thus, the general substitution effect of the price changes serves as the deflator of the specific substitution effect by transforming absolute prices into relative (Frisch-deflated) prices.

2.6 Price Coefficients and Specific Substitutes and Complements

The coefficient of the jth relative price in (2.23) is $\phi \theta_{ij}$, which will be called the (i, j)th price coefficient. The θ_{ij}'s will be called *normalized* price coefficients because they add up to 1 (see eq. [2.26]). It follows from (2.24), the condition that $\phi < 0$, and the symmetric negative definiteness of **U** that the $n \times n$ matrix $[\theta_{ij}]$ is symmetric positive definite. Also, the sum of the θ_{ij}'s in each equation is equal to the corresponding marginal share (see eq. [2.25]). A simple interpretation of the θ_{ij}'s is obtained by inverting $[\theta_{ij}]$ and writing θ^{ij} for the (i, j)th element of this inverse:

$$(2.28) \qquad \theta^{ij} = \frac{\phi M}{\lambda} \, \frac{\partial^2 u}{\partial(p_i q_i) \partial(p_j q_j)} \qquad i, j = 1, \ldots, n.$$

Since $\partial u/\partial(p_i q_i)$ is the marginal utility of a dollar spent on the ith good, the second-order derivative on the right in (2.28) describes the effect on this marginal utility of an extra dollar spent on the jth good. Thus, (2.28) shows that $[\theta_{ij}]$ is inversely proportional to the Hessian matrix of the utility function in expenditure terms.

The separation of the total substitution effect into specific and general components is from Houthakker [194], who also defined the following specific substitution and complementarity relations. We conclude from (2.23) and the condition that $\phi < 0$, that if $\theta_{ij} < 0$, an increase in the jth relative price (real income remaining constant) raises the demand for the ith good. Since $\theta_{ij} < 0$ implies $\theta_{ji} < 0$ (because of the symmetry of $[\theta_{ij}]$), an increase in the ith relative price also raises the demand for the jth good. The two goods are then said to be *specific substitutes*. If θ_{ij} and θ_{ji} are both positive, so that an increase in the relative price of either good reduces the demand for the other, the two goods are called *specific complements*.

These definitions are not identical to those of Hicks's substitutes and complements, which are based on total substitution effects. It follows from (2.20) and (2.27) that the substitution term of (2.23) is equal to

$$(2.29) \qquad \phi \sum_{j=1}^{n} (\theta_{ij} - \theta_i \theta_j) d(\log p_j).$$

Hicks's definitions are based on the sign of $\theta_{ij} - \theta_i \theta_j$ rather than that of θ_{ij}. Also, Slutsky symmetry amounts to symmetry of $[\theta_{ij} - \theta_i \theta_j]$, but this is of course equivalent to symmetry of $[\theta_{ij}]$. As an example, consider the following 3×3 normalized price coefficient matrix:

$$(2.30) \qquad [\theta_{ij}] = \begin{bmatrix} 0.5 & 0.1 & -0.1 \\ 0.1 & 0.4 & -0.2 \\ -0.1 & -0.2 & 0.5 \end{bmatrix} \begin{matrix} \text{good 1} \\ \text{good 2} \\ \text{good 3.} \end{matrix}$$

Here good 1 and good 2 are specific complements of each other, whereas (1, 3) and (2, 3) are two pairs of specific substitutes. The row sums of $[\theta_{ij}]$ yield the following marginal shares: $\theta_1 = 0.5$, $\theta_2 = 0.3$, $\theta_3 = 0.2$ (see eq. [2.25]). By combining these shares with (2.30) we obtain

$$(2.31) \qquad [\theta_{ij} - \theta_i \theta_j] = \begin{bmatrix} 0.25 & -0.05 & -0.20 \\ -0.05 & 0.31 & -0.26 \\ -0.20 & -0.26 & 0.46 \end{bmatrix} \begin{matrix} \text{good 1} \\ \text{good 2} \\ \text{good 3.} \end{matrix}$$

All off-diagonal elements are negative; hence the three goods are all substitutes of each other in Hicks's sense.

The formulation (2.23) is in relative prices. When we replace the substitution term of (2.23) by (2.29), which contains $d(\log p_j)$ in undeflated form, we obtain the absolute price formulation. Both formulations have their merits in particular situations. We shall find in sections 13.5 and 13.6 that the absolute price version plays a role in empirical implementation. On the other hand, the use of the relative price version can contribute to a reduction of the number of unknowns (see the next section). Also, this version will appear to be particularly attractive in relation to parallel developments in the theory of the firm (see chapters 4 and 5).

It follows directly from $\sum_i \theta_i = 1$, (2.25), and the symmetry of $[\theta_{ij}]$ that the sum over i of the substitution term (2.29) vanishes. On combining this with (2.11), we conclude that summation of (2.23) over i yields $d(\log Q) = d(\log Q)$. This shows that (2.23) must be viewed as an allocation model.

2.7   Preference Independence and Block Independence

Under the preference independence condition (2.13), both $\mathbf{U}$ and $\mathbf{U}^{-1}$ are diagonal matrices, so that $\theta_{ij} = 0$ for $i \neq j$ (see eq. [2.24]) and $\theta_{ii} = \theta_i$ (see eq. [2.25]), which proves that (2.23) then takes the form (2.16). Under preference independence, no good is a specific substitute or complement of any other good. Also, θ_{ii} must be positive because it is a diagonal element of a positive definite matrix. Hence $\theta_{ii} = \theta_i$ implies that the marginal share of each good must be positive. This rules out inferior goods under preference independence.

It is also instructive to divide both sides of (2.16) by w_i:

$$(2.32) \qquad d(\log q_i) = \frac{\theta_i}{w_i} d(\log Q) + \frac{\phi \theta_i}{w_i} d\left(\log \frac{p_i}{P'}\right).$$

This equation shows that θ_i/w_i is the income elasticity of the demand for the ith good, in agreement with (2.18), and that $\phi \theta_i/w_i$ is the own-price elasticity of this demand: the elasticity of the demand for this good with respect to its Frisch-deflated price. We conclude that under preference independence the own-price elasticities are proportional to the corresponding income elasticities, with ϕ as (negative) proportionality coefficient.[7]

However, preference independence is too restrictive an assumption for the real world. A weaker version is obtained when we apply the additive specification (2.13) to groups of goods. Let there be $G < n$ groups,

7. This is an exact version of what Deaton [100] calls Pigou's law. The difference is that in our version prices are Frisch-deflated, which makes the proportionality exact rather than approximate.

written $S_1, \ldots, S_G$, in such a way that each good belongs to exactly one
group. Let the utility function be the sum of G group utility functions,[8]

(2.33) $$u(\mathbf{q}) = u_1(\mathbf{q}_1) + \cdots + u_G(\mathbf{q}_G),$$

where $\mathbf{q}_g$ is a subvector of $\mathbf{q}$ which consists of the q_i's that fall under
S_g $(g = 1, \ldots, G)$. Under (2.33) the marginal utility of each good depends
only on the quantities consumed of the goods that belong to the same
group. Hence, when the goods are appropriately numbered, the Hessian $\mathbf{U}$
and its inverse become block-diagonal, so that the same holds for $[\theta_{ij}]$ in
view of (2.24). Therefore, if i belongs to S_g, equations (2.23) and (2.25) can
now be written as

(2.34) $$w_i d(\log q_i) = \theta_i d(\log Q) + \phi \sum_{j \in S_g} \theta_{ij} d\left(\log \frac{p_j}{P'}\right),$$

(2.35) $$\sum_{j \in S_g} \theta_{ij} = \theta_i \quad \text{if} \quad i \in S_g.$$

We shall refer to the utility specification (2.33) as that of *block independence* with G blocks. Since all θ_{ij}'s with i and j in different groups vanish,
no good is a specific substitute or complement of any good that belongs
to a different group. If S_g consists of only one good, (2.34) reduces to the
preference independence version (2.16).

The zero values of the θ_{ij}'s corresponding to goods of different groups
illustrate how the block independence approach succeeds in reducing the
number of unknown parameters. The approach achieves this desirable
objective without making the overly restrictive assumption of preference
independence. However, it should be noted that we are not yet entitled
to speak about parameters at this stage, because (2.34) is in differentials
and its coefficients (ϕ, θ_i, θ_{ij}) are not necessarily constant. The application
of demand systems to statistical data is a separate matter which will be
discussed in chapter 13.

8. It is actually sufficient that the utility function can be written in this
additive form after an appropriate monotonic transformation [see the discussion following (2.3)].

Three

The Cost of Utility

In this chapter we take a different approach to the consumer's problem. One result will be the development of the concept of the cost of utility, which provides a basis for the economic theory of price and real-income indexes. This concept also provides a link with the cost of production in the theory of the firm. A second result will be certain other methods of generating demand equation systems in addition to the two approaches discussed in chapter 2.

3.1 The Indirect Utility Function and Roy's Theorem

Substitution of the demand system (2.1) in the utility function gives

$$(3.1) \qquad u = u(\mathbf{q}^0(M, \mathbf{p})) = u_I(M, \mathbf{p}).$$

The function $u_I(\ )$ of income and prices is called the *indirect utility function*. This function specifies the maximum utility level that can be attained when income is M and prices are $\mathbf{p}$. For example, in the case of the linear expenditure system we substitute (2.5) in (2.3), which yields the indirect utility function

$$(3.2) \qquad u_I(M, \mathbf{p}) = k + \log \left(M - \sum_{i=1}^{n} p_i b_i \right) - \sum_{i=1}^{n} a_i \log p_i,$$

where k is the constant $\sum_i a_i \log a_i$.

Differentiation of (3.1) with respect to M and p_i gives

$$(3.3) \qquad \frac{\partial u_I}{\partial M} = \lambda, \qquad \frac{\partial u_I}{\partial p_i} = -\lambda q_i,$$

which may be verified by applying the chain rule to (3.1) and using (2.2); see Appendix B. Note that the first equation in (3.3) confirms the role of λ as the marginal utility of income. Also note that (3.3) implies

$$(3.4) \qquad q_i = -\frac{\partial u_I/\partial p_i}{\partial u_I/\partial M} \qquad i = 1, \ldots, n.$$

This result is known as Roy's [338] theorem; it expresses the ith quantity as minus the ratio of two derivatives of the indirect utility function. The reader may want to write down these derivatives for (3.2) in order to verify that (3.4) yields an equation which is equivalent to (2.5).

3.2   The Consumer's Cost Function

The cost function $C(U, \mathbf{p})$ is defined as the smallest amount of expenditure which enables the consumer to enjoy the utility level U at the price vector $\mathbf{p}$. (We indicate utility by an uppercase U when it plays the role of an independent variable.) The introduction of this cost function implies that we view the consumer as a producer of utility; he buys certain goods and services which he transforms into utility. The function $C(\ )$ is sometimes called the expenditure function, but we shall not use this term because it has the disadvantage of not reflecting the analogy with the firm's cost function (see section 4.2).

One way of deriving the consumer's cost function is by substituting U for $u_I(\ )$ and $C(\ )$ for M in the indirect utility function. When we apply this to (3.2), we obtain

$$(3.5) \qquad C(U, \mathbf{p}) = \sum_{i=1}^{n} p_i b_i + e^{U-k} \prod_{i=1}^{n} p_i^{a_i},$$

which shows that under the (direct) utility specification (2.3) the cost of utility consists of two parts. One part, $\sum_i p_i b_i$, is independent of U (fixed cost) and is equal to the amount which the consumer needs for his initial purchases before he proceeds to supernumerary spending (see the discussion following eq. [2.5]). The other part increases with U and involves a weighted geometric mean of the prices; the weights are the a_i's, which are the (constant) marginal shares of the linear expenditure system.

The consumer's cost function has been playing an increasingly important role in the theoretical literature of recent years. One major reason is duality: maximizing utility subject to the budget constraint is equivalent to minimizing expenditure subject to the constraint that a given utility level be attained. These two extremum problems, one involving $u(\ )$ and the other involving $C(\ )$, are dual to each other. In fact, it can be shown that if the budget constraint is linear (i.e., if the consumer takes the prices of all goods as given), the cost function provides a complete description of the consumer's preferences insofar as these are relevant to his behavior. The mathematical analysis of the cost function tends to be rather abstract (see, for example, Diewert [117]), but the following properties of this function are nevertheless important.

First, C is an increasing function of both U and the elements of $\mathbf{p}$; it costs more to be better off, and it also costs more to be as well off when prices rise. Second, C is homogeneous of degree 1 in $\mathbf{p}$, which means that when all prices change proportionately, the cost of utility changes in the same proportion. It is easily verified that both properties are satisfied by the cost function (3.5). Third, when prices do not change proportionately, minimizing cost for any given price vector yields the result that C is concave in $\mathbf{p}$,

$$(3.6) \qquad C(U, k_1\mathbf{p}_1 + k_2\mathbf{p}_2) \geq k_1 C(U, \mathbf{p}_1) + k_2 C(U, \mathbf{p}_2),$$

where $k_1 \geq 0$, $k_2 \geq 0$, and $k_1 + k_2 = 1$.

When derivatives exist, as is assumed here, we have both $\partial C/\partial U$, which is the marginal cost of utility, and $\partial C/\partial \mathbf{p}$, which satisfies

$$(3.7) \qquad \frac{\partial C(U, \mathbf{p})}{\partial \mathbf{p}} \equiv \mathbf{q}(U, \mathbf{p}).$$

We shall refer to (3.7) as Shephard's lemma for the consumer, but results of this kind actually date back to Hotelling [190]. The lemma implies that differentiation of the cost of utility with respect to prices yields a system of demand equations which express the quantities in terms of utility and prices. Note the difference between the demand system $\mathbf{q}(U, \mathbf{p})$ and that of (2.1), $\mathbf{q}^0(M, \mathbf{p})$.

3.3   The True Index of the Cost of Living

Consider two price vectors, $\mathbf{p}_1 = [p_{1i}]$ and $\mathbf{p}_2 = [p_{2i}]$. We want to make a cost-of-living comparison of these price situations. If the two price vectors are scalar multiples of each other, such a comparison is straightforward: $\mathbf{p}_2 = 1.05\,\mathbf{p}_1$ means that the cost of living in the second price situation exceeds that in the first by 5%. The challenging case is that in which $\mathbf{p}_1$ and $\mathbf{p}_2$ are not scalar multiples of each other. For this purpose we define

$$(3.8) \qquad P(\mathbf{p}_2, \mathbf{p}_1 | U) = \frac{C(U, \mathbf{p}_2)}{C(U, \mathbf{p}_1)}$$

as the *true cost-of-living* index which compares $\mathbf{p}_2$ with $\mathbf{p}_1$ at the utility level U. Thus, (3.8) states that if the cost of U at prices $\mathbf{p}_2$ exceeds the cost of the same U at prices $\mathbf{p}_1$ by 6%, the true index takes the value 1.06. Note that this numerical value varies with the utility level U that is selected for the comparison of $\mathbf{p}_1$ and $\mathbf{p}_2$.[1]

The application of (3.8) to the cost function (3.5) of the linear expenditure system is in principle straightforward, but an interesting result emerges only when we select a particular utility level. Our selection can be described as follows: First, we extend the vectors $\mathbf{p}_1$ and $\mathbf{p}_2$ by including the associated income values, so that we have two income-price situations, $(M_1, \mathbf{p}_1)$ and $(M_2, \mathbf{p}_2)$. The utility level which we select is that of the first situation, $U_1 = u_I(M_1, \mathbf{p}_1)$ (see eq. [3.1]). Next, we define ρ_1 as the ratio of supernumerary income to total income in $(M_1, \mathbf{p}_1)$,

$$(3.9) \qquad \rho_1 = \frac{M_1 - \sum_{i=1}^{n} p_{1i}b_i}{M_1},$$

and s_i as the budget share of the ith good at the price vector $\mathbf{p}_1$ and zero supernumerary income:

$$(3.10) \qquad s_i = \frac{p_{1i}b_i}{\sum_{j=1}^{n} p_{1j}b_j} \qquad i = 1, \ldots, n.$$

The result is that the true index (3.8) at $U_1 = u_I(M_1, \mathbf{p}_1)$ equals[2]

$$(3.11) \qquad P(\mathbf{p}_2, \mathbf{p}_1 | U_1) = \rho_1 \prod_{i=1}^{n} \left(\frac{p_{2i}}{p_{1i}}\right)^{a_i} + (1 - \rho_1) \sum_{i=1}^{n} s_i \frac{p_{2i}}{p_{1i}}.$$

The right-hand side is a weighted average of two price indexes with weights ρ_1 and $1 - \rho_1$. The first of these indexes is a weighted geometric mean of the price ratios with the a_i's as weights; the second is a weighted arithmetic mean of the same ratios with the s_i's as weights. The discussion of this result will continue in section 3.5, where we shall find that these weights make perfect sense.

1. The definition (3.8) dates back, at least, to an article in Russian by Konüs (see [222] for an English translation). References should also be made to Kloek [219], Lloyd [253], Malmquist [264], Pollak [323], Rajaoja [336], and Samuelson and Swamy [347]. Among surveys and books on index number theory (which include approaches not based on utility theory) we mention Afriat [4], Allen [8], Banerjee [16], Diewert [118], Eichhorn and Voeller [125], Fisher and Shell [133], Fisher [135], and Frisch [143].

2. For proofs of (3.11) and other results stated in this chapter, see Theil [397, chapter 3].

3.4   The True Index of Real Income

The ratio of M to $P(\ )$ of (3.8) would seem a rather obvious volume index, but note that this amounts to an indirect definition of the volume index (via the true cost-of-living index). In fact, a direct definition of a true volume index on the basis of the consumer's cost function is impossible because $C(U, \mathbf{p})$ does not involve quantities; we shall pursue this matter along different lines in section 6.4. However, the cost function does enable us to compare utility levels, which yields what may be called a true index of real income.

Consider again the income-price situations $(M_1, \mathbf{p}_1)$ and $(M_2, \mathbf{p}_2)$ and the associated utility levels $U_1 = u_I(M_1, \mathbf{p}_1)$ and $U_2 = u_I(M_2, \mathbf{p}_2)$. We define

$$(3.12) \qquad\qquad Q(U_2, U_1|\mathbf{p}) = \frac{C(U_2, \mathbf{p})}{C(U_1, \mathbf{p})}$$

as the *true index of real income* which compares U_2 with U_1 at the price vector $\mathbf{p}$. Thus, if the minimum expenditures needed for the utility levels U_2 and U_1 at prices $\mathbf{p}$ are \$10,500 and \$10,000, respectively, the true index of real income at $\mathbf{p}$ equals 1.05. This index depends on $\mathbf{p}$ in the same way that the index (3.8) depends on U.

For example, for the linear expenditure system we can write the index which compares $U_2 = u_I(M_2, \mathbf{p}_2)$ with $U_1 = u_I(M_1, \mathbf{p}_1)$ at the price vector $\mathbf{p}_1$ in the form

$$(3.13) \quad Q(U_2, U_1|\mathbf{p}_1) - 1 = (\rho_2 - \rho_1) + \rho_2 \left[\frac{M_2/M_1}{\prod\limits_{i=1}^{n} (p_{2i}/p_{1i})^{a_i}} - 1 \right],$$

where ρ_2 is the ratio of supernumerary income to total income in $(M_2, \mathbf{p}_2)$, which is obtained by substituting 2 for the subscript 1 in (3.9). If this ratio is larger than that of $(M_1, \mathbf{p}_1)$, i.e., if $\rho_2 - \rho_1 > 0$, an increased affluence in $(M_2, \mathbf{p}_2)$ is implied. This is the interpretation of the first right-hand term in (3.13), which, if positive, thus contributes to a positive excess of $Q(\ )$ over 1 on the left. The other term on the right deals with the ratio of the two incomes, deflated by the same price index which also occurs in the first term of (3.11). This second term will be discussed further at the end of the next section.

3.5   The True Marginal Price Index

In (3.8) we made a cost-of-living comparison of $\mathbf{p}_2$ and $\mathbf{p}_1$ at the utility level U. Let us raise this level by dU. What are the additional expenditures needed to obtain $U + dU$ rather than U in the two price situations? The answer for $\mathbf{p}_2$ is

$$C(U + dU, \mathbf{p}_2) - C(U, \mathbf{p}_2) = C'(U, \mathbf{p}_2)dU,$$

and that for $\mathbf{p}_1$ is $C'(U, \mathbf{p}_1)dU$, where $C'(U, \mathbf{p})$ is defined as $\partial C/\partial U$ evaluated at $(U, \mathbf{p})$. The ratio of these additional expenditures,

$$(3.14) \qquad\qquad P'(\mathbf{p}_2, \mathbf{p}_1 | U) = \frac{C'(U, \mathbf{p}_2)}{C'(U, \mathbf{p}_1)},$$

is the *true marginal price index* which compares $\mathbf{p}_2$ with $\mathbf{p}_1$ at the utility level U. Since $C' = \partial C/\partial U$ is the marginal cost of utility, the index (3.14) is simply the ratio of two values of this marginal cost: those evaluated at $(U, \mathbf{p}_2)$ and at $(U, \mathbf{p}_1)$. Thus, if prices have increased from the first situation to the second so that the additional expenses needed to produce the same utility increment are 9% higher at $(U, \mathbf{p}_2)$ than at $(U, \mathbf{p}_1)$, the index (3.14) equals 1.09. Note that the numerical value depends on U in the same way that (3.8) depends on U. The true marginal price index was first formulated by Frisch [142, pp. 74–82].

For the linear expenditure system the index (3.14) takes the form of the weighted geometric mean $\prod_i (p_{2i}/p_{1i})^{a_i}$, which is independent of U because the a_i's are constant. This index also occurs in the right-hand sides of (3.11) and (3.13), which may be used to clarify these two equations. Suppose that the consumer is poor in $(M_1, \mathbf{p}_1)$, so that ρ_1 takes a small value (see eq. [3.9]) and the index (3.11) is dominated by the second term on the right, which is a weighted mean of price ratios with weights equal to budget shares at zero supernumerary income. These weights emphasize the goods that are bought at a low level of real income, which is as it should be because the $P(\ )$ of equation (3.11) is evaluated at U_1 and the consumer is (by assumption) poor in $(M_1, \mathbf{p}_1)$. Next, suppose that he is very rich in $(M_1, \mathbf{p}_1)$, so that ρ_1 is close to 1 (see eq. [3.9]) and the index (3.11) is dominated by the first term on the right, which is the true marginal price index. This marginal index emphasizes the additional expenses at a high standard of living, which is also as it should be.

The real-income index in (3.13) contains the marginal index in the second term on the right, where it appears as the deflator of M_2/M_1. Hence this deflator emphasizes the goods bought at a high standard of living. Accordingly, the multiplication by ρ_2 of the term in brackets in (3.13) implies that this is relevant for the real-income comparison only in proportion to the amount available for supernumerary spending in $(M_2, \mathbf{p}_2)$.

3.6   The Indexes Used in the Differential Approach

The differential approach considers an income-price situation $(M, \mathbf{p})$ and analyzes the consequences of an infinitesimal change $(dM, d\mathbf{p})$. Thus, an obvious choice of the price vector at which the real-income comparison (3.12) is made is the prevailing price vector $\mathbf{p}$. Similarly, a natural choice of the utility level U of the cost-of-living comparison (3.8) and the marginal price comparison (3.14) is the prevailing utility level $U = u_I(M, \mathbf{p})$. It can be shown that the logarithms of the indexes of the latter two comparisons may be written as follows:

$$(3.15) \qquad \log P(\mathbf{p} + d\mathbf{p}, \mathbf{p} | u_I(M, \mathbf{p})) = \sum_{i=1}^{n} w_i d(\log p_i),$$

$$(3.16) \qquad \log P'(\mathbf{p} + d\mathbf{p}, \mathbf{p} | u_I(M, \mathbf{p})) = \sum_{i=1}^{n} \theta_i d(\log p_i).$$

Similarly,

$$(3.17) \qquad \log Q(U_2, U_1 | \mathbf{p}) = \sum_{i=1}^{n} w_i d(\log q_i),$$

where

$$(3.18) \qquad U_1 = u_I(M, \mathbf{p}), \qquad U_2 = u_I(M + dM, \mathbf{p} + d\mathbf{p}).$$

A comparison of these results with (2.10), (2.11), and (2.20) shows that the indexes used in the differential approach can all be interpreted as true indexes. The Divisia volume index $d(\log Q)$ is the true index of real income which compares the utility level of $(M + dM, \mathbf{p} + d\mathbf{p})$ with that of $(M, \mathbf{p})$ at the prevailing prices $\mathbf{p}$. The Divisia price index $d(\log P)$ is the true cost-of-living index which compares $\mathbf{p} + d\mathbf{p}$ with $\mathbf{p}$ at the prevailing utility level $u_I(M, \mathbf{p})$, and $d(\log P')$ is the true marginal price index which compares the same two price vectors at the same utility level. The term *Frisch price index* for $d(\log P')$ is selected because of Frisch's contribution to the theory of the true marginal price index (3.14).

The true index of real income is independent of the price vector at which it is evaluated if and only if all n goods have income elasticities identically equal to 1. This condition is also necessary and sufficient for the true cost-of-living index to be independent of the utility level at which it is evaluated.

Obviously, this is a very restrictive condition.[3] A more general result is

(3.19) $$\frac{\partial[\log P(\mathbf{p}_2, \mathbf{p}_1 | U)]}{\partial U} = k\left[1 - \frac{P(\mathbf{p}_2, \mathbf{p}_1 | U)}{P'(\mathbf{p}_2, \mathbf{p}_1 | U)}\right],$$

where $k = \partial[\log C(U, \mathbf{p}_2)]/\partial U > 0$. We conclude from (3.19) that when
the cost of living is evaluated at a higher utility level, the index takes a
larger (smaller) value when it is below (above) the true marginal index, or,
equivalently, that the true cost-of-living index moves in the direction of the
true marginal index when evaluated at a higher utility level. This reflects the
fact that budget shares (w_i in eq. [3.15]) move in the direction of the corres-
sponding marginal shares (θ_i in eq. [3.16]) when the consumer becomes
richer.

3.7   Two Other Methods of Generating Demand Equation Systems

Since the consumer's cost function provides a full description of his
preferences (if he takes prices as given), we can select a particular algebraic
form of $C(U, \mathbf{p})$ to generate demand systems. It follows from (3.7) that
once this selection is made, we obtain such a system by differentiating $C(\ )$
with respect to $\mathbf{p}$. Note that this demand system involves utility rather than
income. Therefore, as a second step we have to express utility in terms of
income and prices, using the indirect utility function, which yields a
demand equation system in income and prices. This approach was particularly recommended by Deaton [104].

An alternative approach consists of an algebraic specification of the
indirect utility function. Roy's theorem (3.4) shows how demand equations
can be obtained immediately from this function. In fact, this approach is
older than that of specifying the cost function, and its convenience was
recently emphasized and illustrated by Lau [235]. For example, Houthakker
[194] proposed

(3.20) $$u_I(M, \mathbf{p}) = -\sum_{i=1}^{n} A_i \left(\frac{p_i}{M}\right)^{\alpha_i},$$

which is known as the *addilog indirect utility function*. By applying (3.4)

---

3. If $b_i = 0$ for each i in (3.9), then $\rho_1 = 1$ and the cost-of-living index (3.11)
becomes identical to the true marginal price index. This agrees with the fact
that the utility function (2.3) then takes the Cobb-Douglas form, which is
characterized by income elasticities of all goods identically equal to 1. Such a
case of "homothetic preferences" is of very limited empirical value.

and multiplying by p_i/M, we obtain

$$(3.21) \qquad w_i = \frac{B_i(p_i/M)^{\alpha_i}}{\sum\limits_{j=1}^{n} B_j(p_j/M)^{\alpha_j}} \qquad i = 1, \ldots, n,$$

where $B_i = A_i \alpha_i$, which should be positive for each i in order that the n quantities be positive. Also,

$$(3.22) \qquad \alpha_i < 1 \qquad i = 1, \ldots, n$$

should hold for the existence of a budget-constrained utility maximum. The allocation model (3.21) was proposed earlier by Leser [239] and Somermeyer [366, 367] before Houthakker provided the link with the indirect utility function (3.20).

Note that prices and income occur in (3.20) only in ratio form. This reflects the requirement that a proportionate increase in income and all prices should not affect the maximum utility level that can be attained. The following function, known as the *translog indirect utility function* and proposed by Christensen, Jorgenson, and Lau [83], has the same feature:

$$(3.23) \qquad u_I(M, \mathbf{p}) = \sum_{i=1}^{n} \beta_i \log \frac{p_i}{M} + \frac{1}{2} \sum_{i=1}^{n} \sum_{j=1}^{n} \beta_{ij} \log \frac{p_i}{M} \log \frac{p_j}{M}.$$

Application of (3.4) to (3.23) yields

$$(3.24) \qquad w_i = \frac{\beta_i + \sum\limits_{j=1}^{n} \beta_{ij} \log (p_j/M)}{\sum\limits_{k=1}^{n} \beta_k + \sum\limits_{k=1}^{n} \sum\limits_{j=1}^{n} \beta_{kj} \log (p_j/M)},$$

which should be compared with (2.8). Note that the translog function (2.6) with constant coefficients (c's and d's) is not equivalent to the indirect translog function (3.23) with constant β's. This is expressed by saying that the translog specification in consumption theory is not "self-dual"; an example of self-duality will be given in section 4.2.

Four

The Single-Product Firm

In this chapter we consider a firm which makes one product (or output) and uses n production factors (or inputs). We write z for the quantity produced and $\mathbf{p} = [p_1, \ldots, p_n]'$ and $\mathbf{q} = [q_1, \ldots, q_n]'$ for the price and quantity vectors of the inputs. The firm's technology is described by a production function. We write this function in logarithmic form,

$$(4.1) \qquad \log z = h(\mathbf{q}),$$

and assume that $h(\ )$ has positive first-order derivatives and continuous second-order derivatives. The two major problems considered in this chapter are the following: Given output z and the input prices $\mathbf{p}$, how should the firm behave in order to minimize the amount spent on the inputs? Given input prices $\mathbf{p}$ and a certain price obtained for the product, how should the firm behave in order to maximize profit? We assume that the function (4.1) yields unique positive quantity solutions in both extremum problems.

4.1 Algebraic Specifications of the Production Function

The best-known specification of the function (4.1) is the *Cobb-Douglas production function* [91],

$$(4.2) \qquad h(\mathbf{q}) = a + \sum_{i=1}^{n} b_i \log q_i,$$

where $a, b_1, \ldots, b_n$ are constants, with $b_1 + \cdots + b_n$ equaling the elasticity of scale (the elasticity of output with respect to a proportionate change in all inputs). By adding quadratic terms to (4.2), we obtain the *translog production function* which was proposed by Christensen, Jorgenson, and Lau [82]:

$$(4.3) \qquad h(\mathbf{q}) = a + \sum_{i=1}^{n} b_i \log q_i + \frac{1}{2} \sum_{i=1}^{n} \sum_{j=1}^{n} c_{ij} \log q_i \log q_j.$$

A different generalization of (4.2) is the constant-elasticity-of-substitution (CES) production function.[1] For $n = 2$ inputs this function takes the form

$$(4.4) \qquad h(\mathbf{q}) = a - \frac{1}{\gamma k} \log [b q_1^{-k} + (1 - b) q_2^{-k}],$$

where a, b, k, and γ are constants ($0 < b < 1$ and $\gamma > 0$). The reciprocal of γ is the elasticity of scale, while k exceeds -1 and is related to the elasticity of substitution k' via $k' = 1/(1 + k)$.[2] It can be shown that for $k' = 1$ (implying $k = 0$) the CES function (4.4) takes the Cobb-Douglas form (4.2) with $n = 2$. As $k' \to 0$, the CES function becomes a Leontief-type production function with L-shaped isoquants.

Other algebraic specifications of the production function are described in Appendix A.

4.2   The Firm's Cost Function

The first problem to be considered is that of minimizing total input expenditure, $\mathbf{p}'\mathbf{q} = \sum_i p_i q_i$, subject to the technology constraint (4.1) for given output z and given input prices. This yields demand functions for the inputs which express the q_i's in terms of z and the p_i's. When these functions are substituted for the q_i's in $\sum_i p_i q_i$, we obtain the smallest amount of input expenditure which enables the firm to produce z at the input prices $\mathbf{p}$. This minimum amount is the firm's cost function, $C(z, \mathbf{p})$. The properties of this function are identical to those of the cost-of-utility function introduced in section 3.2; the only change is that the argument U of $C(U, \mathbf{p})$ now becomes z. In particular, Shephard's lemma for the firm takes the form

$$(4.5) \qquad \frac{\partial C(z, \mathbf{p})}{\partial \mathbf{p}} \equiv \mathbf{q}(z, \mathbf{p}),$$

1. The CES function has become particularly popular since the appearance of the article by Arrow et al. [12], but it had been discovered by Dickinson [111] several years earlier. See Nerlove [293] for further historical details.

2. The elasticity of substitution between two inputs is defined as the proportionate change in q_1/q_2 corresponding to a unit proportionate change in the ratio of their marginal products for constant output.

which enables us to obtain a system of input demand equations from an algebraically specified cost function. The function $C(z, \mathbf{p})$ provides a complete description of the firm's behavior under competitive conditions; see McFadden [273], who uses the term "sufficient statistic" to summarize this property of the cost function.

One particular form is the translog cost function; it amounts to writing $\log C$ as a quadratic function of the logarithms of z and the p_i's. Note that this function and (4.3) are not self-dual, i.e., the translog cost function with constant coefficients does not imply a translog production function (and vice versa). Also note that the translog cost specification does not satisfy the concavity condition (see eq. [3.6]) for all positive values of z and the p_i's.[3]

The Cobb-Douglas and CES functions do have the self-dual property. For example, output has a constant elasticity with respect to each input under (4.2) and the associated cost function has constant elasticities with respect to z (equal to $\sum_j b_j$) and to p_i (equal to $b_i / \sum_j b_j$).

4.3 Factor Shares and the Elasticity of Scale

Minimizing $\mathbf{p'q}$ with respect to $\mathbf{q}$ subject to the production function constraint yields a proportionality of marginal products and input prices; the proportionality coefficient is $1/(\partial C/\partial z)$, i.e., the reciprocal of marginal cost. This well-known result may be viewed as the firm's version of the proportionality (2.2) for the consumer. It is easily shown that if we use the logarithmic formulation (4.1), the proportionality of the marginal products and the input prices can be written as

$$(4.6) \qquad \frac{\partial h}{\partial \log q_i} = \frac{f_i}{\gamma} \qquad i = 1, \ldots, n,$$

where f_i is the ith factor share (the share of the ith input in total cost),

$$(4.7) \qquad f_i = \frac{p_i q_i}{C} \qquad i = 1, \ldots, n,$$

and γ is the elasticity of cost with respect to output:

$$(4.8) \qquad \gamma = \frac{\partial \log C}{\partial \log z}.$$

3. Similarly, the translog utility function (2.6) is not globally quasi-concave. The quasi concavity is required for the existence of a budget-constrained utility maximum.

It follows from (4.1) that the sum of the left-hand derivative in (4.6) over i equals the elasticity of scale. Since the f_i's add up to 1, summation of (4.6) over i thus yields the result that γ is not only the output elasticity of cost but also the reciprocal of the elasticity of scale, both at the point of minimum total input expenditure. Note that the interpretation of $1/\gamma$ as the elasticity of scale agrees with the role of γ in the CES function (4.4). However, whereas γ is a constant in (4.4), we shall allow it to be variable in the differential approach that will now be considered. The account which follows is based on Theil [398].

4.4   The Change in Marginal Cost

Since total cost depends on output and on input prices, so does marginal cost. To analyze the nature of this dependence, we introduce the share of the ith input in marginal cost as well as an input price index which uses these shares as weights:

$$(4.9) \qquad \theta_i = \frac{\partial(p_i q_i)/\partial z}{\partial C/\partial z} \qquad i = 1, \ldots, n,$$

$$(4.10) \qquad d(\log P') = \sum_{i=1}^{n} \theta_i d(\log p_i).$$

We shall refer to θ_i as the marginal share of the ith input, which is the firm's version of the consumer's θ_i (see eq. [2.17]), and to $d(\log P')$ as the Frisch price index of the inputs, which is the firm's version of the analogous index (2.20) of the consumer. The subject of the true indexes of the firm will be discussed in section 6.2.

It can be shown (see the next paragraph) that when input prices and output change infinitesimally, the logarithmic change in marginal cost equals

$$(4.11) \qquad d\left(\log \frac{\partial C}{\partial z}\right) = \left(\frac{\gamma}{\psi} - 1\right) d(\log z) + d(\log P'),$$

where ψ is a positive coefficient whose reciprocal is defined as

$$(4.12) \qquad \frac{1}{\psi} = 1 + \frac{1}{\gamma^2} \frac{\partial^2 \log C}{\partial(\log z)^2}.$$

We conclude from (4.11) that the input price component of the logarithmic change in marginal cost equals the Frisch index (4.10), and that the output elasticity of marginal cost equals $\gamma/\psi - 1$. If the output elasticity of C and hence γ (see eq. [4.8]) are constant, as is the case for the CES function (4.4), the second-order derivative in (4.12) vanishes, and hence $\psi = 1$. If the output elasticity of C increases (decreases) with increasing output, ψ is smaller (larger) than 1. Thus, ψ may be viewed as a measure of the curvature of the logarithmic cost function.

The result (4.11), together with the input demand equations that will be described in the next section, is obtained by differentiating the first-order conditions and the production function with respect to z and $\mathbf{p}$, arranging these derivatives in partitioned matrix form, and solving the matrix equation.[4] This equation may be viewed as the firm's version of Barten's fundamental matrix equation (2.21); we shall not discuss this equation here because a more general result will appear in section 5.3 for the multiproduct firm.

A sufficient condition for a minimum of $\sum_i p_i q_i$ subject to (4.1) is the following: Let $\mathbf{F}$ be the $n \times n$ diagonal matrix which contains the factor shares $f_1, \ldots, f_n$ on the diagonal. Let $\mathbf{H}$ be the $n \times n$ logarithmic Hessian matrix of the function (4.1):

$$(4.13) \qquad \mathbf{H} = \left[\frac{\partial^2 h}{\partial(\log q_i)\partial(\log q_j)} \right].$$

A sufficient condition for a minimum of $\sum_i p_i q_i$ subject to (4.1) is that $\mathbf{F} - \gamma\mathbf{H}$ is symmetric positive definite, where $\mathbf{F}$, γ, and $\mathbf{H}$ are all evaluated at the point corresponding to the first-order conditions (4.6). This condition is the firm's version of the symmetric negative definiteness of $\mathbf{U}$ (see the discussion following eq. [2.21]). Further details are provided in Appendix C.

4.5   Demand Equations for Inputs

It is possible to formulate demand equations for the firm's inputs that are quite similar to the consumer demand equation (2.23). Recall from (2.15) that the left-hand variable of (2.23) is the quantity component of the change in the ith budget share. For the ith input of the firm we take the differential of its factor share, using (4.7):

$$(4.14) \qquad df_i = f_i d(\log p_i) + f_i d(\log q_i) - f_i d(\log C).$$

---

4. This solution provides one reason why (4.1) is formulated in logarithmic terms. The matrix equation which I developed earlier [384, p. 305] involves the Hessian matrix of the nonlogarithmic production function, which is singular under constant returns to scale, but the inverse of this matrix is needed if we want to proceed as in (2.22). No such problems arise when the analysis is formulated in logarithmic terms.

Also recall from (2.11) that the left-hand variable of (2.23) is the contribution of the ith good to the consumer's Divisia volume index. Therefore, for the inputs of the firm we take the differential of $C = \sum_i p_i q_i$,

$$dC = \sum_{i=1}^{n} q_i dp_i + \sum_{i=1}^{n} p_i dq_i,$$

which we divide by C to obtain

(4.15) $d(\log C) = d(\log P) + d(\log Q),$

where the two terms on the right are the Divisia price and volume indexes of the inputs:

(4.16) $d(\log P) = \sum_{i=1}^{n} f_i d(\log p_i),$

(4.17) $d(\log Q) = \sum_{i=1}^{n} f_i d(\log q_i).$

We conclude from (4.17) and (4.14) that $f_i d(\log q_i)$ is the contribution of the ith input to the Divisia input volume index and also the quantity component of the change in the ith factor share. Accordingly, we select $f_i d(\log q_i)$ as the left-hand variable of the ith input demand equation that is obtained by minimizing $\sum_i p_i q_i$ subject to (4.1) for given output and given input prices. The result is

(4.18) $f_i d(\log q_i) = \gamma \theta_i d(\log z) - \psi \sum_{j=1}^{n} \theta_{ij} d\left(\log \frac{p_j}{P'}\right),$

where

(4.19) $[\theta_{ij}] = \frac{1}{\psi} \mathbf{F}(\mathbf{F} - \gamma \mathbf{H})^{-1} \mathbf{F},$

(4.20) $\sum_{j=1}^{n} \theta_{ij} = \theta_i \quad i = 1, \ldots, n,$

(4.21) $\sum_{i=1}^{n} \sum_{j=1}^{n} \theta_{ij} = \sum_{i=1}^{n} \theta_i = 1.$

Note that the results (4.18) to (4.21) are quite similar to those given in (2.23) to (2.26) for the consumer. The θ_{ij}'s are defined in (4.19) in the form of an $n \times n$ matrix. This matrix is symmetric positive definite because of the analogous property of $\mathbf{F} - \gamma\mathbf{H}$ and the positive sign of ψ. The θ_{ij}'s are normalized price coefficients because they add up to 1 when summed over both subscripts (see eq. [4.21]). When we take the sum of the n normalized coefficients that occur in the ith equation, we obtain the ith marginal share (see eq. [4.20]).

The most important difference between (4.18) and (2.23) is the fact that the latter equation represents an allocation model and the former represents a different kind of model. We assume that the consumer takes the total amount available for spending, M, as given. Consequently, (2.23) is an allocation equation which describes the change in the demand for the ith good in terms of the given changes in M and the prices. The firm, on the other hand, does not take total input expenditure C as given; its objective is to minimize C. However, it is possible to separate the firm's input decision into two steps, one of which is an allocation decision that is more directly comparable to (2.23).

For this purpose we sum (4.18) over i, which gives $d(\log Q)$ on the left in view of (4.17). Since the θ_i's on the right add up to 1 and the substitution term yields zero when summed over i,[5] the result is

$$(4.22) \qquad\qquad d(\log Q) = \gamma d(\log z).$$

We shall refer to this equation as the firm's *total-input decision*. It describes the total change in the inputs, measured by their Divisia volume index, which is implied by the given change in the output. Note that this component of the firm's input decision does not involve changes in input prices.

Next we substitute (4.22) in (4.18):

$$(4.23) \qquad f_i d(\log q_i) = \theta_i d(\log Q) - \psi \sum_{j=1}^{n} \theta_{ij} d\left(\log \frac{p_j}{P'}\right).$$

This is the *input allocation decision* for the ith input, which describes the change in the demand for this input as a function of the change in the total input volume and the changes in the relative input prices. Thus, by writing (4.18) in the form (4.22) and (4.23), we separate the firm's input decision into a total-input decision, which involves the change in output but not the changes in the input prices, and an input allocation decision, which involves these price changes in addition to the input volume index.

The reader should note that the allocation decision (4.23) is equivalent to the consumer demand equation (2.23) after appropriate reinterpretations: consumer goods become inputs, budget shares become factor shares,

5. This may be verified using $\sum_i \theta_{ij} = \theta_j$, which follows from (4.20) and the symmetry of $[\theta_{ij}]$, and (4.10) and $\sum_j \theta_j = 1$.

the negative income flexibility ϕ becomes $-\psi$ (also negative), and so on. We shall use this analogy by defining the ith and jth inputs as specific substitutes (complements) when θ_{ij} is negative (positive) (see the discussion following eq. [2.28]). By inverting (4.19) and writing $[\theta^{ij}] = [\theta_{ij}]^{-1}$, we obtain

$$(4.24) \qquad\qquad \mathbf{F}[\theta^{ij}]\mathbf{F} = \psi\mathbf{F} - \gamma\psi\mathbf{H},$$

which shows that the inverse of the normalized price coefficient matrix, when pre- and postmultiplied by the diagonal factor share matrix, is proportional to $\mathbf{H}$ as far as the off-diagonal elements are concerned. The off-diagonal elements of $\mathbf{H}$ measure the sensitivity of the elasticity of output with respect to one input for variations in another input (see eq. [4.13]). The result (4.24) is similar to (2.28) for the consumer, but note that the diagonal in (4.24) contains an extra term equal to $\psi\mathbf{F}$.

By dividing (4.23) by f_i we find that the ratio θ_i/f_i is the elasticity of the demand for the ith input with respect to the Divisia volume index of all inputs. We shall refer to this ratio as the *Divisia elasticity* of the ith input. This is the input version of the income elasticity of a consumer good (see eq. [2.18]).

4.6   Special Cases

The Hessian matrix (4.13) is a zero matrix for the Cobb-Douglas function (4.2), and it is a diagonal matrix for the translog function (4.3) when the c_{ij}'s with different subscripts all vanish. The case of a diagonal Hessian is of special interest. Let the logarithmic production function (4.1) take the additive form

$$(4.25) \qquad\qquad h(\mathbf{q}) = h_1(q_1) + \cdots + h_n(q_n),$$

which will be called *input independence*. It implies that the elasticity of output with respect to each input is independent of all other inputs, so that $\mathbf{H}$ in (4.13) becomes diagonal. Given that $\mathbf{F}$ is diagonal by construction, $[\theta_{ij}]$ in (4.19) is then also diagonal and (4.20) becomes $\theta_{ii} = \theta_i$. Therefore, under input independence the input allocation decision (4.23) takes the form

$$(4.26) \qquad f_i d(\log q_i) = \theta_i d(\log Q) - \psi\theta_i d\left(\log \frac{p_i}{P'}\right),$$

which is similar to the consumer demand equation (2.16) under the preference independence condition (2.13). When there is input independence, no input is a specific substitute or complement of any other input. It is possible to extend the input independence concept to groups of inputs, similar to the block independence approach described in section 2.7, but this extension will be postponed until section 9.5.

Next consider the CES function (4.4) with q_1 interpreted as K (capital) and q_2 as L (labor). It can be shown after some algebra that the associated 2×2 normalized price coefficient matrix $[\theta_{ij}]$ takes the form

$$(4.27) \qquad \begin{bmatrix} f_K - (1 - k')f_K f_L & (1 - k')f_K f_L \\ (1 - k')f_K f_L & f_L - (1 - k')f_K f_L \end{bmatrix} \begin{matrix} \text{capital} \\ \text{labor,} \end{matrix}$$

where f_K is the factor share of capital, f_L that of labor ($f_K + f_L = 1$), and k' the elasticity of substitution (see the discussion following eq. [4.4]). The off-diagonal elements in (4.27) are negative (positive) when k' is larger (smaller) than 1. Hence, capital and labor are specific substitutes (complements) when their elasticity of substitution is larger (smaller) than 1.

Alternatively, let the production function take the translog form

$$(4.28) \quad \log z = \text{constant} + \alpha \log K + \beta \log L + \xi(\alpha\beta)^{1/2} \log K \log L,$$

where α, β, ξ are constants ($\alpha, \beta > 0$). We choose units so that $K = L = 1$ holds at the optimum. Then it can be shown after some algebra that the matrix $[\psi\theta_{ij}]$ takes the form

$$(4.29) \qquad \frac{1}{1 - \xi^2} \begin{bmatrix} f_K & \xi(f_K f_L)^{1/2} \\ \xi(f_K f_L)^{1/2} & f_L \end{bmatrix} \begin{matrix} \text{capital} \\ \text{labor,} \end{matrix}$$

and that $\xi^2 < 1$ is implied by the condition of a positive definite matrix $\mathbf{F} - \gamma\mathbf{H}$. We conclude from (4.29) that capital and labor are specific substitutes (complements) when ξ is negative (positive), i.e., when the elasticity of output with respect to either input is a decreasing (increasing) function of the other input (see eq. [4.28]).

The row sums of the matrix (4.27) are the factor shares f_K and f_L; hence (4.20) implies that capital and labor have unitary Divisia elasticities under the CES technology (4.4). This result may be generalized as follows: A technology with production function (4.1) is said to be *homothetic* when a monotone increasing transformation of $h(\ )$ exists which is homogeneous of degree 1 in the inputs; the CES function (4.4) is an example of a homothetic technology. The inputs of such a technology all have unitary Divisia elasticities. For a proof see Theil [398].

4.7   Profit Maximization

Until this point our criterion has been that of minimizing input expenditure $\mathbf{p'q}$ by varying $\mathbf{q}$ subject to (4.1) for given z and $\mathbf{p}$. We now assume that output z is sold at price y, that output sold equals output produced, and that the objective is to maximize profit, $yz - \mathbf{p'q}$. This problem is solved by equating marginal cost to marginal revenue. If the selling price y is exogenous from the firm's point of view, marginal revenue is identical to this price so that

$$(4.30) \qquad\qquad \frac{\partial C}{\partial z} = y.$$

This implies that we can equate the left-hand side of (4.11) to $d(\log y)$, which yields the supply equation of the firm's product,

$$(4.31) \qquad\qquad d(\log z) = \frac{\psi}{\gamma - \psi} d\left(\log \frac{y}{P'}\right),$$

so that $\psi/(\gamma - \psi)$ is the price elasticity of the firm's supply: the elasticity of this supply with respect to the price of the product deflated by the Frisch price index of the inputs. This elasticity is positive because $\gamma > \psi$ is the second-order condition for a profit maximum. When we substitute (4.31) in (4.18) and (4.22), we obtain the change in the demand for each input and the Divisia input volume index expressed in terms of the $n + 1$ input and output price changes.

Remarks

1. It follows from (4.30) that under profit maximization equation (4.9) can be simplified to

$$(4.32) \qquad\qquad \theta_i = \frac{\partial(p_i q_i)}{\partial(yz)} \qquad i = 1, \ldots, n,$$

so that θ_i is now the additional expenditure on the ith input caused by an additional dollar of output revenue. The reader should note the similarity of (4.32) to the consumer's formula (2.17).

2. Since the right-hand side of (4.8) equals $(\partial C/\partial z)(z/C)$, another implication of (4.30) is $\gamma = yz/C$: the ratio of revenue to cost at the point of maximum profit. Hence, if $\gamma \leq 1$, revenue is smaller than or equal to cost, in which case the firm would do better or just as well by not producing and selling anything. Therefore, the validity of the supply equation (4.31) requires $\gamma > 1$.

3. It may seem that the objective of profit maximization represents a departure of the theory of the firm from that of the consumer. Recall that we pictured the consumer as a producer of utility in section 3.2. He transforms n goods into utility, which he enjoys but does not sell. By contrast, the firm transforms n inputs into an output, which it sells at a certain price so as to maximize profit. However, there is an interesting way in which the consumer can also be viewed as a seller and a profit maximizer. This matter will be pursued in section 6.1.

4.8   Direct and Two-Step Approaches to the Theory of the Profit-Maximizing Firm

Our strategy in this chapter may be summarized as follows. First, we minimized input expenditure subject to the technology constraint (4.1) for given output and given input prices, which yields the differential demand equation (4.18). Second, we maximized profit by varying output, which yields the supply equation (4.31). An alternative approach is to maximize profit directly. This amounts to maximizing $yz - \mathbf{p'q}$ subject to the production function (4.1) by varying z and $\mathbf{q}$ for given y and $\mathbf{p}$. This approach, which expresses supply and demand in terms of input and output prices, is indicated by the vertical arrow in figure 1. The two-step procedure of this chapter is represented by the two arrows on the left in this figure. One advantage of this procedure is that it yields the input allocation decision (4.23) which is directly comparable to the consumer demand equation (2.23). Therefore, we shall continue to use this two-step procedure for the multiproduct firm in chapter 5, which will provide us with a system of output supply equations, one for each product, in addition to a system of input demand equations. However, the application-oriented reader may want to follow the advice given in the Preface by proceeding to chapter 7 after completing the present chapter.

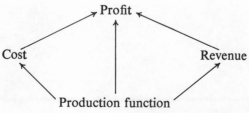

Figure 1   Three approaches to the theory of the profit-maximizing firm

Another advantage of the two-step procedure is that when random disturbances are added to these equations, the supply disturbances appear to be stochastically independent of the demand disturbances under appropriate conditions. When supply and demand are both expressed in terms of input and output prices, as is the case when profit is maximized in one step (see the vertical arrow of fig. 1), the associated disturbances do not have this attractive independence property. These matters will be pursued in sections 8.5 and 8.6.

It should be noted that the two-step procedure of this chapter is not the only possible one. An alternative approach, indicated by the two arrows on the right in figure 1, is the following: First, we maximize output revenue subject to the production function constraint by varying outputs for given output prices and input quantities. Second, we maximize profit by adjusting the input quantities. The first step yields output supply equations which describe supply changes in terms of output price and input quantity changes; the second gives input demand equations that describe the change in demand in terms of input and output price changes. This formulation refers to the multiproduct firm, because the supply equation of the single-product firm which results from the first (revenue-maximizing) step degenerates to a differential form of the production function. However, the revenue-maximizing approach is of interest for the multiproduct firm and is described in Appendix D.

Five

The Multiproduct Firm

In this chapter we extend the analysis of chapter 4 to a firm which makes more than one product. This holds for most firms in the real world, but few authors considered this problem until rather recently. One of the early exceptions is Klein's [215, 216] two-output analysis of U.S. railroads. The outputs are the amount of freight carried in ton-miles (z_1) and the number of passenger-miles (z_2). The production function used by Klein is of the Cobb-Douglas type,

$$(5.1) \qquad z_1 z_2^\alpha = A \prod_{i=1}^{n} q_i^{\beta_i},$$

where α, A, and the β's are positive constants and the q's are inputs used to produce the two outputs jointly. This is an example of an algebraically specified production function. The main objective of this chapter will be the differential approach to the theory of the multiproduct firm. The account which follows is largely based on Laitinen and Theil [229].

5.1   The Firm's Technology

Let the firm make m products. We write $\mathbf{z} = [z_1, \ldots, z_m]'$ for the output vector and describe the firm's technology by means of an implicit production function,

$$(5.2) \qquad h(\mathbf{q}, \mathbf{z}) = 0,$$

where $\mathbf{q} = [q_1, \ldots, q_n]'$ is the input vector. We assume that the second-order derivatives of $h(\ )$ are continuous and that the first-order derivatives with respect to the first n arguments (the inputs) are positive and those with respect to the last m (the outputs) are negative. We also assume that (5.2) can be solved for each product, say z_r, which is interpreted as the maximum output obtainable from the inputs $q_1, \ldots, q_n$ when these inputs are also used to produce the quantities $z_1, \ldots, z_{r-1}, z_{r+1}, \ldots, z_m$ of the other products. In the case of (5.1) this is simply a matter of dividing both sides by z_2^α, which gives the solution for z_1, and dividing by z_1 and then taking αth roots, which gives the solution for z_2. The same assumption is made for the inputs, so that (5.2) can be solved for q_i, which yields the smallest amount of the ith input needed to produce $z_1, \ldots, z_m$ when the q_j's of the other inputs ($j \neq i$) are given.

The production function (4.1) of the single-product firm can be written as

$$(5.3) \qquad\qquad h(\mathbf{q}) - \log z = 0,$$

where z is a scalar. If we reinterpret the left-hand side of (5.3) as $h(\mathbf{q}, z)$, we have $\partial h / \partial(\log z) \equiv -1$, which means that $h(\ )$ is in output-homogeneous form. For the purpose of extending the results of chapter 4 to the multiproduct firm it is convenient to use the output-homogeneous form for $h(\ )$ of (5.2) also, which implies that this function satisfies

$$(5.4) \qquad\qquad \sum_{r=1}^{m} \frac{\partial h}{\partial \log z_r} \equiv -1.$$

It will be shown in section 6.3 that there is no loss of generality when we describe the firm's technology by a production function (5.2) which satisfies (5.4). In the case of (5.1) this is simply a matter of raising both sides to the power $1/(1 + \alpha)$ and taking logarithms.

5.2 Demand Equations for the Inputs of a Multiproduct Firm

Our first objective is to minimize $\sum_i p_i q_i$ by varying the q_i's subject to (5.2) for given p_i's and z_r's. This yields input demand equations that are quite similar to the single-product equation (4.18), but they will obviously contain m output changes. We now have m marginal costs, $\partial C / \partial z_1, \ldots, \partial C / \partial z_m$; so we extend the marginal share of (4.9) to

$$(5.5) \qquad\qquad \theta_i^r = \frac{\partial(p_i q_i)/\partial z_r}{\partial C/\partial z_r} \qquad r = 1, \ldots, m,$$

$$i = 1, \ldots, n,$$

which is the share of the ith input in the marginal cost of the rth product.

Note further that $z_r(\partial C/\partial z_r)$ may be viewed as the dollar value of the rth output evaluated at its marginal cost, and that $\sum_r z_r(\partial C/\partial z_r)$ is "total marginal cost," each product being evaluated at its marginal cost. Therefore,

$$(5.6) \qquad g_r = \frac{z_r(\partial C/\partial z_r)}{\sum\limits_{s=1}^{m} z_s(\partial C/\partial z_s)} \qquad r = 1, \ldots, m$$

is the share of the rth product in total marginal cost, and

$$(5.7) \qquad d(\log Z) = \sum_{r=1}^{m} g_r d(\log z_r)$$

is a Divisia volume index of the outputs. This index emerges when we apply the Divisia decomposition to total marginal cost.[1]

The shares defined in (5.5) and (5.6) occur in the output term of the multiproduct input demand equations, the derivation of which will be outlined in the next section. The result is

$$(5.8) \qquad f_i d(\log q_i) = \gamma \sum_{r=1}^{m} \theta_i^r g_r d(\log z_r) - \psi \sum_{j=1}^{n} \theta_{ij} d\left(\log \frac{p_j}{P'}\right),$$

where γ is the elasticity of cost with respect to a proportionate increase in all outputs,

$$(5.9) \qquad \gamma = \sum_{r=1}^{m} \frac{\partial \log C}{\partial \log z_r},$$

and ψ is a positive coefficient whose reciprocal is defined as

$$(5.10) \qquad \frac{1}{\psi} = 1 + \frac{1}{\gamma^2} \sum_{r=1}^{m} \sum_{s=1}^{m} \frac{\partial^2 \log C}{\partial(\log z_r)\partial(\log z_s)}.$$

Equations (5.9) and (5.10) are the multiproduct extensions of (4.8) and (4.12), respectively, and the substitution term in (5.8) takes the same form as that in (4.18). Therefore, as in the single-product case, we can define specific substitution and complementarity relations for pairs of inputs by means of the signs of the θ_{ij}'s.

---

1. The corresponding price index is $\sum_r g_r(\partial C/\partial z_r)$, but this index plays no role in this chapter. Under profit maximization (see section 5.6) total marginal cost becomes the firm's revenue from all m products, g_r becomes a revenue share, and $d(\log Z)$ becomes the volume index obtained from the Divisia decomposition of revenue.

Recall that the total-input decision (4.22) of the single-product firm is obtained by summation of (4.18) over i. When we apply this to (5.8), using $\sum_i \theta_i^r = 1$ and (5.7) as well as the fact that the substitution term of (5.8) becomes zero when summed over i, we obtain

$$(5.11) \qquad\qquad d(\log Q) = \gamma d(\log Z).$$

This is the total-input decision of the multiproduct firm; its only difference from the single-product result (4.22) is the occurrence of the Divisia output index on the right. The input allocation decision of the multiproduct firm will be considered in section 5.5.

5.3   Outline of the Derivation of the Demand Equations

The result (5.8) is proved in Appendix C, but the main steps of the proof can be summarized as follows: The minimization of $\sum_i p_i q_i$ subject to (5.2) is performed by means of the Lagrangean function $\sum_i p_i q_i - \rho h(\mathbf{q}, \mathbf{z})$. We differentiate this function with respect to $\log q_i$ and equate the derivative to zero, which yields the first-order conditions:

$$(5.12) \qquad\qquad p_i q_i - \rho \frac{\partial h}{\partial \log q_i} = 0 \qquad i = 1, \ldots, n.$$

Next we differentiate (5.2) and (5.12) with respect to the logarithms of the z_r's and p_j's. The result can be written in the following form, which is the firm's version of the consumer's fundamental matrix equation (2.21):

$$(5.13) \qquad
\begin{bmatrix} \mathbf{F}^{-1}(\mathbf{F} - \gamma \mathbf{H})\mathbf{F}^{-1} & \boldsymbol{\iota} \\ \boldsymbol{\iota}' & 0 \end{bmatrix}
\begin{bmatrix} \mathbf{F}\dfrac{\partial \log \mathbf{q}}{\partial \log \mathbf{z}'} & \mathbf{F}\dfrac{\partial \log \mathbf{q}}{\partial \log \mathbf{p}'} \\[2mm] -\dfrac{\partial \log \rho}{\partial \log \mathbf{z}'} & -\dfrac{\partial \log \rho}{\partial \log \mathbf{p}'} \end{bmatrix}
$$

$$= \begin{bmatrix} \gamma \mathbf{F}^{-1}\mathbf{H}^* & -\mathbf{I} \\ \gamma \mathbf{g}' & 0 \end{bmatrix}.$$

On the left, $\mathbf{F}$ is the diagonal $n \times n$ matrix with the factor shares $f_1, \ldots f_n$ on the diagonal and $\mathbf{H}$ is the $n \times n$ matrix (4.13), where $h(\ )$ now refers to (5.2), while $\boldsymbol{\iota}$ is a column vector consisting of n unit elements. In the middle, $\partial(\log \mathbf{q})/\partial(\log \mathbf{z}')$ is the $n \times m$ matrix whose (i, r)th element is $\partial(\log q_i)/$

$\partial(\log z_r)$. On the right, $\mathbf{g}'$ is the m-element row vector whose rth element is given in (5.6), while $\mathbf{H}^*$ is the $n \times m$ matrix

$$(5.14) \qquad \mathbf{H}^* = \left[\frac{\partial^2 h}{\partial(\log q_i)\partial(\log z_r)} \right].$$

The result (5.8) is then obtained by solving (5.13) for its derivatives and making appropriate rearrangements. As in the single-product case, we assume that $\mathbf{F} - \gamma\mathbf{H}$ is symmetric positive definite, which is a sufficient condition for the existence of a constrained minimum of $\sum_i p_i q_i$.

Recall that the denominator in (5.6) equals total marginal cost. The value of the Lagrangean multiplier ρ at the point of the constrained minimum can be shown to be equal to this total marginal cost:

$$(5.15) \qquad \rho = \sum_{r=1}^{m} z_r \frac{\partial C}{\partial z_r} = \sum_{r=1}^{m} \frac{\partial C}{\partial \log z_r}.$$

The last member shows that ρ may also be interpreted as the marginal cost of a proportionate increase in all outputs. By combining (5.15), (5.5), and (5.6) we obtain

$$(5.16) \qquad \sum_{r=1}^{m} g_r \theta_i^r = \theta_i \qquad i = 1, \ldots, n,$$

where θ_i is the share of the ith input in the marginal cost of a proportionate output increase:

$$(5.17) \qquad \theta_i = \frac{1}{\rho} \sum_{r=1}^{m} \frac{\partial(p_i q_i)}{\partial \log z_r} \qquad i = 1, \ldots, n.$$

The single-product results (4.19) to (4.21) all apply to the substitution term of (5.8), provided ψ and θ_i are interpreted as shown in (5.10) and (5.17).

5.4   The Elasticities of Proportionate Output

Consider the differential of (5.2) in logarithmic form:

$$(5.18) \qquad \sum_{i=1}^{n} \frac{\partial h}{\partial \log q_i} d(\log q_i) + \sum_{r=1}^{m} \frac{\partial h}{\partial \log z_r} d(\log z_r) = 0.$$

Let the inputs change proportionally and let this also be true for the outputs, so that $d(\log q_i)$ and $d(\log z_r)$ can both be put before their summation

signs in (5.18). It follows from (5.4) that each logarithmic output change is
then equal to the following multiple of each logarithmic input change:

$$(5.19) \qquad \sum_{i=1}^{n} \frac{\partial h}{\partial \log q_i} = \sum_{i=1}^{n} \frac{p_i q_i}{\rho} = \frac{C}{\rho}.$$

The first equal sign in (5.19) is based on (5.12). We conclude from (5.19) that
C/ρ is the elasticity of proportionate output with respect to proportionate
input at the constrained minimum or, more briefly, the elasticity of scale of
the multiproduct firm at this point. But the reciprocal of C/ρ is the elasticity
of cost with respect to proportionate output changes (see [5.15]), and this
elasticity equals γ defined in (5.9). Therefore, γ is both the elasticity of cost
with respect to proportionate output changes and the reciprocal of the
elasticity of scale. This is an extension of the corresponding single-product
interpretations of γ (see the paragraph following eq. [4.8]).

Next consider (5.18) with $d(\log q_j) = 0$ for each $j \neq i$ and $d(\log z_r)$
independent of r. It then follows from (5.4) that $\partial h/\partial(\log q_i)$ can be interpreted as the elasticity of proportionate output with respect to the ith
input. A diagonal $\mathbf{H}$ (see eq. [4.13]) thus implies that the elasticity of
proportionate output with respect to each input has a zero rate of change
for variations in all other inputs. If $\mathbf{H}$ is diagonal, then $\theta_{ij} = 0$ for $i \neq j$ and
$\theta_{ii} = \theta_i$ (see eqs. [4.19] and [4.20]), so that (5.8) takes the form

$$(5.20) \qquad f_i d(\log q_i) = \gamma \sum_{r=1}^{m} \theta_i^r g_r d(\log z_r) - \psi \theta_i d\left(\log \frac{p_i}{P'}\right),$$

which is the input-independent version of the demand equation for the ith
input of the multiproduct firm.

5.5   Input-Output Separability and the
Input Allocation Decision

A multiproduct technology is said to be *input-output separable* when $h(\ )$
of (5.2) can be separated additively into functions of $\mathbf{q}$ and $\mathbf{z}$: $h(\mathbf{q}, \mathbf{z}) \equiv$
$h_q(\mathbf{q}) - h_z(\mathbf{z})$.[2] Klein's production function (5.1) has this property, which
may be verified by taking logarithms of both sides. It is shown in Appendix

2. This separation need not apply to the output-homogeneous production
function; it is sufficient that this separation apply to some implicit production
function that describes the firm's technology. If it applies to the output-
homogeneous function, then $\mathbf{H^*} = \mathbf{0}$ [see eq. (5.14)], but the weaker version
implies only that $\mathbf{F^{-1}H^*}$ consists of identical rows, from which (5.21) follows
directly; see Appendix C.

C that if a multiproduct technology is input-output separable, the marginal
shares of each input are the same for all outputs:

(5.21) $\theta_i^r = \theta_i$ $r = 1, \ldots, m,$

                                $i = 1, \ldots, n.$

When we substitute (5.21) and (5.7) in (5.8), we obtain

(5.22) $f_i d(\log q_i) = \gamma \theta_i d(\log Z) - \psi \sum_{j=1}^{n} \theta_{ij} d\left(\log \frac{p_j}{P'}\right),$

which is the ith input demand equation under input-output separability.
This equation is a direct extension of (4.18) with $d(\log z)$ replaced by the
Divisia volume index of m outputs. Note that (5.22) contains effectively
only one output term plus n relative price terms, whereas under input
independence we have only one relative price term plus m output terms
(see eq. [5.20]).

   It is easily verified that the input allocation decision takes the single-
product form (4.23) under input-output separability; this is a matter of
substituting (5.11) in (5.22). When there is no such separability so that
(5.21) does not hold, the input allocation decision of the multiproduct firm
has an extra term in the form of a covariance which allows a simple interpretation. To show this we substitute (5.11), multiplied by θ_i, in (5.8), with
the result that the right-hand side takes the following form:

(5.23) $\theta_i d(\log Q) + \gamma \sum_{r=1}^{m} g_r(\theta_i^r - \theta_i) d(\log z_r) - \psi \sum_{j=1}^{n} \theta_{ij} d\left(\log \frac{p_j}{P'}\right).$

It follows from (5.16) and (5.7) that θ_i and $d(\log Z)$ are weighted means of
θ_i^r and $d(\log z_r)$, respectively, with the g_r's as weights. The corresponding
covariance is

(5.24) $\Gamma_i = \sum_{r=1}^{m} g_r(\theta_i^r - \theta_i)[d(\log z_r) - d(\log Z)].$

It is readily verified that the second term in (5.23) equals $\gamma \Gamma_i$. Therefore,

(5.25) $f_i d(\log q_i) = \theta_i d(\log Q) + \gamma \Gamma_i - \psi \sum_{j=1}^{n} \theta_{ij} d\left(\log \frac{p_j}{P'}\right),$

which is the input allocation decision for the ith input of a multiproduct
technology in the general case in which inputs and outputs are not necessarily separable.

The difference between (5.25) and (4.23) is the extra term $\gamma\Gamma_i$. It follows from (5.24) that this term vanishes under input-output separability (see eq. [5.21]) and also when the m outputs change proportionately. Thus, the term $\gamma\Gamma_i$ measures the effect on the input allocation of nonproportionate changes in the outputs when these are not separable from the inputs. This term implies that a change in outputs increases (decreases) the demand for the ith input in excess of the value $\theta_i d(\log Q)$ that is implied by the Divisia input volume index when the output changes are positively (negatively) correlated with the marginal shares of this input. Note that this correlation is a weighted correlation with the g_r's as weights (see eq. [5.24]).

5.6   Conditions for a Profit Maximum

Let $\mathbf{y} = [y_1, \ldots, y_m]'$ be the vector of prices which the firm receives for its products, so that its gross revenue is $R = \mathbf{y}'\mathbf{z} = \sum_r y_r z_r$. We assume in the remainder of this chapter that the firm's objective is to maximize its profit, $R - C$, by varying $\mathbf{q}$ and $\mathbf{z}$ subject to (5.2) for given $\mathbf{p}$ and $\mathbf{y}$. Suppose, then, that we know the solution of $\mathbf{z}$, so that $R = \mathbf{y}'\mathbf{z}$ is also known because $\mathbf{y}$ is given. Maximizing $R - C$ is then equivalent to minimizing $\mathbf{p}'\mathbf{q}$ by varying $\mathbf{q}$ subject to (5.2) with $\mathbf{z}$ specified according to the given solution. This problem has been considered above and it yields the input demand equation (5.8). Evidently, it is sufficient to find the output changes in (5.8) which maximize profit.

For this purpose we consider profit as a function of $\mathbf{z}$ and express the maximum condition in the form

$$(5.26) \qquad \frac{\partial(R - C)}{\partial\mathbf{z}} = \mathbf{0},$$

and a negative definite matrix $\partial^2(R - C)/\partial\mathbf{z}\partial\mathbf{z}'$. The latter condition is equivalent to a positive definite $\partial^2 C/\partial\mathbf{z}\partial\mathbf{z}'$ because $\partial^2 R/\partial\mathbf{z}\partial\mathbf{z}' = \mathbf{0}$ follows from the assumption that $\mathbf{y}$ is fixed.[3]

Condition (5.26) yields $\partial C/\partial z_r = y_r$, so that (5.15) and (5.6) imply

$$(5.27) \qquad \rho = \sum_{r=1}^{m} y_r z_r = R,$$

$$(5.28) \qquad g_r = \frac{y_r z_r}{R} \quad r = 1, \ldots, m.$$

3. The production function (5.1) does not satisfy the second-order condition for maximum profit (but it is applicable to cost minimization). Hasenkamp [176, 177] applied a CES-type production function to Klein's railroad data.

Hence ρ is now equal to the firm's revenue and g_r is the share of the rth product in this revenue, so that $d(\log Z)$ in (5.7) is the Divisia volume index of the outputs which is associated with output revenue. By taking the differential of (5.28) we obtain

$$(5.29) \qquad dg_r = g_r d(\log y_r) + g_r d(\log z_r) - g_r d(\log R),$$

which shows that $g_r d(\log z_r)$ is the quantity component of the change in the rth revenue share. In the next section we shall use this component as the left-hand variable of the rth supply equation, in agreement with the analogous procedure for the consumer demand equation (2.23) and the input demand equation (4.18).

Recall from the discussion following equation (5.19) that ρ/C equals γ. Therefore, (5.27) implies that under profit maximization γ is equal to the ratio of revenue to cost:

$$(5.30) \qquad\qquad \gamma = \frac{R}{C}.$$

Also, $\partial C/\partial z_r = y_r$ implies that the marginal share in (5.5) can be written in the form $\partial(p_i q_i)/\partial(y_r z_r)$, which is a direct multiproduct extension of equation (4.32). These marginal shares enter as weights in

$$(5.31) \qquad d(\log P'^r) = \sum_{i=1}^{n} \theta_i^r d(\log p_i) \qquad r = 1, \ldots, m,$$

which is the Frisch input price index for the production of the rth product. The weighted mean of these indexes, with the g_r's as weights, is equal to

$$(5.32) \qquad\qquad \sum_{r=1}^{m} g_r d(\log P'^r) = d(\log P'),$$

which follows from (5.16).

5.7 Supply Equations of Outputs

It is shown in Appendix C that if the firm maximizes profit for given input and output prices, the supply equation for the rth product can be written as

$$(5.33) \qquad\qquad g_r d(\log z_r) = \psi^* \sum_{s=1}^{m} \theta_{rs}^* d\left(\log \frac{y_s}{P'^s}\right),$$

where ψ^* is a positive coefficient and θ_{rs}^* is an element of a symmetric positive definite matrix of order $m \times m$ which is normalized so that its elements add up to 1:

(5.34) $$\theta_{rs}^* = \frac{1}{\psi^* R}\, y_r c^{rs} y_s \qquad r, s = 1, \ldots, m,$$

(5.35) $$\sum_{r=1}^{m} \sum_{s=1}^{m} \theta_{rs}^* = 1,$$

with c^{rs} defined as the (r, s)th element of $(\partial^2 C/\partial \mathbf{z} \partial \mathbf{z}')^{-1}$. The similarity of (5.34) and (2.24) should be noted. When we write (5.34) in matrix form and invert both sides, we obtain

(5.36) $$\theta^{*rs} = \psi^* R\, \frac{\partial^2 C}{\partial(y_r z_r)\partial(y_s z_s)} \qquad r, s = 1, \ldots, m,$$

where θ^{*rs} is the (r, s)th element of $[\theta_{rs}^*]^{-1}$. Hence the normalized price coefficient matrix $[\theta_{rs}^*]$ of the output supply equations is inversely proportional to the matrix of second derivatives of the cost function with respect to outputs measured in dollars. This should be compared with (2.28). In what follows we shall systematically use asterisks in order to distinguish output supply from input demand.

Equation (5.33) extends the supply equation (4.31) of the single-product firm to a system of m supply equations, each of which describes the change in the supply of a product in terms of changes in deflated output prices. The left-hand side of (5.33) is the contribution of the rth product to the Divisia volume index (5.7), and it is also the quantity component of the change in the rth revenue share (see eq. [5.29]). A new element is the fact that each output price has its own deflator in (5.33). This is in contrast to the input demand equations which use $d(\log P')$ as the deflator of all input prices. To understand this more thoroughly, we must turn to the total-output decision and the output allocation decision which are associated with (5.33).

For this purpose we define

(5.37) $$\theta_r^* = \sum_{s=1}^{m} \theta_{rs}^* \qquad r = 1, \ldots, m$$

as the marginal share of the rth product. This agrees with $\theta_i = \sum_j \theta_{ij}$ for consumer goods and the firm's inputs; a more direct justification will be given in remark (1) at the end of this section, but we note here that the θ_r^*'s add up to 1, as marginal shares should do, in view of (5.35). Next we define the Frisch output price index,

$$(5.38) \qquad d(\log Y') = \sum_{r=1}^{m} \theta_r^* d(\log y_r),$$

and a Frisch-weighted mean of the input price indexes defined in (5.31):[4]

$$(5.39) \qquad d(\log P'') = \sum_{r=1}^{m} \theta_r^* d(\log P''^r).$$

It is then easily verified from the symmetry of $[\theta_{rs}^*]$ that summation of (5.33) over r yields

$$(5.40) \qquad d(\log Z) = \psi^* d\left(\log \frac{Y'}{P''}\right),$$

which is the *total-output decision* of the multiproduct firm. Equation (5.40) shows that ψ^* may be interpreted as the price elasticity of the supply of the firm's output as a whole—that is, the elasticity of this supply with respect to the output price index (5.38) deflated by the input price index (5.39). Note that (5.40) is a multiproduct extension of the single-product supply equation (4.31) in aggregate (Divisia index) form.

Next we subtract (5.40), multiplied by θ_r^*, from (5.33). The result can be written (after minor rearrangements) in the form

$$(5.41) \qquad g_r d(\log z_r) = \theta_r^* d(\log Z) + \psi^* \sum_{s=1}^{m} \theta_{rs}^* d\left(\log \frac{y_s/P'^s}{Y'/P''}\right),$$

which is the *output allocation decision* for the rth product. The deflator in its price term is

$$(5.42) \qquad d\left(\log \frac{Y'}{P''}\right) = d(\log Y') - d(\log P''),$$

which is the same for each $d[\log (y_s/P'^s)]$ that is deflated in (5.41). Thus, by separating the output supply system (5.33) into the total-output decision (5.40) and the output allocation decision (5.41), we eliminate the presence of different deflators. In fact, (5.41) is of entirely the same form as the consumer demand equation (2.23), which suggests that we can extend the notion of specific substitution and complementarity relations to outputs.

4. The double prime of $d(\log P'')$ in (5.39) serves to indicate that Frisch weights are used twice, both in (5.31) and in (5.39). By contrast, $d(\log P')$ is shown in (5.32) as a Divisia-weighted mean of the Frisch indexes of (5.31). Under input-output separability both the index (5.31) for each r and the index (5.39) are all equal to $d(\log P')$; see remark (2) at the end of this section.

Recall from section 2.6 that such relations for pairs of consumer goods are based on the signs of the θ_{ij}'s. These relations refer to demand. We extend this to the firm's supply side by defining the rth and sth products as specific substitutes (complements) *in supply* when θ_{rs}^* is negative (positive). Thus, given that $\psi^* > 0$ in (5.33), an increase in the price of a product reduces (raises) the supply of another product when the two are specific substitutes (complements) in supply.

By dividing (5.41) by g_r we find that the ratio θ_r^*/g_r is the elasticity of the supply of the rth product with respect to the Divisia volume index of all products. We shall refer to this ratio as the Divisia elasticity of the rth product; this is the analogue of the Divisia elasticity θ_i/f_i of the ith input. These elasticities are of interest in relation to the price elasticity ψ^* of the firm's total supply, which may be explained as follows. In Appendix C we prove

$$(5.43) \qquad\qquad \mathbf{g}'(\psi^*\mathbf{\Theta}^*)^{-1}\mathbf{g} = \frac{\gamma - \psi}{\psi},$$

which implies $\gamma > \psi$ because $\psi^*\mathbf{\Theta}^* = [\psi^*\theta_{rs}^*]$ is positive definite. In the next paragraph we shall prove that $\mathbf{g}'\mathbf{\Theta}^{*-1}\mathbf{g} \geq 1$, with equality if and only if all products have unitary Divisia elasticities. On combining this with (5.43) and $\gamma > \psi$, we obtain

$$(5.44) \qquad\qquad \psi^* \geq \frac{\psi}{\gamma - \psi} > 0.$$

Hence the price elasticity of total supply equals the ratio $\psi/(\gamma - \psi)$ under this condition of unitary Divisia elasticities, and it is larger than this ratio otherwise. Note that this result contains (4.31) as a special case because the Divisia elasticity of a product must be identically equal to 1 for a single-product firm.

To prove the inequality for $\mathbf{g}'\mathbf{\Theta}^{*-1}\mathbf{g}$, we note that all products have unitary Divisia elasticities if and only if $\mathbf{g}$ equals $\mathbf{\Theta}^*$ postmultiplied by a vector of unit elements (see eq. [5.37]). Since $\mathbf{\Theta}^*$ is symmetric positive definite, and since the elements of both $\mathbf{\Theta}^*$ and $\mathbf{g}$ add up to 1, it is thus sufficient to prove the following lemma: If the elements of a matrix $\mathbf{A}$ and those of a vector $\mathbf{b}$ add up to 1, $\iota'\mathbf{A}\iota = \iota'\mathbf{b} = 1$, and if $\mathbf{A}$ is symmetric positive definite, then $\mathbf{b}'\mathbf{A}^{-1}\mathbf{b} \geq 1$, with equality if and only if $\mathbf{b} = \mathbf{A}\iota$. For $\mathbf{b} = \mathbf{A}\iota$ we have $\mathbf{b}'\mathbf{A}^{-1}\mathbf{b} = \iota'\mathbf{A}\mathbf{A}^{-1}\mathbf{A}\iota = \iota'\mathbf{A}\iota = 1$. For $\mathbf{b} \neq \mathbf{A}\iota$ we write $\mathbf{b} = \mathbf{A}(\iota + \mathbf{v})$ with $\mathbf{v} \neq \mathbf{0}$, which must satisfy $\iota'\mathbf{A}\mathbf{v} = 0$ because

$$1 = \iota'\mathbf{b} = \iota'\mathbf{A}(\iota + \mathbf{v}) = 1 + \iota'\mathbf{A}\mathbf{v},$$

after which $\mathbf{b}'\mathbf{A}^{-1}\mathbf{b} = 1 + \mathbf{v}'\mathbf{A}\mathbf{v} > 1$ follows directly.

Remarks

1. The interpretation of θ_r^* as the marginal share of the rth product can be verified from (5.41). Suppose that output prices do not change so that $d(\log Z) = d(\log R)$ and the first term on the right in (5.41) becomes $(\theta_r^* dR)/R$. Also suppose that the input prices change proportionately so that the second term in (5.41) vanishes. Since the left-hand side of (5.41) equals $(y_r dz_r)/R$, we thus have $y_r dz_r = \theta_r^* dR$, which shows that θ_r^* can be interpreted as the proportion of an additional dollar of total revenue which is accounted for by the rth product.

2. Since (5.21) holds under input-output separability, the indexes (5.31) and (5.39) are equal to $d(\log P')$ under this condition. This implies that the price term of the output allocation decision (5.41) is simplified to

$$\psi^* \sum_{s=1}^{m} \theta_{rs}^* d\left(\log \frac{y_s}{Y'}\right),$$

which does not contain changes in input prices. Therefore, under input-output separability the output allocation decision is independent of the changes in the input prices. This result is the "output version" of an analogous result obtained in section 5.5, viz., that under this separability the input allocation decision does not involve the output changes which occur in the covariance Γ_i (see eqs. [5.24] and [5.25]).

3. In remark (2) at the end of section 4.7 we noted that under profit maximization, γ equals the ratio of revenue to cost, and that the validity of the supply equation requires $\gamma > 1$. Both results also apply to the profit-maximizing multiproduct firm (see eq. [5.30]).

5.8   The Multiproduct Cost Function and Output Independence

The cost function of the multiproduct firm is a straightforward extension of the single-product cost function. Shephard's lemma (4.5) applies also to several outputs when z is interpreted as a vector. Two special cases should be mentioned. First, under input-output separability the cost function $C(\mathbf{z}, \mathbf{p})$ takes the form $C(f(\mathbf{z}), \mathbf{p})$, where $f(\mathbf{z})$ is a scalar function of the output vector. The second case is that in which $C(\ )$ can be written as the sum of m functions, one for each product:

$$(5.45) \qquad\qquad C(\mathbf{z}, \mathbf{p}) = \sum_{r=1}^{m} C_r(z_r, \mathbf{p}).$$

In this case $\partial^2 C/\partial \mathbf{z}\partial \mathbf{z}'$ and $[\theta_{rs}^*]$ are diagonal matrices (see eq. [5.34]), and

(5.37) becomes $\theta_r^* = \theta_{rr}^*$, so that the supply equation (5.33) becomes

$$(5.46) \qquad\qquad g_r d(\log z_r) = \psi^* \theta_r^* d\left(\log \frac{y_r}{P'^r}\right),$$

which shows that no product has a specific supply substitution or complementarity relation with any other product.

Hall [169] has shown that (5.45) is a necessary and sufficient condition for the technology of the multiproduct firm to be *output-independent* in the following sense.[5] Consider m single-output production functions:

$$(5.47) \qquad\qquad \log z_r = h^r(q_1^r, \ldots, q_n^r) \qquad r = 1, \ldots, m.$$

Output independence means that functions (5.47) exist so that, first, if (5.2) holds, there exists a factor allocation

$$(5.48) \qquad\qquad q_i^1 + \cdots + q_i^m = q_i \qquad i = 1, \ldots, n$$

such that (5.47) holds for each of $h^1(\ )$, ..., $h^m(\ )$, and second, if (5.47) holds, then (5.2) holds for the z_r's of (5.47) and the q_i's of (5.48). Thus, output independence means that the multiproduct firm with technology (5.2) could be broken up into m single-product firms, each with one of the production functions (5.47), and that these m single-product firms, independently adjusting output so as to maximize profit, would use the same aggregate level of each input and produce the same level of output as the multiproduct firm.

5.9 An Example

We use a particular form of the multiproduct cost function to illustrate some of the concepts introduced above.[6] The form chosen is a translog cost function with two inputs and two outputs,

$$(5.49) \qquad\qquad \log C = f_1(\mathbf{z}) + f_2(\mathbf{p}) + f_3(\mathbf{z}, \mathbf{p}),$$

---

5. The term used by Hall is nonjoint rather than output-independent, but "nonjoint" is not fully satisfactory. As interpreted by Hall and by Hirota and Kuga [185] and (originally) by Samuelson [344], it means that there are no economies or diseconomies of jointness for any pair of outputs in the production function. This leaves no provision for disjointness of one group of outputs from another. We shall refer to that case as block independence of outputs (see section 9.6).

6. We could also use an algebraic specification of the production function, but this does not make any difference because of the duality of the production and cost functions. The firm's behavior under competitive conditions can be derived equivalently from either function.

where

$$f_1(\mathbf{z}) = A_1 \log z_1 + A_2 \log z_2 + \tfrac{1}{2}A_1 A_2 \left[\left(\log \frac{z_1}{z_2} \right)^2 + k^*(\log z_1 z_2)^2 \right],$$

$$f_2(\mathbf{p}) = \beta_1 \log p_1 + \beta_2 \log p_2 + \tfrac{1}{2}\beta_1 \beta_2 (1 - a) \left(\log \frac{p_1}{p_2} \right)^2,$$

$$f_3(\mathbf{z}, \mathbf{p}) = \tfrac{1}{2}kA(\beta_1 \beta_2)^{1/2}(\log z_1 z_2) \log \frac{p_1}{p_2}.$$

In the equation for $f_1(\mathbf{z})$, A_1 and A_2 are positive constants with sum $A = A_1 + A_2 > 1$; k^* is a constant larger than $-1 + 1/A$. In the equation for $f_3(\mathbf{z}, \mathbf{p})$, the β's are positive constants with unit sum and k is a constant less than 1 in absolute value. In the equation for $f_2(\mathbf{p})$, a equals the ratio of $1 - k^2$ to $1 + 4k^*A_1 A_2/A^2$. Units are chosen so that $p_1 = p_2 = z_1 = z_2 = 1$ holds at the point of maximum profit.

It can be shown after some algebra that the normalized price coefficient matrix of the output supply equations is

$$(5.50) \qquad [\theta_{rs}^*] = \frac{1}{b} \begin{bmatrix} g_1(A - 1 + k^*Ag_1) & -k^*Ag_1 g_2 \\ -k^*Ag_1 g_2 & g_2(A - 1 + k^*Ag_2) \end{bmatrix},$$

where g_1 and g_2 are the output revenue shares at the point of maximum profit and

$$(5.51) \qquad b = A - 1 + k^*A(g_1 - g_2)^2 > 0.$$

We conclude from (5.50) that the two products are specific substitutes (complements) in supply when k^* is positive (negative). If $k^* = 0$, the supply equations take the output-independent form (5.46). Also, $k^* = 0$ implies that the two products have unitary Divisia elasticities and that ψ^* (the price elasticity of the supply of the firm's output as a whole) equals the reciprocal of $A - 1$ at this point.

The normalized price coefficient matrix of the input demand equations is

$$(5.52) \qquad [\theta_{ij}] = \begin{bmatrix} f_1[1 + 2k(f_1 f_2)^{1/2}] & k(f_2 - f_1)(f_1 f_2)^{1/2} \\ k(f_2 - f_1)(f_1 f_2)^{1/2} & f_2[1 - 2k(f_1 f_2)^{1/2}] \end{bmatrix}$$

and the marginal share vectors arranged in partitioned matrix form are

$$(5.53) \qquad [\boldsymbol{\theta}^1 \quad \boldsymbol{\theta}^2] = \begin{bmatrix} f_1 + [k(f_1 f_2)^{1/2}]/2g_1 & f_1 + [k(f_1 f_2)^{1/2}]/2g_2 \\ f_2 - [k(f_1 f_2)^{1/2}]/2g_1 & f_2 - [k(f_1 f_2)^{1/2}]/2g_2 \end{bmatrix},$$

where $\boldsymbol{\theta}^r = [\theta_1^r \quad \theta_2^r]'$ and f_1 and f_2 are the factor shares of the inputs at the point of maximum profit. We conclude from the matrix (5.52) that the input demand equations take the input-independent form (5.20) when these shares are equal and also when $k = 0$. In the latter case all marginal shares are identical to the corresponding factor shares (see eq. [5.53]), which amounts to input-output separability and unitary Divisia elasticities of the inputs at the point of maximum profit.

Six

The Firm and the Consumer Further Considered

The successive developments in chapters 4 and 5 have shown that the theories of the consumer and the firm have much in common. The objective of this chapter is the discussion of certain topics which show other similarities.

6.1 The Consumer as a Profit-Maximizing Seller of Utility

Consider a single-product firm with technology (4.1). If the firm takes the output price y and the input price vector $\mathbf{p}$ as given, its profit function takes the form

$$(6.1) \qquad \pi(y, \mathbf{p}) = \max (yz - \mathbf{p'q}),$$

where the maximization takes place over z and $\mathbf{q}$ subject to (4.1). The function $\pi(\ )$ is convex and homogeneous of degree 1 in y and $\mathbf{p}$. Shephard's lemma for the profit function states that

$$(6.2) \qquad \frac{\partial \pi}{\partial y} = z, \qquad \frac{\partial \pi}{\partial \mathbf{p}} = -\mathbf{q}.$$

If the firm makes m products rather than one, the only modification which (6.1) and (6.2) require is a vector interpretation of y and z.

Although the profit concept specifically refers to a firm, it can be applied to a consumer also.[1] In section 3.2 we described the consumer as a pro-

---

1. The developments in the remainder of this section were suggested by Professor Angus Deaton, who attributed them to Professor W. M. Gorman.

ducer of utility. Imagine, then, that he sells this utility to himself at a price y, which implies the following profit:

$$(6.3) \qquad \pi(y, \mathbf{p}) = \max_{\mathbf{q}} \ [yu(\mathbf{q}) - \mathbf{p}'\mathbf{q}].$$

A comparison of the expression in brackets with the Lagrangean function $u(\mathbf{q}) - \lambda(\mathbf{p}'\mathbf{q} - M)$ of section 2.1 shows that y (the price of utility) can be identified with the reciprocal of the marginal utility of income:

$$(6.4) \qquad y = \frac{1}{\lambda}.$$

Shephard's lemma (6.2) applied to (6.3) yields

$$(6.5) \qquad \frac{\partial \pi}{\partial y} = u, \qquad \frac{\partial \pi}{\partial \mathbf{p}} = -\mathbf{q},$$

while the homogeneity of $\pi(\ )$ implies

$$(6.6) \qquad \frac{\partial^2 \pi}{\partial p_i \partial y} y + \sum_{j=1}^{n} \frac{\partial^2 \pi}{\partial p_i \partial p_j} p_j = 0 \qquad i = 1, \ldots, n.$$

It is shown in Appendix B that the differential demand equation (2.23) can be expressed in terms of derivatives of the profit function, with normalized price coefficients of the following form:

$$(6.7) \qquad \theta_{ij} = \frac{p_i p_j}{y^2} \frac{\partial^2 \pi / \partial p_i \partial p_j}{\partial^2 \pi / \partial y^2} \qquad i, j = 1, \ldots, n$$

The case of block independence is particularly instructive. As in section 2.7, we write $\mathbf{q}_g$ for the subvector of $\mathbf{q}$ which consists of the q_i's of S_g; let $\mathbf{p}_g$ be the corresponding price subvector. Then, if (2.33) holds, we can write (6.3) as

$$
\begin{aligned}
(6.8) \qquad \pi(y, \mathbf{p}) &= \max_{\mathbf{q}} \left[y \sum_{g=1}^{G} u_g(\mathbf{q}_g) - \mathbf{p}'_g \mathbf{q}_g \right] \\
&= \sum_{g=1}^{G} \max_{\mathbf{q}_g} \ [yu_g(\mathbf{q}_g) - \mathbf{p}'_g \mathbf{q}_g].
\end{aligned}
$$

When we define $\pi_g(y, \mathbf{p}_g)$ as the expression after the summation sign on the second line, we see immediately that $[\partial^2 \pi / \partial p_i \partial p_j]$ is now a block-diagonal matrix. It thus follows from (6.7) that $[\theta_{ij}]$ is also block-diagonal, which yields (2.34).

6.2   The Theory of True Indexes
Applied to the Firm

The extension of the theory of the true indexes of chapter 3 to the firm's inputs is straightforward. For example, if the firm makes one product, the extension of the true cost-of-living index (3.8) is

$$(6.9) \qquad P(\mathbf{p}_2, \mathbf{p}_1 | z) = \frac{C(z, \mathbf{p}_2)}{C(z, \mathbf{p}_1)},$$

which is the true cost-of-production index that compares the input price vectors $\mathbf{p}_2$ and $\mathbf{p}_1$ at the output rate z. The true index of real input expenditure that compares the outputs z_2 and z_1 at the input price vector $\mathbf{p}$ is

$$(6.10) \qquad Q(z_2, z_1 | \mathbf{p}) = \frac{C(z_2, \mathbf{p})}{C(z_1, \mathbf{p})}.$$

This is the firm's input version of the consumer's true real-income index (3.12). Similarly, the true marginal-cost index which compares $\mathbf{p}_2$ with $\mathbf{p}_1$ at z is defined as

$$(6.11) \qquad P'(\mathbf{p}_2, \mathbf{p}_1 | z) = \frac{C'(z, \mathbf{p}_2)}{C'(z, \mathbf{p}_1)},$$

where $C'(z, \mathbf{p})$ equals $\partial C / \partial z$ evaluated at $(z, \mathbf{p})$. The index (6.11) is the extension of the consumer's index (3.14).

When input expenditure is minimized for given z and $\mathbf{p}$, we have

$$(6.12) \qquad \log P(\mathbf{p} + d\mathbf{p}, \mathbf{p} | z) = \sum_{i=1}^{n} f_i d(\log p_i),$$

$$(6.13) \qquad \log Q(z + dz, z | \mathbf{p}) = \sum_{i=1}^{n} f_i d(\log q_i),$$

$$(6.14) \qquad \log P'(\mathbf{p} + d\mathbf{p}, \mathbf{p} | z) = \sum_{i=1}^{n} \theta_i d(\log p_i),$$

where θ_i is defined in (4.9). The above results are immediate extensions of equations (3.15) to (3.17). We conclude that the firm's Divisia indexes of the inputs and also the Frisch price index (4.10) can all be interpreted as true indexes based on the firm's cost function.

The multiproduct extension of (6.9) to (6.14) is a matter of interpreting the z's as vectors, but (6.11) is replaced by

$$(6.15) \qquad P_r'(\mathbf{p}_2, \mathbf{p}_1|\mathbf{z}) = \frac{C_r'(\mathbf{z}, \mathbf{p}_2)}{C_r'(\mathbf{z}, \mathbf{p}_1)},$$

which is the true marginal-cost index of the rth product that compares $\mathbf{p}_2$ and $\mathbf{p}_1$ at $\mathbf{z}$, with $C_r'(\mathbf{z}, \mathbf{p})$ defined as $\partial C / \partial z_r$ at $(\mathbf{z}, \mathbf{p})$. The implied modification of (6.14) is

$$(6.16) \qquad \log P_r'(\mathbf{p} + d\mathbf{p}, \mathbf{p}|\mathbf{z}) = \sum_{i=1}^{n} \theta_i^r d(\log p_i),$$

where θ_i^r is defined in (5.5).

There are similar indexes for the outputs of the multiproduct firm, which are based on the revenue rather than the cost function. The revenue function is defined in Appendix D.

6.3   The Distance Function

In addition to the real-income index (3.12) there are volume indexes based on the so-called distance function. This function, from Shephard [358], is considered in the present section, after which the associated volume indexes will be described in section 6.4.

Figure 2 illustrates the consumer's quantity space for $n = 2$ (the extension for larger n is straightforward). The curve $L(U)$ is the indifference curve

Fig. 2   Fig. 3

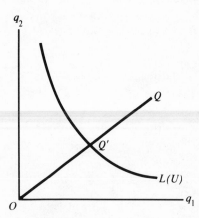
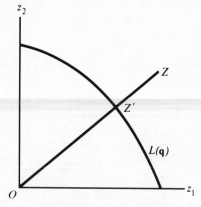

Figures 2 and 3   The distance function and its
                                        output version for the
                                        multiproduct firm

at which utility equals U. The coordinates of Q form a vector $\mathbf{q}$, and Q' is the intersection point of the ray OQ and the indifference curve $L(U)$. The distance function $t(U, \mathbf{q})$ is defined as the ratio of the distances of Q and Q' from the origin:

(6.17) $$t(U, \mathbf{q}) = \frac{OQ}{OQ'}.$$

The value of this function is 1 when Q is located on the indifference curve $L(U)$:

(6.18) $$t(U, \mathbf{q}) = 1 \quad \text{if and only if} \quad u(\mathbf{q}) = U.$$

This result shows that the distance function $t(U, \mathbf{q})$ is equivalent to the utility function $u(\mathbf{q})$ in that both describe the consumer's preferences. The two functions differ from each other in that the distance function is homogeneous of degree 1 in the quantities:

(6.19) $$t(U, k\mathbf{q}) \equiv kt(U, \mathbf{q}) \quad \text{for any} \quad k > 0.$$

To verify this we multiply the vector OQ in figure 2 by k and note that this multiplication does not affect the intersection point Q'. Therefore, the ratio in (6.17) is multiplied by k, which confirms (6.19).

The extension of the distance function for the inputs of a firm is straightforward; the only adjustments needed are the reinterpretation of $L(U)$ in figure 2 as $L(z)$, the locus of all input combinations that yield a given output z, and the replacement of U by z in (6.17). If the firm makes m products rather than one, all we have to do is interpret z as a vector.

Figure 3 illustrates a different kind of distance function for a two-product firm (the extension for a larger number of products is again straightforward). The variables measured along the axes are the two outputs, and the curve $L(\mathbf{q})$ is the locus of all output combinations that can be produced from a given input vector $\mathbf{q}$. We define

(6.20) $$t^*(\mathbf{q}, z) = \frac{OZ'}{OZ},$$

where Z is the point whose coordinates are the elements of the vector z and Z' is the intersection point of the ray OZ and the curve $L(\mathbf{q})$. It is evident from equation (6.20) and figure 3 that

(6.21) $$t^*(\mathbf{q}, z) = 1$$

is necessary and sufficient in order that z can be produced from $\mathbf{q}$. Hence (6.21) is a description of the multiproduct technology in the same way that $t(U, \mathbf{q}) = 1$ is a description of the consumer's preferences (see eq. [6.18]).

Equation (6.21) can be used to show that the multiproduct technology can be represented by a production function (5.2) which has the output-homogeneous property (5.4). The clue is the fact that $t^*(\ )$ is homogeneous of degree -1 in the outputs:

$$(6.22) \qquad t^*(\mathbf{q}, k\mathbf{z}) \equiv (1/k)t^*(\mathbf{q}, \mathbf{z}) \quad \text{for any} \quad k > 0.$$

This may be verified by multiplying the vector OZ in figure 3 by k, which has the effect of multiplying the right-hand side of (6.20) by $1/k$. An implication of the homogeneity is

$$(6.23) \qquad \sum_{r=1}^{m} \frac{\partial t^*}{\partial z_r} z_r = -t^*.$$

Next we take logarithms of both sides of (6.21),

$$(6.24) \qquad \log t^*(\mathbf{q}, \mathbf{z}) = 0,$$

and define $h(\mathbf{q}, \mathbf{z})$ as $\log t^*(\mathbf{q}, \mathbf{z})$. It is then readily verified that (6.24) and (6.23) are equivalent to (5.2) and (5.4), respectively. Therefore, the output-homogeneous property (5.4) can be imposed on the production function $h(\ )$ of a multiproduct technology by means of (6.20), which is simply an output version of the firm's distance function.

6.4 Volume Indexes Based on the Consumer's Distance Function

The homogeneity of degree 1 of the distance function $t(U, \mathbf{q})$ in the quantities (see [6.19]) should be contrasted with the corresponding property of the cost function $C(U, \mathbf{p})$ in the prices (see section 3.2). The indexes developed in chapter 3 are all based on the cost function; in this section we shall proceed similarly on the basis of the distance function. The exposition is in part based on Deaton [105], but Malmquist [264] should be mentioned as a precursor. It will be convenient to reproduce the indexes (3.8) and (3.12),

$$(6.25) \qquad P(\mathbf{p}_2, \mathbf{p}_1 | U) = \frac{C(U, \mathbf{p}_2)}{C(U, \mathbf{p}_1)},$$

$$(6.26) \qquad Q(U_2, U_1 | \mathbf{p}) = \frac{C(U_2, \mathbf{p})}{C(U_1, \mathbf{p})},$$

as well as equations (3.15) and (3.17) in the slightly modified form

(6.27) $$\log P(\mathbf{p} + d\mathbf{p}, \mathbf{p}|u_t(M, \mathbf{p})) = d(\log P),$$

(6.28) $$\log Q(U + dU, U|\mathbf{p}) = d(\log Q),$$

where $U = u_t(M, \mathbf{p})$ and $U + dU = u_t(M + dM, \mathbf{p} + d\mathbf{p})$.

Figure 4 contains two quantity points (Q_1 and Q_2) and the intersection points (Q_1' and Q_2') of the rays OQ_1 and OQ_2 with the indifference curve $L(U)$. Since Q_1' and Q_2' are on the same indifference curve, they are equivalent from the consumer's point of view. Therefore, a natural choice for the volume index which compares the quantity points Q_2 and Q_1 is the ratio of OQ_2/OQ_2' to OQ_1/OQ_1'. It follows from (6.17) that this amounts to

(6.29) $$Q_A(\mathbf{q}_2, \mathbf{q}_1|U) = \frac{t(U, \mathbf{q}_2)}{t(U, \mathbf{q}_1)},$$

which is the true volume index that compares $\mathbf{q}_2$ with $\mathbf{q}_1$ at the utility level U. This index provides a direct comparison of two quantity vectors for any U in the same way that the true cost-of-living index (6.25) gives a direct comparison of two price vectors for any U. By contrast, the true real-income index (6.26) contains no quantities directly; it provides a comparison of money-metric utilities (Samuelson's term) in that it involves dollar amounts needed to attain certain utility levels.

Fig. 4   Fig. 5

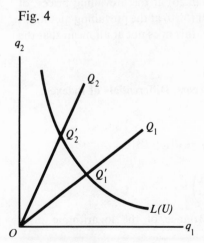

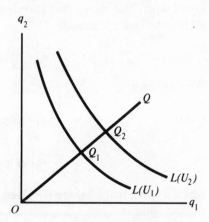

Figures 4 and 5   Two volume indexes based on the consumer's distance function

Note that (6.25) and (6.26) are obtained from each other by interchanging the roles of utility and prices. We can proceed similarly for (6.29) by interchanging the roles of utility and quantities. This yields

$$(6.30) \qquad Q_B(U_2, U_1 | \mathbf{q}) = \frac{t(U_1, \mathbf{q})}{t(U_2, \mathbf{q})},$$

which is another volume index. (Note the subscript 1 in the numerator and 2 in the denominator.) The index (6.30) is illustrated in figure 5. It follows from (6.17) that the right-hand side of (6.30) is equal to the ratio of OQ/OQ_1 to OQ/OQ_2 and thus equals OQ_2/OQ_1. This index compares the points on two indifference curves by means of the distances from the origin at which these curves intersect a particular quantity vector OQ. This is in contrast to the real-income index (6.26), which compares the points on two indifference curves by means of the dollar amounts needed to reach them at a particular price vector $\mathbf{p}$.

By now we have three Q's: equations (6.26), (6.29), and (6.30). How do they compare? One answer is provided by considering infinitesimal changes. Recall from equation (6.28) that the logarithm of the index (6.26) equals the Divisia volume index when evaluated at the prevailing prices. It can be shown that the indexes (6.29) and (6.30) satisfy

$$(6.31) \qquad \log Q_A(\mathbf{q} + d\mathbf{q}, \mathbf{q} | u(\mathbf{q})) = d(\log Q),$$

$$(6.32) \qquad \log Q_B(u(\mathbf{q} + d\mathbf{q}), u(\mathbf{q}) | \mathbf{q}) = d(\log Q).$$

Thus, the first-order terms of the index (6.26) at the prevailing prices, of (6.29) at the prevailing utility level, and of (6.30) at the prevailing quantities are all equal. But, as we shall shortly see, this does not at all mean that the three indexes are identical.

6.5   Second Differentials of Indexes

We introduce

$$(6.33) \qquad \Pi = \sum_{i=1}^{n} w_i [d(\log p_i) - d(\log P)]^2$$

$$= \sum_{i=1}^{n} w_i \left[d \left(\log \frac{p_i}{P} \right) \right]^2,$$

which is the budget-share-weighted variance of the logarithmic price changes, and

$$(6.34) \qquad \Pi' = \sum_{i=1}^{n} \sum_{j=1}^{n} \theta_{ij} d \left(\log \frac{p_i}{P'} \right) d \left(\log \frac{p_j}{P'} \right),$$

which is a positive definite quadratic form in the Frisch-deflated price changes with $[\theta_{ij}]$ as matrix.

Laitinen [223] proved the following extension of (6.27):

(6.35) $\log P(\mathbf{p} + \Delta\mathbf{p}, \mathbf{p}|u_I(M, \mathbf{p})) \approx d(\log P) + \frac{1}{2}(\Pi + \phi\Pi')$.

Note that we have $\Delta\mathbf{p}$ rather than $d\mathbf{p}$ on the left and that $\approx$ indicates "equal to up to terms of the second order." The first term on the right is the Divisia price index. This is the leading term and it agrees with (6.27). The last term in (6.35) is the second-order term; it emerges when we consider second differentials, and it will be further considered at the end of this section.

The analogous extension of (6.28) is

(6.36) $\log Q(U + \Delta U, U|\mathbf{p})$

$$\approx d(\log Q) - \frac{1}{2}(\Pi + \phi\Pi') + d(\log Q)d\left(\log \frac{P}{P'}\right),$$

where $U = u_I(M, \mathbf{p})$ and $U + \Delta U = u_I(M + \Delta M, \mathbf{p} + \Delta\mathbf{p})$. The first term on the right in (6.36) is the leading term, which confirms (6.28). The second-order term consists of two components, the first of which is equal to the second-order term in (6.35), apart from sign.

When we proceed similarly for (6.31) and (6.32), replacing $d\mathbf{q}$ by $\Delta\mathbf{q}$ and evaluating second differentials, we find that the second-order terms are different from each other and also different from that in (6.36). Thus, the Q's of (6.26), (6.29), and (6.30) are all pairwise different, although their first-order terms are all equal to the Divisia volume index. The second-order terms of both Q_A and Q_B contain the square of the Divisia volume index multiplied by a coefficient which involves second derivatives of the distance function. The interested reader should consult Appendix B on this matter.

The results (6.35) and (6.36) were derived by Laitinen under the condition that the logarithms of income and prices are the independent variables; this is a natural procedure in the differential approach to consumption theory.[2] Note that the second-order terms in (6.35) and (6.36) are indeed of the second order in the changes in these logarithms. This is immediately obvious for Π and Π', which are linear combinations of squares and products of logarithmic changes in prices (see eqs. [6.33] and [6.34]). It is also

---

2. The specification of the independent variables is an important matter. If a (positive) variable x is an independent variable, its second differential vanishes but that of $\log x$ does not vanish. If $\log x$ is an independent variable, the second differential of $\log x$ vanishes but $d^2x = x[d(\log x)]^2$. See Allen [6, section 17.8)].

true for the last term of (6.36), because $d(\log Q)$ equals $d(\log M)$ − $d(\log P)$; hence that term is of the second order in the logarithmic changes in both M and the p_i's. In the remainder of this section we shall clarify these second-order terms, mainly for (6.35); those of (6.36) are similar except for the last term, which will be considered at the end of section 6.6.

The component $\frac{1}{2}\phi\Pi'$ of the second-order term in (6.35) is obviously due to price substitution. This component is negative when prices do not change proportionally, reflecting the fact that substitution enables the consumer to attain the utility level $u_l(M, \mathbf{p})$ of (6.35) with a smaller amount of expenditure than would be possible if there were no substitution. At the same time, this substitution enables the consumer to attain a higher utility level, which explains the positive sign of the substitution component $-\frac{1}{2}\phi\Pi'$ in the real-income comparison (6.36). This comparison also shows that the substitution effect is of the second order relative to the change in real income, since the latter change is represented by the leading term $d(\log Q)$ in (6.36). Therefore, the analysis of second differentials is useful not only as a refinement of first-order effects, but also as a tool for verifying which effects dominate other effects.

The interpretation of the other component $(\frac{1}{2}\Pi)$ of the second-order term in (6.35) is simplified when we combine it with the leading term. We write (6.33) in the equivalent form

$$\Pi = \sum_{i=1}^{n} w_i d\left(\log \frac{p_i}{P}\right) d(\log p_i),$$

which gives

$$(6.37) \qquad d(\log P) + \tfrac{1}{2}\Pi = \sum_{i=1}^{n} \left[w_i + \tfrac{1}{2}w_i d\left(\log \frac{p_i}{P}\right) \right] d(\log p_i).$$

The expression on the left is the leading term of (6.35) plus the component $\frac{1}{2}\Pi$ of the second-order term. Next we use (2.9) to write (2.15) in the form

$$(6.38) \qquad dw_i = w_i d\left(\log \frac{p_i}{P}\right) + w_i d\left(\log \frac{q_i}{Q}\right),$$

which shows that the term in brackets in (6.37) is the arithmetic mean of the ith budget share and the changed value of this share when the effect of quantity changes (the second term in eq. [6.38]) is ignored. Thus, $\frac{1}{2}\Pi$ in (6.35) can be viewed as a correction of $d(\log P)$ which alters the budget shares in accordance with the changes in prices.

Why is the effect of quantity changes ignored in (6.37)? The answer is that this effect must be ignored because it is represented by the term $\frac{1}{2}\phi\Pi'$

in (6.35). To verify that this is so, we note that when the second term of (6.38) is not ignored, (6.37) obtains an extra term equal to

$$(6.39) \qquad \frac{1}{2} \sum_{i=1}^{n} w_i d\left(\log \frac{q_i}{Q}\right) d(\log p_i).$$

We have $d(\log Q) = 0$ because utility is fixed at the level $u_i(M, \mathbf{p})$ in (6.35). Therefore, (6.39) is simplified to

$$(6.40) \qquad \frac{1}{2} \sum_{i=1}^{n} w_i d(\log q_i) d(\log p_i) = \frac{1}{2}\phi \sum_{i=1}^{n} \sum_{j=1}^{n} \theta_{ij} d(\log p_i) d\left(\log \frac{p_j}{P'}\right),$$

where the equal sign is based on (2.23) and $d(\log Q) = 0$. It is readily verified that the right-hand side of (6.40) equals $\frac{1}{2}\phi\Pi'$.

6.6   More on Second Differentials in Consumption Theory

The variance Π defined in (6.33) vanishes when all prices change proportionally, and it takes an increasing positive value when the prices change more disproportionately. A finite-change version of Π was used by Törnqvist [412] some forty years ago. More recently Parks [302] analyzed Dutch and American data and noted that the disproportionality of price changes tends to increase when the price level is subject to larger changes (either upward or downward). One of the models which he used to describe this phenomenon is

$$(6.41) \qquad \Pi = \alpha_0 + \alpha_1 [d \log P)]^2,$$

where α_0 and α_1 are positive coefficients. Parks also related Π to problems of unanticipated inflation.

Under preference independence ($\theta_{ij} = 0$ for $i \neq j$ and $\theta_{ii} = \theta_i$) we can simplify Π' of (6.34) to

$$(6.42) \qquad \Pi' = \sum_{i=1}^{n} \theta_i [d(\log p_i) - d(\log P')]^2$$

$$= \sum_{i=1}^{n} \left[\theta_i d\left(\log \frac{p_i}{P'}\right)^2\right].$$

This is a weighted variance of the logarithmic price changes, but unlike (6.33) it uses marginal shares as weights. To distinguish between these two sets of weights, we shall refer to (6.42) as the *Frisch variance* of the price changes, and to (6.33) as the *Divisia variance* of these changes. If we have preference independence so that (6.42) applies, and if the use of different weights does not make much difference, the sign of the second-order term in (6.35) is determined by the value of ϕ. Applied studies tend to confirm that ϕ is negative and less than 1 in absolute value. If this is true, and if the two conditions mentioned above are satisfied, the positive Π in (6.35) will dominate the negative $\phi\Pi'$. See Theil [397, section 13.4] for further details.

We obtain additional insight by considering the Divisia decomposition of the consumer's income,

$$d(\log M) = \sum_{i=1}^{n} w_i d(\log p_i) + \sum_{i=1}^{n} w_i d(\log q_i),$$

and then taking the differential of both sides. Laitinen [228] showed that this yields the following result:

(6.43) $$\sum_{i=1}^{n} w_i d^2(\log q_i) = -\sum_{i=1}^{n} w_i [d(\log w_i)]^2.$$

The left-hand side is the Divisia mean (the weighted mean with budget shares as weights) of the second differentials of the logarithms of the quantities. The analogous mean of the first differentials is the Divisia volume index, which is unrestricted in sign, but (6.43) shows that the mean of the second differentials is nonpositive and equal to minus the Divisia-weighted second moment of the logarithmic changes in the budget shares. Actually, this second moment is the Divisia variance because the corresponding mean vanishes:

$$\sum_{i=1}^{n} w_i d(\log w_i) = \sum_{i=1}^{n} w_i \frac{dw_i}{w_i} = 0.$$

The variance in the right-hand side of (6.43) is a measure of the change in the allocation of income; it vanishes when the allocation proportions (the budget shares) remain unchanged, and it takes increasing positive values when the changes in these proportions are larger. We shall find it useful to pursue this matter a little further. From $w_i = p_i q_i / M$ we obtain

$$d(\log w_i) = d(\log p_i) + d(\log q_i) - d(\log M)$$

$$= [d(\log p_i) - d(\log P)] + [d(\log q_i) - d(\log Q)].$$

Using the expression in the second line, we find

$$(6.44) \qquad \sum_{i=1}^{n} w_i[d(\log w_i)]^2 = \Pi + K + 2\Gamma,$$

where Π is defined in (6.33), while K is the Divisia variance of the quantity changes and Γ is the Divisia covariance of the price and quantity changes:

$$(6.45) \qquad K = \sum_{i=1}^{n} w_i\left[d\left(\log \frac{q_i}{Q}\right)\right]^2,$$

$$(6.46) \qquad \Gamma = \sum_{i=1}^{n} w_i d\left(\log \frac{p_i}{P}\right) d\left(\log \frac{q_i}{Q}\right).$$

Thus, (6.43) shows that the Divisia mean of the second differentials of the quantity logarithms is equal to minus the Divisia variance of the logarithmic changes in the budget shares, while (6.44) states that this variance is equal to the sum of the Divisia variances of the logarithmic price and quantity changes plus twice the Divisia covariance of the latter changes. Needless to say, when we divide goods into groups of goods, we can also apply the familiar variance and covariance decompositions between groups and within groups; see Theil [384, 397] for examples of such decompositions.

Substitution of (2.23) in (6.46) yields

$$(6.47) \qquad \Gamma = \phi\Pi' - d(\log Q)d\left(\log \frac{P}{P'}\right),$$

where the first term on the right ($\phi\Pi'$) is the substitution component of Γ and the second is the real-income component. Hence $\phi\Pi'$ in the second-order terms of (6.35) and (6.36) can be identified with the substitution component of the Divisia covariance of the price and quantity changes. This component is negative (unless all prices change proportionately), which agrees with the intuitive notion that price changes and quantity changes should be negatively correlated because of the consumer's tendency to substitute in favor of those goods that have become relatively cheaper.

However, Γ may be positive when its real-income component is positive. This component is the second term on the right in (6.47) and it is also the last term (apart from sign) in (6.36). Its sign and magnitude are determined by the price changes of luxuries relative to those of necessities, combined with the question of whether real income increases or decreases. Suppose that real income increases, $d(\log Q) > 0$, which shifts the composition of the consumer's basket away from necessities toward luxuries. Also suppose that the prices of luxuries increase relative to those of necessities so that $d(\log P') > d(\log P)$ (see the discussion following eq. [2.20]). Then two things will happen:

1. The product of the two differentials on the right in (6.47) is negative, which means that Γ has a positive real-income component. This is as it should be, because the increase in real income raises the quantities consumed of luxuries relative to those of necessities in spite of the increased prices of the former relative to those of the latter. This parallel development of prices and quantities (those of luxuries both increasing and those of necessities both decreasing) contributes to a positive rather than a negative covariance of price and quantity changes.

2. The positive real-income component of Γ implies a negative value for the last term in (6.36). This negative value means that the leading term $d(\log Q)$ in (6.36) overstates the true increase in real income. The reason is that this leading term fails to take into consideration the fact that the shift toward luxuries caused by the real-income increase amounts to a shift to relatively more expensive goods.

6.7 Extensions to the Theory of the Firm

Many of the developments of section 6.6 can be extended to the theory of the firm. In fact, we met several Divisia- and Frisch-weighted moments in chapter 5: the Divisia covariance Γ_i in (5.24), θ_i as the Divisia-weighted mean of the θ_i^r's in (5.16), $d(\log P')$ as the Divisia-weighted mean of the m price indexes $d(\log P'^1), \ldots, d(\log P'^m)$ in (5.32), and $d(\log P'')$ as the Frisch-weighted mean of the same m indexes in (5.39). However, in the interest of brevity we shall confine ourselves here to the most important subject for subsequent developments: the profit (and its first two differentials) of a multiproduct firm, with the logarithms of the n input prices and the m output prices treated as independent variables.

It follows from (5.30) that profit measured as a fraction of revenue equals

$$(6.48) \qquad \frac{R - C}{R} = 1 - \frac{1}{\gamma}.$$

The first differential of profit, expressed as a fraction of revenue, equals

$$(6.49) \qquad \frac{d(R - C)}{R} = d(\log Y) - \frac{1}{\gamma} d(\log P),$$

where $d(\log Y)$ is the Divisia price index of the outputs:

(6.50) $$d(\log Y) = \sum_{r=1}^{m} g_r d(\log y_r).$$

The result (6.49) may be verified by applying the Divisia decomposition to dR and dC and then using the total-input decision (5.11).

Laitinen and Theil [229] proved that the second differential of profit, also expressed as a fraction of revenue, can be written as

(6.51) $\dfrac{d^2(R - C)}{R}$

$$= \sum_{r=1}^{m} g_r [d(\log y_r)]^2 - \frac{1}{\gamma} \sum_{i=1}^{n} f_i [d(\log p_i)]^2 + \psi^*\Pi^* + \frac{\psi}{\gamma}\Pi',$$

where Π' is defined in (6.34), with the p_i's now interpreted as input prices, while Π^* is a quadratic form in the output price changes deflated by their Frisch input price indexes:

(6.52) $$\Pi^* = \sum_{r=1}^{m} \sum_{s=1}^{m} \theta_{rs}^* d\left(\log \frac{y_r}{P'_r}\right) d\left(\log \frac{y_s}{P'_s}\right).$$

To interpret these results we note that (6.48) contains no price changes; that the first differential (6.49) contains these changes in the form of the two Divisia indexes; and that the second differential (6.51) consists of four terms, each of which is a quadratic form in price changes. The first two terms in (6.51) are in absolute price changes, whereas the last two are in relative price changes. The first two quadratic forms in (6.51) result from the homogeneity of degree 1 of the profit function in the $n + m$ input and output prices, which may be clarified as follows: The terms immediately to the right of the equal signs in (6.48), (6.49), and (6.51) may be viewed as Divisia moments of logarithmic output price changes of order 0, 1, and 2, respectively, while the next terms in these three equations are the corresponding moments of the input price changes, multiplied by $-1/\gamma$. If all input and output prices change by a factor k so that $d(\log p_i) = d(\log y_r) = \log k$ holds for each i and r, a Taylor expansion based on (6.48), (6.49), and (6.51) yields

$$\left(1 - \frac{1}{\gamma}\right)[1 + \log k + \tfrac{1}{2}(\log k)^2 + \cdots].$$

This is the Taylor expansion of $(1 - \gamma^{-1})e^{\log k} = (1 - \gamma^{-1})k$, which agrees with the homogeneity of the profit function in the input and output prices.

The last two terms in (6.51) are quadratic forms in input or output price changes deflated by Frisch input price indexes. Both terms are positive (unless all prices change proportionately); they represent the gain from price substitution. Under input independence Π' takes the form (6.42), which is the sum of n terms, one for each input. Under output independence (see section 5.8) we can simplify (6.52) to

$$(6.53) \qquad \Pi^* = \sum_{r=1}^{m} \theta_r^* \left[d\left(\log \frac{y_r}{P'^r} \right) \right]^2,$$

which is the sum of m terms, one for each output. Therefore, when the firm is both input and output independent, (6.51) describes the second differential of its profit as the sum of $2m + 2n$ terms, each of which is associated with one input or output. This property will be of crucial importance for the independence transformation of the multiproduct firm (see section 11.2).

Seven

Rational Random Behavior

7.1 Introduction

There are few if any consumers who actually go through the mathematics of utility maximization in order to decide on their purchases. Some authors, particularly Friedman [141], would argue that it does not matter whether consumers actually maximize utility; what counts is whether we get good predictions by assuming that consumers behave as if they maximize utility. These predictions will obviously not be perfect, but this imperfection can in principle be handled by means of random disturbances added to the demand equations. Whether we accept Friedman's position or not, in both cases it is appropriate to ask, Does utility theory have anything to say about the distribution of these demand disturbances? Allen and Bowley [9] considered this problem in an informal way; they computed correlation coefficients of residuals around Engel curves in order to verify whether goods are substitutes or complements in Hicks's sense. The subject was considered from a theoretical angle by Theil and Neudecker [407]. More recently it was further considered by Ashenfelter and Heckman [13], Barbosa [17], Barten [29], Jovanovic [208], Laitinen and Theil [229], Pessemier [310], Phlips and Rouzier [312, 316], and Theil [388, 394, 396, 397].

This subject is at least as relevant for the firm as it is for the consumer. In section 4.5 we separated the firm's input decision into a total-input decision and an input allocation decision. But suppose that random disturbances are added to the equations representing the latter two decisions, and that these disturbances are correlated. In that case the total-input and input allocation decisions are stochastically dependent and therefore not really separate.

The introduction of random disturbances in behavioral equations can be justified in various ways. In this chapter we discuss the theory of rational random behavior, from Theil and Barbosa, which provides a unified framework for any decision-maker under certain conditions. The account which follows in this chapter and the first two sections of chapter 8 may be viewed as a digression on decision-making in general, but specific examples will be discussed in section 7.4 and in later sections of chapter 8. Alternative approaches will be considered in section 15.1.

7.2   The Approach of the Theory of Rational Random Behavior

Let $\mathbf{x} = [x_1, \ldots, x_k]'$ be the vector of variables controlled by a decision-maker who may be (but need not be) a consumer or a firm. We assume that $\mathbf{x}$ can vary continuously over some region J (the feasible region of the decision vector). Let $\bar{\mathbf{x}}$ ($\bar{\mathbf{x}} \in J$) be the optimal value of the decision vector and $l(\mathbf{x}, \bar{\mathbf{x}})$ the loss function which describes the decision-maker's loss when his decision is $\mathbf{x}$ rather than $\bar{\mathbf{x}}$. For example, $\bar{\mathbf{x}}$ may be the input quantity vector which minimizes input expenditure given input prices and outputs, in which case $l(\mathbf{x}, \bar{\mathbf{x}})$ is the excess of input expenditure over the attainable minimum.

The optimal decision $\bar{\mathbf{x}}$ typically depends on numerous factors which are relevant for the decision process (such as the prices of many goods and services). We assume that the decision-maker does not know the values of all these factors, so that he does not know $\bar{\mathbf{x}}$, either. To emphasize this feature, we shall refer to $\bar{\mathbf{x}}$ as the *theoretically optimal decision*; it is optimal under perfect knowledge. The decision-maker's knowledge is actually imperfect, but he can improve on this by acquiring information. If information were a free good, the decision-maker would obviously acquire it to such a degree that he knows $\bar{\mathbf{x}}$ and would act accordingly. Here we shall assume that information is not necessarily free, in which case the decision-maker will either acquire no information at all or some finite amount at a certain cost.

If no information is acquired, we describe the decision made as random with density function $p_0(\mathbf{x})$, which will be called the *prior density function*. The justification of the assumption of randomness is the fact that the decision-maker is *uncertain* as to the values of the factors determining $\bar{\mathbf{x}}$. There is at this stage no need to consider the problem of how the prior density function should be specified; examples will be provided in sections 7.3 and 7.4. It will appear in chapter 8 that there is an important class of cases in which the decision-maker's behavior is effectively independent of the function $p_0(\ )$.

If the decision-maker acquires information on the factors determining $\bar{\mathbf{x}}$, the density function $p_0(\ )$ is transformed into $p(\ )$, which is the density function of the decision distribution selected by the decision-maker. Our problem is to find this $p(\ )$, for which purpose an appropriate criterion

must be formulated. First, we must define information. The definition
used is[1]

(7.1) $$I = \int_J p(\mathbf{x}) \log \frac{p(\mathbf{x})}{p_0(\mathbf{x})} \, dx_1 \cdots dx_k,$$

which is the amount of information received when the distribution with
density function $p_0( )$ is transformed into the distribution with density
function $p( )$. We shall prove in section 7.5 that $I = 0$ if $p(\mathbf{x}) = p_0(\mathbf{x})$
for each $\mathbf{x} \in J$, and that $I > 0$ otherwise. Thus, no information is received
when the two distributions are identical, and a positive amount of information is received when they are not identical.

Information is not costless. We write

(7.2) $$c = c(I)$$

for the cost of acquiring information. Since this information depends on
$p( )$ (see eq. [7.1]), so does the cost of information $c(I)$. This cost will be
one consideration for the selection of $p( )$; the other is the expected loss,

(7.3) $$\bar{l} = \int_J l(\mathbf{x}, \bar{\mathbf{x}}) p(\mathbf{x}) dx_1 \cdots dx_k.$$

If the cost $c(I)$ and the expected loss $\bar{l}$ are measured in the same unit
(dollars or any other unit), the obvious solution is the decision distribution
with density function $p( )$ which minimizes their sum, $c(I) + \bar{l}$.

7.3   The Optimal Decision Distribution

The following assumptions are made. First, the theoretically optimal
decision is unique:

(7.4) $$l(\mathbf{x}, \bar{\mathbf{x}}) = 0 \quad \text{if} \quad \mathbf{x} = \bar{\mathbf{x}}$$

$$> 0 \quad \text{if} \quad \mathbf{x} \neq \bar{\mathbf{x}}.$$

1. The definition (7.1) is from information theory. It is the continuous
version of a discrete information measure which can be justified by means of an
additivity axiom. Tribus [413] provides a forceful defense of such measures.
The discrete version will be discussed in section 14.1 in the context of the
evaluation of the fit of allocation models. The approach described here is, of
course, different from what has become known as the economics of information (see Stigler [374]), but a more detailed comparison would be desirable,
particularly for the case in which the marginal costs of search and information
are small.

Second, the prior density function $p_0(\mathbf{x})$ is differentiable around $\mathbf{x} = \bar{\mathbf{x}}$, and it takes a positive value for each $\mathbf{x} \in J$. Third, the cost of information (7.2) is differentiable with a positive first derivative, $dc/dI > 0$, and a non-negative second derivative, $d^2c/dI^2 \geq 0$. Since dc/dI is the marginal cost of information, we thus assume that this marginal cost is positive and non-decreasing.

Our objective is the decision distribution which minimizes $c(I) + I$. We shall prove in section 7.5 that under the above conditions the density function of this distribution is

$$(7.5) \qquad p(\mathbf{x}) \propto p_0(\mathbf{x}) \exp\left[-\frac{l(\mathbf{x}, \bar{\mathbf{x}})}{c'} \right] \quad \text{if} \quad \mathbf{x} \in J,$$

where $c' = dc/dI$ and $\propto$ is the "Bayesian" proportionality symbol, the proportionality coefficient being independent of the vector $\mathbf{x}$. Behavior generated by the random process (7.5) is called *rational random behavior*. There is considerable similarity between (7.5) and the Bayesian derivation of the posterior density function of a parameter vector. Indeed, rational random behavior and Bayesian inference both describe learning processes based on acquiring information, but the two theories are not quite the same.[2]

The limiting cases in which information is either free or very expensive are of special interest. Let us specify the latter case as that in which the marginal cost of information increases beyond bounds: $c' \to \infty$. The exponent in (7.5) will then converge to $e^0 = 1$ so that $p(\mathbf{x}) \equiv p_0(\mathbf{x})$ and no information is acquired ($I = 0$ in eq. [7.1]). This agrees with intuition. Alternatively, let c' converge to zero. We shall prove in chapter 8 that the random decision with distribution (7.5) ceases to be random in the limit as $c' \to 0$. The non-random decision which the decision-maker selects is the theoretically optimal decision $\bar{\mathbf{x}}$, which also agrees with intuition.

A simple example of the proportionality (7.5) is instructive. Consider a quadratic loss function for one decision variable:

$$(7.6) \qquad l(x, \bar{x}) = \tfrac{1}{2}(x - \bar{x})^2.$$

2. There are two similarities between (7.5) and the Bayesian formula for the posterior density function of a parameter vector. One is the occurrence of the prior density function on the right. The other is the presence of c' (which depends on the information acquired) in the exponent of (7.5); this should be compared with the role of the likelihood function (which represents the information obtained from the sample) in the Bayesian formula. The major difference is the occurrence of the unknown constant $\bar{\mathbf{x}}$ in the exponent of (7.5). The likelihood function involves no unknown constant in Bayesian analysis. This function is determined by the parameter vector, which is viewed as random, and the sample, which is viewed as a set of known constants for the derivation of the posterior density function.

If the prior density function $p_0(x)$ equals a constant independent of x, application of (7.5) to (7.6) yields

$$(7.7) \qquad p(x) \propto \exp\left[-\frac{1}{2}\frac{(x - \bar{x})^2}{c'}\right] \quad \text{if} \quad x \in J,$$

which is the density function of a truncated normal distribution over the range J. When J is sufficiently large, (7.7) is approximately equivalent to the density function of a normal distribution whose mean equals the theoretically optimal decision ($\bar{x}$) and whose variance equals the marginal cost of information (c'). This result is intuitively plausible: when information is cheap in the sense that its marginal cost is small, it is profitable to make an extensive search for the theoretical optimum, which yields a decision distribution that is tight around $\bar{x}$.

The discussion of this example will continue in chapter 8. We shall find there that the approximate normality of the decision distribution (with a mean equal to the theoretically optimal decision) is a much more general phenomenon that does not require the assumption of a quadratic loss function.

7.4   Application to the Linear Expenditure System

As a second example we take the utility function (2.3) which yields the linear expenditure system (2.5). The budget constraint introduces a new element because the analysis of this chapter considered no such constraint so far. However, we can use this constraint to eliminate the quantity of the nth good from (2.3). With the utility function thus modified, we define the loss function as the excess of the maximum utility level over the level that is actually attained.

The simplest result emerges when the consumer's decision variables are defined as

$$(7.8) \qquad x_i = \frac{p_i q_i - p_i b_i}{M - \sum\limits_{j=1}^{n} p_j b_j} \qquad i = 1, \ldots, n - 1,$$

which are the shares of the goods in supernumerary income (for short, the supernumerary shares). The linear expenditure system in the form (2.5) implies that $x_i = a_i$, where a_i is the (constant) marginal share of the ith good. Under rational random behavior the decision variable x_i does not take a fixed value but is random; the value a_i then becomes the theoretically optimal value of x_i. Barbosa [17] applied (7.5) under the assumption that $p_0(\mathbf{x})$ equals a constant independent of $\mathbf{x}$, and obtained

$$(7.9) \qquad p(\mathbf{x}) \propto \left(1 - \sum_{i=1}^{n-1} x_i\right)^{a_n/c'} \prod_{i=1}^{n-1} x_i^{a_i/c'},$$

which is the density function of a Dirichlet distribution.
The means and variances of this distribution are

$$(7.10) \qquad\qquad \mathscr{E}x_i = \frac{a_i + c'}{1 + nc'},$$

$$(7.11) \qquad \operatorname{var} x_i = c' \frac{(a_i + c')[1 - a_i + (n-1)c']}{(1 + nc')^2[1 + (n+1)c']},$$

and the covariances $(i \neq j)$ are

$$(7.12) \qquad \operatorname{cov}(x_i, x_j) = -c' \frac{(a_i + c')(a_j + c')}{(1 + nc')^2[1 + (n+1)c']}.$$

Remarks

1. The mean given in (7.10) differs from the theoretically optimal decision a_i. This is equivalent to saying that if the decision distribution (7.9) is represented by a disturbance added to the right-hand side of (2.5), this disturbance has nonzero expectation. However, the disturbance has zero mode, which follows from the general proposition that the decision distribution (7.5) has a mode at $\bar{\mathbf{x}}$ when $p_0(\mathbf{x})$ equals a constant for each $\mathbf{x} \in J$. This proposition is implied by (7.4).

2. If the marginal cost of information is small, (7.10) becomes approximately $\mathscr{E}x_i = a_i$. Hence the disturbance considered in remark (1) has approximately zero expectation for small c'. Also, the variance-covariance structure given in (7.11) and (7.12) can for small c' be simplified to

$$(7.13) \qquad \operatorname{cov}(x_i, x_j) = c'a_i(1 - a_i) \quad \text{if} \quad i = j$$

$$= -c'a_i a_j \qquad \text{if} \quad i \neq j.$$

3. The decision distributions (7.7) and (7.9) are both based on the assumption that the prior density function $p_0(\mathbf{x})$ equals a constant for each $\mathbf{x} \in J$. Generalizations are possible. For example, if the prior distribution of the supernumerary shares is a Dirichlet distribution, then (7.5) will

also yield a distribution of the Dirichlet type, but the parameters of the latter distribution differ from those of (7.9); see Barbosa [17]. However, we shall prove in chapter 8 that the prior distribution is actually irrelevant when the marginal cost of information is sufficiently small.

7.5   Derivations

The nonnegativity of information (see eq. [7.1]) can be derived from the simple lemma which states that, for any positive A,[3]

$$(7.14) \qquad \log A = A - 1 \quad \text{if} \quad A = 1$$

$$< A - 1 \quad \text{if} \quad A \neq 1.$$

Hence, for $A = p_0(\mathbf{x})/p(\mathbf{x})$,

$$\log \frac{p_0(\mathbf{x})}{p(\mathbf{x})} = \frac{p_0(\mathbf{x})}{p(\mathbf{x})} - 1 \quad \text{if} \quad p_0(\mathbf{x}) = p(\mathbf{x})$$

$$< \frac{p_0(\mathbf{x})}{p(\mathbf{x})} - 1 \quad \text{if} \quad p_0(\mathbf{x}) \neq p(\mathbf{x}),$$

which we multiply by $p(\mathbf{x})$:

$$(7.15) \qquad p(\mathbf{x}) \log \frac{p_0(\mathbf{x})}{p(\mathbf{x})} = p_0(\mathbf{x}) - p(\mathbf{x}) \quad \text{if} \quad p_0(\mathbf{x}) = p(\mathbf{x})$$

$$< p_0(\mathbf{x}) - p(\mathbf{x}) \quad \text{if} \quad p_0(\mathbf{x}) \neq p(\mathbf{x}).$$

When we integrate this over $\mathbf{x}$, we obtain $-I$ on the left (see eq. [7.1]) and

$$\int_J p_0(\mathbf{x}) dx_1 \cdots dx_k - \int_J p(\mathbf{x}) dx_1 \cdots dx_k = 1 - 1 = 0$$

on the right. Thus, the equal and less-than signs in (7.15) show that $-I = 0$ if $p_0(\ )$ and $p(\ )$ are identical, and that $-I < 0$ if these density functions are not identical.

The remainder of this section concerns the proof of (7.5), which will be presented in the form of a pedestrian version of the calculus of variations.

---

3. Lemma (7.14) is easily verified by comparing the curve $y = \log A$ (natural logarithm) with the straight line $y = A - 1$ for $0 < A < \infty$.

We write $p(\ )$ for the (unknown) density function of the optimal decision distribution and $p^*(\ )$ for some other density function, and write

$$(7.16) \qquad\qquad p^*(\mathbf{x}) = p(\mathbf{x}) + \delta f(\mathbf{x}),$$

where δ is independent of $\mathbf{x}$. Thus, we write the difference between $p^*(\mathbf{x})$ and $p(\mathbf{x})$ in the form $\delta f(\mathbf{x})$, and we concentrate the dependence of this difference on $\mathbf{x}$ in the function $f(\mathbf{x})$, which must satisfy

$$(7.17) \qquad\qquad \int_J f(\mathbf{x}) dx_1 \cdots dx_k = 0$$

because of (7.16) and the fact that both $p(\ )$ and $p^*(\ )$ have unit integrals.

It follows from (7.3) and (7.16) that the expected loss associated with $p^*(\ )$, to be written l^*, is a linear function of δ:

$$(7.18) \qquad\qquad l^* = l + \delta \int_J l(\mathbf{x}, \bar{\mathbf{x}}) f(\mathbf{x}) dx_1 \cdots dx_k.$$

We write similarly I^* for the information (7.1) associated with $p^*(\ )$:

$$(7.19) \qquad\qquad I^* = \int_J p^*(\mathbf{x}) \log \frac{p^*(\mathbf{x})}{p_0(\mathbf{x})} dx_1 \cdots dx_k.$$

We shall prove in the last paragraph of this section that

$$(7.20) \qquad\qquad I^* - I = k_1 \delta + \tfrac{1}{2} k_2 \delta^2 + O(\delta^3),$$

where I is the information (7.1) associated with $p(\ )$ and

$$(7.21) \qquad\qquad k_1 = \int_J f(\mathbf{x}) \log \frac{p(\mathbf{x})}{p_0(\mathbf{x})} dx_1 \cdots dx_k,$$

$$(7.22) \qquad\qquad k_2 = \int_J \frac{[f(\mathbf{x})]^2}{p(\mathbf{x})} dx_1 \cdots dx_k.$$

We use (7.20) to apply a Taylor expansion to $c(I^*)$, writing $c' = dc/dI$ and $c'' = d^2c/dI^2$ for the derivatives of $c(\ )$ at the I of $p(\ )$:

$$c(I^*) = c(I) + (k_1 \delta + \tfrac{1}{2} k_2 \delta^2) c' + \tfrac{1}{2} k_1^2 \delta^2 c'' + O(\delta^3)$$

$$= c(I) + \delta k_1 c' + \tfrac{1}{2} \delta^2 (k_2 c' + k_1^2 c'') + O(\delta^3).$$

Next we add this to (7.18):

$$(7.23) \quad c(I^*) + \bar{l}^* = c(I) + \bar{l} + \delta \left[k_1 c' + \int_J l(\mathbf{x}, \bar{\mathbf{x}}) f(\mathbf{x}) dx_1 \cdots dx_k \right]$$

$$+ \tfrac{1}{2} \delta^2 (k_2 c' + k_1^2 c'') + O(\delta^3).$$

Since $p(\ )$ is optimal by assumption, the left-hand side of (7.23) must exceed the sum of the first two terms on the right for any δ and any $f(\ )$ that satisfies (7.17). This implies (1) that the expression in brackets in (7.23) must vanish for any $f(\ )$ satisfying (7.17); and (2) that the co-efficient of δ^2 must be positive. Condition (2) is satisfied when $c'' \geq 0$ (a nondecreasing marginal cost of information) because (7.22) shows that $k_2 > 0$ when $f(\mathbf{x}) \neq 0$ for some $\mathbf{x}$. It follows from (7.21) that condition (1) amounts to a zero value of the integral

$$\int_J \left[c' \log \frac{p(\mathbf{x})}{p_0(\mathbf{x})} + l(\mathbf{x}, \bar{\mathbf{x}}) \right] f(\mathbf{x}) dx_1 \cdots dx_k.$$

This integral vanishes, given (7.17), when the expression in brackets is a constant independent of $\mathbf{x}$, which yields the solution (7.5) immediately.

To prove (7.20) we write the integrand of (7.19) as

$$(7.24) \qquad p^* \log \frac{p^*}{p_0} = p^* \left(\log \frac{p^*}{p} + \log \frac{p}{p_0} \right)$$

$$= p^* \log \frac{p^*}{p} + p \log \frac{p}{p_0} + \delta f \log \frac{p}{p_0},$$

where the second step is based on (7.16). Also,

$$p^* \log \frac{p^*}{p} = (p + \delta f) \log \left(1 + \frac{\delta f}{p} \right)$$

$$= (p + \delta f) \left(\frac{\delta f}{p} - \frac{\delta^2 f^2}{2p^2} \right) + O(\delta^3)$$

$$= \delta f + \frac{\delta^2 f^2}{2p} + O(\delta^3),$$

which we substitute in (7.24):

$$p^* \log \frac{p^*}{p_0} = p \log \frac{p}{p_0} + \delta f \left(1 + \log \frac{p}{p_0} \right) + \frac{\delta^2 f^2}{2p} + O(\delta^3).$$

We obtain (7.20) from this equation by writing f and the p's as $f(\mathbf{x})$, $p(\mathbf{x})$, $p^*(\mathbf{x})$, and $p_0(\mathbf{x})$, followed by integration over $\mathbf{x} \in J$ and application of (7.17).

Eight

Asymptotic Decision Distributions

The result (7.5) clearly shows that the decision distribution of rational random behavior involves three determinants: the prior density function, the loss function, and the marginal cost of information. In this chapter we shall analyze the case in which the marginal cost of information takes a small value. Such a small marginal cost extends the applicability of the theory considerably, which will be illustrated for both the consumer and the firm.

8.1 A Small Marginal Cost of Information

The marginal cost of information (c') obviously depends on I and hence also on $p(\ )$ (see eqs. [7.2] and [7.1]); hence c' in (7.5) should be interpreted as the marginal cost of information evaluated at the solution $p(\ )$. Moreover, this marginal cost will depend on the prices of certain goods and services which the decision-maker buys in order to acquire his information. Imagine that these prices decrease so that c' also decreases. It will be shown in section 8.2 that as $c' \to 0$ the optimal decision distribution (7.5) collapses with all of its mass concentrated at $\bar{\mathbf{x}}$, irrespective of the form of the prior density function $p_0(\ )$. This result should be intuitively obvious, because if information becomes a free good in the sense that its marginal cost converges to zero, minimizing $c(I) + \bar{l}$, becomes equivalent to minimizing $\bar{l}$, which yields $\mathbf{x} \equiv \bar{\mathbf{x}}$ in view of (7.3) and (7.4).

A much stronger result emerges when we make the following assumptions in addition to those stated in the first paragraph of section 7.3. First, the derivatives of the loss function $l(\mathbf{x}, \bar{\mathbf{x}})$ with respect to $\mathbf{x}$ exist up to those of the third order, the third derivatives being all continuous functions of $\mathbf{x}$ for each $\mathbf{x} \in J$. Second, the gradient vanishes at $\mathbf{x} = \bar{\mathbf{x}}$,

(8.1)
$$\frac{\partial}{\partial \mathbf{x}} l(\mathbf{x}, \bar{\mathbf{x}}) = \mathbf{0} \quad \text{at} \quad \mathbf{x} = \bar{\mathbf{x}},$$

and the Hessian matrix at $\mathbf{x} = \bar{\mathbf{x}}$ is a positive definite matrix $\mathbf{A}$:

(8.2) $$\frac{\partial^2}{\partial\mathbf{x}\partial\mathbf{x}'} l(\mathbf{x}, \bar{\mathbf{x}}) = \mathbf{A} \quad \text{at} \quad \mathbf{x} = \bar{\mathbf{x}}.$$

These assumptions may be viewed as regularity conditions which imply that when the elements of $\mathbf{x} - \bar{\mathbf{x}}$ are not too far from zero, $l(\mathbf{x}, \bar{\mathbf{x}})$ is approximately a quadratic function of these elements with a minimum (zero) at $\mathbf{x} - \bar{\mathbf{x}} = \mathbf{0}$.

It will be shown in section 8.2 that under these conditions, as $c' \to 0$, the density function (7.5) converges to

(8.3) $$\bar{p}(\mathbf{x}) \propto \exp\left[-\frac{1}{2}(\mathbf{x} - \bar{\mathbf{x}})'\left(\frac{1}{c'}\mathbf{A}\right)(\mathbf{x} - \bar{\mathbf{x}})\right],$$

which is the density function of the multinormal decision distribution with mean vector $\bar{\mathbf{x}}$ and covariance matrix $c'\mathbf{A}^{-1}$. When we apply this result to the linear expenditure system, we find that the supernumerary shares (7.8) have asymptotically $(c' \to 0)$ a multinormal distribution with means $\mathscr{E}x_i = a_i$ and covariances of the form (7.13). When we apply (8.3) to the example of a quadratic loss function discussed in section 7.3, we obtain the univariate normal decision distribution with mean $\bar{x}$ and variance c'. The density function (7.7) is that of a truncated normal distribution, but the truncation becomes irrelevant as $c' \to 0$. Also, the decision distributions (7.7) and (7.9) have been derived under the condition that the prior density function $p_0(\mathbf{x})$ equals a constant for each $\mathbf{x} \in J$, but this assumption is not needed for the asymptotic distribution (8.3), which is independent of $p_0(\ )$.

Given c', the asymptotic decision distribution (8.3) is completely determined by two characteristics of the loss function: the theoretically optimal decision $\bar{\mathbf{x}}$ and the Hessian matrix $\mathbf{A}$ at $\mathbf{x} = \bar{\mathbf{x}}$. If the decision vector is a scalar, the covariance matrix $c'\mathbf{A}^{-1}$ becomes a variance of the form c' divided by the second derivative of the loss function at the theoretically optimal decision. This illustrates that when the loss function has a flat minimum, the variance of the asymptotic decision distribution is larger than when the minimum is sharply peaked—which is intuitively plausible, given that in the former case the decision-maker can afford large deviations from the theoretical optimum with a modest loss.

The more general situation of an arbitrary number of decision variables can be clarified by means of the concentration ellipsoid associated with the distribution (8.3):

(8.4) $$\tfrac{1}{2}(\mathbf{x} - \bar{\mathbf{x}})'\mathbf{A}(\mathbf{x} - \bar{\mathbf{x}}) = \text{constant}.$$

It follows from (8.1) and (8.2) that the left-hand side of (8.4) is approximately equal to $l(\mathbf{x}, \bar{\mathbf{x}})$ for $\mathbf{x} - \bar{\mathbf{x}}$ close to a zero vector. Since $\mathbf{A}$ is symmetric positive definite by assumption, a nonsingular matrix $\mathbf{Q}$ exists such that $\mathbf{Q'Q} = \mathbf{A}$. Hence (8.4) can be written as $\frac{1}{2}\xi'\xi =$ constant, where $\xi = \mathbf{Q}(\mathbf{x} - \bar{\mathbf{x}})$ is a linear transformation of the decision vector, so that the loss function equals one-half of the sum of the squares of the transformed decision variables (for $\mathbf{x} - \bar{\mathbf{x}}$ and hence ξ close to zero). In addition, the distribution (8.3) implies that the transformed decision variables have zero covariances and equal variances (all equal to c'). This is quite sensible. Given that the loss function $\frac{1}{2}\xi'\xi$ contains only squares and no products, there is no reason why the decision distribution should contain a nonzero covariance for any pair of elements of ξ; and given that $\frac{1}{2}\xi'\xi$ assigns equal weights to all squares, there is no reason why the decision distribution should assign different variances to different elements of ξ.

The decision distribution (8.3) should be compared with the large-sample normal distribution of a statistical estimator. In fact, it can be shown that the asymptotic version ($c' \to 0$) of rational random behavior is equivalent to large-sample maximum-likelihood estimation of the theoretically optimal decision, with a large sample interpreted as a small marginal cost of information.[1] Another statistical comparison of interest is that with Kadane's [209] small-σ asymptotics, which consists of an asymptotic series of a multiple σ of the variance of the disturbance of a structural equation. If this equation is a behavioral equation of a decision-maker, this approach is equivalent to the asymptotic version of rational random behavior when we identify σ with c'. A third statistical comparison is that with the theorem which states that out of all distributions with a given mean vector and a given covariance matrix, the multinormal distribution has the largest entropy. The link between this theorem and (8.3) is the information definition (7.1); both (7.1) and the entropy are measures from information theory. However, note that the normal distribution (8.3) is not obtained by imposing a given mean and a given covariance matrix a priori.

When we use the asymptotic distribution (8.3) rather than the exact distribution (7.5), we commit an approximation error which is acceptable when the marginal cost of information is sufficiently small. This approximation is an improvement over the conventional approach which assumes that the decision-maker selects the theoretically optimal decision with probability 1 (which amounts to assuming $c' = 0$). The asymptotic result is more convenient than the exact result in two important respects:

1. The asymptotic result (8.3) is independent of the prior density function $p_0(\ )$ which occurs in (7.5). This independence reflects the fact that

---

1. I formulated this result in an earlier work [397, section 2.8] in terms of the entropy of the decision distribution, but it can also be done in terms of the cost of information. In both approaches the clue is the similar role played by the Hessian matrix (8.2) of the loss function and the information matrix of maximum-likelihood theory.

when the marginal cost of information is small, the decision-maker acquires so much information that his behavior is dominated by this information and is no longer affected by his prior ideas on how to behave before he obtained this information.[2]

2. Whereas (7.5) requires a complete specification of the loss function $l(\mathbf{x}, \bar{\mathbf{x}})$, (8.3) requires only two characteristics of this function: $\bar{\mathbf{x}}$ and $\mathbf{A}$. For example, the differential approach to consumer demand theory does not specify an algebraic form of the utility function, so that (7.5) cannot be used, but the asymptotic version can be applied and yields a simple and elegant result (see section 8.3).

8.2   Proof of the Asymptotic Results

We take the logarithm of (7.5),

$$(8.5) \qquad \log p(\mathbf{x}) = \text{constant} + \log p_0(\mathbf{x}) - \frac{l(\mathbf{x}, \bar{\mathbf{x}})}{c'},$$

and substitute $\bar{\mathbf{x}}$ for $\mathbf{x}$ in (8.5), using (7.4):

$$(8.6) \qquad \log p(\bar{\mathbf{x}}) = \text{constant} + \log p_0(\bar{\mathbf{x}}).$$

Since the constants in these two equations are equal, subtraction of (8.5) from (8.6) yields

$$(8.7) \qquad \log \frac{p(\bar{\mathbf{x}})}{p(\mathbf{x})} = \log \frac{p_0(\bar{\mathbf{x}})}{p_0(\mathbf{x})} + \frac{l(\mathbf{x}, \bar{\mathbf{x}})}{c'}.$$

It follows from (7.4) that as $c' \to 0$, the second term on the right increases beyond bounds for any $\mathbf{x} \neq \bar{\mathbf{x}}$, so that the same must be true for $p(\bar{\mathbf{x}})/p(\mathbf{x})$ on the left. Hence, as $c' \to 0$ the density $p(\mathbf{x})$ becomes zero for each $\mathbf{x} \neq \bar{\mathbf{x}}$, which proves that the random decision with density function (7.5) converges in probability to $\bar{\mathbf{x}}$.

To verify the asymptotic distribution (8.3), we define the vector

$$(8.8) \qquad \mathbf{v} = \frac{1}{\sqrt{c'}}(\mathbf{x} - \bar{\mathbf{x}}),$$

so that $l(\mathbf{x}, \bar{\mathbf{x}})$ becomes $l(\bar{\mathbf{x}} + \sqrt{c'}\mathbf{v}, \bar{\mathbf{x}})$. Next we apply a Taylor expansion

---

2. This result is similar to that of Bayesian inference for a large sample; the posterior density function is then dominated by the likelihood function and is no longer affected by the prior density function.

to $l(\mathbf{x}, \bar{\mathbf{x}})/c'$, using (8.1) and (8.2):

(8.9) $$\frac{l(\mathbf{x}, \bar{\mathbf{x}})}{c'} = \frac{1}{c'} \left[\tfrac{1}{2}(\sqrt{c'}\mathbf{v})'\mathbf{A}(\sqrt{c'}\mathbf{v}) + O(c'^{3/2})\right]$$

$$= \tfrac{1}{2}\mathbf{v}'\mathbf{A}\mathbf{v} + O(\sqrt{c'}).$$

Since $p_0(\mathbf{x})$ is assumed to be positive and differentiable around $\bar{\mathbf{x}}$, we can apply a Taylor expansion to $\log p_0(\mathbf{x})$ and write it as the sum of $\log p_0(\bar{\mathbf{x}})$ and a linear remainder term in $\mathbf{x} - \bar{\mathbf{x}}$. It follows from (8.8) that this can be written as

$$\log p_0(\mathbf{x}) = \log p_0(\bar{\mathbf{x}}) + O(\sqrt{c'}).$$

On combining this result with (8.5) and (8.9) we conclude that $\log p(\mathbf{x})$ is equal to a constant minus $\tfrac{1}{2}\mathbf{v}'\mathbf{A}\mathbf{v}$ plus the sum of two remainder terms which both converge to zero as $c' \to 0$. The result (8.3) is then obtained by substituting (8.8) for $\mathbf{v}$ in $\tfrac{1}{2}\mathbf{v}'\mathbf{A}\mathbf{v}$.

8.3   Application to Consumer Demand Systems

The remainder of this chapter is devoted to the application of the asymptotic decision distribution (8.3) to the theories of the consumer and the firm. It should be understood that from now on, and also in later chapters, rational random behavior will be interpreted asymptotically, for a small marginal cost of information, so that (8.3) is the density function of the distribution selected by the decision-maker.

Let $u(\mathbf{q})$ be the consumer's utility function. To obtain the covariance matrix $c'\mathbf{A}^{-1}$ of the distribution (8.3), we use the budget constraint to eliminate q_n from $\mathbf{q}$ so that utility becomes a function of the remaining q_i's. We define the consumer's loss as the maximum of this function minus the value attained for arbitrary values of these q_i's, and $\mathbf{A}$ as the Hessian matrix of this loss function at the point of zero loss. When this algebra is performed (see Theil [397, sections 2.6 and 2.7]), covariances emerge of the form

(8.10) $$\operatorname{cov}(q_i, q_j) = -k\left(\lambda u^{ij} - \frac{\lambda}{\partial\lambda/\partial M}\frac{\partial q_i}{\partial M}\frac{\partial q_j}{\partial M}\right),$$

where k is a positive coefficient which is independent of i and j and proportional to the marginal cost of information. A comparison with (2.22) shows that the covariance of q_i and q_j is proportional to the substitution component (specific plus general) of $\partial q_i/\partial p_j$.

We apply this result to the addilog indirect utility function (3.20). The corresponding direct utility function need not be specified; the substitution effects of price changes are all we need. The result can be summarized as follows. We write (3.21) in the form

$$(8.11) \qquad \bar{w}_i = \frac{B_i(p_i/M)^{\alpha_i}}{\sum\limits_{k=1}^{n} B_k(p_k/M)^{\alpha_k}} \qquad i = 1, \ldots, n,$$

where the bar of $\bar{w}_i$ indicates that this is the theoretically optimal value of the ith budget share. For the actual values of these shares we have

$$(8.12) \qquad \log \frac{w_i}{w_j} = \log \frac{B_i}{B_j} + \alpha_i \log \frac{p_i}{M} - \alpha_j \log \frac{p_j}{M} + u_i - u_j,$$

where u_i and u_j are random variables. It was shown by Barbosa [17] that the asymptotic decision distribution (8.3) is in this case equivalent to the independence and normality of $u_1, \ldots, u_n$ with zero means and variances proportional to $(1 - \alpha_i)/\bar{w}_i$. The positive sign of these variances follows from (3.22).

Next consider the differential demand equation (2.23) with a disturbance ε_i added on the right:

$$(8.13) \qquad w_i d(\log q_i) = \theta_i d(\log Q) + \phi \sum_{j=1}^{n} \theta_{ij} d\left(\log \frac{p_j}{P'}\right) + \varepsilon_i.$$

The decision variable is here the quantity component of the change in the ith budget share. This first-difference formulation implies that the theory of rational random behavior must be interpreted conditionally; that is, this theory describes the distribution of today's decision variables, given yesterday's values of the quantities bought.

The right-hand side of (8.13) excluding ε_i is the theoretically optimal value of the ith decision variable. The distribution (8.3) implies that the ε_i's follow a multinormal distribution with zero means and variances and covariances of the form

$$(8.14) \qquad \text{cov}\,(\varepsilon_i, \varepsilon_j) = \sigma^2(\theta_{ij} - \theta_i\theta_j) \qquad i, j = 1, \ldots, n,$$

where σ^2 is a coefficient which is proportional to the marginal cost of information. The coefficient θ_{ij} in (8.14) corresponds to λu^{ij} in (8.10), and $-\theta_i\theta_j$ corresponds to the other term in parentheses in (8.10).

It is obviously of interest to verify whether the covariance specification (8.14) is in agreement with actual data. This matter is pursued in figure 6 for a demand system formulated in terms of fourteen groups of consumer goods.[3] Since these groups differ substantially in size, a double-log scale is in order. This eliminates the covariances ($i \neq j$), many of which are negative so that their logarithms do not exist. Accordingly, the fourteen small circles in the figure refer to the variance of ε_i (for $i = 1, \ldots, 14$), which (8.14) predicts to be proportional to $\theta_{ii} - \theta_i^2$. The variable along the horizontal axis is the estimate of $\theta_{ii} - \theta_i^2$ which is obtained from the coefficient estimates of (8.13); the variable measured vertically is the mean square of the associated residuals, which is used as an estimate of the variance of ε_i. On a double-log scale the proportionality between var ε_i and $\theta_{ii} - \theta_i^2$ becomes a linear relation with unit slope. The figure shows that the fourteen points are indeed scattered around such a line, which is encouraging. (The line drawn corresponds to $\sigma^2 = 10^{-4}$ in eq. [8.14].) In sections 13.6 and

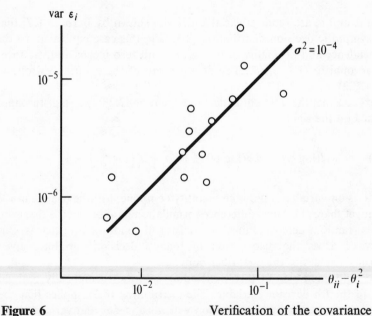

Figure 6   Verification of the covariance
                                                 specification (8.14)

3. The 14 groups are (1) bread, (2) groceries, (3) dairy products, (4) vegetables and fruit, (5) meat, (6) fish, (7) beverages, (8) tobacco products, (9) pastry, chocolate, etc., (10) clothing and other textiles, (11) footwear, (12) other durables, (13) water, light, and heat, and (14) other goods and services. Figure 6 is based on annual Dutch data for the period 1922–63 excluding World War II and the immediate postwar period during which there was rationing.

14.2 we shall have more to say about this result, which is based on a particular parametrization in finite (rather than infinitesimal) changes. Further evidence on the validity of the covariance structure of (8.3) will be presented in section 9.4; see also Ashenfelter and Heckman [13].

Note the implication of (2.25) that the sum of the covariance (8.14) over j vanishes. This means that (8.14) is the (i, j)th element of a singular covariance matrix of order $n \times n$. The cause of the singularity is the fact that $\varepsilon_1 + \cdots + \varepsilon_n = 0$ holds with probability 1. This is as it should be, because the differential demand system is an allocation model even in its stochastic form (8.13); that is, summation of (8.13) over i must yield $d(\log Q) = d(\log Q)$, in agreement with the corresponding result described at the end of section 2.6 for the nonstochastic version of (8.13).

However, it is possible to describe the covariance structure (8.14) in terms of a nonsingular covariance matrix. The clue is the correspondence of θ_{ij} in (8.14) to λu^{ij} in (8.10), and of $-\theta_i \theta_j$ in (8.14) to the other term in parentheses in (8.10). Given the interpretation of these two terms in (8.10) as specific and general substitution components, this means that the covariance (8.14) can be viewed as consisting of a specific component $(\sigma^2 \theta_{ij})$ and a general component $(-\sigma^2 \theta_i \theta_j)$. In fact, this decomposition can be applied to each random demand disturbance individually. To show this we write

$$(8.15) \qquad \varepsilon_i = \bar{\varepsilon}_i - \theta_i \overline{E} \qquad i = 1, \ldots, n,$$

$$(8.16) \qquad \overline{E} = \sum_{i=1}^{n} \bar{\varepsilon}_i,$$

where $\bar{\varepsilon}_1, \ldots, \bar{\varepsilon}_n$ are normal variates with zero means and the following covariance structure:

$$(8.17) \qquad \text{cov}\,(\bar{\varepsilon}_i, \bar{\varepsilon}_j) = \sigma^2 \theta_{ij} \qquad i, j = 1, \ldots, n.$$

It is readily verified that this specification is equivalent to the normality of $\varepsilon_1, \ldots, \varepsilon_n$ with zero means and covariance structure (8.14).

We shall refer to $\bar{\varepsilon}_i$ in (8.15) as the *specific component* of ε_i and to $-\theta_i \overline{E}$ as its *general component*. The covariance matrix of $\bar{\varepsilon}_1, \ldots, \bar{\varepsilon}_n$ that is implied by (8.17) is nonsingular. The sign of the covariance of two specific components $\bar{\varepsilon}_i$ and $\bar{\varepsilon}_j$ is determined by the question of whether the ith and jth goods are specific substitutes or complements. Under preference independence we can simplify (8.17) to var $\bar{\varepsilon}_i = \sigma^2 \theta_i$ and cov $(\bar{\varepsilon}_i, \bar{\varepsilon}_j) = 0$ for $i \neq j$. Therefore, the implication of the decision distribution (8.3) for the differential demand system under preference independence can be described as follows: The specific components of the demand disturbances are n independent normal variates with zero means and variances that are proportional to the corresponding marginal shares.

8.4 Application to the Differential Input Demand System

We proceed to apply (8.3) to the input demand equation (4.18) by adding a disturbance on the right:

$$(8.18) \qquad f_i d(\log q_i) = \gamma \theta_i d(\log z) - \psi \sum_{j=1}^{n} \theta_{ij} d\left(\log \frac{p_j}{P'}\right) + \varepsilon_i.$$

The decision-maker's loss is now interpreted in terms of the firm's input expenditure rather than the consumer's utility. Jovanovic [208] proved that under this interpretation (8.3) yields the result that $\varepsilon_1, \ldots, \varepsilon_n$ of (8.18) have a multinormal distribution with zero means and covariances of precisely the same form (8.14) which also applies to the differential consumer demand equations. Therefore, the separation of the demand disturbances into specific and general components is also applicable to input demand disturbances. In particular, under input independence the specific components of the input demand disturbances are independent normal variates with zero means and variances that are proportional to the marginal shares $\theta_1, \ldots, \theta_n$ of the inputs. All these results hold for the multiproduct firm also; this is a matter of adding a disturbance to equation (5.8).

In the previous section we clarified the singular property of the covariance structure (8.14) by pointing out that (8.13) is an allocation model. By contrast, (8.18) is not an allocation model, so that the singular property of its covariance structure requires an explanation. For this purpose we sum (8.18) over i, which yields the stochastic version of the total-input decision. But since (8.14) combined with (4.20) implies that the ε_i's have zero sum with probability 1, summation of (8.18) yields

$$(8.19) \qquad\qquad d(\log Q) = \gamma d(\log z),$$

which is the total-input decision in its original nonstochastic form (4.22). By substituting (8.19) in (8.18), we find

$$(8.20) \qquad f_i d(\log q_i) = \theta_i d(\log Q) - \psi \sum_{j=1}^{n} \theta_{ij} d\left(\log \frac{p_j}{P'}\right) + \varepsilon_i,$$

so that the input allocation decision fully accounts for the random disturbances of the input demand system (8.18). This explains why the latter disturbances must have a singular covariance matrix.

But why does the total-input decision remain nonstochastic under rational random behavior? The answer is that this decision is equivalent to a differential version of the firm's production function, which is nonstochastic; this holds for the multiproduct firm also.[4] Rational random behavior is not concerned with random variations in the firm's technology. Instead, it deals with "errors in optimization" or, more precisely, with the random variations in behavior which are caused by the fact that the decision-maker must take the cost of information, $c(I)$, into account. By proceeding in this way, the firm will raise the amount of input expenditure, $\sum_i p_i q_i$, above the theoretically attainable minimum. Similarly, when $d(\log z)$ in (8.18) is specified in accordance with the associated supply equation, the firm will reduce its profit below the theoretically attainable maximum. In sections 8.5 and 8.6 we shall consider the output supply equations of a multiproduct firm under rational random behavior, after which the effect on the firm's profit will be discussed in section 8.7.

It is of interest to note that the covariance structure (8.14) can be expressed in terms of partial elasticities of substitution. Recall that we considered the elasticity of substitution between two inputs in the discussion following equation (4.4). This concept can be extended to the case of n inputs in various ways, but the version known as the Allen or Allen-Uzawa partial elasticity of substitution is the most useful for our present purpose. The value of this elasticity between the ith and jth inputs $(i \neq j)$ at the point of minimum input expenditure is

$$(8.21) \qquad\qquad -\psi \frac{\theta_{ij} - \theta_i \theta_j}{f_i f_j}.$$

Next we divide both sides of (8.20) by f_i so that we obtain $d(\log q_i)$ on the left and ε_i/f_i on the far right. It then follows from (8.14) and (8.21) that the covariance of $d(\log q_i)$ and $d(\log q_j)$ is proportional to the partial elasticity of substitution between the two inputs. An analogous result holds in consumption theory.[5]

In section 7.1 we raised the question whether the total-input decision and the input allocation decision are stochastically independent when random disturbances are introduced. The answer is provided by equation

4. This follows from (5.18) and the values f_i/γ and $-g_r$ of the derivatives of $h(\ )$ with respect to $\log q_i$ and $\log z_r$, respectively, at the point of minimum input expenditure.

5. The partial elasticity of substitution between the ith and jth consumer goods is equal to $\phi(\theta_{ij} - \theta_i \theta_j)/w_i w_j$ at the point of the budget-constrained utility maximum (see Powell [332, pp. 12–14]). By dividing (8.13) by w_i we find that (8.14) implies a covariance of the logarithmic changes in q_i and q_j which is proportional to their partial elasticity of substitution.

(8.19). When the change in output is taken as fixed, the total-input decision is nonstochastic and therefore (trivially) independent of the input allocation decision (8.20). In the next section we shall extend this to the multiproduct firm with the output changes expressed in supply equations containing random disturbances. The result will be that the Divisia volume index $d(\log Q)$ is random but stochastically independent of the disturbances of the input allocation equations.

8.5 Application to the Differential Demand and Supply System of the Multiproduct Firm

We now apply (8.3) to the multiproduct firm, with the decision-maker's loss interpreted in terms of (minus) the profit of this firm. This requires that we add a random disturbance to the input demand equation (5.8),

$$(8.22) \quad f_i d(\log q_i) = \gamma \sum_{r=1}^{m} \theta_i^r g_r d(\log z_r) - \psi \sum_{j=1}^{n} \theta_{ij} d\left(\log \frac{p_j}{P'}\right) + \varepsilon_i,$$

and also to the output supply equation (5.33):

$$(8.23) \qquad\qquad g_r d(\log z_r) = \psi^* \sum_{s=1}^{m} \theta_{rs}^* d\left(\log \frac{y_s}{P's}\right) + \varepsilon_r^*.$$

The following results were proved by Laitinen and Theil [229]. First, all $n + m$ disturbances $(\varepsilon_1, \ldots, \varepsilon_n, \varepsilon_1^*, \ldots, \varepsilon_m^*)$ are normally distributed with zero means. Second, the demand disturbance vector $(\varepsilon_1, \ldots, \varepsilon_n)$ has a multinormal distribution with covariance matrix (8.14). Third, the demand disturbance vector is stochastically independent of the supply disturbance vector $(\varepsilon_1^*, \ldots, \varepsilon_m^*)$. Fourth, the supply disturbance vector has a multinormal distribution with variances and covariances of the following form:

$$(8.24) \qquad\qquad \operatorname{cov}(\varepsilon_r^*, \varepsilon_s^*) = \frac{\sigma^2 \psi^*}{\gamma \psi} \theta_{rs}^* \qquad r, s = 1, \ldots, m.$$

We conclude from (8.24) that under output independence (see section 5.8) the supply disturbances are m independent normal variates with zero means and variances proportional to the marginal shares $\theta_1^*, \ldots, \theta_m^*$. This independence may be viewed as an extension of Hall's [169] theorem according to which the multiproduct firm can be broken up into m single-product firms which maximize their profits independently.[6]

The independence property just mentioned holds only in the case of output independence. The stochastic independence of the input demand disturbance vector $(\varepsilon_1, \ldots, \varepsilon_n)$ and the output supply disturbance vector $(\varepsilon_1^*, \ldots, \varepsilon_m^*)$ holds generally under (8.3); it does *not* require input-output separability. The implication is that the firm's input demand decisions and output supply decisions can be viewed as a *two-stage block-recursive decision system*. The first stage consists of (8.23), which yields the m output changes, and the second consists of (8.22), which yields the n input changes when the output changes are given.

Since the ε_i's of the input demand equations have covariances of the form (8.14) and thus have zero sum, we obtain the following result by summing (8.22) over i:

$$(8.25) \qquad\qquad d(\log Q) = \gamma d(\log Z).$$

This is the total-input decision in the original form (5.11). Next, by substituting (8.25) in (8.22) we obtain

$$(8.26) \quad f_i d(\log q_i) = \theta_i d(\log Q) + \gamma \Gamma_i - \psi \sum_{j=1}^{n} \theta_{ij} d\left(\log \frac{p_j}{P'}\right) + \varepsilon_i,$$

which is the input allocation decision (5.25) with the disturbance ε_i of (8.22) added. The results (8.25) and (8.26) are immediate extensions of (8.19) and (8.20), respectively, but note that $d(\log Q)$ and Γ_i in (8.26) are no longer nonstochastic because they involve changes in outputs. However, the first two terms on the right in (8.26) are still stochastically independent of the ε_i's so that the input allocation decision remains independent of the total-input decision. This is the second general independence property in addition to that discussed in the previous paragraph.

To prove this second independence property we sum (8.23) over r:

$$(8.27) \qquad d(\log Z) = \psi^* d\left(\log \frac{Y'}{P''}\right) + E^* \quad \text{where} \quad E^* = \sum_{r=1}^{m} \varepsilon_r^*,$$

6. Note the implication of (8.24) that two supply disturbances are positively (negatively) correlated when the corresponding products are specific complements (substitutes) in supply. The covariance structure (8.24) can also be expressed in terms of partial elasticities of transformation (see Powell and Gruen [333] for a definition of such elasticities). Note further that (8.24) is comparable to (8.17), whereas (8.14) is comparable to equation (8.31) below. This illustrates that the supply equation (8.23) is not an allocation model $(r = 1, \ldots, m)$.

which is the stochastic version of the total-output decision (5.40). On combining (8.27) with (8.25) we find that the random component of $d(\log Q)$ is γE^*, which is independent of ε_i because E^* is the sum of the supply disturbances and these are independent of the ε_i's. Next we substitute (8.23) in (5.24):

$$(8.28) \quad \Gamma_i = \psi^* \sum_{r=1}^{m} \sum_{s=1}^{m} \theta_{rs}^*(\theta_i^r - \theta_i)d\left(\log \frac{y_s}{P'^s}\right) + \sum_{r=1}^{m} (\theta_i^r - \theta_i)\varepsilon_r^*.$$

Hence the disturbance component of Γ_i is a linear combination of output supply disturbances and is thus stochastically independent of the disturbances of the input allocation system (8.26).

The third general independence property is the independence of the total-output decision and the output allocation decision. The former decision is shown in (8.27) and the latter is obtained by multiplying (8.27) by θ_r^* and subtracting the result from (8.23). This yields

$$(8.29) \quad g_r d(\log z_r) = \theta_r^* d(\log Z) + \psi^* \sum_{s=1}^{m} \theta_{rs}^* d\left(\log \frac{y_s/P'^s}{Y'/P''}\right) + \varepsilon_r^{**},$$

which is the stochastic version of (5.41), with ε_r^{**} defined as

$$(8.30) \quad \varepsilon_r^{**} = \varepsilon_r^* - \theta_r^* E^* \qquad r = 1, \ldots, m.$$

It is readily verified from (8.24), (5.35), and (5.37) that

$$(8.31) \quad \text{cov}(\varepsilon_r^{**}, \varepsilon_s^{**}) = \frac{\sigma^2 \psi^*}{\gamma \psi}(\theta_{rs}^* - \theta_r^* \theta_s^*) \qquad r, s = 1, \ldots, m,$$

$$(8.32) \quad \text{cov}(E^*, \varepsilon_r^{**}) = 0 \qquad r = 1, \ldots, m.$$

The independence of the total-output and the output allocation decisions follows directly from (8.32) combined with the normal distribution of the disturbances in (8.27) and (8.29).

8.6   The Implied Hierarchy within the Firm

It is instructive to summarize the results of the previous section in terms of the following hierarchy. At the top is the output manager who makes the total-output decision, using (8.27) and data on the price indexes $d(\log Y')$ and $d(\log P'')$. Once this decision is made, the aggregate input requirement in terms of the Divisia input volume index is determined (see eq. [8.25]).

The output manager has an assistant who makes the output allocation decision, using (8.29) and the decision on $d(\log Z)$ made by his superior as well as the data on input and output prices needed for the second right-hand term in (8.29). Given $d(\log Z)$, the assistant can make this decision independently because ε_r^{**} in (8.29) is stochastically independent of E* in the total-output decision (8.27).

Next comes the input manager who reports to the office of the output manager. One of the tasks of the input manager is to provide this office with the input price data needed for the output allocation decision.[7] His other task is to make the input decision, using (8.22) and the decision on $g_r d(\log z_r)$ made by the output manager's assistant as well as the input price data that are needed for the second right-hand term in (8.22). Given $g_r d(\log z_r)$ for $r = 1, \ldots, m$, the input manager can make this decision independently because ε_i is stochastically independent of the output supply disturbances of the two earlier decisions.

The hierarchy outlined above, which can be extended to more layers under appropriate block structures for inputs and outputs (see section 9.6), views the output manager as the superior of the input manager. This is the result of our approach which maximizes profit in two steps, the first consisting of input-expenditure minimization for given outputs and the second consisting of an adjustment of the outputs so that profit is maximized. We mentioned in section 4.8 that an alternative two-step procedure can be used with a first step consisting of revenue-maximization for given inputs. This second approach also yields output supply disturbances that are stochastically independent of the input demand disturbances (see Appendix D), but there is an important difference in that the new approach views the input manager as the superior of the output manager. Therefore, by deciding on either a cost-minimizing or a revenue-maximizing approach to profit maximization, the firm selects a particular hierarchy for its input and output managers.

We also mentioned in section 4.8 that the firm can maximize profit in one step rather than two, which yields input demand and output supply equations in terms of input and output prices. Such equations can be derived from (8.22) and (8.23). The latter equation describes the change in supply directly in terms of input and output price changes; hence it needs no modification. The corresponding demand equation in input and output price changes is considered in the next paragraph, and the result is that the associated demand and supply disturbances are not necessarily independent. This means that the one-step approach to profit maximization has

7. Note that this task need not be performed under input-output separability because the output allocation decision is then independent of the changes in the input prices [see remark (2) at the end of section 5.7].

the disadvantage of not yielding an independence property which the firm can use to design a hierarchy of independently operating input and output managers.

To verify the lack of independence we substitute (8.23) in (8.22),

$$(8.33) \qquad f_i d(\log q_i) = \gamma \psi^* \sum_{r=1}^{m} \theta_i^r \sum_{s=1}^{m} \theta_{rs}^* d\left(\log \frac{y_s}{P'_s}\right)$$

$$- \psi \sum_{j=1}^{n} \theta_{ij} d\left(\log \frac{p_j}{P'}\right) + \varepsilon_i + \gamma \sum_{r=1}^{m} \theta_i^r \varepsilon_r^*,$$

which shows that $\varepsilon_i + \gamma \sum_r \theta_i^r \varepsilon_r^*$ is the disturbance in the equation that describes the change in the demand for the ith input in terms of input and output price changes. Using (8.24) and the independence of the ε_i's and ε_r^*'s, we find that the covariance of this disturbance and the sth supply disturbance is

$$(8.34) \qquad \text{cov}\left(\varepsilon_i + \gamma \sum_{r=1}^{m} \theta_i^r \varepsilon_r^*, \varepsilon_s^*\right) = \frac{\sigma^2 \psi^*}{\psi} \sum_{r=1}^{m} \theta_i^r \theta_{rs}^*,$$

which is in general nonzero.

8.7 The Firm's Profit under Rational Random Behavior

When the firm maximizes profit subject to the technology constraint (5.2) but without further restrictions, the disturbances ε_i and ε_r^* in (8.22) and (8.23) are both zero. The occurrence of disturbances with positive variances under rational random behavior is caused by the fact that the firm takes the cost of information, $c(I)$, into account, which reduces profit below the attainable maximum. This reduction will be the objective of this section.

The simplest approach is in terms of the differentials of profit which we considered earlier in section 6.7. Laitinen and Theil [229] proved that equations (6.48) and (6.49) for profit and its first differential (measured as a fraction of revenue) remain unchanged, but that (6.51) for the second differential is affected. Hence rational random behavior, like price substitution, has a second-order effect on the firm's profit. The new result for the second differential of profit, measured as a fraction of revenue, can be conveniently written as the sum of three terms,

$$(8.35) \qquad \frac{d^2(R - C)}{R} = B_1 + B_2 + B_3,$$

where B_1 consists of quadratic forms in absolute price changes,

$$(8.36) \qquad B_1 = \sum_{r=1}^{m} g_r[d(\log y_r)]^2 - \frac{1}{\gamma} \sum_{i=1}^{n} f_i[d(\log p_i)]^2,$$

while B_2 contains quadratic forms in relative price changes,

$$(8.37) \qquad B_2 = \psi^* \sum_{r=1}^{m} \sum_{s=1}^{m} \theta_{rs}^* d\left(\log \frac{y_r}{P'_r}\right) d\left(\log \frac{y_s}{P'_s}\right)$$

$$+ \frac{\psi}{\gamma} \sum_{i=1}^{n} \sum_{j=1}^{n} \theta_{ij} d\left(\log \frac{p_i}{P'}\right) d\left(\log \frac{p_j}{P'}\right),$$

and B_3 consists of quadratic forms in disturbances,

$$(8.38) \qquad B_3 = -\frac{1}{\psi^*} \sum_{r=1}^{m} \sum_{s=1}^{m} \theta^{*rs} \varepsilon_r^* \varepsilon_s^* - \frac{1}{\gamma\psi} \sum_{i=1}^{n} \sum_{j=1}^{n} \theta^{ij} \varepsilon_i \varepsilon_j,$$

where $[\theta^{*rs}] = [\theta_{rs}^*]^{-1}$ and $[\theta^{ij}] = [\theta_{ij}]^{-1}$.

A comparison of these results with (6.51) shows that the latter equation contains only B_1 and B_2, which means that B_3 is the component of the second differential that is due to rational random behavior. The positive definiteness of $[\theta_{ij}]$ and $[\theta_{rs}^*]$ implies that this component is negative with probability 1, which should come as no surprise. In fact, it can be shown that B_3 is distributed as a multiple $-\sigma^2/\gamma\psi$ of a χ^2 variate with $m + n - 1$ degrees of freedom.

If the firm is both input and output independent, each of the terms B_1, B_2, and B_3 consists of $m + n$ components, each of which is associated with one input or one output. This matter will be further considered in section 11.2 for the independence transformation of the multiproduct firm.

Nine

Block Structures

When the number of consumer goods is not very small, the implementation of their demand equations to statistical data requires constraints on the utility function. The most important source of constraints consists of separability assumptions on this function. The separation amounts to combining goods into groups of goods in such a way that group utility functions play a role. This approach was pioneered by Sono [371] and Leontief [237, 238], and was further elaborated by Strotz [378, 379], Goldman and Uzawa [154], Barten and Turnovsky [39], and Gorman [158, 160]. Geary and Morishima [149] provided a good survey of the literature until about 1970. An extensive treatment in monograph form was recently published by Blackorby, Primont, and Russell [61].

The first four sections of this chapter deal with the theory of the consumer and the next two with that of the firm. The last section provides a brief description of some block structures that have not been discussed in the earlier sections.

9.1 The Demand for Groups of Goods under Block Independence

Let there be G groups of goods, $S_1, \ldots, S_G$, such that each good belongs to exactly one group. We assume that the consumer's preferences can be represented by a utility function of the form (2.33), which is reproduced here,

$$(9.1) \qquad u(\mathbf{q}) = u_1(\mathbf{q}_1) + \cdots + u_G(\mathbf{q}_G),$$

where $\mathbf{q}_g$ is the subvector of $\mathbf{q}$ which consists of the q_i's that fall under S_g. We also reproduce the demand equation (2.34) for $i \in S_g$, with a disturbance ε_i added as in (8.13),

$$(9.2) \qquad w_i d(\log q_i) = \theta_i d(\log Q) + \phi \sum_{j \in S_g} \theta_{ij} d\left(\log \frac{p_j}{P'}\right) + \varepsilon_i,$$

as well as the constraint (2.35):

$$(9.3) \qquad \sum_{j \in S_g} \theta_{ij} = \theta_i \quad \text{if} \quad i \in S_g.$$

Our first objective is to derive a demand equation for S_g, i.e., a composite demand equation for all goods of that group. For this purpose we define

$$(9.4) \qquad W_g = \sum_{i \in S_g} w_i, \qquad \Theta_g = \sum_{i \in S_g} \theta_i, \qquad E_g = \sum_{i \in S_g} \varepsilon_i,$$

so that W_g is the budget share and Θ_g is the marginal share of the group as a whole. We also define the Divisia volume index and the Frisch price index of S_g:

$$(9.5) \qquad d(\log Q_g) = \sum_{i \in S_g} \frac{w_i}{W_g} d(\log q_i),$$

$$(9.6) \qquad d(\log P'_g) = \sum_{i \in S_g} \frac{\theta_i}{\Theta_g} d(\log p_i).$$

Note that θ_i/Θ_g exists because

$$(9.7) \qquad \Theta_g > 0$$

holds under block independence. This may be verified by summing (9.3) over $i \in S_g$ and using the positive definiteness of $[\theta_{ij}]$. Also note that the indexes (9.5) and (9.6) satisfy

$$(9.8) \qquad d(\log Q) = \sum_{g=1}^{G} W_g d(\log Q_g),$$

$$(9.9) \qquad d(\log P') = \sum_{g=1}^{G} \Theta_g d(\log P'_g).$$

Summation of both sides of (9.2) over $i \in S_g$ yields $W_g d(\log Q_g)$ on the left and $\Theta_g d(\log Q)$ and E_g for the first and last terms on the right (see eqs. [9.4] and [9.5]). For the substitution term we obtain

$$\phi \sum_{j \in S_g} \left(\sum_{i \in S_g} \theta_{ij} \right) d\left(\log \frac{p_j}{P'} \right) = \phi \sum_{j \in S_g} \theta_j [d(\log p_j) - d(\log P')]$$

$$= \phi \Theta_g [d(\log P'_g) - d(\log P')],$$

where the first step is based on $\sum_i \theta_{ij} = \theta_j$ (sum over $i \in S_g$), which follows from (9.3) and the symmetry of $[\theta_{ij}]$, and the second on (9.6). Therefore, when we add the demand equations of all goods of S_g, we obtain

$$(9.10) \qquad W_g d(\log Q_g) = \Theta_g d(\log Q) + \phi\Theta_g d\left(\log \frac{P'_g}{P'}\right) + E_g,$$

which is the composite demand equation for S_g as a group. We conclude that the change in the allocation of the consumer's income to the G groups does not require knowledge of the price changes of all n goods. The substitution term of (9.10) requires only the Frisch price indexes of the G groups; the deflator in that term can be obtained directly from these indexes in view of (9.9).[1]

9.2   A Weaker Condition: Blockwise Dependence

Next we consider the case in which the consumer's preferences can be represented by a utility function $u(\mathbf{q})$ which is some increasing function $f(\ )$, rather than the sum, of the group utility functions:

$$(9.11) \qquad\qquad u(\mathbf{q}) = f(u_1(\mathbf{q}_1), \ldots, u_G(\mathbf{q}_G)).$$

Under condition (9.1) the marginal utility of each good is independent of the quantities of all goods that belong to different groups. This does not hold under condition (9.11), but the following weaker result can be proved.

Consider $\partial u/\partial(p_i q_i)$, the marginal utility of a dollar spent on the ith good, and the second derivative $\partial^2 u/\partial(p_i q_i)\partial(p_j q_j)$, which measures the change in this marginal utility caused by an extra dollar spent on the jth good. Under condition (9.1) such second derivatives vanish whenever i and j belong to different groups. They do not vanish under condition (9.11), but we do have the following result at the point of the budget-constrained utility maximum:

$$(9.12) \qquad \frac{\partial^2 u}{\partial(p_i q_i)\partial(p_j q_j)} = a_{gh} \quad \text{if}\quad i \in S_g, j \in S_h, g \neq h.$$

1. Gorman [158] considered conditions on the utility function under which the change in the allocation to the groups is determined by only one price index for each group. His conditions include homogeneity properties and are much stronger than those used here (particularly those of section 9.2). These seemingly different results are reconciled when we recognize that the present approach uses two price indexes for each group: Divisia and Frisch. The Divisia price index is not explicitly represented in (9.10), but it must be used when we transform the left-hand variable of (9.10) into dW_g. This may be verified by summing (2.15) over $i \in S_g$.

This means that the change in the marginal utility of a dollar spent on the ith good ($i \in S_g$) caused by an extra dollar spent on the jth good which belongs to a different group ($j \in S_h$, $g \neq h$) equals a_{gh}; i.e., this effect is independent of i and j and, hence, is the same for all pairs of goods in the two groups. Thus, if food and clothing are two such groups, an extra dollar spent on either bread or butter has the same effect on the marginal utility of a dollar spent on any good within the clothing group. The utility interaction of two goods of different groups is therefore a matter of the groups rather than the individual goods, which explains why condition (9.11) is described as *blockwise dependence*. ("Weak separability" is also used.) For proofs of (9.12) and the results which follow in the next two sections, see Theil [397, chap. 8]; some of these results were obtained earlier by Barten [32].

Under blockwise dependence the demand equation (9.10) for S_g is extended so that it includes the Frisch price indexes of all groups. Also, the demand equation (9.2) for an individual good must be modified under blockwise dependence because (9.12) implies that the Hessian matrix of the utility function in expenditure terms (and hence also $[\theta_{ij}]$) ceases to be block-diagonal if $a_{gh} \neq 0$ for some $g \neq h$. These matters will be considered in the next section.

9.3 The Demand for Goods and for Groups of Goods under Blockwise Dependence

The exposition is simplified when we start with the composite demand equations for groups of goods. The extension of (9.10) under blockwise dependence is

$$(9.13) \quad W_g d(\log Q_g) = \Theta_g \, d(\log Q) + \phi \sum_{h=1}^{G} \Theta_{gh} d\left(\log \frac{P_h'}{P'}\right) + \mathrm{E}_g,$$

where Θ_{gh} is an element of a normalized symmetric positive definite price coefficient matrix of order $G \times G$. This element is defined as

$$(9.14) \quad \Theta_{gh} = \sum_{i \in S_g} \sum_{j \in S_h} \theta_{ij} \qquad g, h = 1, \ldots, G,$$

and it satisfies

$$(9.15) \quad \sum_{h=1}^{G} \Theta_{gh} = \Theta_g \qquad g = 1, \ldots, G,$$

$$(9.16) \quad \sum_{g=1}^{G} \sum_{h=1}^{G} \Theta_{gh} = \sum_{g=1}^{G} \Theta_g = 1.$$

A comparison with (2.23) to (2.26) shows that these results constitute an "uppercase version" of the demand equations of the individual goods. Since Θ_{gh} equals the sum of the θ_{ij}'s over all goods of the two groups (see [9.14]), it is natural to call S_g and S_h specific substitutes (complements) when Θ_{gh} is negative (positive). Note that the group demand equation (9.10) of block independence is the uppercase version of the individual demand equation (2.16) of preference independence. We have $\Theta_{gh} = 0$ for $g \neq h$ in (9.10), so that under block independence no group is a specific substitute or complement of any other group.

The distribution of the group demand disturbances $E_1, \ldots, E_G$ under rational random behavior is easily obtained. Since the ε_i's are normally distributed with zero means and covariances of the form (8.14), and since E_g in (9.13) equals the sum of ε_i over $i \in S_g$, the E_g's are also normal with zero means. The covariance of E_g and E_h is found by summation of (8.14) over $i \in S_g$ and $j \in S_h$. Using (9.14) and $\sum_i \theta_i = \Theta_g$ (see [9.4]), we obtain

$$(9.17) \qquad \mathrm{cov}\,(E_g, E_h) = \sigma^2(\Theta_{gh} - \Theta_g \Theta_h) \qquad g, h = 1, \ldots, G,$$

which is simply the uppercase version of (8.14).

The result (9.13) is subject to the proviso that the Frisch price indexes of the groups cannot be defined as shown in (9.6). The reason is that (9.6) contains θ_i/Θ_g and that Θ_g may be zero under blockwise dependence. However, we can write

$$(9.18) \qquad\qquad\qquad \theta_i = \theta_i' \Theta_g \quad \text{if} \quad i \in S_g.$$

The θ_i' in this equation exists under blockwise dependence and is equal to θ_i/Θ_g if Θ_g does not vanish.[2] Therefore, we replace θ_i/Θ_g by θ_i' in (9.6) and elsewhere when there is blockwise dependence rather than block independence. In particular, the Frisch price index of S_g becomes

$$(9.19) \qquad\qquad\qquad d(\log P_g') = \sum_{i \in S_g} \theta_i' d(\log p_i).$$

We shall refer to θ_i' as the *conditional marginal share* of the ith good within its group. This share answers the following question: If income increases by one dollar so that the additional amount spent on S_g is Θ_g, what is the proportion of that amount allocated to the ith good?

---

2. It can be shown that if $\Theta_g = 0$, then $\theta_i = 0$ for each $i \in S_g$ under blockwise dependence. The positive definiteness of the $G \times G$ matrix $[\Theta_{gh}]$ does not exclude a negative Θ_g either; hence a group may be inferior under blockwise dependence [see the discussion following eq. (2.18)]. Inferior groups cannot occur under block independence.

Finally, we turn to the demand equation for an individual good under blockwise dependence. For $i \in S_g$ the equation is

$$(9.20) \qquad w_i d(\log q_i) = \theta_i d(\log Q) + \phi \sum_{j \in S_g} \theta_{ij} d\left(\log \frac{p_j}{P'}\right)$$

$$+ \phi \theta_i' \sum_{h \neq g} \Theta_{gh} d\left(\log \frac{P_h'}{P'}\right) + \varepsilon_i,$$

which shows that the substitution term consists of two parts. The first part is identical to the substitution term of the block independent demand equation (9.2). The second part contains the changes in the deflated prices of the goods outside S_g. However, these prices occur only in the form of Frisch price indexes of the groups, thus displaying the blockwise dependence at the level of the demand equations for the individual goods.

9.4   The Conditional Demand for a Good within Its Group

We multiply (9.13) by θ_i' and subtract the result from (9.20) so that the term involving $d(\log Q)$ cancels out (see [9.18]). After some further rearrangements we obtain

$$(9.21) \qquad w_i d(\log q_i) = \theta_i' W_g d(\log Q_g) + \phi \sum_{j \in S_g} \theta_{ij} d\left(\log \frac{p_j}{P_g'}\right) + \varepsilon_i',$$

where

$$(9.22) \qquad\qquad \varepsilon_i' = \varepsilon_i - \theta_i' E_g \quad \text{if} \quad i \in S_g.$$

We shall refer to (9.21) as the *conditional demand equation* for the ith good within its group. This terminology is motivated by the fact that all variables of (9.21) are confined to S_g; that is, whereas (9.20) contains the Divisia volume index of total expenditure and also the Frisch price indexes of groups other than S_g, these indexes are all absent from (9.21). The simplest comparison of (9.21) is with the block independent demand equation (9.2), although (9.21) is actually valid under the weaker condition of blockwise dependence. The left-hand variables in (9.2) and (9.21) are identical, but the real-income term of (9.2) is replaced in (9.21) by the conditional marginal share θ_i' multiplied by the left-hand variable of the group demand equation (9.13). The substitution terms in (9.2) and (9.21) are the same except that the price deflator in (9.21) is not the Frisch price index of all n goods but the Frisch price index of the goods of S_g.

These results suggest that under blockwise dependence the consumer can solve his allocation problem in two steps. First, he uses (9.13) to allocate his income to each of the G groups, which requires knowledge of the change in his real income and of the price indexes of the groups. It does not require knowledge of price changes of individual goods. Second, given the allocation of income to the groups, the consumer uses (9.21) to allocate the total expenditure of each group to the goods within that group. This requires knowledge of the change in the consumption volume of the group (which is obtained in the first step) and of the price changes of all goods of the group.

However, this separation of the allocation into two steps requires that the disturbance E_g of the group demand equation (9.13) be stochastically independent of the disturbance ε_i' of the conditional equation (9.21). Fortunately, this is the case under rational random behavior. The reason is

$$(9.23) \qquad \text{cov}(\varepsilon_i', E_h) = 0 \qquad i \in S_g; g, h = 1, \ldots, G,$$

which means that *each* conditional demand disturbance is uncorrelated with (and hence, given the normality, independent of) *all* group disturbances $E_1, \ldots, E_G$. Also, for ε_i' of (9.22) and $\varepsilon_j' = \varepsilon_j - \theta_j' E_h$ with $j \in S_h$, we have

$$(9.24) \qquad \text{cov}(\varepsilon_i', \varepsilon_j') = 0 \quad \text{if} \quad i \in S_g, j \in S_h, g \neq h.$$

We conclude from (9.23) that we can indeed separate the group allocation decision from all conditional allocation decisions within the groups, and from (9.24) that we can also separate all within-group decisions for different groups. Therefore, when the blockwise dependence specification is combined with the theory of rational random behavior, the consumer can separate his allocation decision into $G + 1$ subsystems: one for the groups and G for the goods within groups.

In addition, we have the following covariance structure for (9.21) when i and j belong to the same group:

$$(9.25) \qquad \text{cov}(\varepsilon_i', \varepsilon_j') = \sigma^2(\theta_{ij} - \Theta_{gg}\theta_i'\theta_j') \quad \text{if} \quad i, j \in S_g.$$

If S_g consists of n_g goods, (9.25) defines a covariance matrix of order $n_g \times n_g$. This matrix is singular because ε_i' yields zero with probability 1 when summed over $i \in S_g$. This zero-sum property reflects the fact that (9.21) is an allocation model within the group. Actually, it is not difficult to prove that summation of both sides of (9.21) yields $W_g d(\log Q_g) = W_g d(\log Q_g)$, which provides another confirmation of its allocation character.

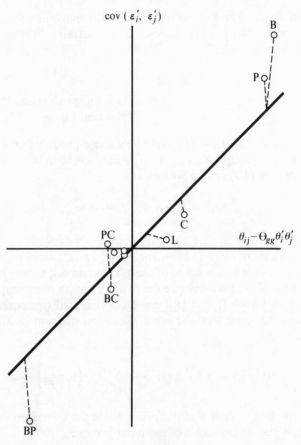

Figure 7   Verification of the covariance
                                                specification (9.25)

Figure 7, which is similar to figure 6 in section 8.3 (except that it does not use a logarithmic scale), provides an informal test of the covariance specification (9.25). The variable along the horizontal axis is $\theta_{ij} - \Theta_{gg}\theta_i'\theta_j'$, represented by an estimate of this expression, and the variable measured vertically is the corresponding disturbance covariance, represented by the mean product of the associated residuals. The data used in the figure refer to meats (annual U.S. data for the period 1950–72). The small circles in the positive quadrant correspond to $i = j$ in (9.25) with B, P, C, and L indicating beef, pork, chicken, and lamb, respectively. The six circles to the left of the vertical axis correspond to $i \neq j$, with BP indicating that of beef and pork. The figure shows that the ten circles are not very far from the upward-sloping line through the origin, which is encouraging for the

validity of (9.25). The line corresponds to the maximum-likelihood estimates obtained when (9.25) is imposed as a constraint. Further details can
be found in section 13.8.

9.5 Block Independent and Blockwise Dependent Inputs

Next we consider the n inputs bought by a single-product firm and arrange
these into input groups, $S_1, \ldots, S_G$. The firm's version of (9.1) is the case
in which $h(\mathbf{q})$ of (4.1) can be written as

$$(9.26) \qquad h(\mathbf{q}) = h_1(\mathbf{q}_1) + \cdots + h_G(\mathbf{q}_G),$$

where $\mathbf{q}_g$ is a subvector of $\mathbf{q}$ consisting of the q_i's of S_g. We shall refer to
(9.26) as the case of *block independent inputs*. The elasticity of output with
respect to q_i is then independent of the q_j's that do not belong to the same
group as that of the ith input (see the first paragraph of section 4.6).

Under (9.26) both $\mathbf{H}$ and $[\theta_{ij}]$ are block-diagonal (see eqs. [4.13] and
[4.19]) with the result that the input allocation decision (8.20) for $i \in S_g$
takes the form

$$(9.27) \qquad f_i d(\log q_i) = \theta_i d(\log Q) - \psi \sum_{j \in S_g} \theta_{ij} d\left(\log \frac{p_j}{P'}\right) + \varepsilon_i,$$

which is the firm's version of (9.2). We define the combined factor share
and the Divisia volume index of the input group S_g,

$$(9.28) \qquad F_g = \sum_{i \in S_g} f_i, \qquad d(\log Q_g) = \sum_{i \in S_g} \frac{f_i}{F_g} d(\log q_i),$$

and we sum (9.27) over $i \in S_g$,

$$(9.29) \qquad F_g d(\log Q_g) = \Theta_g d(\log Q) - \psi \Theta_g d\left(\log \frac{P'_g}{P'}\right) + E_g,$$

which is the firm's version of (9.10), with Θ_g, E_g, and $d(\log P'_g)$ defined in
(9.4) and (9.6) but now interpreted as referring to the input group S_g.
Clearly, (9.29) for $g = 1, \ldots, G$ is the firm's allocation decision in terms
of input groups under block independence.

The firm's version of (9.11) is

$$(9.30) \qquad h(\mathbf{q}) = f(h_1(\mathbf{q}_1), \ldots, h_G(\mathbf{q}_G)),$$

which is the case of *blockwise dependent inputs*. An example is Sato's [348] two-level CES production function,

$$(9.31) \qquad z = [aq_1^{-k} + (1 - a)z'^{-k}]^{-1/k},$$

where

$$(9.32) \qquad z' = [bq_2^{-k'} + (1 - b)q_3^{-k'}]^{-1/k'},$$

with a, b, k, and k' all positive constants (a, $b < 1$). The technology represented by (9.31) and (9.32) can be written in the form

$$\log z = f(h_1(q_1), h_2(q_2, q_3)),$$

with $h_1(\ )$, $h_2(\ )$, and $f(\ )$ specified as

$$h_1(q_1) = q_1^{-k}, \qquad h_2(q_2, q_3) = bq_2^{-k'} + (1 - b)q_3^{-k'},$$

$$f(h_1, h_2) = -\frac{1}{k} \log [ah_1 + (1 - a)h_2^{k/k'}].$$

The implications of (9.30) for the elasticities of output with respect to the inputs are similar to those of (9.11) for the marginal utilities. Consider the (i, j)th element of the Hessian matrix (4.13),

$$(9.33) \qquad \frac{\partial^2 h}{\partial(\log q_i)\partial(\log q_j)},$$

which describes the change in the elasticity of output with respect to q_i caused by a change in q_j at the point of minimum input expenditure. MaCurdy [262] proved that if i and j belong to different groups ($i \in S_g$, $j \in S_h$, $g \neq h$), the derivative (9.33) takes the form $b_{gh}f_if_j$, where b_{gh} is independent of i and j. This shows that the productive interaction of inputs of different groups is indeed blockwise.

MaCurdy also proved that under blockwise dependence the group and conditional equations for inputs take the same form as those for consumer goods. The input allocation equation for S_g is an extension of (9.29) and is also the firm's version of (9.13),

$$(9.34) \qquad F_g d(\log Q_g) = \Theta_g d(\log Q) - \psi \sum_{h=1}^{G} \Theta_{gh} d\left(\log \frac{P'_h}{P'}\right) + E_g,$$

and the condition allocation equation for the ith input within S_g is the firm's version of (9.21),

$$(9.35) \qquad f_i d(\log q_i) = \theta'_i F_g d(\log Q_g) - \psi \sum_{j \in S_g} \theta_{ij} d\left(\log \frac{p_j}{P'_g}\right) + \varepsilon'_i,$$

where Θ_{gh}, θ'_i, $d(\log P'_g)$, and ε'_i are defined in (9.14), (9.18), (9.19), and

(9.22), respectively. In addition, the implications (9.17) and (9.23)–(9.25) of rational random behavior hold for (9.34) and (9.35) also, so that the input allocation for groups is independent of the G conditional allocations within the groups and the latter allocations are all mutually independent.

Block structures also have implications for the partial elasticity of substitution which is shown in (8.21). This elasticity takes the form $\psi \theta_i \theta_j / f_i f_j$ when i and j belong to different groups under block independence. Hence, if a firm's input structure is block independent, two inputs belonging to different groups have a partial elasticity of substitution which is proportional to their Divisia elasticities (θ_i / f_i and θ_j / f_j), and the proportionality coefficient equals ψ. This can be generalized as follows for the weaker condition of blockwise dependence. Let S_g and S_h be different groups and let $i \in S_g$ and $j \in S_h$; then the partial elasticity of substitution between i and j is proportional to the ith and jth Divisia elasticities, but the proportionality coefficient depends on g and h (i.e., on the groups to which the two inputs belong). This result illustrates the blockwise dependence at the level of the partial elasticities of substitution. See also Berndt and Christensen [46] and Russell [339].

9.6   Extensions for the Multiproduct Firm

Chapter 5 has shown that the input structure of the multiproduct firm is an immediate extension of that of the single-product firm, provided that the elasticities of output with respect to inputs are interpreted as elasticities of proportionate output. The results (9.34) and (9.35) can be generalized straightforwardly to the multiproduct firm, including the independence results stated in the discussion following equation (9.35). The implication is that the firm can extend the hierarchy described in section 8.6 by providing the input manager with subordinates who make the conditional input allocation decisions within the G groups.

The outputs of a multiproduct firm may also be subject to a block structure; such structures were considered by Burmeister and Turnovsky [73]. Let each of the m outputs belong to one of several output groups. The case of block independent outputs is defined as that in which the firm's cost function is the sum of a number of cost functions, one for each output group. Thus, for three groups we have

$$(9.36) \qquad\qquad C(\mathbf{z}, \mathbf{p}) = \sum_{v=1}^{3} C_v(\mathbf{z}_v, \mathbf{p}),$$

where $\mathbf{z}_v$ is the subvector of $\mathbf{z}$ which consists of the z_r's that belong to the vth output group. It can be shown along the lines of Hall's [169] proof that the m-product firm can be broken up into a number of firms, one for each product group (see section 5.8). Also, (9.36) implies that the matrix $\partial^2 C/\partial \mathbf{z} \partial \mathbf{z}'$ is block-diagonal so that the supply disturbances of products of different groups are stochastically independent under rational random behavior (see eqs. [5.34] and [8.24]). This enables the firm to extend the hierarchy of its output management by appointing persons who make the conditional allocation decisions within the output groups.

A weaker version of (9.36) is that in which the firm's cost function can be written as an increasing function $f(\ )$, rather than the sum, of the C_v's. The implications of this condition (that of blockwise dependent outputs) have not yet been explored.

9.7   Other Block Structures

Pearce [306, 307] considered the utility structure (9.11) under the additional specification that the group utility function $u_g(\mathbf{q}_g)$ can be written as the sum of certain functions, one for each q_i that falls under S_g. This amounts to blockwise dependence with respect to groups of goods, and preference independence for the group utility function with respect to the goods of the group. The conditional demand equations of the goods of such a group contain only one relative price change; a generalization of this result will be described in section 15.6.

A different type of constraint may be described as follows. We use (2.28) to write $[\theta_{ij}]^{-1}$ as a scalar multiple $\phi M/\lambda$ of $\mathbf{P}^{-1}\mathbf{U}\mathbf{P}^{-1}$, where $\mathbf{P}$ is the diagonal matrix which contains the prices $p_1, \ldots, p_n$ on the diagonal. Under block independence certain off-diagonal elements of $\mathbf{P}^{-1}\mathbf{U}\mathbf{P}^{-1}$ are zero and others are nonzero. Barten [24] considered the situation in which the nonzero off-diagonal elements are small in absolute value relative to the square root of the product of the corresponding diagonal elements. If this is the case, the (i, j)th element of $(\mathbf{P}^{-1}\mathbf{U}\mathbf{P}^{-1})^{-1}$ and hence θ_{ij} are approximately zero when the (i, j)th element of $\mathbf{P}^{-1}\mathbf{U}\mathbf{P}^{-1}$ is zero, which may be verified by expanding the inverse of $\mathbf{P}^{-1}\mathbf{U}\mathbf{P}^{-1}$. This condition ("almost additive preferences") is another tool which serves to reduce the number of co-efficients in demand equations.

There are several other types of block structures, including "implicit" or "quasi" separability; in consumption theory this amounts to a separability of the cost function $C(U, \mathbf{p})$ with respect to the price subvectors of different groups of goods. It is also possible to include the theory of the true price indexes of groups in the analysis. We considered this theory in various sections of chapters 3 and 6, but the developments in these sections are confined to true indexes for all n consumer goods or all n inputs. The reader who has a taste for abstract mathematics should consult the monograph of Blackorby, Primont, and Russell [61] for further details.

Ten

The Input
Independence
Transformation

Gorman and his associates [66, 156, 157, 162] and Lancaster [231, 232] asked the question whether it is possible to express the consumer's preferences in terms of certain "basic characteristics." This question can be answered in various ways. For example, we may use statistical techniques such as factor analysis or principal component analysis. A solution which is based more directly on economic theory can be obtained from the differential approach to demand analysis. A first solution was formulated by Theil [384] and a second by Brooks [68]; the latter solution was subsequently justified axiomatically by Theil [397, chap. 12]. Recent work by Theil [398] and Laitinen and Theil [229] has shown that this transformation is also applicable to the firm.

To simplify the exposition, we start with the input independence transformation of a single-product firm. Extensions for the multiproduct firm and the consumer will be described in chapter 11.

10.1 The Objective of the Input
Independence Transformation

We reproduce the input demand equation (8.18),

$$(10.1) \qquad f_i d(\log q_i) = \gamma \theta_i d(\log z) - \psi \sum_{j=1}^{n} \theta_{ij} d \left(\log \frac{p_j}{P'} \right) + \varepsilon_i,$$

and also the input allocation equation (8.20):

$$(10.2) \qquad f_i d(\log q_i) = \theta_i d(\log Q) - \psi \sum_{j=1}^{n} \theta_{ij} d \left(\log \frac{p_j}{P'} \right) + \varepsilon_i.$$

If the firm is input independent, i.e., if

(10.3) $h(\mathbf{q}) = h_1(q_1) + \cdots + h_n(q_n),$

we can simplify (10.1) to

(10.4) $f_i d(\log q_i) = \gamma \theta_i d(\log z) - \psi \theta_i d\left(\log \dfrac{p_i}{P'}\right) + \varepsilon_i,$

and, similarly, (10.2) to

(10.5) $f_i d(\log q_i) = \theta_i d(\log Q) - \psi \theta_i d\left(\log \dfrac{p_i}{P'}\right) + \varepsilon_i.$

Note that (10.5) for $i = 1, \ldots, n$ constitutes an input allocation model with only $n + 1$ unconstrained coefficients. These include $n - 1$ unconstrained marginal shares (one θ_i is determined by $\theta_1 + \cdots + \theta_n = 1$) as well as ψ and the coefficient σ^2 of the covariance specification (8.14). Also note that if (10.3) holds, this covariance specification can be formulated in terms of specific components of input demand disturbances that are independently and normally distributed and have zero means and variances $\sigma^2\theta_1, \ldots, \sigma^2\theta_n$ (see the discussion following eq. [8.18]). Since the general component of the ith disturbance equals the sum of the specific components multiplied by $-\theta_i$ (see eq. [8.15]), the distribution of the disturbances is thus completely determined by σ^2 and the marginal shares.

The objective of the input independence transformation is to change the observed inputs into transformed inputs so that at the point of minimum input expenditure, the elasticity of output with respect to each such input has zero rates of change for variations in all other transformed inputs. This agrees with (10.3), and it yields equations of the form (10.4) and (10.5) which contain the change in only one relative price. Equivalently, the transformation yields inputs none of which is a specific substitute or complement of any other input; it yields input demand equations with random disturbances that have independent specific components; and it yields, for all pairs of inputs, partial elasticities of substitution that are proportional to the Divisia elasticities of the two inputs (see the last paragraph of section 9.5).

Transformed inputs should be visualized as composite goods similar to ordinary aggregates which represent groups of goods. The main difference between a transformed input and such an aggregate is that the former may represent an observed input with a negative sign (see the next paragraph). We shall define a transformed input in terms of its logarithmic price and quantity changes and the amount which the firm spends on it. We shall not define a level of a price or a quantity of a transformed input. This would be futile in the same way that it is futile to try to define a price or a quantity of an aggregate such as textile. There is no "price of textile," but only a price index with an arbitrary base.

In addition to the amount spent on each transformed input and its logarithmic price and quantity changes, we shall be able to derive its Divisia elasticity as well as the composition matrix of the transformation. This matrix expresses the amount spent on each transformed input in terms of the amounts spent on the observed inputs (such as capital and labor) and vice versa. It will usually occur that a composition matrix contains negative elements, which means that one or more transformed inputs represent an observed input negatively. Examples will be discussed in section 10.5 after the transformation has been derived in sections 10.2 to 10.4.

The transformation of (10.1) and (10.2) into equations of the form (10.4) and (10.5) involves a diagonalization of the normalized price coefficient matrix $[\theta_{ij}]$, which reduces the number of relative price terms to one in each equation. The positive definiteness of $[\theta_{ij}]$ implies that we shall obtain as many (n) transformed inputs as there are observed inputs. But the diagonalization of a symmetric positive definite matrix such as $[\theta_{ij}]$ is not unique. To obtain a unique transformation, we shall impose a constraint on the associated aggregate money flow and the price and volume components of its logarithmic change. For the input independence transformation this flow is the firm's total cost C. Its logarithmic change is given in (4.15), which is reproduced here:

$$(10.6) \qquad d(\log C) = d(\log P) + d(\log Q).$$

The constraints imposed on the input independence transformation are invariance conditions on total cost and the two components of its logarithmic change as shown in (10.6): the Divisia price and volume indexes of the inputs. This will be clarified in section 10.2. For the supply side of the multiproduct firm and for the consumer we shall proceed analogously with constraints on total revenue R and on income M, respectively. These two transformations will be considered in chapter 11.

10.2   The Constraints on the Transformation

We imagine that a dollar spent on the jth observed input results in r_{ij} dollars spent on the ith transformed input, where r_{ij} is to be determined but is not yet defined. Hence, when $p_j q_j$ dollars are spent on the jth observed input, the expenditure on the ith transformed input is $r_{ij} p_j q_j$

dollars insofar as it originates with the jth observed input. Summation over j gives the total amount spent on the transformed input:

(10.7)   Expenditure on ith transformed input $= \sum_{j=1}^{n} r_{ij} p_j q_j.$

By summing (10.7) over i we obtain $\sum_j (\sum_i r_{ij}) p_j q_j$, which is total cost expressed in transformed inputs. The first constraint requires total cost to be invariant, which implies $\sum_i r_{ij} = 1$ for each j or, in matrix notation,

(10.8) $\iota' \mathbf{R} = \iota',$

where $\mathbf{R}$ is the $n \times n$ matrix $[r_{ij}]$ and ι is a column vector consisting of n unit elements.

When we divide (10.7) by C, we obtain the factor share of the ith transformed input on the left. On the right we obtain $\sum_j r_{ij} f_j$, which is the ith element of the vector $\mathbf{RF}\iota$, where $\mathbf{F}$ is the diagonal matrix with the factor shares $f_1, \ldots, f_n$ on the diagonal. Therefore,

(10.9) $\mathbf{F}_T \iota = \mathbf{RF}\iota,$

where $\mathbf{F}_T$ is the diagonal matrix which contains the factor shares $f_{T1}, \ldots, f_{Tn}$ of the transformed inputs on the diagonal.

We write π and $\varkappa$ for the n-element column vectors whose ith elements are $d(\log p_i)$ and $d(\log q_i)$, respectively. The second constraint states that the logarithmic price and quantity changes of the transformed inputs are linear transformations of their observed counterparts, $\pi_T = \mathbf{S}_1 \pi$ and $\varkappa_T = \mathbf{S}_2 \varkappa$, in such a way that the Divisia price and volume indexes (4.16) and (4.17) are invariant. The price index (4.16) equals $\iota' \mathbf{F} \pi$ and its transformed counterpart is $\iota' \mathbf{F}_T \pi_T = \iota' \mathbf{F}_T \mathbf{S}_1 \pi$, which equals $\iota' \mathbf{FR}' \mathbf{S}_1 \pi$ (see eq. [10.9]). Therefore, the invariance of the Divisia price index requires $\mathbf{R}' \mathbf{S}_1 = \mathbf{I}$ and hence that $\mathbf{S}_1$ be the inverse of $\mathbf{R}'$. We can proceed similarly for the volume index, which yields the same result for $\mathbf{S}_2$. Therefore, the price and quantity transformations use the same matrix,

(10.10) $\pi_T = \mathbf{S}\pi, \qquad \varkappa_T = \mathbf{S}\varkappa,$

with $\mathbf{S}$ satisfying

(10.11) $\mathbf{R}' \mathbf{S} = \mathbf{I},$

which requires $\mathbf{R}$ and $\mathbf{S}$ to be nonsingular. It will be convenient to assume temporarily that this is true, but the singular case is important and will be discussed in section 11.5.

Note that (10.11) implies $\mathbf{R}' = \mathbf{S}^{-1}$. Since $\mathbf{R}'\iota = \iota$ follows from (10.8), this yields $\mathbf{S}^{-1}\iota = \iota$ and hence, after premultiplication by $\mathbf{S}$,

(10.12) $\mathbf{S}\iota = \iota$.

An important and desirable implication of (10.10) and (10.12) is that when the prices (quantities) of all observed inputs change proportionately, the price (quantity) of each transformed input changes in the same proportion. This is easily verified by noting that a proportionate price change of the observed inputs implies $\boldsymbol{\pi} = k\iota$ (k = scalar), so that (10.10) and (10.12) yield $\boldsymbol{\pi}_T = \mathbf{S}(k\iota) = k\mathbf{S}\iota = k\iota$.

10.3   The Diagonalization of the Input Allocation Decision

We write $\boldsymbol{\Theta} = [\theta_{ij}]$ for the normalized price coefficient matrix and $\boldsymbol{\theta} = [\theta_i]$ for the marginal share vector, so that the equation $\sum_j \theta_{ij} = \theta_i$ for $i = 1, \ldots, n$ can be written as $\boldsymbol{\Theta}\iota = \boldsymbol{\theta}$ and the Frisch price index takes the form

(10.13) $$d(\log P') = \sum_{i=1}^{n} \theta_i d(\log p_i) = \boldsymbol{\theta}'\boldsymbol{\pi} = \iota'\boldsymbol{\Theta}\boldsymbol{\pi}.$$

We can now write the input allocation decision (10.2) for $i = 1, \ldots, n$ as

(10.14) $\mathbf{F}\boldsymbol{\varkappa} = (\iota'\mathbf{F}\boldsymbol{\varkappa})\boldsymbol{\Theta}\iota - \psi\boldsymbol{\Theta}(\mathbf{I} - \iota\iota'\boldsymbol{\Theta})\boldsymbol{\pi} + \boldsymbol{\varepsilon}$,

where $\iota'\mathbf{F}\boldsymbol{\varkappa} = d(\log Q)$ and $\boldsymbol{\varepsilon} = [\varepsilon_1, \ldots, \varepsilon_n]'$ is the disturbance vector.
    Next we premultiply (10.14) by $\mathbf{R}$:

$$\mathbf{R}\mathbf{F}\boldsymbol{\varkappa} = (\iota'\mathbf{F}\boldsymbol{\varkappa})\mathbf{R}\boldsymbol{\Theta}\iota - \psi\mathbf{R}\boldsymbol{\Theta}(\mathbf{I} - \iota\iota'\boldsymbol{\Theta})\boldsymbol{\pi} + \mathbf{R}\boldsymbol{\varepsilon}.$$

The left-hand side equals $\mathbf{R}\mathbf{F}\mathbf{R}'\mathbf{S}\boldsymbol{\varkappa} = \mathbf{R}\mathbf{F}\mathbf{R}'\boldsymbol{\varkappa}_T$ in view of (10.11) and (10.10). When we proceed similarly on the right and use (10.8) also, we obtain

(10.15)

$$\mathbf{R}\mathbf{F}\mathbf{R}'\boldsymbol{\varkappa}_T = (\iota'\mathbf{F}\boldsymbol{\varkappa})(\mathbf{R}\boldsymbol{\Theta}\mathbf{R}')\iota - \psi\mathbf{R}\boldsymbol{\Theta}\mathbf{R}'[\mathbf{I} - \iota\iota'(\mathbf{R}\boldsymbol{\Theta}\mathbf{R}')]\boldsymbol{\pi}_T + \mathbf{R}\boldsymbol{\varepsilon}.$$

Since the Divisia volume index is invariant by construction ($\iota'\mathbf{F}\boldsymbol{\varkappa} = \iota'\mathbf{F}_T\boldsymbol{\varkappa}_T$), (10.15) is an allocation model of the same form as (10.14), with logarithmic price and quantity changes $\boldsymbol{\pi}_T$ and $\boldsymbol{\varkappa}_T$, provided $\mathbf{R}\mathbf{F}\mathbf{R}'$ on the left can be identified with the diagonal factor share matrix $\mathbf{F}_T$. The new normalized price coefficient matrix is $\mathbf{R}\boldsymbol{\Theta}\mathbf{R}'$, which occurs in the same three places in

(10.15) as $\boldsymbol{\Theta}$ does in (10.14). (The matrix $\mathbf{R\Theta R'}$ is a normalized matrix because $\iota'\mathbf{R\Theta R'}\iota = \iota'\boldsymbol{\Theta}\iota = 1$.) Therefore, the two conditions

$$(10.16) \qquad\qquad \mathbf{RFR'} = \mathbf{F}_T, \qquad \mathbf{R\Theta R'} = \text{diagonal}$$

are sufficient to ensure that the transformed allocation model takes the form (10.5). These are two conditions on $\mathbf{R}$, which must also satisfy (10.8).

10.4   The Solution of the Transformation

The problem of finding the matrix $\mathbf{R}$ which satisfies these three conditions was solved by Theil [398]. Here we confine ourselves to stating the solution and its implications and verifying that the conditions are satisfied.

Consider the diagonalization of the normalized price coefficient matrix $\boldsymbol{\Theta}$ relative to the diagonal factor share matrix $\mathbf{F}$,

$$(10.17) \qquad\qquad (\boldsymbol{\Theta} - \lambda_i\mathbf{F})\mathbf{x}_i = 0 \qquad i = 1, \ldots, n,$$

where λ_i is a latent root and $\mathbf{x}_i$ is a characteristic vector associated with this root. The normalization of the characteristic vectors is

$$(10.18) \qquad\qquad \mathbf{x}_i'\mathbf{Fx}_j = 1 \quad \text{if} \quad i = j$$
$$= 0 \quad \text{if} \quad i \neq j.$$

It will prove useful to present this diagonalization in two alternative forms. We define $\mathbf{F}^{-1/2}$ as the diagonal $n \times n$ matrix whose diagonal elements are the reciprocal square roots of the factor shares: $1/\sqrt{f_1}, \ldots,$ $1/\sqrt{f_n}$. We premultiply (10.17) by $\mathbf{F}^{-1/2}$ to obtain

$$(10.19) \qquad (\mathbf{F}^{-1/2}\boldsymbol{\Theta}\mathbf{F}^{-1/2} - \lambda_i\mathbf{I})\mathbf{F}^{1/2}\mathbf{x}_i = 0 \qquad i = 1, \ldots, n,$$

which shows that $\lambda_1, \ldots, \lambda_n$ are ordinary latent roots of the symmetric positive definite matrix $\mathbf{F}^{-1/2}\boldsymbol{\Theta}\mathbf{F}^{-1/2}$. This proves that the λ_i's are real and positive and also that the diagonalizations (10.17) and (10.19) are unique when the λ_i's are all distinct.

For the third form of the diagonalization we introduce the $n \times n$ matrix $\mathbf{X}$ whose ith column is the characteristic vector $\mathbf{x}_i$. Hence (10.18) can now be written as $\mathbf{X'FX} = \mathbf{I}$. We also introduce the $n \times n$ diagonal matrix $\boldsymbol{\Lambda}$ with the successive latent roots $\lambda_1, \ldots, \lambda_n$ on the diagonal. Then (10.17) in the form $\boldsymbol{\Theta}\mathbf{x}_i = \lambda_i\mathbf{Fx}_i$ for $i = 1, \ldots, n$ can be written as $\boldsymbol{\Theta}\mathbf{X} = \mathbf{FX\Lambda}$, which we premultiply by $\mathbf{X'}$: $\mathbf{X'\Theta X} = \mathbf{X'FX\Lambda}$. This can be simplified to $\mathbf{X'\Theta X} = \boldsymbol{\Lambda}$

because $\mathbf{X'FX} = \mathbf{I}$. Therefore, (10.17) and (10.18) can be written in the following form:

(10.20) $\mathbf{X'\Theta X} = \mathbf{\Lambda}, \quad \mathbf{X'FX} = \mathbf{I}.$

This amounts to a simultaneous diagonalization of $\mathbf{\Theta}$ and $\mathbf{F}$, $\mathbf{\Theta}$ being transformed into $\mathbf{\Lambda}$ and $\mathbf{F}$ into $\mathbf{I}$, both $\mathbf{\Lambda}$ and $\mathbf{I}$ being diagonal matrices.

The solution of $\mathbf{R}$ is

(10.21) $\mathbf{R} = (\mathbf{X^{-1}\iota})_\Delta \mathbf{X'},$

where $(\mathbf{X^{-1}\iota})_\Delta$ stands for the vector $\mathbf{X^{-1}\iota}$ written in the form of a diagonal matrix. We proceed to prove that this solution satisfies the three conditions listed at the end of section 10.3. Condition (10.8) in the transposed form $\mathbf{R'\iota} = \iota$ is satisfied by (10.21) because $\mathbf{X(X^{-1}\iota)}_\Delta\iota = \mathbf{XX^{-1}\iota} = \iota$. Also, (10.21) implies

$$\mathbf{RFR'} = (\mathbf{X^{-1}\iota})_\Delta \mathbf{X'FX}(\mathbf{X^{-1}\iota})_\Delta = (\mathbf{X^{-1}\iota})_\Delta^2,$$

where the last step is based on (10.20). Therefore, the first condition in (10.16) is implemented in the form

(10.22) $\mathbf{RFR'} = \mathbf{F}_T = (\mathbf{X^{-1}\iota})_\Delta^2 = \text{diagonal}.$

The second condition is similarly implemented in the form

(10.23) $\mathbf{R\Theta R'} = (\mathbf{X^{-1}\iota})_\Delta^2 \mathbf{\Lambda} = \text{diagonal},$

which follows from (10.21), $\mathbf{\Theta} = (\mathbf{X'})^{-1}\mathbf{\Lambda X^{-1}}$ (see eq. [10.20]) and the fact that diagonal matrices are commutative in multiplication.

We conclude from (10.22) and (10.23) that the transformed allocation model (10.15), after premultiplication by $(\mathbf{RFR'})^{-1} = (\mathbf{X^{-1}\iota})_\Delta^{-2}$, becomes

(10.24) $\mathbf{\varkappa}_T = (\iota'\mathbf{F\varkappa})\mathbf{\Lambda\iota} - \psi\mathbf{\Lambda}(\mathbf{I} - \iota'\mathbf{R\Theta R'})\mathbf{\pi}_T + \text{disturbance}.$

We write $d(\log q_{Ti})$ and $d(\log p_{Ti})$ for the ith element of $\mathbf{\varkappa}_T$ and $\mathbf{\pi}_T$, respectively. The expression which is subtracted in the substitution term of (10.24) represents the deflation by the Frisch price index, which is invariant in the same way that the Divisia price index is invariant.[1] Therefore, the

---

1. The marginal share vector of the transformed inputs is obtained from that of the observed inputs by premultiplication by $\mathbf{R}$, which follows from the first right-hand term in (10.15) combined with (10.8). The invariance of the Frisch price index then follows from (10.10), (10.11), and (10.13).

scalar form of (10.24) is

$$(10.25) \quad d(\log q_{Ti}) = \lambda_i d(\log Q) - \psi\lambda_i d\left(\log \frac{p_{Ti}}{P'}\right) + \text{disturbance,}$$

which shows that λ_i is the Divisia elasticity of the ith transformed input and that $-\psi\lambda_i$ is its own-price elasticity (the elasticity with respect to its Frisch-deflated price). Note that ψ is invariant under the transformation. This is not surprising, because ψ is a property of the cost function (see eq. [4.12]), and total cost is constrained to be invariant. Another invariance property is that of σ^2 of the covariance model. It can be shown that this model takes the input independent form; that is, the disturbances of the transformed input demand system have stochastically independent specific components.[2]

We noted in the discussion following equation (10.19) that the λ_i's must be distinct in order that the transformation be unique. Given the interpretation of the λ_i's as the Divisia elasticities of the transformed inputs, this means that *transformed inputs are identified by their Divisia elasticities.* If two elasticities are equal, $\lambda_i = \lambda_j$ for $i \neq j$, the characteristic vectors $\mathbf{x}_i$ and $\mathbf{x}_j$ are not uniquely determined and it is impossible to separate the ith and jth transformed inputs. See Theil and Laitinen [405] for an analysis of the situation in which the firm moves through such a multiple-root point.

At the beginning of section 10.2 we stated that the expenditure on the ith transformed input is $r_{ij}p_jq_j$ dollars insofar as it originates with the jth observed input. By dividing this by C we obtain $r_{ij}f_j$, which is thus the factor share of the ith transformed input insofar as it originates with the jth observed input. This $r_{ij}f_j$ is the (i, j)th element of the matrix $\mathbf{RF}$, to be written $\mathbf{T}$,

$$(10.26) \qquad\qquad \mathbf{T} = \mathbf{RF} = (\mathbf{X}^{-1}\iota)_\Delta\mathbf{X}^{-1},$$

where the second equal sign is based on (10.21) and $\mathbf{F} = (\mathbf{X}')^{-1}\mathbf{X}^{-1}$ (see eq. [10.20]). Postmultiplication of (10.26) by ι yields $\mathbf{T}\iota = \mathbf{RF}\iota = \mathbf{F}_T\iota$ (see eq. [10.9]); hence the row sums of $\mathbf{T}$ are the factor shares of the transformed inputs. Also, $\iota'\mathbf{T} = \iota'\mathbf{RF} = \iota'\mathbf{F}$, so that the column sums of $\mathbf{T}$ are the factor shares of the observed inputs.

The matrix $\mathbf{T}$ is known as the *composition matrix* of the input independence transformation. The rows of $\mathbf{T}$ show the composition of the factor

2. These disturbances are the elements of the vector $\mathbf{R}\varepsilon$ in (10.15), with $\mathbf{R}$ as specified in (10.21). Obviously, the multiplication of ε by this $\mathbf{R}$ affects neither the normality nor the zero means of the disturbances.

shares of the transformed inputs in terms of those of the observed inputs. The columns of **T** provide the composition of the factor shares of the observed inputs in terms of those of the transformed inputs. These rows and columns, together with the Divisia elasticities $(\lambda_1, \ldots, \lambda_n)$, should be viewed as tools for the interpretation of the transformed inputs.

We conclude by mentioning the following additional results, proofs of which can be found in Theil [397, sections 12.2 and 12.3]. First, by dividing the elements of each column of **T** by the column sum, we obtain **R**. Second, by dividing the elements of each row of **T** by the row sum we obtain **S** of (10.10). Third, the own-price elasticities $-\psi\lambda_1, \ldots, -\psi\lambda_n$ of the transformed inputs are the latent roots of the (asymmetric) price elasticity matrix $[-\psi\theta_{ij}/f_i]$ of the observed inputs, and the rows of **T** are characteristic vectors of this matrix. Note the implication that the sum of the own-price elasticities is invariant under the transformation (because the trace of the price elasticity matrix equals the sum of the latent roots).

10.5   Two Examples

We return to the translog production function (4.28) and use (4.29) to write the price coefficient matrix of the associated input allocation decision (see eq. [10.2]) as

$$
(10.27) \qquad -\psi\Theta = \frac{-1}{1-\xi^2}
\begin{bmatrix}
f_K & \xi(f_K f_L)^{1/2} \\
\xi(f_K f_L)^{1/2} & f_L
\end{bmatrix}
\begin{array}{l} \text{capital} \\ \text{labor.} \end{array}
$$

It may be verified that the matrix

$$
(10.28) \qquad \mathbf{X} = (2f_K f_L)^{-1/2}
\begin{bmatrix}
\sqrt{f_L} & -\sqrt{f_L} \\
\sqrt{f_K} & \sqrt{f_K}
\end{bmatrix}
$$

satisfies $\mathbf{X'FX} = \mathbf{I}$ and that $\mathbf{X'}(\psi\Theta)\mathbf{X}$ is a diagonal matrix whose diagonal elements are the reciprocals of $1 - \xi$ and $1 + \xi$. A comparison with (10.20) and (10.25) shows that the own-price elasticities of the transformed inputs are

$$
(10.29) \qquad -\psi\lambda_1 = \frac{-1}{1-\xi}, \qquad -\psi\lambda_2 = \frac{-1}{1+\xi}.
$$

We have multiple roots for $\xi = 0$, but this is the uninteresting case in which the translog function (4.28) becomes Cobb-Douglas, which is in input independent form (and, hence, requires no transformation).

Substitution of (10.28) in (10.26) yields the composition matrix:

$$(10.30) \qquad \mathbf{T} = \frac{1}{2} \begin{bmatrix} f_K + (f_K f_L)^{1/2} & f_L + (f_K f_L)^{1/2} \\ f_K - (f_K f_L)^{1/2} & f_L - (f_K f_L)^{1/2} \end{bmatrix}.$$

The sums of the elements in the two columns are f_K and f_L. The row sums are the factor shares of the transformed inputs: $\frac{1}{2} + (f_K f_L)^{1/2}$ for the input corresponding to λ_1 and $\frac{1}{2} - (f_K f_L)^{1/2}$ for the input corresponding to λ_2. On comparing this with (10.29) we conclude that the transformed input with own-price elasticity $-(1 - \xi)^{-1}$ has the larger factor share.

The following is a numerical specification of the matrix (10.30), bordered by row and column sums, for $f_K = 0.2$ and $f_L = 0.8$ (with the transformed inputs indicated by T_1 and T_2).

0.3	0.6	0.9	(T_1)
−0.1	0.2	0.1	(T_2)
0.2	0.8	1	
(capital)	(labor)		

This composition matrix shows that both observed inputs are positively represented in T_1, but that this is not true for T_2. Buying more T_2 means that the firm's operation becomes more labor-intensive, each dollar spent on T_2 being equivalent to two dollars' worth of labor compensated by one dollar worth of capital services which is given up. Thus, T_2 is a *contrast* between labor and capital. The occurrence of such contrasts is a regular feature of independence transformations, which will become clear from other applications that will be discussed in chapter 11.

As a second example we take the CES function (4.4) whose normalized price coefficient matrix is shown in (4.27) and is reproduced here:

$$(10.31) \quad \mathbf{\Theta} = \begin{bmatrix} f_K - (1 - k')f_K f_L & (1 - k')f_K f_L \\ (1 - k')f_K f_L & f_L - (1 - k')f_K f_L \end{bmatrix} \begin{matrix} \text{capital} \\ \text{labor.} \end{matrix}$$

It can be shown that the matrix

$$(10.32) \qquad \mathbf{X} = (f_K f_L)^{-1/2} \begin{bmatrix} (f_K f_L)^{1/2} & f_L \\ (f_K f_L)^{1/2} & -f_K \end{bmatrix}$$

satisfies $\mathbf{X'FX} = \mathbf{I}$ and that, for $\mathbf{\Theta}$ defined in (10.31), $\mathbf{X'\Theta X}$ is a diagonal matrix whose diagonal elements are $\lambda_1 = 1$ and $\lambda_2 = k'$. Hence one transformed input has unitary Divisia elasticity and the other has a Divisia elasticity equal to the elasticity of substitution between capital and labor

(k'). Multiple roots occur at $k' = 1$, in which case the CES function becomes Cobb-Douglas.

The inverse of (10.32) is

$$(10.33) \qquad \mathbf{X}^{-1} = \begin{bmatrix} f_K & f_L \\ (f_K f_L)^{1/2} & -(f_K f_L)^{1/2} \end{bmatrix},$$

which implies $\mathbf{X}^{-1}\iota = [1 \quad 0]'$. Hence, using (10.26), we obtain

$$(10.34) \qquad \mathbf{T} = \begin{bmatrix} f_K & f_L \\ 0 & 0 \end{bmatrix},$$

which should be compared with (10.30). The zeros in the second row of (10.34) imply that both capital and labor make a zero contribution to the transformed input whose Divisia elasticity is the elasticity of substitution between the observed inputs. The transformed input with unitary Divisia elasticity absorbs the factor shares of the latter inputs completely. This means that capital and labor collectively behave as one transformed input with unitary Divisia elasticity. If the reader finds this a little mysterious, we can reassure him that we shall reconsider this example in section 11.5, but he can obtain some idea of what is going on by noting that the zero element of $\mathbf{X}^{-1}\iota$ which causes $\mathbf{T}$ to have a zero row in (10.34) will also imply a zero row for $\mathbf{R}$ in (10.21). This means that $\mathbf{R}$ is singular, which is a contradiction of the nonsingularity assumption made in the discussion following equation (10.11).

Eleven

The Independence Transformations for the Consumer and the Multiproduct Firm

The mathematics of the input independence transformation can be applied directly to the consumer's demand equations and the input demand and output supply equations of the multiproduct firm. This matter is pursued in the first four sections of this chapter. The last two sections provide a discussion of the transformation under singularity and a comparison with the principal component technique in statistics.

11.1 The Preference Independence Transformation

We reproduce the differential consumer demand equation (8.13):

$$(11.1) \qquad w_i d(\log q_i) = \theta_i d(\log Q) + \phi \sum_{j=1}^{n} \theta_{ij} d\left(\log \frac{p_j}{P'}\right) + \varepsilon_i.$$

If the consumer is preference independent, i.e., if his preferences can be represented by a utility function of the additive form

$$(11.2) \qquad u(\mathbf{q}) = u_1(q_1) + \cdots + u_n(q_n),$$

we can simplify (11.1) to

$$(11.3) \qquad w_i d(\log q_i) = \theta_i d(\log Q) + \phi \theta_i d\left(\log \frac{p_i}{P'}\right) + \varepsilon_i.$$

The above three equations are the consumer's version of equations (10.2), (10.3), and (10.5) for the inputs of the single-product firm. It is easily seen that the mathematics of the input independence transformation can be immediately applied to the consumer's demand equations after appropriate reinterpretations (factor shares become budget shares, ψ becomes $-\phi$, and so on). We shall refer to this procedure as the preference independence transformation; it changes observed consumer goods into transformed goods so that at the point of the budget-constrained utility maximum, the marginal utility of each such good has zero rates of change with respect to the consumption of all others. The transformation diagonalizes $[\theta_{ij}]$ of (11.1) subject to an invariance constraint on the consumer's income M and the associated Divisia price and volume indexes. The λ's of (10.17) and (10.25) are here the income elasticities of the transformed consumer goods.

We proceed to discuss an application of the preference independence transformation to annual U.S. data on three meats: beef, pork, and chicken. This application is based on an estimated system of demand equations in block independent form (see section 13.8 for further details). Under block independence we can apply the preference independence transformation to each block separately.[1] This is particularly convenient, since it permits us to confine our attention to the three meats.

The transformation is applied to each pair of successive years from 1950 to 1972. In each case we obtain a composition matrix, to be compared with those discussed in section 10.5 for the inputs of the translog and CES production functions. Three bordered composition matrices at 10-year intervals are shown in table 1. The entries in this table represent dollar amounts expressed as fractions of the expenditure on the three-meat group. The column totals show that the share of beef increased (from 43.8 to 53.3 to 56.7 percent) at the expense of the shares of pork and chicken. A major cause is the increase in real income per capita combined with the high income elasticity of the demand for beef relative to those for pork and chicken.

The row sums of the composition matrix are the shares of the transformed meats. One of these, labeled T_1, dominates the others and accounts for about three-fourths of the expenditure on the three-meat group. The behavior of the income elasticities λ_1, λ_2, λ_3 of the transformed meats is shown in figure 8. (More precisely, in this within-group application λ_i is a conditional income elasticity, i.e., the income elasticity of a transformed meat divided by the income elasticity of the three-meat group.) The figure shows that the elasticity λ_1 of T_1 is the lowest of the three, so that T_1 is a necessity relative to the other transformed meats. This result, together with

1. This follows from the fact that the normalized price coefficient matrix is then block-diagonal, so that (10.20) is satisfied by a block-diagonal matrix **X**. This result applies to both the input and the preference independence transformations (and also to the output independence transformation to be discussed in section 11.2). For extensions of this result to the weaker condition of blockwise dependence, see Theil and Laitinen [405].

**The Preference Independence
Transformation**

Table 1   Composition Matrices for Meats

		Beef	Pork	Chicken	Total
			1950–51		
	T_1	0.119	0.407	0.209	0.736
	T_2	0.295	−0.078	−0.003	0.213
	T_3	0.023	0.092	−0.065	0.051
Total		0.438	0.421	0.142	1
			1960–61		
	T_1	0.205	0.370	0.185	0.760
	T_2	0.263	−0.108	0.008	0.164
	T_3	0.065	0.086	−0.075	0.076
Total		0.533	0.348	0.118	1
			1970–71		
	T_1	0.252	0.343	0.184	0.779
	T_2	0.200	−0.107	0.016	0.109
	T_3	0.115	0.084	−0.087	0.112
Total		0.567	0.320	0.113	1

the fact that the observed meats are all positively represented in T_1 (see the first row of each matrix in table 1), indicates that T_1 represents the consumer's demand for affordable meat. Note that λ_1 is subject to an increasing trend, which means that T_1 moved in the direction of a luxury during the 20-year period. This agrees with the fact that T_1 is gradually "beefed up"; the contribution of beef to T_1 steadily increased, mainly at the expense of the contribution of pork (see the first row of each matrix).[2]

The second rows of the composition matrices show that beef contributes positively to T_2, that pork contributes negatively to T_2, and that the contribution of chicken is close to zero. Therefore, T_2 is a contrast between beef and pork similar to the contrast between labor and capital described in the discussion following equation (10.30). The third transformed meat is a contrast between beef and pork on one hand and chicken on the other. Figure 8 shows that T_2 is the most luxurious of the three transformed meats and that the position of T_3 is between T_1 and T_2 in this respect. Note that the three curves in the figure are well separated. If two such curves intersect, we would have a problem in identifying the transformed goods because

2. The contribution of each observed meat to the conditional income elasticity of each transformed meat can also be computed. It appears that the increase in the elasticity λ_1 of T_1 is mainly due to the increase in the contribution of beef; the contributions of pork and chicken to λ_1 are virtually constant. See Theil [397, section 13.3].

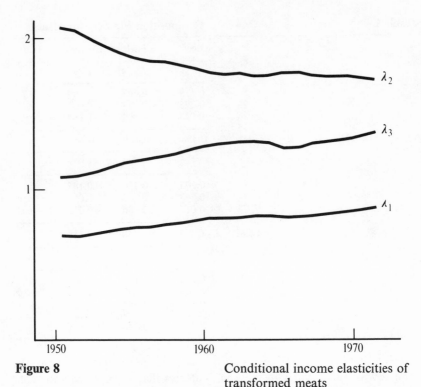

Figure 8   Conditional income elasticities of
                                             transformed meats

these goods are identified by their income elasticities in the same way that
transformed inputs are identified by their Divisia elasticities (see the discussion following eq. [10.25]).

11.2   The Independence Transformation
of the Multiproduct Firm

The generalization of the results of chapter 10 to the multiproduct firm
requires consideration of both the input demand equations and the output
supply equations. The input demand equations take the form (8.22), which
is reproduced here:

$$(11.4) \quad f_i d(\log q_i) = \gamma \sum_{r=1}^{m} \theta_i^r g_r d(\log z_r) - \psi \sum_{j=1}^{n} \theta_{ij} d\left(\log \frac{p_j}{P'}\right) + \varepsilon_i.$$

If the elasticity of proportionate output with respect to each input has a
zero rate of change for variations in all other inputs (see the last paragraph
of section 5.4), we can simplify (11.4) to

$$(11.5) \quad f_i d(\log q_i) = \gamma \sum_{r=1}^{m} \theta_i^r g_r d(\log z_r) - \psi \theta_i d\left(\log \frac{p_i}{P'}\right) + \varepsilon_i.$$

In this case no input is a specific substitute or complement of any other input.

The firm's output supply equations take the form (8.23), which is reproduced here:

$$(11.6) \qquad g_r d(\log z_r) = \psi^* \sum_{s=1}^{m} \theta_{rs}^* d\left(\log \frac{y_s}{P'_s}\right) + \varepsilon_r^*.$$

If the firm is output independent, i.e., if

$$(11.7) \qquad C(\mathbf{z}, \mathbf{p}) = C_1(z_1, \mathbf{p}) + \cdots + C_m(z_m, \mathbf{p}),$$

we can simplify (11.6) to

$$(11.8) \qquad g_r d(\log z_r) = \psi^* \theta_r^* d\left(\log \frac{y_r}{P'_r}\right) + \varepsilon_r^*,$$

in which case no product has a specific supply substitution or complementarity relation with any other product.

The independence transformation of the multiproduct firm changes observed inputs into transformed inputs and observed outputs into transformed outputs in such a way that the input demand and output supply equations take the form (11.5) and (11.8), respectively. This is entirely in agreement with the input independence transformation of chapter 10 and the preference independence transformation of section 11.1, but it is worthwhile to provide further clarification by means of the second differential of profit which we considered earlier in sections 6.7 and 8.7.

We reproduce equation (8.35),

$$(11.9) \qquad \frac{d^2(R - C)}{R} = B_1 + B_2 + B_3,$$

and note that each of the B's is defined in equations (8.36) to (8.38) as the sum of an input term and an output term. Consequently, the left-hand side of (11.9) can also be written as the sum of an input term,

$$(11.10) \quad -\frac{1}{\gamma} \sum_{i=1}^{n} f_i [d(\log p_i)]^2 + \frac{\psi}{\gamma} \sum_{i=1}^{n} \sum_{j=1}^{n} \theta_{ij} d\left(\log \frac{p_i}{P'}\right) d\left(\log \frac{p_j}{P'}\right)$$

$$- \frac{1}{\gamma\psi} \sum_{i=1}^{n} \sum_{j=1}^{n} \theta^{ij} \varepsilon_i \varepsilon_j,$$

and the following output term:

$$(11.11) \quad \sum_{r=1}^{m} g_r [d(\log y_r)]^2 + \psi^* \sum_{r=1}^{m} \sum_{s=1}^{m} \theta_{rs}^* d\left(\log \frac{y_r}{P'_r}\right) d\left(\log \frac{y_s}{P'_s}\right)$$

$$- \frac{1}{\psi^*} \sum_{r=1}^{m} \sum_{s=1}^{m} \theta^{*rs} \varepsilon_r^* \varepsilon_s^*.$$

If the firm is input independent, we can simplify the input term (11.10) to

$$(11.12) \quad -\frac{1}{\gamma} \sum_{i=1}^{n} f_i [d(\log p_i)]^2 + \frac{\psi}{\gamma} \sum_{i=1}^{n} \theta_i \left[d\left(\log \frac{p_i}{P'}\right) \right]^2 - \frac{1}{\gamma\psi} \sum_{i=1}^{n} \frac{\varepsilon_i^2}{\theta_i},$$

which is the sum of $3n$ terms, each of which is associated with one input. Similarly, if the firm is output independent, we can simplify the output term (11.11) to

$$(11.13) \quad \sum_{r=1}^{m} g_r [d(\log y_r)]^2 + \psi^* \sum_{r=1}^{m} \theta_r^* \left[d\left(\log \frac{y_r}{P'^r}\right) \right]^2 - \frac{1}{\psi^*} \sum_{r=1}^{m} \frac{\varepsilon_r^{*2}}{\theta_r^*},$$

which is the sum of $3m$ terms, each of which is associated with one output.

We conclude that if the firm is both input and output independent, the second differential of its profit is the sum of $3n + 3m$ terms, each of which is associated with one input or one output. The profit function may then be viewed as additive in the inputs and outputs as far as the terms up to the second order are concerned. This is what the independence transformation achieves with respect to the firm's profit function. It is entirely analogous to the preference independence transformation in the theory of the consumer. By transforming consumer goods so that the marginal utility of each has a zero rate of change for variations in the consumption of all others, we make the utility function additive in the transformed goods for terms up to the second order. In the consumer's case this Taylor expansion is from the point of the budget-constrained utility maximum. In the firm's case the expansion is from the point of maximum profit constrained by the technology (5.2).

The input independence transformation of chapter 10 can be described in similar terms. The input demand equation (10.1) refers to a single-product firm; the equation results from the firm's objective to minimize input expenditure subject to the technology constraint (4.1). This objective is equivalent to that of the dual problem of maximizing (scalar) output subject to the constraint that a given amount be spent on the inputs. Consider then a Taylor expansion of (4.1):

$$(11.14) \quad \Delta(\log z) = \sum_{i=1}^{n} \frac{\partial h}{\partial \log q_i} \Delta(\log q_i)$$

$$+ \frac{1}{2} \sum_{i=1}^{n} \sum_{j=1}^{n} \frac{\partial^2 h}{\partial(\log q_i)\partial(\log q_j)} \Delta(\log q_i)\Delta(\log q_j) + \cdots$$

The input independence transformation diagonalizes the matrix $[\theta_{ij}]$ and hence also $\mathbf{H}$ (see eq. [4.19]), the (i, j)th element of which appears after the double sum in equation (11.14). Therefore, the transformation changes the firm's production function so that, as far as terms up to the second order are concerned, the logarithm of output is additive in the transformed inputs.

The independence transformation of the multiproduct firm can be
viewed as consisting of two components: an input independence transformation and an output independence transformation. The former yields
transformed inputs so that, at the point of maximum profit, the elasticity
of proportionate output with respect to each transformed input has zero
rates of change for variations in all others. The latter yields transformed
outputs so that, at the same point, the marginal cost of each has zero
rates of change for variations in all other transformed outputs. When the
two transformations have been performed, all specific substitution and
complementarity relations are eliminated, both in supply and demand.

We shall prove in the next paragraph that the two transformations can be
applied separately and independently. This property is obviously very
convenient. The output independence transformation diagonalizes $\Theta^* = [\theta_{rs}^*]$ subject to the constraint that the firm's total revenue R and the associated Divisia price and volume indexes remain invariant. The mathematics of
this transformation is a carbon copy of that of the input independence
transformation of the single-product firm described in chapter 10; it is
simply a matter of adding appropriate asterisks, replacing the diagonal
factor share matrix F by the diagonal revenue share matrix G, and so on.
In particular, (10.20) becomes

$$(11.15) \qquad \mathbf{X}^{*\prime}\mathbf{\Theta}^*\mathbf{X}^* = \mathbf{\Lambda}^*, \qquad \mathbf{X}^{*\prime}\mathbf{G}\mathbf{X}^* = \mathbf{I},$$

where $\mathbf{\Lambda}^*$ is the diagonal matrix with the Divisia elasticities $\lambda_1^*, \ldots, \lambda_m^*$ of
the transformed outputs on the diagonal. Also, (10.26) becomes

$$(11.16) \qquad \mathbf{T}^* = (\mathbf{X}^{*-1}\mathbf{\iota}^*)_\Delta \mathbf{X}^{*-1},$$

where $\mathbf{T}^*$ is the composition matrix of the output independence transformation and $\mathbf{\iota}^*$ is a column vector consisting of m (rather than n) unit
elements. The rows of $\mathbf{T}^*$ display the composition of the revenue shares of
the transformed outputs in terms of those of the observed outputs, while
the columns show the composition of the revenue shares of the latter in
terms of those of the former.

There are two reasons why the input and output independence transformations can be applied separately and independently. One is the fact that
the input term (11.10) is completely separate from the output term (11.11).
The other reason has to do with the proportional output concept. If this
concept had different meanings for transformed and observed outputs, the
output independence transformation would affect the normalized price
coefficient matrix $[\theta_{ij}]$ of the input demand equations,[3] so that the input

---

3. This matrix is defined in (4.19), where H is the matrix (4.13). In the multiproduct case the latter matrix specifies the sensitivity of the n elasticities of
proportionate output for variations in the n inputs.

and output independence transformations could not be implemented independently. However, this is not the case, since the proportional output concept is identical for transformed and observed outputs: if the quantities of all observed outputs change proportionately, the quantity of each transformed output changes in the same proportion. This proposition is the output version of the proposition for the quantities of the inputs which is described at the end of section 10.2.

The input independence transformation of the multiproduct firm is identical to that of the single-product firm. The result is that a substantial number of coefficients and variables are invariant. These include, in addition to total cost and total revenue and their Divisia indexes, profit $(R - C)$, $\gamma = R/C$ (see eq. [5.30]), ψ, ψ^*, and the Frisch indexes $d(\log P')$, $d(\log P'')$, and $d(\log Y')$. The last two indexes play a role in the total-output and output allocation decisions. Another invariance property is that of the second-order Divisia moments of the logarithmic input and output price changes. Such a moment occurs in the first term of each of the expressions (11.10) to (11.13).

11.3   An Example

We use the translog cost function of section 5.9 as an example and reproduce the normalized price coefficient matrices (5.50) and (5.52):

$$(11.17) \quad [\theta_{rs}^*] = \frac{1}{b} \begin{bmatrix} g_1(A - 1 + k^*Ag_1) & -k^*Ag_1g_2 \\ -k^*Ag_1g_2 & g_2(A - 1 + k^*Ag_2) \end{bmatrix},$$

$$(11.18) \quad [\theta_{ij}] = \begin{bmatrix} f_1[1 + 2k(f_1f_2)^{1/2}] & k(f_2 - f_1)(f_1f_2)^{1/2} \\ k(f_2 - f_1)(f_1f_2)^{1/2} & f_2[1 - 2k(f_1f_2)^{1/2}] \end{bmatrix}.$$

If either $k = 0$ or $f_1 = f_2 = \frac{1}{2}$ holds in (11.18), $[\theta_{ij}]$ is diagonal and the input independence transformation is unnecessary. If both $k \neq 0$ and $f_1 \neq f_2$, we define

$$(11.19) \quad \mathbf{X} = \frac{1}{\sqrt{2}} \begin{bmatrix} 1 - (f_2/f_1)^{1/2} & 1 + (f_2/f_1)^{1/2} \\ 1 + (f_1/f_2)^{1/2} & 1 - (f_1/f_2)^{1/2} \end{bmatrix},$$

which satisfies (10.20) with Λ specified by its two diagonal elements:

$$(11.20) \quad \lambda_1 = 1 - k, \quad \lambda_2 = 1 + k.$$

When we substitute (11.19) in (10.26), we obtain the composition matrix of the input independence transformation:

$$(11.21) \quad \mathbf{T} = \frac{1}{2} \begin{bmatrix} f_1 - (f_1f_2)^{1/2} & f_2 + (f_1f_2)^{1/2} \\ f_1 + (f_1f_2)^{1/2} & f_2 - (f_1f_2)^{1/2} \end{bmatrix}.$$

Note that the factor shares of the transformed inputs (the row sums of $\mathbf{T}$) are both $\frac{1}{2}$. Hence, if the factor shares of the observed inputs are not equal $(f_1 \neq \frac{1}{2}, f_2 \neq \frac{1}{2})$ and if $k \neq 0$, the transformation yields inputs with equal shares.

If $k^* \neq 0$ in (11.17), we apply the output independence transformation, for which purpose we define

$$(11.22) \qquad \mathbf{X}^* = \begin{bmatrix} 1 & (g_2/g_1)^{1/2} \\ -1 & (g_1/g_2)^{1/2} \end{bmatrix},$$

which satisfies (11.15) with $\mathbf{\Lambda}^*$ specified by its two diagonal elements:

$$(11.23) \qquad \lambda_1^* = \frac{A - 1 + k^*A}{b}, \qquad \lambda_2^* = \frac{A - 1}{b}.$$

Substitution of (11.22) in (11.16) gives

$$(11.24) \qquad \mathbf{T}^* = \begin{bmatrix} g_1(g_1 - g_2) & -g_2(g_1 - g_2) \\ 2g_1g_2 & 2g_1g_2 \end{bmatrix},$$

which is the composition matrix of the output independence transformation. The row sums of $\mathbf{T}^*$ are $(g_1 - g_2)^2 = 1 - 4g_1g_2$ and $4g_1g_2$. The observed outputs contribute equally to the transformed output corresponding to λ_2^* (see the second row of $\mathbf{T}^*$), whereas the other transformed output is a contrast between the first and the second observed outputs. If the latter two outputs have equal revenue shares $(g_1 = g_2 = \frac{1}{2})$, the first row of $\mathbf{T}^*$ consists of zeros and the firm's total revenue is completely accounted for by the transformed output corresponding to λ_2^*. This special case is similar to that of the transformed inputs of the CES function (see the end of section 10.5). We shall have more to say about such cases in section 11.5.

11.4   Does the Transformation Yield an Input-Output Separable Firm?

In the discussion following equation (5.22) we provided a symmetric description of input independence and input-output separability. We noted that under input independence each input demand equation contains one relative price term plus m output terms, whereas under input-output separability each input demand equation contains one output term plus n relative price terms. Given this symmetry, is it the case that the independence transformation of the multiproduct firm changes this firm into an input-output separable firm?

The answer is no. There is an important difference between input-output separability on one hand and input and output independence on the other in that the latter forms of independence refer to the diagonal form of positive definite matrices (Θ and Θ^*), whereas input-output separability refers to the question of whether the (rectangular) matrix $[\theta_i^r]$ has unit rank (see eq. [5.21]). If a multiproduct firm is input-output separable before the independence transformation, it will be separable after the transformation; if the firm is inseparable before the transformation, it will remain inseparable after the transformation.

In fact, it can be shown that in a particular sense the degree to which a firm is input-output inseparable is invariant under the independence transformation. To clarify this statement we must define the degree of input-output separability. The simplest way in which this can be done is by means of a simultaneous consideration of the cost-minimizing and the revenue-maximizing firms; we refer to Appendix D.

11.5   The Independence Transformation under Singularity

We return to the last paragraph of section 10.5, where we noted that the vector $X^{-1}\iota$ contains a zero element which causes the transformation matrix R to be singular (see eq. [10.21]). The situation described at the end of section 11.3 is completely analogous: if $g_1 = g_2$, the inverse of X^* in (11.22) has the property that the elements of its first row add up to zero, which yields zero for both elements in the first row of T^* in (11.24). The Divisia elasticity of the transformed output that corresponds to the second row of T^* is then $\lambda_2^* = 1$, which may be verified by substituting $g_1 = g_2$ in (5.51) and (11.23). Hence the transformed output which fully accounts for the firm's revenue has unitary Divisia elasticity. This is analogous to the unitary Divisia elasticity of the transformed input which fully accounts for the firm's cost in the CES case described in section 10.5.

The crucial issue is the occurrence of one or more zero elements in the vector $X^{-1}\iota$ or the analogous vector of the output independence transformation. It will be sufficient to clarify this situation for the input independence transformation of a single-product firm. Assume first that $X^{-1}\iota$ contains no zero elements so that $(X^{-1}\iota)_\Delta$ is a nonsingular diagonal matrix. Then (10.11) and (10.21) imply

$$(11.25) \qquad\qquad S = (X^{-1}\iota)_\Delta^{-1}X^{-1},$$

and (10.10) yields

$$(11.26) \qquad\qquad d(\log p_{Ti}) = \sum_{j=1}^{n} s_{ij}d(\log p_j),$$

where s_{ij} is the (i, j)th element of S.

Imagine that the ith element of $\mathbf{X}^{-1}\iota$ takes a small value and then converges to zero because of a perturbation of the firm's technology. (Such a perturbation amounts to a change in the production function [4.1], which affects $\mathbf{X}$ via $\mathbf{H}$ and Θ in view of eqs. [4.13], [4.19], and [10.20].) It follows from (11.25) that the ith row of $\mathbf{S}$ will then consist of elements that increase beyond bounds, so that (11.26) implies that the logarithmic price change of the ith transformed input moves toward $\pm\infty$. If the move is to $+\infty$, the transformed input is priced out of the market, so that nothing is spent on it in the limit. If the move is to $-\infty$, this input becomes a free good; again, nothing is spent on it in the limit. These zero expenditures agree with the zero row of the composition matrix for the CES function (4.4) which is shown in equation (10.34). Transformed inputs on which nothing is spent can be viewed as limiting cases with either zero or infinite prices which result from the firm's technology. A similar explanation applies to transformed outputs with zero revenue shares and also to transformed consumer goods with zero budget shares. In the latter case the perturbation described above refers to the consumer's preferences rather than the firm's technology.

A particularly strong result applies to homothetic technologies of which the CES function (4.4) is an example (see the last paragraph of section 4.6). It was shown by Theil [398] that the following equation holds for any homothetic single-product firm:

$$(11.27) \qquad\qquad \mathbf{F}_T = \Lambda\mathbf{F}_T.$$

This yields $\Lambda = \mathbf{I}$, amounting to a unit root of multiplicity n, when the diagonal elements of $\mathbf{F}_T$ are all nonzero, i.e., when all transformed inputs have positive factor shares. If $\lambda_i \neq 1$, equation (11.27) implies that the associated transformed input has a zero factor share. There must be at least one λ_i equal to 1, because otherwise $\mathbf{F}_T = \mathbf{0}$ would hold, which violates the invariance condition on total cost. Therefore, when there are no multiple roots, a homothetic technology implies that the firm buys only one transformed input, corresponding to $\lambda_1 = 1$.

This may be further clarified by substituting (10.22) in (11.27),

$$(11.28) \qquad\qquad (\mathbf{X}^{-1}\iota)_\Lambda^2 = \Lambda(\mathbf{X}^{-1}\iota)_\Lambda^2,$$

which shows that under a homothetic technology with $\lambda_1 = 1$ and $\lambda_j \neq 1$ for each $j \neq 1$, all elements of $\mathbf{X}^{-1}\iota$ vanish except the first. Hence (10.21) implies that all elements of $\mathbf{R}$ except those in the first row vanish, while (10.8) shows that this first row must consist of unit elements. On combining this with (10.7) we conclude that the expenditure on the transformed input corresponding to $\lambda_1 = 1$ is the sum of the expenditures on all observed inputs. In other words, the observed inputs of a homothetic technology collectively behave as one transformed input with unitary Divisia elasticity. The firm spends no money on any transformed input whose Divisia elasticity differs from 1; such inputs are all limiting cases with zero or infinite prices that result from the homothetic technology.

11.6   A Principal Component Interpretation

The principal component transformation changes a set of n observed correlated variables into a set of uncorrelated variables. This transformation is not unique because it depends on the units of measurement of the observed variables. To make it unique statisticians frequently standardize these variables so that they all have unit variance. Let V be the covariance matrix of the observed variables prior to the standardization. Let $\hat{V}$ be the diagonal matrix whose diagonal is identical to that of V, so that $\hat{V}^{1/2}$ contains the standard deviations of these variables. Then $\hat{V}^{-1/2}V\hat{V}^{-1/2}$ is the covariance matrix after the standardization and also the correlation matrix of the original observed variables. The principal component technique involves the derivation of latent roots (λ_i) from the determinantal equation

$$(11.29) \qquad |\hat{V}^{-1/2}V\hat{V}^{-1/2} - \lambda_i I| = 0 \qquad i = 1, \ldots, n.$$

Having obtained $\lambda_1, \ldots, \lambda_n$, we can derive the principal components and various weight vectors, but these are irrelevant for our present purpose.

A comparison of the independence transformation with the principal component technique is appropriate because this transformation does indeed change a set of (random) variables that are correlated into a set of uncorrelated variables. The diagonalization of $[\theta^*_{rs}]$ performed by the output independence transformation changes the m correlated output supply disturbances into m uncorrelated disturbances (see eq. [8.24]). Similarly, the diagonalization of $[\theta_{ij}]$ performed by the input and preference independence transformations changes the correlated specific components of the n demand disturbances into n uncorrelated specific components; see the last paragraph of section 8.3 and the first of section 8.4.

However, the independence transformation takes a form different from (11.29). It is easily verified that (10.19) implies the following determinantal equation:

$$(11.30) \qquad |F^{-1/2}\Theta F^{-1/2} - \lambda_i I| = 0 \qquad i = 1, \ldots, n.$$

The extension of (11.30) to the output and preference independence transformations is

(11.31) $|\mathbf{G}^{-1/2}\mathbf{\Theta}^*\mathbf{G}^{-1/2} - \lambda_r^*\mathbf{I}| = 0 \qquad r = 1, \ldots, m,$

(11.32) $|\mathbf{W}^{-1/2}\mathbf{\Theta}\mathbf{W}^{-1/2} - \lambda_i\mathbf{I}| = 0 \qquad i = 1, \ldots, n,$

where $\mathbf{W}$ is the diagonal matrix with the consumer's budget shares ($w_1, \ldots,$ w_n) on the diagonal.

In (11.29) the covariance matrix $\mathbf{V}$ is pre- and postmultiplied by $\hat{\mathbf{V}}^{-1/2}$ so that it becomes the correlation matrix. Since the diagonals of $\mathbf{\Theta}$ and $\mathbf{W}$ are in general not identical, the matrix $\mathbf{W}^{-1/2}\mathbf{\Theta}\mathbf{W}^{-1/2}$ in (11.32) is not a correlation matrix. This implies that the preference independence transformation is not equivalent to principal components computed from a standardized version of specific components of disturbances. The presence of $\mathbf{W}$ results from the budget constraint which is imposed on the transformed goods. Similarly, $\mathbf{F}$ in (11.30) and $\mathbf{G}$ in (11.31) result from the invariance constraint on total cost C and total revenue R, respectively. Thus, the independence transformation may be viewed as a constrained principal component transformation: income-constrained for the consumer, cost-constrained for the firm's demand side, and revenue-constrained for the supply side of the multiproduct firm. Such constraints are more natural than the rather arbitrary standardization procedure.

It is common among statisticians to arrange the λ_i's of (11.29) in descending order and to use the first $r < n$ principal components as an approximate description of the behavior of the observed variables. This procedure is not recommended for the independence transformation. If we applied it to the meats of section 11.1 by confining ourselves to the two transformed meats with the largest λ's, we would miss T_1, which accounts for about 75 percent of the expenditure on the three-meat group (see table 1).

The objective of the independence transformation is not a reduction of the number of dimensions. Rather, its objective is to present the consumer's preferences and the firm's technology in the simplest form. For the consumer this amounts to additivity of the utility function around the point of maximum utility. For the supply side of the multiproduct firm it amounts to additivity of the cost function in the outputs around the point of maximum profit. For the demand side of this firm it amounts to an elasticity of proportionate output with respect to each input which is independent of all other inputs (this may be viewed as logarithmic additivity of proportionate output in the inputs). In all cases the transformation eliminates the specific substitution and complementarity relations, both in demand and in supply.

Twelve

The View from the Top and the Descent to Detail

The previous chapter completes our discussion of the system-wide approach to the theories of the consumer and the firm. Before proceeding to the application of this approach to statistical data (in chaps. 13 and 14) and consideration of generalizations of earlier results (in chap. 15), it is appropriate to ask whether the approach provides us with valuable insights in addition to demand and supply equations. These insights are the subject of the present chapter. The results can be conveniently divided into two groups. First, it is possible to define system-wide summary measures such as the change in the quality of consumption and the income elasticity of the demand for quality. Such measures refer to all n consumer goods jointly rather than one in particular; that is why these measures are called system-wide. Second, it is also possible to proceed from the other end by adopting a completely microscopic point of view. This will take place in the last section of this chapter, where we shall consider changes in budget shares of individual goods as well as relations among pairs of budget share changes.

12.1 The Degree of Dependence

When a system of demand or supply equations is formulated in terms of observed consumer goods, inputs, or outputs, it is usually not in independent form. How dependent is such a system? In this section we shall answer this question for the demand and supply systems of the differential approach.

The preference and input independence transformations change the normalized price coefficient matrix $\mathbf{\Theta} = [\theta_{ij}]$ into a diagonal matrix. One way of measuring the degree to which any $n \times n$ symmetric positive definite matrix $\mathbf{\Theta}$ differs from diagonality is by means of

$$(12.1) \qquad \Delta = \sum_{i=1}^{n} \log \theta_{ii} - \log |\mathbf{\Theta}|,$$

where $|\Theta|$ stands for the determinant value of Θ. The coefficient Δ vanishes when Θ is diagonal and is positive otherwise; this follows from the fact that $|\Theta|$ is at most equal to the product of the diagonal elements $\theta_{11}, \ldots, \theta_{nn}$. For example, for the translog specification given in equation (4.28) we have $\Delta = -\log(1 - \xi^2)$, which vanishes at $\xi = 0$ and is a monotonically increasing function of ξ^2. We shall call Δ the *degree of input dependence* in the case of a firm and the *degree of preference dependence* in the consumer's case.

The definition (12.1) has the advantage of a very simple decomposition under blockwise dependence. We reproduce equation (9.14),

$$(12.2) \qquad \Theta_{gh} = \sum_{i \in S_g} \sum_{j \in S_h} \theta_{ij} \qquad g, h = 1, \ldots, G,$$

and recall that $[\Theta_{gh}]$ is the normalized price coefficient matrix of the demand equation system for groups which is given in (9.13). Thus, the extension of (12.1) for groups is

$$(12.3) \qquad \Delta_0 = \sum_{g=1}^{G} \log \Theta_{gg} - \log |\Theta_{gh}|,$$

where $|\Theta_{gh}|$ stands for the determinant value of the $G \times G$ matrix $[\Theta_{gh}]$.

Next we turn to the gth group, S_g, and write Θ_g for the $n_g \times n_g$ principal submatrix of Θ that refers to this group, where n_g is the number of goods in S_g. The sum of the elements of Θ_g equals Θ_{gg} in view of (12.2), so that the price coefficient matrix of the goods of S_g normalized within the group is $(1/\Theta_{gg})\Theta_g$. It thus follows from (12.1) that the within-group degree of dependence for S_g is

$$(12.4) \qquad \Delta_g = \sum_{i \in S_g} \log \frac{\theta_{ii}}{\Theta_{gg}} - \log \left| \frac{1}{\Theta_{gg}} \Theta_g \right|.$$

It was shown by Theil [397, section 12.6] that, in the consumer's case,

$$(12.5) \qquad \Delta = \Delta_0 + \sum_{g=1}^{G} \Delta_g,$$

or, in words, the degree of dependence of the system as a whole equals the degree of dependence among the groups plus the total within-group dependence, the latter being obtained by adding the degrees of dependence within the G groups. When blockwise dependence is strengthened to block independence, the between-group dependence (12.3) vanishes. Similar results were obtained by Verma [422] for the inputs of a firm.

For the supply side of a profit-maximizing multiproduct firm we extend (12.1) to

(12.6) $$\Delta^* = \sum_{r=1}^{m} \log \theta_{rr}^* - \log |\Theta^*|,$$

where $|\Theta^*|$ is the determinant value of the $m \times m$ matrix $\Theta^* = [\theta_{rs}^*]$. This Δ^* is the *degree of output dependence*.

Both Δ and Δ^* are related to correlation matrices of disturbances under rational random behavior. It follows from (8.24) that Δ^* equals minus the logarithm of the determinant value of the correlation matrix of the supply disturbances, and from (8.17) that Δ has the same property with respect to the specific components of the demand disturbances.

12.2 The Measurement of the Quality of Consumption

Frisch price indexes with marginal shares as weights have played a prominent role in earlier chapters, but analogous volume indexes have not yet appeared. We define

(12.7) $$d(\log Q') = \sum_{i=1}^{n} \theta_i d(\log q_i),$$

and proceed to analyze this concept for the consumer. By subtracting the Divisia volume index from both sides of (12.7), we obtain

(12.8) $$d\left(\log \frac{Q'}{Q}\right) = \sum_{i=1}^{n} (\theta_i - w_i) d(\log q_i)$$

$$= \sum_{i=1}^{n} \frac{\partial w_i}{\partial \log M} d(\log q_i),$$

where the second step is based on $\partial w_i/\partial(\log M) = \theta_i - w_i$, which follows directly from (2.15) and (2.18). We conclude from (12.8) that $d[\log (Q'/Q)]$ is a weighted sum of the logarithmic quantity changes with weights equal to the derivatives of budget shares with respect to $\log M$. This is in contrast to the Divisia volume index whose weights are the budget shares rather than derivatives of such shares.

We can write the first line of (12.8) in the following form:

(12.9) $$d\left(\log \frac{Q'}{Q}\right) = \sum_{i=1}^{n} w_i\left(\frac{\theta_i}{w_i} - 1\right) d(\log q_i).$$

Since the income elasticities $\theta_1/w_1, \ldots, \theta_n/w_n$ have a unit weighted mean when the budget shares are used as weights, this result shows that the left-hand sides of (12.8) and (12.9) are equal to the Divisia covariance of the income elasticities and the logarithmic quantity changes of the n goods.[1] This covariance is positive (negative) when the composition of the consumer's basket changes so that the quantities of luxuries increase (decrease) on the average relative to those of necessities (see the discussion following eq. [2.18]).

It is not difficult to argue that the consumer reveals by his own behavior that he considers luxuries more attractive than necessities. When his income increases, prices remaining constant, he allocates a larger proportion of his income to luxuries and a smaller proportion to necessities. Thus, a positive (negative) sign of the covariance in (12.9) indicates that the consumer's basket has become more (less) attractive from his point of view. We shall express this by referring to the left-hand side of (12.9) as the *quality index* of the consumer's basket in differential form. This definition of quality does not involve an outside judgment on what is "good" for the consumer; it measures the desirability of the basket from the consumer's point of view as revealed by his behavior.[2] The quality index is similar to the degree of dependence in that it refers to all n goods jointly; groupwise decompositions will be considered in section 12.3.

Expressing the quality change in terms of income and price changes is a matter of substituting demand equations for quantity changes. We shall use the preference independent form,

$$(12.10) \qquad w_i d(\log q_i) = \theta_i d(\log Q) + \phi \theta_i d\left(\log \frac{p_i}{P'}\right) + \varepsilon_i,$$

which involves no real loss of generality because we can always apply the preference independence transformation so that the consumer's demand

---

1. As in section 6.6, we use the term Divisia variance or covariance when budget shares (or factor shares or revenue shares) are used as weights, while Frisch variances and covariances indicate that the weights are marginal shares.

2. There are several alternative ways of measuring quality. Horsepower, weight, length, and the number of miles per gallon are an example for automobiles. This amounts to measuring quality by means of a vector, which is more complicated than the scalar measure (12.9). The average price paid for a group of goods is another example of a scalar quality measure (see Houthakker [192] and Theil [381]), but it cannot be used for prices of goods whose quantity dimensions are different. Also, when it can be used it is likely to yield results similar to the quality measure based on income elasticities. In Germany, where beer is cheap relative to wine, the income elasticity of beer is only 0.5 and that of wine is 1.3. In Italy, where beer is expensive relative to wine, the income elasticity of beer is 1.1 and that of wine only 0.7. See Cramer [96] for these estimates, which are based on a European household survey in 1963–64.

equations take the form (12.10). It should be understood that in the remainder of this chapter the differential consumer demand equations take this form. Note that the positive sign of the income elasticities of the transformed goods implies that their marginal shares are also positive; hence all Frisch-weighted means, variances, and covariances have positive weights and are thus proper moments of the first or second order.[3]

When we substitute (12.10) in the first line of (12.8) and make minor algebraic rearrangements, we obtain

$$(12.11) \qquad d\left(\log \frac{Q'}{Q}\right) = d(\log Q) \sum_{i=1}^{n} w_i \left(\frac{\theta_i}{w_i} - 1\right)^2$$

$$+ \phi \sum_{i=1}^{n} \theta_i d\left(\log \frac{p_i}{P'}\right) \frac{\theta_i}{w_i} + \sum_{i=1}^{n} \frac{\theta_i}{w_i} \varepsilon_i.$$

The first term on the right is the real-income component of the change in quality. It takes the form of the Divisia volume index multiplied by the Divisia variance of the income elasticities; hence this variance is the *income elasticity of the demand for quality*. The implication is that given any fixed nonzero value of $d(\log Q)$, the quality change is larger when the income elasticities of the n goods are more dispersed. This is as it should be, because a larger dispersion of these elasticities implies that a given change in real income has a larger impact on the consumer's allocation of his income to luxuries and necessities.

The second right-hand term in (12.11) is the substitution component of the change in quality. This term is a multiple ϕ of a weighted covariance of the logarithmic price changes and the income elasticities, but it is a Frisch covariance, not a Divisia covariance, since it uses marginal shares as weights. When prices of luxuries increase relative to those of necessities, this covariance is positive. Hence, given that $\phi < 0$, the substitution component of the quality change is then negative as we would expect it to be. The disturbance term in (12.11) will be considered in section 12.4.

Some numerical evidence is shown in table 2 for the Netherlands, based on an estimated demand model for fourteen commodity groups (about which we shall have more to say in section 13.6). The figures in the table

3. The positive sign of the marginal shares is subject to the proviso that the preference independence transformation does not yield transformed goods with zero budget shares, because the marginal shares will then be zero also. But these shares will never be negative; hence the moments will remain proper moments. It will be convenient to delete transformed goods with zero budget and marginal shares, so that the statement in the text on positive marginal shares is always valid.

Table 2   Change in Volume and Quality of Consumption, the Netherlands, 1922–63

			COMPONENTS OF THE CHANGE IN QUALITY		
PERIOD	CHANGE IN VOLUME	CHANGE IN QUALITY	Real income	Substitution	Disturbance
1922–39	0.104	0.002	0.038	0.020	−0.056
1939–51	−0.062	−0.059	−0.024	−0.041	0.006
1951–63	0.418	0.107	0.113	0.016	−0.023

are changes in natural logarithms, cumulated over successive years. The first column contains the change in real per capita income. The figure on top amounts to a modest 0.6 percent increase per year on the average during the 17-year period prior to World War II ($0.104/17 \approx 0.006$). The next figure shows that real per capita income in 1951 was below the 1939 level, while the last reflects the substantial increase in affluence thereafter.

The other columns of the table contain the change in quality and its components, each corresponding to one of the terms in equation (12.11). There was virtually no change in the quality index between 1922 and 1939, which was the result of small positive real-income and substitution components compensated by a negative disturbance component. The quality index declined from 1939 to 1951 by about 6 percent. The decline of real per capita income was one cause, but a more important contributor was the substitution effect of price controls which allowed prices of luxuries to increase faster than those of necessities. The quality increase after 1951 (about 0.9 percent per year on the average) mainly resulted from the increase in real per capita income.

12.3   A Groupwise Decomposition of the Quality Index

When the preference independence transformation has been applied, the conditional demand equation (9.21) is simplified to

$$(12.12) \qquad w_i d(\log q_i) = \theta_i' W_g d(\log Q_g) + \phi \Theta_g \theta_i' d\left(\log \frac{p_i}{P_g'}\right) + \varepsilon_i',$$

where θ_i' equals the ratio of the marginal shares θ_i and Θ_g, both of which are now positive (see eq. [9.18]). We extend equation (9.19) to quantities:

$$(12.13) \qquad\qquad d(\log Q_g') = \sum_{i \in S_g} \theta_i' d(\log q_i).$$

Using equation (9.5) also, we have

$$(12.14) \qquad d\left(\log \frac{Q'_g}{Q_g}\right) = \sum_{i \in S_g} \left(\theta'_i - \frac{w_i}{W_g}\right) d(\log q_i)$$

$$= \sum_{i \in S_g} \frac{w_i}{W_g} \left(\frac{\theta'_i}{w_i/W_g} - 1\right) d(\log q_i),$$

which is a within-group version of (12.8) and (12.9). The ratio of θ'_i to w_i/W_g is equal to the income elasticity θ_i/w_i of the ith good divided by the income elasticity Θ_g/W_g of the group and is hence the conditional income elasticity of the ith good within its group. The expression on the second line of (12.14) is the Divisia covariance of the conditional income elasticities and the logarithmic quantity changes of this group. Accordingly, we define the left-hand side of (12.14) as the quality index of the group, S_g, in differential form. This index goes up (down) when the composition of this group shifts toward goods that are luxuries (necessities) within the group.

We can evaluate the quality index (12.14) for each of the G groups. To analyze the relationship between these indexes and the index (12.8) for the consumer's basket as a whole, we note that (12.13) and $\theta'_i = \theta_i/\Theta_g$ imply that $d(\log Q')$ equals $\sum_g \Theta_g d(\log Q'_g)$. We combine this with (9.8),

$$d\left(\log \frac{Q'}{Q}\right) = \sum_{g=1}^{G} \Theta_g d(\log Q'_g) - \sum_{g=1}^{G} W_g d(\log Q_g),$$

which we write in the equivalent form

$$(12.15) \; d\left(\log \frac{Q'}{Q}\right) = \sum_{g=1}^{G} (\Theta_g - W_g) d(\log Q_g) + \sum_{g=1}^{G} \Theta_g d\left(\log \frac{Q'_g}{Q_g}\right).$$

The first term on the right is the uppercase version of the corresponding term in (12.8) and can thus be interpreted as the quality index for groups of goods; it measures the shift in the consumer's basket toward luxury groups (with $\Theta_g/W_g > 1$) or necessity groups (with $\Theta_g/W_g < 1$). On comparing (12.15) with (12.14), we conclude that the change in the quality of the basket as a whole is the sum of the quality change between groups and the average within-group quality change. This average is a Frisch-weighted average, that is, the weights are the marginal shares of the groups.

By substituting (12.12) in (12.14) we obtain the three components of the quality index of the group. These components are similar to those shown in (12.11), but the real-income component becomes a volume component in the case of the quality index of a group. This component takes the form of the Divisia variance of the conditional income elasticities multiplied by $d(\log Q_g)$, while the substitution component is also confined to the prices and conditional income elasticities of the group.[4] This decomposition is illustrated in table 3 for the meats which we considered in section 11.1 (beef, pork, and chicken), but with lamb added as a fourth meat. The first column of the table contains a finite-change (year-to-year) version of the Divisia volume index $d(\log Q_g)$ of the four-meat group. The second column corresponds to the left-hand side of (12.14) and the other columns contain the three components of this quality index. The largest quality change took place from 1952 to 1953; its main contributor was the substitution com-

Table 3   Change in Volume and Quality of Meat Consumption, United States, 1950–72

			COMPONENTS OF THE CHANGE IN QUALITY		
PERIOD	CHANGE IN VOLUME	CHANGE IN QUALITY	Volume	Substitution	Disturbance
1950–51	−0.0337	−0.0453	−0.0101	−0.0215	−0.0137
1951–52	0.0557	0.0260	0.0164	−0.0006	0.0101
1952–53	0.0483	0.0802	0.0126	0.0665	0.0011
1953–54	−0.0053	0.0127	−0.0013	0.0006	0.0133
1954–55	0.0398	−0.0094	0.0084	−0.0222	0.0044
1955–56	0.0352	−0.0035	0.0067	−0.0080	−0.0022
1956–57	−0.0384	0.0075	−0.0070	0.0076	0.0069
1957–58	−0.0206	−0.0145	−0.0036	−0.0150	0.0041
1958–59	0.0505	−0.0157	0.0082	−0.0241	0.0002
1959–60	0.0023	0.0137	0.0003	0.0031	0.0103
1960–61	0.0054	0.0074	0.0007	0.0055	0.0012
1961–62	0.0122	−0.0021	0.0015	−0.0038	0.0002
1962–63	0.0392	0.0033	0.0047	0.0005	−0.0018
1963–64	0.0263	0.0060	0.0030	0.0015	0.0015
1964–65	−0.0318	0.0061	−0.0037	0.0121	−0.0023
1965–66	0.0324	0.0051	0.0041	0.0104	−0.0094
1966–67	0.0462	−0.0102	0.0059	−0.0145	−0.0016
1967–68	0.0260	−0.0001	0.0030	−0.0053	0.0021
1968–69	0.0029	−0.0006	0.0003	−0.0019	0.0010
1969–70	0.0267	−0.0032	0.0030	−0.0000	−0.0061
1970–71	0.0253	−0.0112	0.0027	−0.0173	0.0034
1971–72	−0.0054	0.0105	−0.0005	0.0058	0.0052

4. It is also possible to obtain the real-income, substitution, and disturbance components of the quality index for groups, and to relate these components and those of the within-group indexes to the components of the overall index shown in (12.11). See chapter 14 of Theil [397], which also provides further information on tables 2 and 3.

ponent. This resulted from large price decreases of luxury meats relative to those with smaller income elasticities. A comparison of the last three columns clearly shows that the substitution component tends to dominate the two others in the annual changes in the quality index. The decline of the volume components in the later years is mainly caused by the decreasing Divisia variance of the conditional income elasticities.

12.4 More on Income and Divisia Elasticities

In the two previous sections we introduced several system-wide (or subsystem-wide) measures in the form of moments, such as the Frisch-weighted means in equations (12.7) and (12.13) and the last term of equation (12.15); the Divisia covariances in equations (12.9) and (12.14); the Divisia variance in the real-income component of equation (12.11); and the Frisch covariance in the substitution component of equation (12.11). These moments should be viewed as a continuation of the list of moments (Π, K, Γ, etc.) which we introduced in sections 6.5 and 6.6 for the consumer and in section 6.7 for the firm; all these moments are system-wide (or subsystem-wide) summary measures of the differential approach to the theory of the consumer and the firm. In particular, income elasticities play a prominent role in the covariances introduced in sections 12.2 and 12.3. This prominence, and that of the Divisia elasticities in the theory of the firm, is not at all surprising because these elasticities determine the effects both of relative price changes and of the Divisia volume index when the independence transformation has been applied (see eq. [10.25]). In this section we shall provide some further evidence on the role of these elasticities.

Consider the disturbance component $\sum_i (\theta_i/w_i)\varepsilon_i$ of the quality index (12.11). Under rational random behavior this component is a normal variate with zero mean. Its variance can be obtained from equation (8.14), which now takes the form

$$(12.16) \qquad \text{cov}(\varepsilon_i, \varepsilon_j) = \sigma^2\theta_i(1 - \theta_i) \quad \text{if} \quad i = j$$

$$= -\sigma^2\theta_i\theta_j \qquad \text{if} \quad i \neq j,$$

because (12.10) is preference independent. The result is

$$(12.17) \qquad \text{var}\left(\sum_{i=1}^n \frac{\theta_i}{w_i}\varepsilon_i\right) = \sigma^2 \sum_{i=1}^n \theta_i\left(\frac{\theta_i}{w_i} - \sum_{j=1}^n \theta_j\frac{\theta_j}{w_j}\right)^2,$$

which shows that the disturbance component of the quality index has a variance proportional to the Frisch variance of the income elasticities of the n goods. This should be compared with the coefficient of real income in (12.11), which is the Divisia variance (not the Frisch variance) of the same income elasticities.

Reciprocals of income and Divisia elasticities also play a role. For example, under output independence we can write equation (5.43) as

$$(12.18) \qquad \sum_{r=1}^{m} g_r \frac{g_r}{\theta_r^*} = \psi^* \frac{\gamma - \psi}{\psi}.$$

The expression on the left is the Divisia-weighted mean of the reciprocal Divisia elasticities of the firm's products. We know from (5.44) that the right-hand side of (12.18) equals 1 if all products have unitary Divisia elasticities, and exceeds 1 otherwise (this holds also when the firm is not output independent). To understand this in the present context we note that the Divisia-weighted mean on the left in (12.18) is identical to the Frisch-weighted second moment of the reciprocal Divisia elasticities:

$$(12.19) \qquad \sum_{r=1}^{m} g_r \frac{g_r}{\theta_r^*} = \sum_{r=1}^{m} \theta_r^* \left(\frac{g_r}{\theta_r^*} \right)^2 .$$

Since the Frisch-weighted mean of these reciprocal elasticities equals 1,

$$(12.20) \qquad \sum_{r=1}^{m} \theta_r^* \frac{g_r}{\theta_r^*} = 1,$$

both sides of (12.19) must be at least equal to 1, because the second moment on the right in (12.19) exceeds the square of the mean (given in eq. [12.20]) by the corresponding variance. Therefore, the left-hand sides of (12.18) and (12.19) are equal to 1 if this variance vanishes, i.e., if all products have equal Divisia elasticities, and exceed 1 when these elasticities are not all equal. Of course, equal Divisia elasticities of all products mean unitary elasticities.

The consumer's version of equation (12.20) is $\sum_i \theta_i(w_i/\theta_i) = 1$, that is, the Frisch-weighted mean of the reciprocal income elasticities equals 1. In Appendix B we consider a curvature measure of the consumer's distance function which can be expressed in terms of the Frisch variance of the reciprocal income elasticities under preference independence.

12.5   The Geometry of Demand and Supply

Elementary economics textbooks use two-dimensional pictures to illustrate the dependence of demand and supply on price. The system-wide approach requires more dimensions. The reader who is geometrically inclined will find an attractive description of the differential approach in the n-dimensional Euclidean space in chapters 11 and 12 of Theil [397]; this description is confined to the theory of the consumer, but the extension to the firm is straightforward. Some of the merits of this geometric approach are the following:

1. Each of the three terms on the right in equation (12.10) for $i = 1, \ldots, n$ can be represented by a vector in the n-dimensional space: a vector of real-income components, a substitution vector, and a disturbance vector. By adding these three vectors we obtain the vector of left-hand variables, $w_i d(\log q_i)$ for $i = 1, \ldots, n$; this vector describes the change in demand. Summary measures such as the quality index, including their real-income, substitution, and disturbance components, can also be illustrated in this space.

2. Equation (12.10) is based on the preference independence assumption. The independence transformation, too, allows a simple description in the n-dimensional space. This takes place in three steps: first a compression along the axes, next a rotation of the axes, and finally a decompression along the rotated axes.

3. Equation (10.22) shows that the diagonal factor share matrix $\mathbf{F}_T$ of the transformed inputs equals the square of $(\mathbf{X}^{-1}\iota)_\Delta$. This means that the elements of the vector $\mathbf{X}^{-1}\iota$ have the interpretation of (positive or negative) square roots of factor shares. The reader may find the prominent role of such square roots a little mysterious, but if he is geometrically inclined he will readily appreciate the following argument. Factor shares (or budget shares or revenue shares) are nonnegative numbers which add up to 1. Therefore, square roots of such shares are numbers whose sum of squares equals 1, which implies that these square roots can be represented by a point on the unit sphere. In fact, it can be shown that the independence transformation implies an orthogonal transformation of square roots of factor (or budget or revenue) shares. Geometrically, this amounts to a rotation of the axes. With this in mind, the reader is perhaps a bit less mystified by the occurrence of numerous square roots in equations (10.27) to (10.33) and (11.18) to (11.22).

12.6 A Bivariate Analysis of Changes in Shares

We conclude this chapter by showing how the system-wide approach can be used, not only for summary measures describing certain features of all goods (consumer goods, inputs, or outputs) or a group of goods, but also for detailed analysis at a highly disaggregated level. The exposition which follows, based on Theil [397, chap. 16], refers to the consumer, but the reader should have no difficulty in extending the approach to the theory of the firm.

When the ith budget share increases, $dw_i > 0$, some other budget share must decrease. We are interested in the question of how budget share changes can be decomposed in terms of flows from one good to the other. We state the solution here, postponing the justification until the next paragraph. Let g_{ji} be the gross budget share flow from the jth good to the ith and $n_{ji} = g_{ji} - g_{ij}$ the corresponding *net flow*. The gross flow should be viewed as an auxiliary concept; the net flow is what counts. The latter is specified as consisting of four components:

$$(12.21) \qquad n_{ji} = w_i w_j \left(\frac{\theta_i}{w_i} - \frac{\theta_j}{w_j}\right) d(\log Q) + \phi \theta_i \theta_j d\left(\log \frac{p_i}{p_j}\right)$$

$$+ w_i w_j d\left(\log \frac{p_i}{p_j}\right) + (\theta_j \varepsilon_i - \theta_i \varepsilon_j).$$

The first term on the right is the *real-income component* of the net flow from the jth good to the ith. It states that an increase in real income generates a positive net flow to the good with the higher income elasticity, which is a plausible result. The second term is the *substitution component*; it implies that an increase in the relative price of either good generates a positive net flow to the other good. The third term is also a price term but of opposite sign. This term results from the factor p_i in the budget share $w_i = p_i q_i / M$. If p_i increases, q_i and M remaining constant, an increase in w_i is implied. We shall refer to this term as the *direct price component* of n_{ji}. The substitution component is an indirect price component; it involves the price effect on $w_i = p_i q_i / M$ via the factor q_i. The last term in equation (12.21) is the *disturbance component* and will be discussed later in this section (see eq. [12.28] below).

The justification of the specification (12.21) is as follows. As in (6.38), we use (2.9) to write (2.15) in the form

$$(12.22) \qquad dw_i = w_i d\left(\log \frac{p_i}{P}\right) + w_i d\left(\log \frac{q_i}{Q}\right),$$

and we refer to the two terms on the right as the price and volume components of dw_i. We impose the condition that the gross flow g_{ji} consists of a price and a quantity term, the price term being some proportion A_j of the price component of dw_i and the quantity term a proportion B_j of the volume component of dw_i,

$$(12.23) \qquad g_{ji} = A_j w_i d\left(\log \frac{p_i}{P}\right) + B_j w_i d\left(\log \frac{q_i}{Q}\right),$$

where $\sum_j A_j = \sum_j B_j = 1$. The second condition is that the implied price and quantity terms of the corresponding net flow should be independent of the price changes of all goods other than the ith and jth. We now proceed to prove that this implies $A_i = w_i$ and $B_i = \theta_i$, and that this yields the net flow specification (12.21).

For this purpose we note that the price term of the net flow $n_{ji} = g_{ji} - g_{ij}$ which is implied by equation (12.23) is

$$(12.24) \qquad A_j w_i d \left(\log \frac{p_i}{P} \right) - A_i w_j d \left(\log \frac{p_j}{P} \right).$$

The quantity term of n_{ji} is similarly equal to

$$(12.25) \qquad B_j w_i d \left(\log \frac{q_i}{Q} \right) - B_i w_j d \left(\log \frac{q_j}{Q} \right).$$

We assume that preference independence prevails or that the preference independence transformation has been applied. This means that we can use (12.10) to write the quantity term (12.25) as

$$(12.26) \quad B_j \left[(\theta_i - w_i) d(\log Q) + \phi \theta_i d \left(\log \frac{p_i}{P'} \right) + \varepsilon_i \right]$$
$$- B_i \left[(\theta_j - w_j) d(\log Q) + \phi \theta_j d \left(\log \frac{p_j}{P'} \right) + \varepsilon_j \right].$$

The price term (12.24) contains the Divisia price index; the quantity term (12.26) contains the Frisch price index. Since both indexes involve price changes of goods other than the ith and jth, their coefficients must be zero. The coefficient of $d(\log P)$ in (12.24) is $-A_j w_i + A_i w_j$, which vanishes if and only if the A_i's are proportional to the w_i's. The solution $A_i = w_i$ then follows from the unit-sum constraint on the A_i's. The coefficient of $d(\log P')$ in (12.26) is $-B_j \theta_i + B_i \theta_j$ multiplied by ϕ, which similarly yields $B_i = \theta_i$.

Substitution of these solutions and (12.10) in (12.23) yields

$$g_{ji} = \theta_j (\theta_i - w_i) d(\log Q) + \phi \theta_i \theta_j d \left(\log \frac{p_i}{P'} \right) + w_i w_j d \left(\log \frac{p_i}{P} \right) + \theta_j \varepsilon_i,$$

which still contains the Divisia and Frisch price indexes. However, when we subtract the corresponding equation for g_{ij}, we obtain (12.21), in which these indexes no longer occur. Summation of (12.21) over j and i gives

$$(12.27) \qquad \sum_{j=1}^{n} n_{ji} = dw_i, \qquad \sum_{i=1}^{n} n_{ji} = -dw_j,$$

which is easily verified from (12.10) and (12.22). The first summation in
(12.27) is over the origin of the flow and the second is over the destination.

Note that (12.21) does not involve demand disturbances of goods other
than the ith and jth, in spite of the fact that this has not been imposed as a
constraint. Also note that the disturbance combination in (12.21) is equal
to the same linear combination of the specific components of ε_i and ε_j,

$$(12.28) \qquad\qquad \theta_j \varepsilon_i - \theta_i \varepsilon_j = \theta_j \bar{\varepsilon}_i - \theta_i \bar{\varepsilon}_j,$$

which follows directly from (8.15). Under rational random behavior the
disturbance component of n_{ji} is a normal variate with zero mean and a
variance which is proportional to the two marginal shares and their sum:

$$(12.29) \qquad \operatorname{var}(\theta_j \varepsilon_i - \theta_i \varepsilon_j) = \sigma^2 \theta_i \theta_j (\theta_i + \theta_j) \quad \text{if} \quad i \neq j.$$

When two net flows have either the origin or the destination in common
(n_{ij} and n_{ik} or n_{ij} and n_{kj}), their disturbance components have a covariance
equal to $\sigma^2 \theta_i \theta_j \theta_k$. When two net flows have neither the origin nor the destination in common (n_{ij} and n_{hk}, with all four subscripts different), their
disturbance components are independently distributed. These results are
easily verified from equation (12.28) and the fact that under preference
independence $\bar{\varepsilon}_1, \ldots, \bar{\varepsilon}_n$ are independent and have variances $\sigma^2 \theta_1, \ldots, \sigma^2 \theta_n$.

The simplicity of the distribution of these disturbance components adds
to the plausibility of the specification (12.21). We can interpret (12.21) in
the sense that the consumer behaves as if his allocation decision is based on
pairwise comparisons of all goods; this is a direct consequence of the condition described in the discussion following equation (12.23). The approach
can be extended to net flows between groups of goods and conditional net
flows between goods within a group. Rather than providing the mathematics
of these flows, which is spelled out in detail in Theil [397, section 16.2],
we shall illustrate the conditional net flow approach for the three transformed meats of section 11.1, with lamb added as a fourth independent
meat. Recall that the transformed meats are T_1, affordable meat; T_2, the
beef-pork contrast; T_3, the contrast between beef and pork on one hand
and chicken on the other.

The first line of table 4 contains the changes in the conditional budget
shares of these meats from 1950 to 1951 and from 1952 to 1953; these
shares are of the form w_i/W_g, where W_g is the budget share of the four-meat
group. In 1951 the share of T_1 increased by about 1.6 percent, mainly at
the expense of T_2 but also at the expense of lamb. In 1953 the share of T_1
declined by 0.6 percent and that of T_2 increased by about the same amount.
These relatively small changes illustrate that the conditional budget shares
are quite stable.

Table 4   Conditional Net Flows between
                                                    Meats, 1950–51 and 1952–53

	1950–51				1952–53			
	T_1	T_2	T_3	Lamb	T_1	T_2	T_3	Lamb
Changes in Conditional Budget Shares								
	0.0161	−0.0138	0.0009	−0.0032	−0.0060	0.0059	0.0003	−0.0002
Conditional Net Flows								
T_1	0	−0.0135	−0.0001	−0.0025	0	0.0028	0.0029	0.0002
T_2	0.0135	0	0.0008	−0.0005	−0.0028	0	−0.0025	−0.0005
T_3	0.0001	−0.0008	0	−0.0002	−0.0029	0.0025	0	0.0001
Lamb	0.0025	0.0005	0.0002	0	−0.0002	0.0005	−0.0001	0
Volume Components								
T_2	0.0067				−0.0088			
T_3	0.0005	−0.0003			−0.0009	0.0005		
Lamb	0.0006	−0.0001	0.0000		−0.0007	0.0002	−0.0000	
Substitution Components								
T_2	0.0146				−0.0452			
T_3	0.0011	−0.0007			0.0016	0.0079		
Lamb	0.0004	−0.0010	−0.0001		−0.0020	0.0022	−0.0004	
Direct Price Components								
T_2	−0.0166				0.0518			
T_3	−0.0023	0.0005			−0.0033	−0.0057		
Lamb	−0.0006	0.0005	0.0001		0.0033	−0.0013	0.0004	
Disturbance Components								
T_2	0.0088				−0.0007			
T_3	0.0008	−0.0003			−0.0004	−0.0002		
Lamb	0.0021	0.0011	0.0002		−0.0008	−0.0006	−0.0001	

The next four lines contain the conditional net flows in the form of
4×4 matrices. By adding the elements of a column we obtain the corresponding conditional budget share change in the first line. The 1950–51
matrix shows that the increased share of T_1 and the decreased shares of T_2
and lamb are mainly due to the two positive net flows from the latter meats

to T_1. All other net flows are less than 0.1 percent in absolute value. For 1952–53 the situation is slightly more complicated. The increase in the share of T_2 is about equally due to positive net flows from T_1 and T_3. The near-zero change in the share of T_3 results from net flows from T_1 and T_2 which are about equal but of opposite sign. The decrease in the share of T_1 is due to the negative net flows from that meat to T_2 and T_3.

Note that the net-flow matrix is skew-symmetric, and that this is also true for the components of this matrix. Therefore, it is sufficient to present only the elements of these matrices below the diagonal, which is done in the table for the four sets of components of the conditional net flows. The real-income component of equation (12.21) becomes the volume component when we work within the meat group. The Divisia volume index of meat decreased from 1950 to 1951 and increased from 1952 to 1953. Since the income elasticity of T_1 is much smaller than that of T_2 (see fig. 8 in section 11.1), this yields a positive volume component of the flow from T_2 to T_1 in 1950–51 and a negative value in 1952–53. All other volume components in these years are less than 0.1 percent in absolute value.[5]

Some of the price components are much larger than any numbers that we have met so far. The price of T_1 decreased from 1950 to 1951 relative to those of the three other meats, which yields positive elements in the first column of the matrix of substitution components and negative values for the corresponding direct price components. The picture for 1952–53 is just the opposite. The price of T_1 increased substantially relative to that of T_2, yielding a large direct price component of the flow from T_2 to T_1 and an almost equally large (but negative) substitution component.

The first row of the table shows that the net changes in the conditional budget shares from 1950 to 1951 are larger in absolute value than the corresponding values of 1952–53. But when we consider the volume, substitution, and direct price components of the conditional net flows, we find that the 1950–51 values are all smaller in absolute value than the corresponding 1952–53 values. This means that the forces determining the changes in the shares of the meats were more powerful in 1952–53 than in 1950–51, but that they canceled each other out to a larger degree. In particular, the large values of some of the substitution components indicate the extent to which consumers engage in price substitution among meats.

5. A major cause of the small size of these components is the smallness of the conditional budget shares of T_3 and lamb. The volume component can be derived from the real-income component in (12.21) by replacing $w_i w_j$ by the product of the two conditional budget shares, the income elasticities by their conditional counterparts, and $d(\log Q)$ by the Divisia volume index of meat.

Thirteen

The Application of the System-Wide Approach to Statistical Data

In this chapter and the next we shall consider a number of problems that arise when statistical data are used to estimate the coefficients of demand and supply systems and to test theoretical restrictions on such coefficients. This subject is extensively analyzed from various points of view in the monographs listed in the first paragraph of the Preface of this book; it is also considered in several general econometrics texts, such as those by Bridge [67], Desai [108], Intriligator [199], and Theil [387, 399]. The treatment of this subject in these texts and monographs tends to emphasize the consumer rather than the firm. The account which follows is an attempt to provide a symmetric treatment, but this attempt will only be partly successful because much more experience has been obtained on consumer demand systems than on input demand and output supply systems (particularly the latter).

Statistically estimated demand and supply systems can be used for several purposes other than testing the validity of the theory of the consumer and the firm. Forecasting supply and demand is one example. It is also possible to use such systems as inputs in a larger model. The use of consumer demand systems in the theory of optimal taxation is a third example. However, these topics are beyond the scope of this book.

13.1 The Selection of a Functional Form

Chapter 2 and section 3.7 have shown that consumer demand systems can be formulated in many different ways. This is also true for the input demand and output supply systems of a firm. In this section we shall argue that the problem of selecting a functional form is important. We shall also discuss some general problems in the statistical analysis of different functional forms. The translog approach will be a convenient starting point.

Translog specifications have been recommended on the ground that quadratic functions in logarithms can be viewed as second-order Taylor approximations which are accurate when the independent variables take values in sufficiently small regions. This does not, of course, guarantee that the approximation is accurate for large regions. However, even when the quadratic function itself provides a satisfactory approximation in the relevant region, the implied approximation of the demand functions may be very unsatisfactory. The reason is that although the translog function is a second-order approximation, the associated demand functions are only first-order approximations. This is immediately clear for the translog cost function because of Shephard's lemma, which states that demand functions are obtained from the cost function by differentiating with respect to prices; this differentiation reduces any second-order approximation to one of the first order. It is also true for the translog production function, since the demand equations are obtained from the first-order equilibrium conditions which involve derivatives of the production function. In section 13.3 we shall present some numerical evidence on this matter.

The lower quality of approximation of derived results is a more general phenomenon, which may be illustrated with another example. A monopolist makes one product. His cost function is linear, so that marginal cost is a constant with respect to output. We assume that the demand function for the product takes either of two forms, linear or log-linear. Imagine that marginal cost increases by one dollar because of increased prices of raw materials. What is the effect on the monopolist's profit-maximizing price? Under the linear demand specification the answer is one-half dollar, but under the log-linear specification it is more than one dollar,[1] and hence more than twice as much. This result serves as a clear warning that matters of specification should not be taken casually. The linear and log-linear demand specifications can both be viewed as first-order approximations of the true demand function, but the answers which they give to the question raised above are zero-order approximations.

The statistical analysis of specifications raises several important issues. One is the conflict that always exists between the quality of the approximation achieved by a specification and the statistical quality of the estimates of the parameters of this specification. The approximation is usually satisfactory when the independent variables vary very little, but precise parameter estimates require adequate variation in these variables.

A second statistical problem is the fact that many system-wide specifications present a problem of nonnested hypotheses, which may be clarified

1. More precisely, it is $\eta/(\eta + 1) > 1$ dollars, where η is the elasticity of demand (with respect to the price charged by the monopolist) and the " $>$ " sign is implied by $\eta < -1$, which is the second-order condition for maximum profit. See Theil [387, pp. 541–42].

as follows. We reproduce the utility function (2.3) of the linear expenditure system,

$$(13.1) \qquad\qquad u(\mathbf{q}) = \sum_{i=1}^{n} a_i \log (q_i - b_i),$$

and the translog specification (2.6),

$$(13.2) \qquad u(\mathbf{q}) = \sum_{i=1}^{n} c_i \log q_i + \tfrac{1}{2} \sum_{i=1}^{n} \sum_{j=1}^{n} d_{ij} \log q_i \log q_j.$$

It is clear that (13.1) is a special case of (13.2) when all b_i's vanish but not when some b_i's are nonzero. In the latter case neither specification is a special case of the other and the two specifications form a pair of non-nested hypotheses, which used to present insurmountable problems in hypothesis testing. However, in the early 1960s Cox [94, 95] developed a likelihood ratio procedure for a pair of nonnested hypotheses, although it was not noticed by econometricians until the appearance of Pesaran's article [308]. The procedure amounts to the use of two likelihood ratios (properly modified), one for each hypothesis, and it has four possible outcomes: one or the other hypothesis is rejected, neither is rejected, or both are rejected. Deaton [104] gave an elementary exposition of this procedure and an example.

A third statistical problem is presented by the poor quality of the data, which is particularly important for large models. The discussion of this problem is postponed until section 14.2.

13.2   The Application of the Linear Expenditure System

We reproduce the linear expenditure system (2.5) with a disturbance and a time subscript t added:

$$(13.3) \qquad p_{it}q_{it} = p_{it}b_i + a_i \left(M_t - \sum_{j=1}^{n} p_{jt}b_j \right) + \varepsilon_{it}.$$

Let there be T successive observations ($t = 1, \ldots, T$). In his first attempt to estimate the a_i's and b_i's, Stone [376] minimized the residual sum of squares over all n goods and all T observations. Subsequent work by Parks [301] and Solari [364] was more statistical in nature and based on the assumption that $[\varepsilon_{1t}, \ldots, \varepsilon_{nt}]$ for $t = 1, \ldots, T$ are independent random drawings from an n-variate normal distribution with zero means. This assumption permits the use of the maximum-likelihood method.

Note that the ε_{it}'s have zero sum when added over $i = 1, \ldots, n$; this may be verified by summing equation (13.3) over i, which yields $M_t = M_t + \sum_i \varepsilon_{it}$. The zero-sum constraint on the disturbances is a standard problem for allocation models. It can be solved either by deleting one of the n equations or by using an appropriate generalized inverse of the singular disturbance covariance matrix. When the first of these two methods is used, a nonsingular submatrix of the disturbance covariance matrix of order $(n - 1) \times (n - 1)$ emerges, which is estimated by a matrix of mean squares and products of residuals. The latter matrix is singular when $T < n - 1$, which causes a problem because its inverse is needed. Deaton [101] had to face this problem when he estimated a linear expenditure system for 37 goods from 17 years of data. His solution consists of an a priori specified disturbance covariance matrix. Theil and Laitinen [404] suggested a different procedure, namely, replacing the singular sample covariance matrix of the residuals by their maximum-entropy covariance matrix. The latter matrix is always positive definite and it is based on the residuals rather than an a priori specification.

The assumption that the ε_{it}'s of (13.3) have a constant contemporaneous covariance matrix is typically unrealistic. The variable on the left is the amount spent on a good, which is usually subject to a rising trend due to inflation and economic growth; it is therefore more realistic to assume that the variances of the ε_{it}'s are also subject to a rising trend. One way of handling this is by dividing both sides of (13.3) by M_t, so that the left-hand side becomes a budget share, and treating ε_{it}/M_t as homoscedastic.

Another assumption that should be questioned is the independence of the ε_{it}'s over time. It is frequently found that allocation models which are formulated in terms of levels of (rather than changes in) variables, as is the case in (13.3), yield residuals that are strongly positively autocorrelated. A first-difference transformation is the simplest solution. More complicated autoregressive transformations can also be used, but their application to allocation models requires special care (see Berndt and Savin [48]). However, strong autocorrelation may also result from the fact that (13.3) is simply a misspecification. It is an illusion to think that an autoregressive correction of a misspecified model results in a correct model. It seems likely that this will often apply to (13.3) in view of the restrictive assumption of preference independence (see eq. [2.3]).

13.3   The Application of Translog Models

We proceed to consider the translog direct and indirect utility functions and their budget share equations (2.8) and (3.24). Random disturbances and time subscripts are added to these equations, as in (13.3):

$$(13.4) \qquad w_{it} = \frac{c_i + \sum\limits_{j=1}^{n} d_{ij} \log q_{jt}}{\sum\limits_{k=1}^{n} c_k + \sum\limits_{k=1}^{n} \sum\limits_{j=1}^{n} d_{kj} \log q_{jt}} + \varepsilon_{it},$$

$$(13.5) \qquad w_{it} = \frac{\beta_i + \sum\limits_{j=1}^{n} \beta_{ij} \log (p_{jt}/M_t)}{\sum\limits_{k=1}^{n} \beta_k + \sum\limits_{k=1}^{n} \sum\limits_{j=1}^{n} \beta_{kj} \log (p_{jt}/M_t)} + \varepsilon_{it}.$$

The disturbances are assumed to be stochastically independent of the quantities in the case of (13.4) and of the ratios of prices to income in the case of (13.5). Under these assumptions, Christensen, Jorgenson, and Lau [83] applied the translog approach to annual U.S. data on $n = 3$ groups of goods: durables, nondurables, and energy. The authors obtained disappointing results and were led to the conclusion that they could unambiguously reject the theory of demand. This conclusion has the merit of unambiguity, but it is clearly unsatisfactory. Why should utility (direct or indirect) be translog? Since the translog approach is not self-dual, either (13.4) or (13.5) must be an incorrect specification, but it is more likely that both are incorrect to some degree. The disappointing results mentioned above may be due to the poor quality of the approximation rather than to the theory of demand. Also, the different independence assumptions for the disturbances in equations (13.4) and (13.5) make the statistical estimation procedures of these equations very much ad hoc.[2]

Burgess [72] applied the translog approach to aggregated annual U.S. data on three inputs: capital, labor, and imports. Although this application is, strictly speaking, beyond the scope of this book (it is more macro than micro), we will discuss it nevertheless because it provides an interesting comparison of the translog production approach and the translog cost approach. These approaches are not self-dual, but if (1) the translog production function is a close approximation of the true production function, and (2) the translog cost function is a close approximation of the true cost function, we might hope that the implications of the two competing translog approximations are not too far apart. However, Burgess's estimates

2. See Jorgenson and Lau [207, n. 17] and Christensen, Jorgenson, and Lau [83, n. 16]. Several authors abandon these independence assumptions and estimate the coefficients of translog functions by means of instrumental variables, but the selection of these variables is not always as explicitly justified as it should be. Users of the translog approach should also be encouraged to provide more evidence on the autocorrelation (or its absence) of the disturbances in their equations.

(discussed below) deny this and confirm what has been said in section 13.1 about the lower quality of derived results.

The estimates of partial elasticities of substitution at 10-year intervals are shown in table 5. When the translog production function is used, the largest elasticity values are those between capital and imports and the smallest those between labor and imports. This ranking is precisely the opposite when the translog cost function is used. Burgess also presents estimates of the own-price elasticities of the three inputs. For imports these elasticity values range between -1.6 and -2.1 on the basis of the translog production function, suggesting that a devaluation of the U.S. dollar will reduce the expenditure on imports expressed in dollars, but the corresponding values based on the translog cost function range between -0.7 and -0.75, which suggest the opposite. Burgess presented no standard errors which would permit the evaluation of the statistical significance of these differences, but the differences are substantial. We refer to his article for the estimation procedure used, which involves instrumental variables and a correction for autocorrelated disturbances.

Returning to the translog equations (13.4) and (13.5) for the consumer, we should note that their coefficients (the c's, d's, and β's) have no simple economic interpretation. This is a disadvantage compared to the linear

Table 5   Estimates of Partial Elasticities of Substitution between Inputs

Year	Based on Translog Production Function	Based on Translog Cost Function
Between Capital and Labor		
1947	1.55	1.14
1957	1.52	1.14
1967	1.52	1.14
Between Capital and Imports		
1947	4.14	-0.31
1957	3.65	-0.14
1967	2.85	-0.19
Between Labor and Imports		
1947	0.99	1.40
1957	1.04	1.36
1967	1.04	1.39

expenditure system (13.3) whose a_i's are marginal shares and whose b_i's have the interpretation of minimum quantities bought if they are nonnegative. A more serious problem with the translog approach is the fact that the number of parameters tends to increase about proportionally to the square of the number of goods. It is not surprising, therefore, that few users of this approach use more than very few goods. A natural way of solving this problem is by means of block structures of the type discussed in chapter 9. Unfortunately, it was shown by Blackorby, Primont, and Russell [60] that when this idea is applied to the translog approach, the implications are much more restrictive than a casual observer might have expected. Translog specifications (and several other specifications described in Appendix A) are frequently referred to as "flexible functional forms." However, translog utility functions are "separability-inflexible" under blockwise dependence; that is, they are not capable of providing a second-order approximation of an arbitrary blockwise dependent utility function in any neighborhood of a given point.

The quality of the translog approximations has been the subject of several experiments. Gabrielsen constructed a four-equation linear expenditure system;[3] he applied a second-order Taylor expansion to the associated indirect utility function in $\log (p_i/M)$ around $p_i/M = 1$ for $i = 1, \ldots, 4$ in order to obtain a translog approximation of the indirect utility function. This approximation appears satisfactory for values of p_i/M close to 1, but quite bad for other values; the implied values of some budget shares are negative and those of some others are larger than 1. The quality of the approximation appears to be very sensitive to the selection of the year in which p_i/M is put equal to 1. Also, the approximation errors tend to be strongly positively autocorrelated.

The sensitivity of the translog specification is something of a mystery. Perhaps it is due to the use of squares and products of logarithms, but this is a mere guess and would require further analysis. We shall have more to say about approximations in section 14.4.

13.4   Finite-Change Versions of Divisia Indexes

The application of the differential approach to statistical data requires a formulation in finite rather than infinitesimal changes. For this purpose we define, for any positive variable x, the *log-change* from period $t - 1$ to period t as the change in the natural logarithm of x, and we write Dx_t for

---

3. See Theil and Gabrielsen [401] and, for similar experiences, Griffin [166], Kiefer and MacKinnon [214], and Wales [425].

this log-change:

(13.6) $$Dx_t = \log x_t - \log x_{t-1} = \log \frac{x_t}{x_{t-1}}.$$

The Divisia indexes $d(\log P)$ and $d(\log Q)$ of the consumer are weighted means of logarithmic price or quantity changes with budget shares as weights (see eqs. [2.10] and [2.11]). When we proceed to finite changes, an obvious choice is to replace the infinitesimal logarithmic changes by log-changes (Dp_{it} and Dq_{it}), but we must face the fact that there are two equally likely candidates for the weights: the budget share in $t - 1$, $w_{i,t-1}$, and that in t, w_{it}. The most popular choice is their arithmetic average,

(13.7) $$\bar{w}_{it} = \tfrac{1}{2}(w_{i,t-1} + w_{it}) \qquad i = 1, \ldots, n,$$

which yields the following finite-change versions of the Divisia indexes:[4]

(13.8) $$DP_t = \sum_{i=1}^{n} \bar{w}_{it} Dp_{it}, \qquad DQ_t = \sum_{i=1}^{n} \bar{w}_{it} Dq_{it}.$$

The definition (13.8), which can be found in Fisher [135, p. 473], was particularly advocated by Törnqvist [412]. Recall from equation (2.9) that the sum of the Divisia price and volume indexes equals the logarithmic change in money income. The indexes DP_t and DQ_t of (13.8) do not have the analogous property of adding up to DM_t (the log-change in money income), but it can be shown that the discrepancy between DM_t and $DP_t + DQ_t$ is of a high order of smallness, namely, of the third order in the log-changes in prices and income. Several authors, including Sato [350, 352], Theil [392, 395], and Vartia [421], have redefined the weights in (13.8) so that this discrepancy is of an even higher order of smallness or eliminated altogether. In fact, log-change indexes date back to a period well before Divisia published his results and include a formulation by Walsh [427] early in this century.

Recall from equations (3.17) and (3.18) that $d(\log Q)$ is the true index of real income for infinitesimal changes at the prevailing prices. It can be shown (see Theil [397, section 3.7]) that, apart from a discrepancy of the third order of smallness, DQ_t of (13.8) equals the true index of real income which compares the utility levels of periods t and $t - 1$ at prices equal to the geometric means of those prevailing in these two periods. Similarly,

---

4. Note that DP_t and DQ_t in (13.8) should not be viewed as log-changes in P and Q. They should simply be interpreted as abbreviations of $\sum_i \bar{w}_{it} Dp_{it}$ and $\sum_i \bar{w}_{it} Dq_{it}$, respectively [compare remark (2) at the end of section 2.3].

apart from a discrepancy of the same order, DP_t of (13.8) is equal to the true cost-of-living index which compares the price vectors of t and $t - 1$ at the utility level which corresponds to the geometric means of the incomes and prices in $t - 1$ and t.

Note that the indexes in (13.8) do not involve unknown parameters and can thus be computed directly from price-quantity data in $t - 1$ and t. This is an advantage compared with true indexes based on algebraically specified utility functions, such as (3.11) which corresponds to the linear expenditure system. One disadvantage of (3.11) is that it requires the validity of the utility function underlying this system, which is bound to be an imperfect approximation. A second disadvantage is that (3.11) involves unknown parameters, which must be replaced by imperfect estimates. It is not true that indexes which are theoretically exact under restrictive conditions (such as the linear expenditure system) are preferable to good indexes which are applicable under weaker conditions. See also Diewert [118, 119].

We mentioned above that DP_t of (13.8) refers to the utility level associated with the geometric means of the incomes and prices of $t - 1$ and t. These geometric means obviously change as time proceeds. It is possible to compute constant-utility cost-of-living indexes over longer periods, although such computations do involve estimates of unknown parameters. Basically, it is a matter of adjusting the weight of Dp_{it} in (13.8) so that it corresponds to the utility level selected.

This procedure can also be applied to cost-of-living subindexes for groups of goods. Although the extension of (13.8) to group indexes will not take place before section 13.7, this should be no reason for postponing the discussion of some interesting numerical results. Table 6 shows the cost of

Table 6   Cost of Meat at Two Utility Levels

	COST OF MEAT AT	
YEAR	One-half of Real per Capita Income of 1950	Twice the Real per Capita Income of 1950
1950	100	100
1951	109.3	112.4
1952	107.2	110.2
1953	105.5	99.6
1954	104.3	98.7
1955	95.9	93.2
1956	91.1	89.7
1957	99.4	97.2
1958	107.4	107.5
1959	100.1	103.7
1960	99.2	102.2

meat (consisting of beef, pork, chicken, and lamb) in the United States at two utility levels: one-half the per capita real income of 1950 and twice that year's per capita real income. The results are presented in index form with base 1950 = 100. The sharp drop of the cost of meat at the higher utility level in 1953 (from 110.2 to 99.6) should be contrasted with the much smaller decline at the lower utility level (from 107.2 to 105.5). This difference results from the large price decrease of high income-elastic beef and lamb relative to low income-elastic pork and chicken. Since the former two meats have comparatively large budget shares for people who are better off, this group experienced a much sharper drop of the cost of meat than those who were worse off. See Theil [397, section 13.6] for further details.

The meat example is selected here because of the large discrepancies of the price changes of individual meats. Usually these discrepancies are much smaller, in which case the cost-of-living indexes and subindexes are also much less dependent on the utility level selected.

13.5   The Rotterdam Model

We write the demand equation (8.13) in the form

$$w_i d(\log q_i) = \theta_i d(\log Q) + \phi \sum_{j=1}^{n} \theta_{ij}[d(\log p_j) - d(\log P')] + \varepsilon_i.$$

A comparison with (13.8) shows that a finite-change version of this equation is

(13.9) $$\bar{w}_{it} Dq_{it} = \theta_i DQ_t + \sum_{j=1}^{n} \nu_{ij}(Dp_{jt} - DP_t') + \varepsilon_{it},$$

where

(13.10) $$\nu_{ij} = \phi\theta_{ij} \qquad i,j = 1, \ldots, n,$$

and DP_t' is a finite-change version of the Frisch price index:

(13.11) $$DP_t' = \sum_{i=1}^{n} \theta_i Dp_{it}.$$

Equation (13.9) with constant coefficients (the θ_i's and ν_{ij}'s) is known as the *Rotterdam model* for systems of consumer demand equations.[5] It is

5. This terminology was proposed by Parks [300], who referred to the domicile of Barten and Theil at the time when the model was first formulated.

obtained by solving Barten's fundamental matrix equation (2.21) and writing the solution for the quantity changes in the form (2.23), after which infinitesimal changes are replaced by finite changes and the coefficients are postulated to be constants. We shall have more to say about this constancy in sections 14.3 and 14.4. The ν_{ij}'s in (13.9) are the price coefficients of the model (the coefficients of relative prices), but, unlike the θ_{ij}'s, they are not normalized price coefficients. Since $[\theta_{ij}]$ is symmetric positive definite, equation (13.10) combined with $\phi < 0$ implies that the price coefficient matrix $[\nu_{ij}]$ is symmetric negative definite. Summation of (13.10) over j yields

$$(13.12) \qquad \sum_{j=1}^{n} \nu_{ij} = \phi\theta_i \qquad i = 1, \ldots, n,$$

because $\sum_j \theta_{ij} = \theta_i$. Hence the sum of the price coefficients in each demand equation is proportional to the corresponding marginal share, with ϕ as proportionality constant. Summation of (13.12) over i yields the result that ϕ equals the sum of all ν_{ij}'s in the system.

It follows from (13.11) that the substitution term of (13.9) may be written as

$$\sum_{j=1}^{n} \nu_{ij}Dp_{jt} - \left(\sum_{j=1}^{n} \nu_{ij}\right) \sum_{j=1}^{n} \theta_j Dp_{jt} = \sum_{j=1}^{n} (\nu_{ij} - \phi\theta_i\theta_j)Dp_{jt},$$

where the equal sign is based on (13.12). Thus, when we define

$$(13.13) \qquad \pi_{ij} = \nu_{ij} - \phi\theta_i\theta_j \qquad i, j = 1, \ldots, n,$$

we can write (13.9) in the equivalent form

$$(13.14) \qquad \bar{w}_{it}Dq_{it} = \theta_i DQ_t + \sum_{j=1}^{n} \pi_{ij}Dp_{jt} + \varepsilon_{it}.$$

Note that (13.14) contains the prices in undeflated form, whereas in (13.9) Dp_{jt} is deflated by DP_t'. Accordingly, (13.9) is known as the *relative price version* of the Rotterdam model and (13.14) as the *absolute price version*.

Substitution of (13.10) in (13.13) yields

$$(13.15) \qquad \pi_{ij} = \phi(\theta_{ij} - \theta_i\theta_j) \qquad i, j = 1, \ldots, n,$$

which shows that π_{ij} may be identified with the coefficient of $d(\log p_j)$ in the substitution term (2.29). The π_{ij}'s are known as the *Slutsky coefficients* of the Rotterdam model. The $n \times n$ Slutsky matrix $[\pi_{ij}]$ is symmetric negative semidefinite of rank $n - 1$. This matrix satisfies

$$(13.16) \qquad \sum_{j=1}^{n} \pi_{ij} = 0,$$

which follows from (13.15) and $\sum_j \theta_{ij} = \theta_i$.

The covariance structure of rational random behavior can be expressed in terms of Slutsky coefficients in a particularly simple manner. By combining equations (13.15) and (8.14), we find that the disturbances of (13.14) satisfy

$$(13.17) \qquad \text{cov}(\varepsilon_{it}, \varepsilon_{jt}) = \frac{\sigma^2}{\phi} \pi_{ij} \qquad i, j = 1, \ldots, n,$$

or, in words, all disturbance covariances (including the variances) are proportional to the corresponding Slutsky coefficients. The disturbances $\varepsilon_{1t}, \ldots, \varepsilon_{nt}$ add up to zero and thus have a singular covariance matrix, which agrees with equations (13.16) and (13.17) and the fact that the Rotterdam model is an allocation model.

13.6   The Application of the Rotterdam Model

A major convenience of the absolute price version (13.14) is its linearity in the parameters (the θ_i's and π_{ij}'s), which explains its popularity for small demand systems (small n). The standard procedure is to estimate (13.14) by the least-squares method, test for Slutsky symmetry ($\pi_{ij} = \pi_{ji}$), and impose this symmetry when the test finds that it is an acceptable hypothesis. This procedure considers only the symmetry of $[\pi_{ij}]$, not its negative semidefiniteness, but a method to handle the latter property was recently developed by Barten and Geyskens [37]. If the covariance structure (13.17) of rational random behavior is imposed, the estimate of $[\pi_{ij}]$ is automatically negative semidefinite. An application of this procedure will be discussed in section 13.8.

When n becomes larger, the number of π_{ij}'s grows rapidly and the relative price version (13.9) combined with a block independence assumption becomes more attractive.[6] This assumption implies that the θ_{ij}'s with i and

6. The relative price version requires at least one additional restriction, because it would not be identified otherwise. The simplest way to see this is by means of a comparison with the absolute price version. The latter contains

j in different groups all vanish (see eq. [9.2]), so that the same holds for the ν_{ij}'s of (13.9) in view of (13.10). The relative price version is nonlinear in its parameters,[7] but this problem can be handled by maximum likelihood or by generalized least-squares in iterative form. Even so, the total number of parameters may be quite substantial. For example, Paulus [304] estimated a 14-commodity demand system from Dutch data, using a block independent specification with 37 unconstrained parameters. Since these parameters must all be estimated simultaneously, it is appropriate to provide prior judgments on their numerical values, because otherwise problems of multicollinearity and observational errors will easily yield unrealistic results. One method of incorporating prior judgments is Bayesian inference, but this technique is typically characterized by problems of integration and other difficulties (Barbosa [18] and Kiefer [213] have made first attempts to apply Bayesian inference to the Rotterdam model). Therefore, Paulus used the method of mixed estimation (from Theil and Goldberger [382, 393, 402]), which is easier to apply because it permits the analyst to confine his prior judgments to those parameters about which he feels that he has some prior knowledge. The technique itself amounts to generalized least-squares in a non-Bayesian setting. Barten [24] was the first to apply the mixed estimation technique to a system of demand equations.

Table 7 summarizes the main results obtained by Paulus. Prior judgments are formulated for the θ_i's of (13.9), not for the ν_{ij}'s. Since it is easier to speculate on income elasticities than marginal shares, the former are taken as a starting point. The first line of the table shows that the prior estimate of the income elasticity of the demand for bread is 0.2, with a standard error of 0.1. This amounts to a two-sigma interval (0, 0.4), which indicates that bread is judged to be a necessity but not an inferior good. For groceries the prior estimate is twice as large, but the standard error is also larger. The latter feature reflects the fact that groceries are a more heterogeneous commodity group than bread, which implies greater uncertainty as to the value of the income elasticity of groceries.

(in addition to the marginal shares) the symmetric matrix $[\pi_{ij}]$ constrained by (13.16), whereas the former contains the symmetric matrix $[\nu_{ij}]$ constrained by (13.10), which involves the additional parameter ϕ. This identification problem is related to the lack of invariance of ϕ and $[\nu_{ij}]$ under monotone increasing transformations of the utility function (see Theil [397, section 2.5]). This problem does not arise in the theory of the firm, because ψ can be obtained from equation (5.43) when the firm maximizes profit under competitive conditions; see section 14.7.

7. When all constraints are used to eliminate parameters, the relative price version is cubic in the remaining parameters. This may be verified by substituting (13.11) in (13.9) and using (13.10) to eliminate ν_{ii} and $\sum_i \theta_i = 1$ to eliminate θ_n.

Table 7   Prior, Sample, and Mixed Estimates of Income Elasticities and Marginal Shares

Commodity Group	Prior Estimate of Income Elasticity	Marginal Share			Implied Estimate of Income Elasticity
		Prior Estimate	Sample Estimate	Mixed Estimate	
Bread	0.2 (0.10)	0.0070 (0.0035)	0.0005 (0.0068)	0.0056 (0.0027)	0.16 (0.08)
Groceries	0.4 (0.15)	0.0227 (0.0085)	0.0567 (0.0121)	0.0280 (0.0060)	0.50 (0.11)
Dairy products	0.6 (0.15)	0.0434 (0.0108)	0.0327 (0.0084)	0.0351 (0.0056)	0.49 (0.08)
Vegetables and fruit	0.6 (0.20)	0.0265 (0.0088)	0.0333 (0.0103)	0.0276 (0.0058)	0.62 (0.13)
Meat	1.0 (0.20)	0.0760 (0.0152)	0.0517 (0.0144)	0.0676 (0.0094)	0.89 (0.12)
Fish	0.8 (0.25)	0.0057 (0.0018)	0.0049 (0.0045)	0.0050 (0.0012)	0.71 (0.16)
Beverages	1.5 (0.30)	0.0406 (0.0081)	0.0316 (0.0063)	0.0382 (0.0044)	1.41 (0.16)
Tobacco products	0.6 (0.25)	0.0225 (0.0094)	0.0301 (0.0085)	0.0234 (0.0056)	0.62 (0.15)
Pastry, chocolate, etc.	0.8 (0.25)	0.0249 (0.0078)	0.0227 (0.0068)	0.0243 (0.0041)	0.78 (0.13)
Clothing and other textiles	2.0 (0.40)	0.2656 (0.0531)	0.2353 (0.0203)	0.2263 (0.0159)	1.70 (0.12)
Footwear	1.5 (0.30)	0.0215 (0.0043)	0.0297 (0.0040)	0.0238 (0.0025)	1.66 (0.18)
Other durables	2.0 (0.50)	0.1882 (0.0471)	0.2233 (0.0150)	0.2125 (0.0106)	2.26 (0.11)
Water, light, and heat	0.8 (0.30)	0.0439 (0.0165)	0.0592 (0.0111)	0.0462 (0.0076)	0.84 (0.14)
Other goods and services	0.7 (0.35)	0.2115 (0.1100)	0.1883 (0.0277)	0.2364 (0.0200)	0.75 (0.06)

The prior estimate of the marginal share is obtained by multiplying the prior estimate of the income elasticity by the average budget share of the sample period (1922–63 except the war years and the immediate postwar period). The sample estimates of the marginal shares, computed without using the prior judgments, are shown in the column next to that of the corresponding prior estimates. Note that the sample estimate for bread is weak, so that it is not surprising to find that the corresponding mixed estimate is dominated by the prior judgments. The last column of the table contains the estimates of the income elasticities that are implied by the mixed estimates of the marginal shares. A comparison of these elasticity estimates with the corresponding prior estimates in the first column shows that the point estimates do not differ greatly, but that many of the standard errors are substantially reduced. This means that the sample evidence tends to confirm the prior judgments and makes these judgments more precise. The discussion of Paulus's model will continue in section 14.2.

13.7   Conditional Extensions of the Rotterdam Model

We reproduce the conditional demand equation (9.21),

$$(13.18)\quad w_i d(\log q_i) = \theta_i' W_g d(\log Q_g) + \phi \sum_{j \in S_g} \theta_{ij} d\left(\log \frac{p_j}{P_g'}\right) + \varepsilon_i',$$

where the ith good is part of a group S_g in a block independent or block-wise dependent framework. To obtain a finite-change version of equation (13.18), we must first extend the indexes in (13.8) to groups. We write $W_{gt} = \sum_i w_{it}$ (sum over $i \in S_g$) and define

$$(13.19)\qquad \overline{W}_{gt} = \tfrac{1}{2}(W_{g,t-1} + W_{gt}) = \sum_{i \in S_g} \overline{w}_{it},$$

which is an extension of (13.7) to the group S_g. The group version of (13.8) is then

$$(13.20)\qquad DP_{gt} = \sum_{i \in S_g} \frac{\overline{w}_{it}}{\overline{W}_{gt}} Dp_{it}, \qquad DQ_{gt} = \sum_{i \in S_g} \frac{\overline{w}_{it}}{\overline{W}_{gt}} Dq_{it},$$

which obviously satisfies

$$(13.21)\qquad \sum_{g=1}^{G} \overline{W}_{gt} DP_{gt} = DP_t, \qquad \sum_{g=1}^{G} \overline{W}_{gt} DQ_{gt} = DQ_t.$$

We conclude from (13.19) and (13.20) that the following equation is a finite-change version of (13.18):

$$(13.22) \qquad \bar{w}_{it} Dq_{it} = \theta_i' \overline{W}_{gt} DQ_{gt} + \sum_{j \in S_g} \nu_{ij}(Dp_{jt} - DP_{gt}') + \varepsilon_{it}'.$$

This is a conditional demand equation in relative prices, ν_{ij} being defined in (13.10) and Dp_{jt} being deflated by

$$(13.23) \qquad\qquad DP_{gt}' = \sum_{i \in S_g} \theta_i' Dp_{it},$$

which is a finite-change version of the Frisch price index (9.19). Note that the price coefficients in equation (13.22) are the same as in the unconditional demand equation (13.9), but that the deflators differ. Also note from (13.20) that $\overline{W}_{gt} DQ_{gt}$ in the volume term of (13.22) is equal to the sum of $\bar{w}_{it} Dq_{it}$ over $i \in S_g$. Hence $\overline{W}_{gt} DQ_{gt}$ has a disturbance component of the form $E_{gt} = \sum_i \varepsilon_{it}$ (sum over $i \in S_g$). Under rational random behavior, E_{gt} is stochastically independent of ε_{it}' (see eq. [9.23]), which means that we can view $\overline{W}_{gt} DQ_{gt}$ as a predetermined variable in the conditional demand model (13.22).

As in the case of the unconditional Rotterdam model, the conditional variant has both an absolute and a relative price version. To derive the absolute price version from (13.22), we use[8]

$$(13.24) \qquad\qquad \sum_{j \in S_g} \theta_{ij} = \Theta_{gg} \theta_i' \quad \text{if} \quad i \in S_g.$$

On combining this with (13.10) and (13.23), we find that the substitution term of (13.22) can be written as $\phi \sum_j (\theta_{ij} - \Theta_{gg} \theta_i' \theta_j') Dp_{jt}$. Therefore, equation (13.22) is equivalent to

$$(13.25) \qquad \bar{w}_{it} Dq_{it} = \theta_i' \overline{W}_{gt} DQ_{gt} + \sum_{j \in S_g} \pi_{ij}^g Dp_{jt} + \varepsilon_{it}',$$

where

$$(13.26) \qquad\qquad \pi_{ij}^g = \phi(\theta_{ij} - \Theta_{gg} \theta_i' \theta_j') \qquad i, j \in S_g,$$

which is a conditional Slutsky coefficient for two goods within the group S_g.

Equation (13.25) is the absolute price version of our conditional variant of the Rotterdam model. As in the case of the unconditional model, this

---

8. Under block independence the left-hand side of (13.24) equals $\Theta_g \theta_i'$ (see [9.3] and [9.18]), which confirms (13.24) because Θ_{gg} equals Θ_g under that condition. The reader may verify (13.24) under the weaker condition of blockwise dependence, using $\theta_{i1} + \cdots + \theta_{in} = \theta_i = \Theta_g \theta_i'$ as well as (9.20) and (9.15).

absolute price version is linear in the parameters, but note that the Slutsky coefficients differ in (13.25) and (13.14), whereas the price coefficients in the relative price versions (13.22) and (13.9) are the same. Since $\overline{W}_{gt}DQ_{gt}$ is stochastically independent of ε'_{it}, we can estimate (13.25) in the same way that we can estimate its unconditional counterpart (13.14). However, it will prove useful to dig a little deeper before considering the application of conditional demand models to statistical data.

By dividing both sides of (13.18) by W_g, we obtain

$$(13.27) \qquad \frac{w_i}{W_g} d(\log q_i) = \theta'_i d(\log Q_g) + \frac{\phi}{W_g} \sum_{j \in S_g} \theta_{ij} d\left(\log \frac{p_j}{P'_g}\right) + \frac{\varepsilon'_i}{W_g}.$$

The left-hand side of (13.27) is the quantity component of $d(w_i/W_g)$, that is, of the infinitesimal change in the conditional budget share of the ith good within its group. This follows from

$$(13.28) \qquad d\left(\frac{w_i}{W_g}\right) = \frac{w_i}{W_g} d(\log p_i) + \frac{w_i}{W_g} d(\log q_i) - \frac{w_i}{W_g} d(\log W_g M),$$

which shows that the change in the conditional budget share of a good is the sum of three components, one for the change in its price, one for the change in its quantity, and one for the change in $W_g M$ (i.e., in the amount spent on the group). The result (13.28) is a within-group version of equation (2.15). Note that the quantity component in (13.28), and hence also the left-hand side of (13.27), may be viewed as the contribution of the ith good to the Divisia volume index (9.5).

When we take (13.27) rather than (13.18) as our starting point, the finite-change equation in relative prices becomes

$$(13.29) \qquad \frac{\overline{w}_{it}}{\overline{W}_{gt}} Dq_{it} = \theta'_i DQ_{gt} + \sum_{j \in S_g} v'_{ij}(Dp_{jt} - DP'_{gt}) + \varepsilon''_{it},$$

where ε''_{it} is the finite-change version of $\varepsilon''_i = \varepsilon'_i/W_g$ and

$$(13.30) \qquad v'_{ij} = \frac{v_{ij}}{W_g} = \frac{\phi}{W_g} \theta_{ij} \qquad i, j \in S_g.$$

The corresponding absolute price version is

$$(13.31) \qquad \frac{\overline{w}_{it}}{\overline{W}_{gt}} Dq_{it} = \theta'_i DQ_{gt} + \sum_{j \in S_g} \pi'_{ij} Dp_{jt} + \varepsilon''_{it},$$

where

$$(13.32) \qquad \pi'_{ij} = \frac{\pi^g_{ij}}{W_g} = \frac{\phi}{W_g} (\theta_{ij} - \Theta_{gg}\theta'_i\theta'_j) \qquad i, j \in S_g,$$

which is another conditional Slutsky coefficient.

13.8   The Application of the Conditional Extensions

Choosing between (13.22) and (13.25) on one hand and (13.29) and (13.31) on the other is basically a matter of deciding whether the ν_{ij}'s (and hence ϕ) are constants or proportional to the budget share W_g of the group. In the latter case we should select (13.29) and (13.31) in view of (13.30) and (13.32). Economic theory has little to say about such matters, so that it is appropriate to delegate this problem to the data. An application to annual U.S. data on four meats in the period 1950–72 shows that (13.31) has a better fit than (13.25). Accordingly, (13.31) is selected. (The problem of how to measure the fit will be considered in section 14.1.) The upper part of table 8 displays the symmetry-constrained estimates of the coefficients of (13.31). These estimates are obtained under the assumption that DQ_{gt} is predetermined, which is justified by the theory of rational random behavior.

The covariances in (9.25) are proportional to $\theta_{ij} - \Theta_{gg}\theta_i'\theta_j'$ and hence, in view of (13.32), also to π_{ij}'. The disturbance of (13.31) is obtained by dividing ε_i' by W_g (see eq. [13.27]), but this division does not affect the proportionality. Accordingly, the horizontal coordinates of the ten small circles of figure 7 in section 9.4 are obtained from the point estimates in the upper half of table 8, while the vertical coordinates are the mean squares and products of the residuals associated with these estimates. A likelihood ratio test indicates that the proportionality (9.25) is acceptable at the 10 percent significance level. The straight line through the origin in figure 7 contains the maximum-likelihood estimates constrained by (9.25); the broken lines in the figure show how the estimates are affected by this constraint. The lower part of table 8 contains these new estimates. They are close to the corresponding figures in the upper part except for the coefficients which involve lamb. The constraint forces the estimates of the latter coefficients all in zero direction.

In fact, it appears that those coefficients ν_{ij}' in the relative price version (13.29) which refer to lamb and any of the other meats are all close to zero. When we force these coefficients to be zero and impose (9.25) also, we obtain a maximum-likelihood estimate of the 4×4 price coefficient matrix equal to

$$(13.33) \quad [\nu_{ij}'] = \begin{bmatrix} -0.5286 & 0.0804 & 0.0109 & 0 \\ & -0.2425 & 0.0282 & 0 \\ & & -0.0802 & 0 \\ & & & -0.0270 \end{bmatrix} \begin{array}{l} \text{beef} \\ \text{pork} \\ \text{chicken} \\ \text{lamb,} \end{array}$$

as well as estimates of the conditional marginal shares (θ_i') equal to 0.684 for beef, 0.209 for pork, 0.064 for chicken, and 0.042 for lamb. It follows

Table 8

Conditional Demand Model for Meats

Meat	θ'_i	π'_{i1}	π'_{i2}	π'_{i3}	π'_{i4}
		Symmetry-constrained Estimates			
Beef	0.692 (0.049)	−0.227 (0.019)	0.164 (0.014)	0.033 (0.009)	0.029 (0.010)
Pork	0.199 (0.044)		−0.214 (0.014)	0.038 (0.007)	0.012 (0.004)
Chicken	0.059 (0.021)			−0.084 (0.009)	0.013 (0.005)
Lamb	0.050 (0.012)				−0.055 (0.014)
		Maximum-Likelihood Estimates Constrained by (9.25)			
Beef	0.703 (0.040)	−0.216 (0.015)	0.173 (0.012)	0.034 (0.009)	0.008 (0.007)
Pork	0.201 (0.040)		−0.216 (0.013)	0.035 (0.008)	0.007 (0.004)
Chicken	0.058 (0.024)			−0.079 (0.010)	0.009 (0.005)
Lamb	0.039 (0.014)				−0.024 (0.008)

Table 9   Demand Elasticities of Meats

MEAT	CONDITIONAL INCOME ELASTICITY	ELASTICITY WITH RESPECT TO THE FRISCH-DEFLATED PRICE OF			
		Beef	Pork	Chicken	Lamb
Beef	1.37	−1.06	0.16	0.02	0
Pork	0.60	0.23	−0.69	0.08	0
Chicken	0.53	0.09	0.23	−0.66	0
Lamb	1.54	0	0	0	−0.98

from (13.29) that division of these four figures by the averages of the corresponding conditional budget shares in the sample period yields estimates of the conditional income elasticities. These estimates are shown in the first column of table 9 and indicate that beef and lamb are luxuries relative to pork and chicken. The other columns of the table are estimates of price elasticities, obtained by dividing the elements in each row in (13.33) by the average of the corresponding conditional budget shares in the sample period.

It follows from (13.30) and $\phi < 0$ that the positive off-diagonal elements of the matrix (13.33) declare beef, pork, and chicken to be pairwise specific substitutes, while the zero off-diagonal elements in the last column imply that lamb is neither a specific substitute nor a specific complement of any other meat. The composition matrices of table 1 in section 11.1 are based on the leading 3×3 submatrix of the matrix (13.33). Additional details can be found in Theil's monograph [397, chap. 7], but we should mention that further results were obtained by Kenneth Laitinen since this monograph appeared. One result is that the speed of the convergence procedures can be much improved by the use of Newton's method. The asymptotic standard errors in the lower part of table 8 are another new result. They are obtained from the information matrix of maximum-likelihood theory; the implementation involves the leading 3×3 submatrix of the disturbance covariance matrix (see eq. [9.25]), the inverse of which is written as the product of diagonal and upper triangular matrices. See also Barnett [19] and Berndt et al. [43].

Fourteen

Further Discussion
of Applications

The discussion of chapter 13 is incomplete in several respects. We mentioned in section 13.8 that one demand model has a better fit than another, but how should we measure the fit of a *system* of demand equations? Also, the applications discussed in chapter 13 are all based on national (or per capita) aggregates, whereas the theory of the consumer and the firm refers to individual units. What are the implications of aggregation over consumers or firms? Furthermore, the applications described in sections 13.6 and 13.8 treat price changes as predetermined variables. Is it also possible to treat quantity changes as predetermined, and when is it appropriate to do so? These are among the problems discussed in this chapter, the last two sections of which are devoted to a parametrization of the multiproduct firm similar to the Rotterdam model of the consumer.

14.1 Measuring the Fit of an Allocation Model

The standard measure of fit in econometrics is the multiple correlation coefficient. Since this coefficient refers to a single equation, its use is unattractive when the objective is to measure the fit of several equations that are estimated simultaneously. It is possible, however, to generalize the multiple correlation coefficient for an equation system. This can be done in several ways; we refer to a recent article by McElroy [270] for a comparison of three different generalizations.

Below we discuss a measure of fit from information theory which is specifically applicable to allocation models, that is, models which serve to explain positive proportions that add up to 1 such as budget or factor or revenue shares. Let $w_{1t}, \ldots, w_{nt}$ be the observed budget shares of n goods in period t ($\sum_i w_{it} = 1$) and $\hat{w}_{1t}, \ldots, \hat{w}_{nt}$ the predicted or adjusted budget shares implied by some allocation model ($\sum_i \hat{w}_{it} = 1$). The *information inaccuracy* of these predictions is defined as

$$(14.1) \qquad\qquad I_t = \sum_{i=1}^{n} w_{it} \log \frac{w_{it}}{\hat{w}_{it}},$$

which vanishes when the predictions are perfect ($\hat{w}_{it} = w_{it}$ for $i = 1, \ldots, n$) and is positive otherwise.[1] The larger I_t is, the worse the predictions $\hat{w}_{1t}, \ldots,$ $\hat{w}_{nt}$ are as approximations of the observed budget shares. When we expand the natural logarithm in (14.1), we find that the leading term is quadratic:

$$(14.2) \qquad\qquad I_t \approx \frac{1}{2} \sum_{i=1}^{n} \frac{(\hat{w}_{it} - w_{it})^2}{w_{it}}.$$

This shows that the information inaccuracy is approximately proportional to a chi-square as long as the prediction errors are small. Note that (14.1) evaluates the predictions of all n budget shares for one period. When we have data on several periods ($t = 1, \ldots, T$), we can use the average of $I_1,$ $\ldots, I_T$ as an overall measure of inaccuracy. The arithmetic mean is the obvious choice because information measures are additive.

Table 10, from Parks [300], provides an example of the use of average information inaccuracies, based on annual Swedish data on eight groups

Table 10   Average Information Inaccuracies of
                                          Five Demand Models for Sweden

Period	No-Change Extrapolation	Rotterdam Model	Addilog Model	Linear Expenditure System No Trend	Linear Expenditure System With Trend
Sample period	0.310	0.199	0.260	0.308	0.260
1863–1901	0.233	0.224	0.243	0.309	0.295
1902–1914	0.198	0.103	0.122	0.170	0.148
1920–1940	0.367	0.175	0.284	0.250	0.253
1941–1955	0.390	0.220	0.329	0.310	0.326

NOTE: All entries are to be divided by 100.

1. The definition (14.1) is the discrete version of the amount of information given in (7.1). The use of (14.1) is not confined to the evaluation of allocation predictions. For example, Fane [128] uses a measure similar to (14.1) for factor shares under Cobb-Douglas and CES technologies. Other applications, including the measurement of income inequality and industrial concentration, are described in Theil [389]. For applications to accounting and related areas, see references [14], [186], and [244]–[252] by Lev and others.

of goods from the early 1860s until 1955.[2] The first column contains the average of (14.1) for no-change extrapolation, that is, for the case in which $\hat{w}_{it}$ is interpreted as $w_{i,t-1}$. To clarify this we return to infinitesimal changes and use equation (2.15) to conclude that no change in w_i (i.e., $dw_i = 0$) implies

$$w_i d(\log q_i) = w_i d(\log M) - w_i d(\log p_i).$$

This can be written in the form

$$(14.3) \qquad w_i d(\log q_i) = w_i d\left(\log \frac{M}{P}\right) - w_i d\left(\log \frac{p_i}{P}\right),$$

which is equivalent to the preference independent demand equation (2.14) in the special case $\phi = -1$ and $\theta_i = w_i$ for each i (so that the Divisia and Frisch price indexes are identical). Therefore, no-change extrapolation of budget shares is equivalent to assuming that all goods and the marginal utility of income have unitary income elasticities (see eq. [2.19]).

We should expect that more sophisticated attempts to model consumer demand will yield lower average information inaccuracies. This was verified by Parks for four models: the absolute price version (13.14) of the Rotterdam model, the addilog indirect utility model (3.21), the linear expenditure system (13.3), and the linear expenditure system in which the coefficients $b_1, \ldots, b_n$ are assumed to be linear functions of calendar time. In each case the model provides a prediction of Δw_{it} (the change in the budget share from $t - 1$ to t), which is added to the observed $w_{i,t-1}$ in order to yield the implied prediction $\hat{w}_{it}$ of w_{it}:

$$(14.4) \qquad \hat{w}_{it} = w_{i,t-1} + \text{prediction of } \Delta w_{it}.$$

The prediction of Δw_{it} is in all cases conditional on the observed changes in income and prices.

The average information inaccuracies of the entire sample period are shown in the first line of table 10. The results indicate that the Rotterdam model has a considerably better fit than all other models. The next rows contain average information inaccuracies for selected subperiods; they show that the Rotterdam model is also the only model which consistently beats no-change extrapolation. We should add the qualification that the number of parameters adjusted by the Rotterdam model exceeds those of

2. The data refer to the value of output devoted to final consumption for the following production sectors: (1) agriculture, (2) manufacturing, (3) transportation and communications, (4) commerce and insurance, (5) domestic services, (6) housing services, (7) public services, and (8) imported goods.

the other models. This problem will be considered in remark (2) at the end of this section.

The information inaccuracy (14.1) can be extended in several ways. If the analyst is interested in the performance of the allocation model with respect to the ith good only, all he has to do is lump all other goods together. This yields

$$(14.5) \qquad I_{it} = w_{it} \log \frac{w_{it}}{\hat{w}_{it}} + (1 - w_{it}) \log \frac{1 - w_{it}}{1 - \hat{w}_{it}},$$

which is the information inaccuracy for the ith good and its complement. Needless to say, this idea can be applied to any grouping of the n goods. Note that I_t of (14.1) is never below I_{it}. This is so because $I_t - I_{it}$ is equal to a positive fraction of an information inaccuracy in a conditional sense; see Theil [397, section 5.5].

The conditional interpretation of (14.1) is another extension. Let W_{gt} be the budget share of a group of goods and w_{it}/W_{gt} the conditional share of the ith good within this group. When a conditional allocation model provides a prediction of the change in such a conditional share, we can add this prediction to the observed value of $w_{i,t-1}/W_{g,t-1}$ in order to obtain the implied prediction of w_{it}/W_{gt}. This approach is applied in table 11 to the conditional demand models (13.25) and (13.31) of meat. The figures shown are the conditional version of (14.1) for $n = 4$, averaged over the 22-year sample period. They indicate that both demand models are superior to no-change extrapolation, but that (13.31) has a better fit than (13.25). The next four lines provide the conditional version of (14.5) for each of the four meats. They show that (13.31) is also superior to (13.25) with respect to the individual equations except that for lamb.

Table 11   Average Information Inaccuracies of
                                             Conditional Demand Models for
                                             Meats: United States, 1950–72

Meat	No-Change Extrapolation	Model (13.25)	Model (13.31)
All four meats	0.337	0.237	0.196
Beef	0.221	0.142	0.109
Pork	0.165	0.127	0.095
Chicken	0.071	0.047	0.042
Lamb	0.059	0.044	0.045

NOTE: All entries are to be divided by 1000.

Remarks

1. It can be shown that if the parameters of the Rotterdam model (13.9) or (13.14) are known, the prediction $\hat{w}_{it} - w_{it}$ is simply minus the disturbance,[3] so that (14.2) yields

$$(14.6) \qquad I_t \approx \frac{1}{2} \sum_{i=1}^{n} \frac{\varepsilon_{it}^2}{w_{it}}.$$

If we take the expectation of ε_{it}^2 and use (8.14), we obtain an approximate expectation of I_t, written $\bar{I}_t$, under rational random behavior:

$$(14.7) \qquad \bar{I}_t = -\frac{\sigma^2}{2\phi} \left(-\phi \sum_{i=1}^{n} \frac{\theta_{it}}{w_{it}} + \phi \sum_{i=1}^{n} \frac{\theta_i^2}{w_{it}} \right).$$

The first expression in parentheses is the sum of the absolute values of the own-price elasticities, which is verified by dividing both sides of (2.23) by the ith budget share. The second expression is a multiple ϕ of the Frisch-weighted mean of the income elasticities (which is identical to the Divisia-weighted second moment of the same elasticities). Both expressions are invariant under the preference independence transformation.

2. When the coefficients are unknown, (14.6) is replaced by

$$(14.8) \qquad I_t \approx \frac{1}{2} \sum_{i=1}^{n} \frac{e_{it}^2}{w_{it}},$$

where e_{it} is a residual associated with the coefficient estimates. The result (14.8) suggests a simple correction for degrees of freedom. Since each observation yields $n - 1$ degrees of freedom for an allocation model consisting of n equations, the total number of degrees of freedom supplied by T observations is $(n - 1)T$. This is the number of degrees of freedom prior to the statistical adjustment of the coefficients. The correction of the average information inaccuracy consists of a multiplication by the ratio of the numbers of degrees of freedom before and after the adjustment. The latter number is obtained from the former by subtracting the number of

---

3. The simplest way to verify this is in terms of infinitesimal changes. It follows from (2.15) and (8.13) that dw_i is equal to a linear combination of income and price changes plus ε_i. Since we operate conditionally on these changes and on the level of w_i, the error of the predicted budget share change is thus equal to $-\varepsilon_i$ when the coefficients of (8.13) are known. If these coefficients are unknown and replaced by estimates, the prediction error becomes minus the residual associated with these estimates, which yields (14.8).

unconstrained coefficients. The number of these coefficients is equal to $\frac{1}{2}(n - 1)(n + 2)$ for the absolute price version of the Rotterdam model, which is 35 in the case of table 10 ($n = 8$). The correction raises 0.199 in the first row of table 10 to about 0.21, which is well below the other figures in this row. (The latter figures are of course also raised by the correction.) In the case of table 11 no correction is needed because (13.25) and (13.31) adjust the same number of coefficients.

14.2   On the Difference between Large and Small Models

Paulus [304] used the information inaccuracy to simplify the fourteen-commodity demand system which we considered earlier in section 13.6. His initial specification contains 37 unconstrained parameters, but he reduced this number step-by-step by breaking up groups into smaller groups, using the average information inaccuracy (corrected for degrees of freedom) as one of his criteria. Figure 6 in section 8.3 is based on the final specification selected, which contains only one group that consists of more than one commodity. Although the scatter in this figure is encouraging for the covariance model (8.14), a likelihood ratio test rejects this model. This should be contrasted with the more positive result for meats which we reported in section 13.8. The difference is not entirely surprising, because the meat data are much more accurate than those of several commodity groups listed in table 7 in section 13.6. The theory of rational random behavior which yields the covariance specification (8.14) predicts random *behavior*; it is not concerned with random or nonrandom errors in the *measurement* of behavior. As we shall shortly see, observational errors present serious problems in the evaluation of statistical test results for theoretical constraints on coefficients of demand equation systems, particularly when such systems are large.

The application to the four meats described in section 13.8 is an example of a small model. A model ceases to be small when the number of goods (n) approaches 10, while Paulus's model ($n = 14$) is large by present standards. There is an important difference between small and large models in that small models typically yield no problems with respect to the acceptance of standard results of demand theory, whereas large models frequently do present problems. In particular, the homogeneity condition, which states that proportionate changes in income and prices do not affect demand, is frequently rejected by the data in the case of large models. This condition is represented by equation (13.16) for the Rotterdam model. On the other hand, Slutsky symmetry ($\pi_{ij} = \pi_{ji}$) tends to be much more acceptable.

These results are surprising because homogeneity is a very weak condition, but Laitinen has shown that they are in fact misleading.[4] The problem is that the standard F test for homogeneity becomes an asymptotic χ^2 test when the contemporaneous covariance matrix of the disturbances is unknown. This asymptotic test is seriously biased toward rejecting the homogeneity hypothesis. For example, the value of the test statistic for the Dutch data used by Paulus ($n = 14$) is 267.8, which is highly significant for $\chi^2(13)$ at any reasonable significance level, but the correct 5 percent significance limit is 306.3, which accepts the homogeneity hypothesis. This correct limit is based on the finite-sample distribution of the test statistic, which is a multiple

$$\frac{(n - 1)(T - n - 1)}{T - 2n + 1}$$

of F with $n - 1$ and $T - 2n + 1$ degrees of freedom, T being the number of observations. The bias of the asymptotic χ^2 approximation is particularly large when n approaches $\frac{1}{2}T$, but it is also noticeable for smaller values of n. Laitinen illustrated his results with several sampling experiments.

The accuracy of the price data should also be considered. Testing for homogeneity requires that prices be introduced in absolute (undeflated) form, which typically yields a considerable degree of multicollinearity. When some of the prices are also poorly measured, estimates produced by standard techniques have doubtful validity. This is particularly serious for large systems with numerous unknown coefficients. On the other hand, prices are typically more accurate, and the multicollinearity problem is less severe, for small demand subsystems such as that of the meats which we considered in section 13.8. This is one reason why it is attractive to work with such subsystems. Another reason is that subsystems usually avoid large residual items. For example, it is appropriate to be skeptical about the price of "other goods and services" (see table 7 in section 13.6); this item accounts for about 30 percent of the Dutch budget.

14.3   Aggregation over Consumers and the Constancy of Coefficients

The aggregation of demand equations over consumers is another matter of concern. Sonnenschein [369, 370] has shown that little is known about aggregate demand functions except for the (negative) result that such

4. "Why Is Demand Homogeneity So Often Rejected?" *Economics Letters* 1 (1978): 187–91. Laitinen's results also apply to the testing of constant terms in the Rotterdam model, which serve as time trends (because the model is in first differences). The asymptotic test of zero constant terms is biased toward rejecting this hypothesis, particularly for large systems.

functions are not integrable to a "community utility function." He notes that his proofs provide a striking indication that the budget and homogeneity restrictions largely exhaust the empirical implications of the utility hypothesis for market (aggregate) demand functions; Slutsky symmetry is not among the properties of these functions. This holds even under the strong condition that the incomes of all consumers change proportionately.

As could be expected under such circumstances, others have formulated different approaches in order to rescue demand systems at the aggregate level. Below we shall discuss Barnett's [21] approach, for which purpose we return to the individual consumer. If this consumer's utility function has continuous derivatives of the third order, his demand equations have continuous derivatives of the second order. We can then apply Young's theorem to the ith demand equation:

$$(14.9) \qquad \frac{\partial^2 q_i}{\partial p_j \partial M} = \frac{\partial^2 q_i}{\partial M \partial p_j} \qquad i, j = 1, \ldots, n.$$

The derivative $\partial q_i/\partial M$ equals θ_i/p_i in the notation of the differential approach; hence the derivative of $\partial q_i/\partial M$ with respect to p_j vanishes for $i \neq j$ and equals $- \theta_i/p_i^2$ for $i = j$ if θ_i *is a constant*. It can be shown that the other cross-derivative in equation (14.9) takes a different value when all other coefficients of the differential approach are also constant. The only exception is the uninteresting case in which all goods have income elasticities identically equal to 1. Since the Rotterdam model is based on the differential approach and uses constant coefficients, this has led some writers to the belief that the model must have unitary income elasticities. This conclusion goes much too far. Below we discuss Barnett's response, but the discussion of this issue will continue in section 14.4.

Barnett [21] noted that the Rotterdam model is nearly always applied to aggregate data rather than data on individual consumers. Thus, the question is not whether the model is applicable to one consumer; it is whether the model is applicable (with constant coefficients) to per capita data. For this purpose, Barnett performed a sophisticated aggregation analysis based on an infinitesimal version of (13.14) for an individual consumer, with an additional subscript attached to the coefficients in order to identify this consumer. These microcoefficients are not assumed constant; they may depend on the consumer's income and tastes, on the prices which he pays for goods and services, and so on. The tool for the aggregation analysis is a random-coefficient model.

The result is that the Rotterdam model with constant θ_i's and π_{ij}'s provides a Taylor series approximation to a new theoretical construct which exists at the per capita level under conditions far weaker than those necessary for aggregate integrability (see the first paragraph of this section).

This holds even when there is no individual consumer whose differential demand equations have constant coefficients. Given that the theoretical foundations of the per capita Rotterdam model do not depend on aggregate integrability, any results derived from this integrability (such as homotheticity of a community utility function and unitary aggregate income elasticities) are acquired from assumptions stronger than those maintained by this model. By contrast, most other available models approximate the demand of a "representative consumer," which exists only under the very restrictive assumptions that are necessary for the integrability of aggregate demand functions.

14.4   Models as Approximations

The reader will have noticed a difference in tone between the two previous sections. Section 14.3 deals with high theory and uses such terms as community utility function, integrability, Young's theorem, a random-coefficient model, and a representative consumer. On the other hand, section 14.2 discusses data problems and uses such unappealing terms as observational errors in prices. The purpose of this section is to strike a balance between these extremes. After two general observations we shall discuss (1) the problem of how one model can be expressed in terms of another model, (2) statistical implications of approximations, and (3) evidence on the income flexibility.

The first general observation, which is perhaps superfluous, is that the result on unitary income elasticities does not apply to the differential approach (see the discussion following eq. [14.9]). The differential approach to the theory of the consumer and the firm does not postulate constancy for any of its coefficients. It is only under this constancy that (14.9) yields unitary income elasticities.

Barnett's analysis, described in section 14.3, is based on aggregation considerations. The second general observation is that if we do not invoke such considerations, we can always view the Rotterdam model as an approximation. We reproduce the absolute price version (13.14),

$$(14.10) \qquad \bar{w}_{it} Dq_{it} = \theta_i DQ_t + \sum_{j=1}^{n} \pi_{ij} Dp_{jt} + \varepsilon_{it},$$

which clearly shows that the model is a linear approximation (linear in DQ_t, Dp_{1t}, ..., Dp_{nt}). Such approximations are standard practice in econometrics.[5] Approximations are not unique; we have seen in sections

5. Examples are the translog approach and Kmenta's [221] quadratic approximation of the CES production function. Kmenta's approximation and that of the Rotterdam model are both approximations in the parameter space, whereas translog is an approximation in the space of the variables (quantities, prices, or price-income ratios).

13.7 and 13.8 that conditional demand equations can be parametrized differently. It is perfectly proper to make the choice dependent on the goodness of fit. None of the demand studies based on the Rotterdam model have ever produced exclusively unitary income elasticities. There is no reason why they should.

It is appropriate to discuss how the Rotterdam model fares when in fact some other model is the correct model. This comparison is similar to Gabrielsen's experiment in which the linear expenditure system is taken as the correct model and a translog specification is the subject of analysis (see section 13.3). The differential approach, which does not postulate a particular form of the utility function, has considerable merits for such comparisons. The reason is that since the consumer's true utility function is unknown, it is advantageous to use an approach which can accommodate different types of utility functions without being exactly appropriate for any particular type. Such robustness is desirable, and this is exactly what the differential approach performs. Deaton [99] used this idea for the estimation of several models, including the linear expenditure system and an addilog model, in a comparable way by writing them all in "Rotterdam format."

We proceed to show how this comparison works for Nasse's [290] generalization of the linear expenditure system. This generalization is based on the indirect utility function

$$(14.11) \qquad u_I(M, \mathbf{p}) = \log f(M, \mathbf{p}) - \sum_{i=1}^{n} a_i \log p_i,$$

where

$$(14.12) \qquad f(M, \mathbf{p}) = M - \sum_{i=1}^{n} \sum_{j=1}^{n} b_{ij}(p_i p_j)^{1/2},$$

which is equivalent to the indirect utility function (3.2) of the linear expenditure system when $[b_{ij}]$ is a diagonal matrix with $b_1, \ldots, b_n$ on the diagonal. Application of Roy's theorem to (14.11) gives

$$(14.13) \qquad p_i q_i = \sum_{j=1}^{n} b_{ij}(p_i p_j)^{1/2} + a_i f(M, \mathbf{p}),$$

which extends the linear expenditure system to a model that expresses the expenditure on each good as a linear function of income plus a quadratic function of the square roots of the prices. The marginal shares $(a_1, \ldots, a_n)$ are constants as in the original linear expenditure system.

It appears after some algebra (see Theil [397, section 3.2]) that the income flexibility and the normalized price coefficients associated with (14.11) take the form

$$(14.14) \qquad \phi = -\frac{f(M, \mathbf{p})}{M}, \quad \theta_{ij} = -\frac{b_{ij}(p_i p_j)^{1/2}}{2f(M, \mathbf{p})} \quad \text{if} \quad i \neq j,$$

$$(14.15) \qquad \theta_{ii} = a_i + \frac{1}{2f(M, \mathbf{p})} \sum_{j \neq i} b_{ij}(p_i p_j)^{1/2}.$$

Hence ϕ and the θ_{ij}'s of Nasse's model depend on the levels of income and prices. In particular, θ_{ij} for $i \neq j$ equals the constant $-b_{ij}$ multiplied by a homogeneous function (of degree zero) of income and prices, while θ_{ii} equals the constant a_i minus the sum of the nonconstant coefficients $\theta_{i1}, \ldots, \theta_{i,i-1}, \theta_{i,i+1}, \ldots, \theta_{in}$.

We can write (14.13) in differential form by dividing both sides by M, which gives w_i on the left, and taking differentials, which changes w_i into dw_i. Then, by subtracting the price and income components of dw_i from both sides, we have transformed Nasse's model into the familiar differential form. The equation which emerges has a constant marginal share ($\theta_i = a_i$), but ϕ and the θ_{ij}'s are not constant. The Rotterdam model is a finite-change version of Nasse's differential model in which the nonconstant ϕ and θ_{ij}'s are approximated by constants. Note that b_{ij} in (14.12) has the dimension of $(q_i q_j)^{1/2}$ and that all coefficients of the Rotterdam model are dimensionless. Thus, the approximation achieved by the latter model is in terms of dimensionless coefficients. This has some advantages, particularly when results for different countries (and hence different currencies) are compared.[6]

Nasse's model is just one example. Other utility specifications can be introduced for which the marginal shares are also nonconstant. In all such cases the Rotterdam model can be viewed as a linear approximation. What can be said about this approximation when the coefficients are in fact not constant? To avoid irrelevant algebra we shall answer this question under the simplifying assumption that prices change proportionally during each of the periods $t = 1, \ldots, T$. It follows from (13.16) that (14.10) then becomes

$$(14.16) \qquad \bar{w}_{it} Dq_{it} = \theta_i DQ_t + \varepsilon_{it} \qquad t = 1, \ldots, T.$$

6. The quantity dimensions of $(q_i q_j)^{1/2}$ are usually handled by measuring quantities as expenditures in prices of some base year. This means that b_{ij} for France is measured in francs and for Britain in pounds.

We estimate θ_i by the least-squares method:

(14.17)
$$\hat{\theta}_i = \frac{\sum\limits_{t=1}^{T} DQ_t(\bar{w}_{it}Dq_{it})}{\sum\limits_{t=1}^{T} (DQ_t)^2}.$$

Suppose now that θ_i is not constant. We take this into account by replacing equation (14.16) by

(14.18) $\bar{w}_{it}Dq_{it} = \theta_{it}DQ_t + \varepsilon_{it} \qquad t = 1, \ldots, T,$

which we interpret as the true specification. The subscript t added to θ_i indicates that this marginal share may depend on the levels of income, prices, and any other (nonstochastic) variables. Then, by substituting (14.18) in (14.17) and taking the expectation (under the assumption that the DQ_t's are nonrandom and the ε_{it}'s are random with zero mean), we obtain

(14.19)
$$\mathscr{E}\hat{\theta}_i = \frac{\sum\limits_{t=1}^{T} (DQ_t)^2\theta_{it}}{\sum\limits_{t=1}^{T} (DQ_t)^2},$$

which shows that the expectation of the marginal share estimator of the Rotterdam model is a weighted average of the marginal shares in the individual periods. The weights are proportional to the squared log-changes in real income. These weights are perfectly sensible, because the coefficient θ_{it} of DQ_t should have a larger weight when DQ_t is farther from zero.

The treatment of ϕ as a constant in the Rotterdam model is in conflict with Frisch's conjecture that ϕ is a function of real income (see the end of section 2.4). Several authors have tried to verify this conjecture, but the results are not impressive.[7] This is not surprising. The reciprocal of ϕ is the income elasticity of the marginal utility of income. This marginal utility is

7. Theil and Brooks [400] and Paulus [304] obtained statistically insignificant results for the effect of real income on ϕ. De Janvry and others [97] collected a large number of estimates of ϕ obtained by different authors and claimed that these confirm Frisch's conjecture, but the uncritical acceptance of these estimates makes the claim of doubtful validity. Lluch, Powell, and Williams [259, pp. 74–81] also report positive results, based on cross-section data for various countries. However, the validity of these results is reduced by the authors' reliance on the linear expenditure system. See also Biørn [51], Theil [397, section 15.4], and Van Praag [420].

the first derivative of utility with respect to income; its income elasticity involves the second derivative, so that the dependence of this elasticity of the level of real income involves the third derivative. The empirical relevance of derivatives gradually disappears when they are of higher order.

On the more positive side, a fair degree of consensus has developed that ϕ is of the order of $-\frac{1}{2}$, which amounts to an income elasticity of the marginal utility of income of about -2. Such knowledge is useful for obtaining an informal estimate of the own-price elasticity of a commodity group under block independence. For example, if we assume that food is block independent of all other consumption goods and use an income elasticity of the demand for food equal to 0.6, the implied own-price elasticity of food is $-\frac{1}{2}$ of 0.6, and hence -0.3, which may be verified by dividing both sides of equation (9.10) by W_g. This own-price elasticity is the elasticity of the Divisia volume index of food with respect to the Frisch-deflated Frisch price index of food.

14.5   Which Variables Are Predetermined?

Most statistical procedures used for demand equation systems are based on the assumption that prices are predetermined variables. However, it is well known (see Fox [140]) that when a single good is considered, the inter-action of demand and supply may be such that the quantity consumed becomes predetermined and the price becomes an endogenous variable. For this to be true it is necessary that suppliers react to price changes with a time lag and that supply and demand disturbances be independently distributed. When the quantity consumed is used as a predetermined variable, the estimated price sensitivity of demand is larger than under the assumption of a predetermined price. These results will now be clarified for the general case of n goods.

We enlarge the set of n demand equations of the Rotterdam model by adding n supply equations, each of which describes the change in the supply of a good in terms of lagged price changes and possibly other variables. We assume that the latter variables are all predetermined; that the change in the supply of each good always equals the change in demand; that the supply disturbance vector is stochastically independent of the demand disturbance vector in each period; and that these vectors are also independently distributed over time. The result is that the n quantity changes in the demand system are now predetermined, whereas the n price changes are endogenous. Since the quantity changes occur on the left in the Rotterdam model, we thus have the rather unusual situation in which the n left-hand variables of this model are all predetermined.

Although this situation is unusual, it can be handled easily by means of the simple device of using these predetermined variables as instrumental variables in the statistical estimation. We proceed to illustrate this for the meats of section 13.8, for which purpose we reproduce equation (13.31):

$$(14.20) \qquad \frac{\overline{w}_{it}}{\overline{W}_{gt}} Dq_{it} = \theta'_i DQ_{gt} + \sum_{j \in S_g} \pi'_{ij} Dp_{jt} + \varepsilon''_{it}.$$

We assume that the change in the supply of each meat equals the change in demand in each year. When it is also true that the suppliers of meats react to changes in meat prices with a one-year time lag, and that the relevant disturbances are appropriately independent, the variable on the left in equation (14.20) is predetermined. When we use these variables as instrumental variables and impose Slutsky symmetry, we obtain the estimates shown in the upper part of table 12. The lower part contains the corresponding estimates under predetermined price changes, which are reproduced from table 8. Note that the Slutsky estimates in the upper part all have the same sign as, but are larger than, the corresponding estimates in the lower part of the table. This illustrates that predetermined quantity changes yield a greater price sensitivity of demand than do predetermined price changes. Also note that the standard errors of the Slutsky estimates in the upper part exceed those in the lower part but that the t ratios are pairwise fairly close.

Remarks

1. The assumption that the left-hand variable in (14.20) is predetermined implies that DQ_{gt} on the right is also predetermined (see eq. [13.20]). In section 13.8 we justified the assumption of a predetermined DQ_{gt} on the basis of the theory of rational random behavior, but this is unnecessary under the present approach. A justification of the assumption of a predetermined DQ_t in the unconditional Rotterdam model will be given in section 15.2.

2. Instead of using the left-hand variables of the Rotterdam model as instrumental variables, we can also proceed as follows: We write equation (13.9) for $i = 1, \ldots, n$ in vector form and premultiply this equation system by the inverse of $[\nu_{ij}]$. This yields the result that the Frisch-deflated price log-change of each good becomes a linear function of $\overline{w}_{jt} Dq_{jt}$ for $j = 1, \ldots, n$. The coefficient matrix of this reciprocal Rotterdam model is a generalized inverse of the Slutsky matrix. If $\overline{w}_{jt} Dq_{jt}$ is predetermined, we can estimate the reciprocal model and obtain the Slutsky matrix from its generalized inverse. However, it appears that this alternative approach is more complicated than that based on instrumental variables; see Theil

Table 12

Estimates for Meats under Predetermined Price and Quantity Changes

Meat	θ'_i	π'_{i1}	π'_{i2}	π'_{i3}	π'_{i4}
		Estimates under Predetermined Quantity Changes			
Beef	0.669 (0.057)	−0.306 (0.031)	0.171 (0.018)	0.047 (0.013)	0.089 (0.027)
Pork	0.183 (0.047)		−0.239 (0.015)	0.040 (0.008)	0.028 (0.009)
Chicken	0.067 (0.024)			−0.105 (0.011)	0.018 (0.009)
Lamb	0.081 (0.022)				−0.135 (0.035)
		Estimates under Predetermined Price Changes			
Beef	0.692 (0.049)	−0.227 (0.019)	0.164 (0.014)	0.033 (0.009)	0.029 (0.010)
Pork	0.199 (0.044)		−0.214 (0.014)	0.038 (0.007)	0.012 (0.004)
Chicken	0.059 (0.021)			−0.084 (0.009)	0.013 (0.005)
Lamb	0.050 (0.012)				−0.055 (0.014)

[397, chap. 9]. For a related approach, based on the Antonelli matrix, see
Salvas-Bronsard, Leblanc, and Bronsard [340].

3. We noted in section 2.2 that equation (2.8) cannot be considered as a
demand equation because it contains more than one quantity. However,
when we divide both sides of (2.8) by q_i, we obtain p_i/M on the left and a
function of quantities on the right. This amounts to an inverted demand
model which describes price-income ratios in terms of quantities demanded.

4. Theil [397, chap. 10] extended the Rotterdam demand model by
means of a conjugate supply model. This involves an additional parameter
which varies between 0 and 1, the two limits corresponding to predetermined
price changes or predetermined quantity changes. When this parameter is
between the limits, both price changes and quantity changes are endogenous. Given any fixed value of this parameter, consistent estimates of
marginal shares and Slutsky coefficients can be obtained. See Clements [88]
for a different procedure, involving the linear expenditure system, for estimation with both prices and quantities as endogenous variables.

14.6   A Parametrization of the Multi-
product Firm

Since the Rotterdam model has been widely applied to consumer demand,
a natural question is whether a similar model can be formulated for input
demand and output supply of a firm. An adequate response to this question
requires recognition of the fact that the firm's position is different from the
consumer in that output is measurable and utility is not. It is therefore in
principle possible to consider the firm's production function or cost function directly. However, in the interest of brevity we shall ignore this issue
and confine ourselves to the formulation of Rotterdam-type input demand
and output supply equations. The account which follows in this section
and the next is an extension of a paper by Theil and Laitinen [403].

We reproduce the output supply equation (8.23),

$$(14.21) \qquad g_r d(\log z_r) = \psi^* \sum_{s=1}^{m} \theta_{rs}^* d\left(\log \frac{y_s}{P'_s}\right) + \varepsilon_r^*,$$

and write the input demand equation (8.22) in absolute price form,

$$(14.22) \quad f_i d(\log q_i) = \gamma \sum_{r=1}^{m} \theta_i^r g_r d(\log z_r) + \sum_{j=1}^{n} \pi_{ij} d(\log p_j) + \varepsilon_i,$$

where π_{ij} is the (i, j)th Slutsky coefficient of the firm,

$$(14.23) \qquad \pi_{ij} = -\psi(\theta_{ij} - \theta_i \theta_j) \qquad i, j = 1, \ldots, n,$$

which is the firm's version of equation (13.15) for the consumer.

Recall from (5.30) that under profit maximization γ equals the revenue-cost ratio:

(14.24)
$$\gamma = \frac{R}{C}.$$

Also recall that the demand and supply disturbance vectors are independent and that their covariance matrices are as shown in equations (8.14) and (8.24), which are reproduced here:

(14.25) $\text{cov}\,(\varepsilon_i, \varepsilon_j) = \sigma^2(\theta_{ij} - \theta_i\theta_j) \qquad i, j = 1, \ldots, n,$

(14.26) $\text{cov}\,(\varepsilon_r^*, \varepsilon_s^*) = \dfrac{\sigma^2\psi^*}{\gamma\psi}\,\theta_{rs}^* \qquad r, s = 1, \ldots, m.$

Our objective is to formulate a finite-change version of the results summarized in the two previous paragraphs. This requires a definition of finite-change versions of Divisia indexes. For this purpose we extend (13.7) and (13.8) to the inputs and outputs of the multiproduct firm, which yields

(14.27) $DP_t = \displaystyle\sum_{i=1}^{n} \bar{f}_{it}Dp_{it}, \qquad DQ_t = \sum_{i=1}^{n} \bar{f}_{it}Dq_{it},$

(14.28) $DY_t = \displaystyle\sum_{r=1}^{m} \bar{g}_{rt}Dy_{rt}, \qquad DZ_t = \sum_{r=1}^{m} \bar{g}_{rt}Dz_{rt},$

where $\bar{f}_{it}$ and $\bar{g}_{rt}$ are, respectively, the average factor share of the ith input in $t - 1$ and t, and the average revenue share of the rth product in $t - 1$ and t:

(14.29) $\bar{f}_{it} = \frac{1}{2}(f_{i,t-1} + f_{it}), \qquad \bar{g}_{rt} = \frac{1}{2}(g_{r,t-1} + g_{rt}).$

We consider first the input demand equation (14.22) and note that γ in its output term is not a constant because (14.24) shows that γ varies with revenue and cost. We use (14.24) to define

(14.30)
$$\gamma_t = \left(\frac{R_{t-1}R_t}{C_{t-1}C_t}\right)^{1/2}$$

as the γ value which prevails during the transition from $t - 1$ to t. Using equations (14.27) to (14.29) also, we conclude that the following finite-change version of (14.22) is suggested:

(14.31) $\bar{f}_{it}Dq_{it} = \displaystyle\sum_{r=1}^{m} \theta_i^r(\gamma_t\bar{g}_{rt}Dz_{rt}) + \sum_{j=1}^{n} \pi_{ij}Dp_{jt} + \varepsilon_{it}.$

Summation of (14.31) over i yields $DQ_t = \gamma_t DZ_t$. This is a finite-change version of the total-input decision (8.25), which is reproduced here:

$$(14.32) \qquad d(\log Q) = \gamma d(\log Z).$$

A problem with the finite-change version $DQ_t = \gamma_t DZ_t$ is that it will usually be violated by the definitions of DQ_t, DZ_t, and γ_t in equations (14.27), (14.28), and (14.30). One explanation is in terms of technical change. Equation (14.32) is equivalent to a differential form of the firm's production function, but there may be technical change from $t-1$ to t. To take this possibility into account, we write the finite-change version of (14.32) as

$$(14.33) \qquad DQ_t = \gamma_t DZ_t + E_t,$$

where E_t is a residual which can be computed directly from price-quantity data on inputs and outputs, given the above definitions of DQ_t, DZ_t, and γ_t. Note that (14.33) is similar to the Jorgenson-Griliches [205] procedure for the measurement of productivity change at the level of the aggregate U.S. economy.[8]

Next we subtract E_t from Dq_{it} in the left-hand side of (14.31):

$$(14.34) \qquad \bar{f}_{it}(Dq_{it} - E_t) = \sum_{r=1}^{m} \theta_i^r(\gamma_t \bar{g}_{rt} Dz_{rt}) + \sum_{j=1}^{n} \pi_{ij} Dp_{jt} + \varepsilon_{it}.$$

Summation of (14.34) over i yields $DQ_t - E_t = \gamma_t DZ_t$, which is true in view of (14.33). The subtraction of E_t from each Dq_{it} amounts to a proportional adjustment of the quantities of all inputs in order to accommodate the residual E_t in the observed relation between the firm's aggregate input and output changes. This proportional adjustment may be interpreted as a form of neutral technical change.

Equation (14.34) with constant marginal shares and Slutsky coefficients (θ_i^r and π_{ij}) is a finite-change input demand equation, to be compared with the consumer's equation (13.14). We use (14.23) and (14.25) to write the disturbance covariances in the form

$$(14.35) \qquad \text{cov}(\varepsilon_{it}, \varepsilon_{jt}) = -k\pi_{ij} \qquad i,j = 1, \ldots, n,$$

8. Also note that there will be a residual in (14.33) even when there is no technical change, because the finite-change version of (14.32) is an approximation; see the discussion following equation (13.8) for the analogous case in consumption theory. Therefore, what Jorgenson and Griliches measured was a combination of a (presumably small) finite-change error and technical change.

where

(14.36)
$$k = \frac{\sigma^2}{\psi} > 0.$$

Hence, by postulating that k is a constant we ensure that the input demand system (14.34) for $i = 1, \ldots, n$ has homoscedastic disturbances.

We proceed analogously for the output supply system and note that a finite-change version of equation (14.21) is

(14.37)
$$\bar{g}_{rt} Dz_{rt} = \psi^* \sum_{s=1}^{m} \theta_{rs}^* \left(Dy_{st} - \sum_{i=1}^{n} \theta_i^s Dp_{it} \right) + \varepsilon_{rt}^*,$$

where $\sum_i \theta_i^s Dp_{it}$ is a finite-change version of the Frisch index $d(\log P'^s)$. But note that the covariance (14.26) involves γ, which is not constant over time when we use the definition (14.30). To avoid heteroscedastic supply disturbances, we multiply (14.37) by γ_t,

(14.38)
$$\gamma_t \bar{g}_{rt} Dz_{rt} = \sum_{s=1}^{m} \alpha_{rs} \left(Dy_{st} - \sum_{i=1}^{n} \theta_i^s Dp_{it} \right) + \zeta_{rt}^*,$$

where

(14.39)
$$\alpha_{rs} = \gamma_t \psi^* \theta_{rs}^* \qquad r, s = 1, \ldots, m,$$

(14.40)
$$\zeta_{rt}^* = \gamma_t \varepsilon_{rt}^* \qquad r = 1, \ldots, m.$$

The covariance of $\gamma \varepsilon_r^*$ and $\gamma \varepsilon_s^*$ equals $\sigma^2 \gamma \psi^* \theta_{rs}^* / \psi = k \gamma \psi^* \theta_{rs}^*$ in view of (14.26) and (14.36). It thus follows from (14.39) and (14.40) that the covariance structure of the output supply system (14.38) is

(14.41)
$$\mathrm{cov}\,(\zeta_{rt}^*, \zeta_{st}^*) = k\alpha_{rs} \qquad r, s = 1, \ldots, m.$$

Given the assumption that k is constant, we obtain homoscedastic supply disturbances when $[\alpha_{rs}]$ is a matrix of constants. We shall have more to say about the constancy of this matrix at the end of section 14.7.

14.7   Statistical Discussion of the Parametrization

The input demand system (14.34) with the covariance structure (14.35) is quite similar to the absolute price version (13.14) of the Rotterdam model in consumption theory. Since the disturbances in the system (14.34) are stochastically independent of those of the supply system (14.38), we can view $\gamma_t \bar{g}_{rt} D z_{rt}$ as a predetermined variable in (14.34). This means that the estimation of the input demand system may be viewed as a direct extension of that of the Rotterdam model in absolute prices. However, this statement is subject to the qualification that the marginal shares of the inputs occur not only in (14.34) but also in the supply system (14.38); hence a joint estimation of (14.34) and (14.38) is appropriate in spite of the independence of their disturbances. In addition, (14.38) is nonlinear in the parameters. The model consisting of (14.34) and (14.38) is therefore a nontrivial extension of the Rotterdam model.

We proceed to discuss three hypotheses: input independence, output independence, and input-output separability. Each of these can be tested and/or imposed on the estimates. Testing for output independence or input-output separability amounts to testing linear constraints on parameters: $\alpha_{rs} = 0$ for each $r \neq s$ in (14.38) for the former hypothesis, and θ_i^r independent of r in both (14.34) and (14.38) for the latter. When output independence is imposed, (14.38) is simplified to

$$(14.42) \qquad \gamma_t \bar{g}_{rt} D z_{rt} = \alpha_r \left(D y_{rt} - \sum_{t=1}^{n} \theta_i^r D p_{it} \right) + \zeta_{rt}^*,$$

where $\alpha_r = \gamma_t \psi^* \theta_r^*$, while $\zeta_{1t}^*, \ldots, \zeta_{mt}^*$ are now independently distributed (see eq. [14.41]). When input-output separability is imposed, we delete the superscripts from the marginal shares in both (14.34) and (14.38) with the result that (14.34) now contains the log-change in the output volume index:

$$(14.43) \qquad \bar{f}_{it}(D q_{it} - E_t) = \theta_i(\gamma_t D Z_t) + \sum_{j=1}^{n} \pi_{ij} D p_{jt} + \varepsilon_{it}.$$

This equation is of the same form as (13.14) when $\bar{f}_{it}(D q_{it} - E_t)$ is identified with $\bar{w}_{it} D q_{it}$ and $\gamma_t D Z_t$ with $D Q_t$.

The discussion of input independence is simplified when we consider first how it can be imposed. We reproduce equation (5.43),

$$\mathbf{g}'(\psi^* \Theta^*)^{-1} \mathbf{g} = \frac{\gamma - \psi}{\psi},$$

which shows, when combined with (14.39), that we can obtain a value ψ_t of ψ for the transition from $t - 1$ to t by means of

$$(14.44) \qquad \sum_{r=1}^{m} \sum_{s=1}^{m} \alpha^{rs} \bar{g}_{rt} \bar{g}_{st} = \frac{1}{\psi_t} - \frac{1}{\gamma_t},$$

where α^{rs} is the (r, s)th element of $[\alpha_{rs}]^{-1}$. Thus, equation (14.44) defines ψ_t as a function of the unknown parameter matrix $[\alpha_{rs}]$ and the observable values $\gamma_t, \bar{g}_{1t}, \ldots, \bar{g}_{mt}$.

Under input independence we can simplify equation (14.23) to

$$(14.45) \qquad \pi_{ij} = -\psi\theta_i(1 - \theta_i) \quad \text{if} \quad i = j$$

$$= \psi\theta_i\theta_j \qquad \text{if} \quad i \neq j,$$

where θ_i equals $\sum_r g_r\theta_i^r$ in view of (5.16). Therefore, when the firm is input independent, we can write the substitution term $\sum_j \pi_{ij}Dp_{jt}$ of (14.34) in the form

$$(14.46) \qquad -\psi_t\left(\sum_{r=1}^m \bar{g}_{rt}\theta_i^r\right)\left[Dp_{it} - \sum_{j=1}^n \left(\sum_{r=1}^m \bar{g}_{rt}\theta_j^r\right)Dp_{jt}\right],$$

where the expressions in parentheses are the values of θ_i and θ_j during the transition from $t - 1$ to t. The substitution term (14.46) contains no parameters in addition to those which occur elsewhere in the system, because θ_i^r occurs in the output term of (14.34) and ψ_t can be obtained from $[\alpha_{rs}]$ by means of (14.44).

It is possible to use an estimate of (14.34) in order to verify the extent to which input independence is a satisfactory approximation. This amounts to computing the estimate of the difference $\pi_{ij} - \psi\theta_i\theta_j$ for each $i \neq j$ and each observation (see eq. [14.45]), with ψ specified as the ψ_t obtained from equation (14.44) and θ_i and θ_j as the expressions in parentheses in (14.46). When these estimates are sufficiently close to zero, the investigator may decide that input independence is an adequate approximation. This procedure can be extended straightforwardly to block independent inputs.

Note that the difference $\pi_{ij} - \psi\theta_i\theta_j$ $(i \neq j)$ cannot be exactly zero because π_{ij} is treated as a constant in (14.34) while the ψ and θ_i values vary over time. However, it is possible to formulate a formal test of the hypothesis that this difference vanishes at the sample means. Let the sample consist of T observations. We define $\bar{g}_r$ as the arithmetic mean of the T values g_{rt} and $\bar{\gamma}$ as the antilog of the arithmetic mean of the T values $\log(R_t/C_t)$; these definitions are extensions of (14.29) and (14.30). Then, by substituting $\bar{g}_r$ for $\bar{g}_{rt}$ and $\bar{\gamma}$ for γ_t in (14.44), we obtain the implied value for ψ, after which input independence can be tested by means of the $\frac{1}{2}n(n - 1)$ nonlinear restrictions

$$\pi_{ij} = \psi\left(\sum_{r=1}^m \bar{g}_r\theta_i^r\right)\left(\sum_{r=1}^m \bar{g}_r\theta_j^r\right) \quad \text{if} \quad i \neq j.$$

Also note the implication of the constancy of the matrix $[\alpha_{rs}]$ that ψ^* (the price elasticity of the firm's total supply) is proportional to the cost-revenue ratio; this follows from (14.30) and $\sum_r \sum_s \alpha_{rs} = \gamma_t \psi^*$ (see eq. [14.39]). It is an empirical matter whether this proportionality is an acceptable property for ψ^*. An alternative parametrization with a constant ψ^* can also be formulated. This is a matter of dividing both sides of equations (14.34) and (14.38) by γ_t and treating π_{ij}/γ_t and α_{rs}/γ_t as constants. The reader should have no difficulty verifying that the disturbances $\varepsilon_{it}/\gamma_t$ and ζ_{rt}^*/γ_t are homoscedastic under this specification.

Fifteen

Extensions and Possibilities for Future Research

This final chapter, which has a very heterogeneous content, provides brief discussions of generalizations. Many of the issues considered have been insufficiently analyzed and would merit further investigation.

15.1 Changing Preferences and Technologies

In the theoretical part of this book we assumed that the consumer has stable preferences, but applied workers have frequently found it necessary to use time trends to represent changes in tastes. It is also possible to introduce random shifts in preferences. Such shifts yield random disturbances in the demand equations. A particular type of random shift was considered by Theil [397, section 2.7]; the implied disturbance covariance matrix takes the form (8.14) and is thus identical to that of rational random behavior. See also Clements et al. [90], Pessemier [310], Phlips [312], and Phlips and Rouzier [316].

A changing technology is for the firm what changing preferences are for the consumer. There is a vast literature on the economics of technical change and also on randomness in production. It would be interesting to verify whether random shifts of the production function exist which yield the covariance structures (8.14) and (8.24) of the input demand and output supply disturbances. If these shifts are also such that each input demand disturbance is uncorrelated with each output supply disturbance, this result would amount to an extension for the firm of what was described for the consumer in the previous paragraph.

It seems likely that several features of the differential approach are useful for a systematic analysis of technical change. One example is the Jorgenson-Griliches study [205], quoted in section 14.6, on the measurement of productivity change. The input independence transformation is another example. To clarify this we extend equation (4.1) to

$$(15.1) \qquad\qquad \log z_t = h(t, \mathbf{q}_t),$$

which expresses output in period t as a function of the inputs in that period and calendar time. Many applications of (15.1) use a form of neutral technical change, $h(\ )$ being specified as a function of t plus a function of $\mathbf{q}_t$. The Hessian of $h(\ )$, whose order is $(n + 1) \times (n + 1)$, then has zeros in the first row and column except for the leading element. This means that calendar time is an independent (although uncontrolled) input. If $h(\ )$ is not additively separable in this way, we can apply the input independence transformation, which yields $n + 1$ transformed inputs that are combinations of the n observed inputs and calendar time.

Another area that could benefit from the input independence transformation is the analysis of economic growth. Equation (11.14) provides a Taylor expansion of output as a function of inputs in logarithmic form. Since the transformation diagonalizes the matrix of second derivatives, it implies that (apart from third-order terms) the logarithmic growth rate of output equals the sum of a number of terms, each of which represents the contribution of one transformed input to the growth of output.

15.2   Dynamic Extensions

Houthakker and Taylor [197] extended consumption theory by making preferences dependent on stocks, which are either physical inventories (in the case of durable goods) or of a psychological nature ("habits"). Changes in these stocks are approximated by lagged observable variables, including lagged consumption, which yields a dynamic model. For other contributions to this and related approaches see Lee [236], Lluch [255], Maks and Muysken [263], Phlips [313, 314], Pollak and Wales [326], Powell [332, pp. 58–62], and Taylor and Weiserbs [380]. We also refer to Fisher and Shell [133], Muellbauer [278], and Phlips and Sanz-Ferrer [317] for the measurement of the cost of living when there are changes in tastes.

A natural way of introducing dynamic elements in consumption theory is by postulating that the arguments of the utility function include both the present and the future consumption of each good. Tintner [410, 411] considered such an extension of Hicks's theory in the late 1930s. More recently Lluch [255] proposed a particular dynamic structure which extends the linear expenditure system so that savings enter into the picture. A further elaboration can be found in Lluch, Powell, and Williams [259, chap. 2]; see also Keller [212].

The differential approach can also be extended to utility maximization over time. We write $\mathbf{q}_t = [q_{it}]$ for the n-element quantity vector of the current period t. We assume that the consumer has a horizon of three periods,[1] so that $\mathbf{q}_t$, $\mathbf{q}_{t+1}$, and $\mathbf{q}_{t+2}$ are the arguments of the multiperiod utility function, and postulate that this function takes the form

$$(15.2) \qquad u(\mathbf{q}_t, \mathbf{q}_{t+1}, \mathbf{q}_{t+2}) = f(u_1(\mathbf{q}_t), u_2(\mathbf{q}_{t+1}, \mathbf{q}_{t+2})),$$

which amounts to blockwise dependence with two groups: present and future consumption (see eq. [9.11]).

We write $\mathbf{p}$ for the $3n$-element price vector whose subvectors are $\mathbf{p}_t$, $\mathbf{p}_{t+1}$, and $\mathbf{p}_{t+2}$. We define $\mathbf{q}$ analogously and write M for the total amount available for spending in the three periods, so that the budget constraint is $\mathbf{p}'\mathbf{q} = M$. Maximizing (15.2) subject to this constraint is fully equivalent to that of the utility analysis of blockwise dependence in sections 9.2 to 9.4. In particular, since the first group (S_1) in (15.2) consists of the goods of current consumption, (9.13) for $g = 1$ is the demand equation for total current consumption. After dividing both sides of that equation by W_1 we obtain

$$(15.3) \quad d(\log Q_1) = \frac{\Theta_1}{W_1} d(\log Q) + \frac{\phi}{W_1} \sum_{h=1}^{2} \Theta_{1h} d\left(\log \frac{P_h'}{P'}\right) + \frac{E_1}{W_1},$$

where the left-hand side is now the Divisia volume index of current consumption and $d(\log Q)$ has become the corresponding index of three-period consumption. Hence Θ_1/W_1 is the elasticity of the volume of current consumption with respect to M, which is three-period income. Note that (15.3) is nothing but an aggregate consumption function, where aggregate refers to the consumer's total current expenditure.

Next consider the conditional demand equation (9.21) for $i \in S_1$ and divide both sides by W_1:

$$(15.4) \quad \frac{w_i}{W_1} d(\log q_i) = \theta_i' d(\log Q_1) + \frac{\phi}{W_1} \sum_{j \in S_1} \theta_{ij} d\left(\log \frac{p_j}{P_1}\right) + \frac{\varepsilon_i'}{W_1}.$$

It follows from (13.28) that the left-hand side is the quantity component of the change in w_i/W_1, which is now the share of the ith good in the total current expenditure. In fact, (15.4) is nothing but the demand equation (2.23) of the static (one-period) differential approach. Note further that E_1/W_1 in (15.3) is the random component of the Divisia index $d(\log Q_1)$, and recall that E_1 and ε_i' are stochastically independent under rational random behavior (see eq. [9.23]). Therefore, E_1/W_1 and hence $d(\log Q_1)$ are also independent of the disturbance ε_1'/W_1 in (15.4), which implies that

---

1. The extension to any other number of periods is obvious. The utility specification (15.2) was introduced by Koopmans [223] and Koopmans, Diamond, and Williamson [226] under the name "weak time perspective."

the change in real income is a predetermined variable in the static demand equations of the differential approach. The underlying assumptions are the blockwise dependence specification (15.2) and those of rational random behavior.

Note that ϕ in equations (15.3) and (15.4) is not the income flexibility of the static model. To make the distinction we shall add a star to ϕ in these two equations. It follows from (15.3) that the own-price elasticity of the demand for total current consumption is then

$$(15.5) \qquad \frac{\phi^* \Theta_{11}}{W_1} = \frac{\phi^*}{W_1} \sum_{i \in S_1} \sum_{j \in S_1} \theta_{ij},$$

where the equal sign is based on (9.14). Note that the right-hand side of (15.5) is the sum of the coefficients of all Frisch-deflated price changes in the static system (15.4), and that this sum equals ϕ in view of (2.23) and (2.26). Therefore, under the blockwise dependence specification (15.2), *the income flexibility of the static demand model is equal to the own-price elasticity of the demand for total current consumption.* This is a rather unexpected result.

Remarks

1. A plea can be made for the idea that future incomes and prices should be discounted. This has both a substitution and an income effect; see Theil [397, section 8.7]. Note further that the three-period budget constraint associated with (15.2) implies that the consumer is assumed to be able to borrow and lend. Also note that future prices are typically unknown. One way of handling this is by means of the assumption that such prices are random and that the objective is to maximize expected utility. Another possibility is to postulate that future prices are unknown constants about which information can be obtained, and then to apply the theory of rational random behavior. These two approaches present problems which must still be considered.

2. It would be of interest to verify whether a multiperiod version of the firm's production function yields the result that $-\psi$ in the input allocation decision (4.23) has the interpretation as the own-price elasticity of the demand for total current input. This would be the extension for the firm's inputs of the result for ϕ obtained in the discussion following equation (15.5). This extension would be particularly interesting because we know that ψ^* in (5.33) and (5.40) has the interpretation as the own-price elasticity of the supply of total output. Note that when such a multiproduct generalization makes a distinction between outputs produced in different periods, the firm becomes a multiproduct firm even if it makes only one kind of product.

15.3   The Demand for Leisure and the Supply of Labor

Another extension of consumption theory deals with the household's demand for leisure. We write q_0 for the quantity of leisure (measured in time units) and p_0 for its price, so that the household's "full income" is

(15.6)
$$M = \sum_{i=0}^{n} p_i q_i,$$

which includes the market value of the household's time. The utility function has now $n + 1$ arguments. We consider first the case of blockwise dependence,

(15.7)
$$u(q_0, \mathbf{q}) = f(u_1(q_0), u_2(\mathbf{q})),$$

where $\mathbf{q} = [q_1, \ldots, q_n]'$ is the quantity vector of the goods consumed. As in the case of the previous section, this yields a demand equation for total consumption as well as a conditional demand equation for each consumption good which can be identified with (2.23). In addition, we obtain a separate demand equation for leisure, which is equivalent to a supply equation of labor. This result provides a justification of the conventional separation of consumption theory and labor theory.

However, the specification (15.7) may not be realistic. Imagine that there are three goods other than leisure, and that the correct blockwise dependence specification is

(15.8)
$$u(q_0, \mathbf{q}) = f(u_1(q_0, q_1), u_2(q_2, q_3)).$$

In this case $\mathbf{q} = [q_1 \ q_2 \ q_3]'$ is no longer separable from q_0, so that (2.23) is not applicable to the three goods. Under (15.8) differential demand equations for consumer goods involve the change in the price of leisure. On the other hand, since q_2 and q_3 are separated from q_0 in (15.8), conditional demand equations which do not involve leisure exist for these two goods. This would apply to the meats of section 13.8 if these meats are indeed separable from leisure.

Barnett [22, 23] extended the Rotterdam model to include the demand for leisure and applied it to annual U.S. data of the period 1890–1955, using a five-commodity classification: services, perishables, semidurables, durables, and leisure. He found that the data allow a block independent specification, with the latter three goods separated from the former two. The following matrix is a maximum-likelihood estimate of the price coefficient matrix of the three-good group (normalized within the group):

(15.9)
$$\begin{bmatrix} 0.501 & 0.042 & -0.342 \\ 0.042 & 0.560 & -0.419 \\ -0.342 & -0.419 & 1.378 \end{bmatrix} \begin{array}{l} \text{semidurables} \\ \text{durables} \\ \text{leisure.} \end{array}$$

The negative elements in the last row and column show that semidurables and durables are both specific substitutes of leisure. This is not entirely surprising, since many durables are time-saving goods. Examples are vacuum cleaners, washing machines, dishwashers, electric typewriters, and electronic calculators.

Flinn [138] used the matrix (15.9) to apply a preference independence transformation for each pair of successive years. Since this transformation involves leisure, the quantity of which is measured in time units, it bears some resemblance to the input independence transformation under technical change that was mentioned in the discussion following equation (15.1). Below is shown Flinn's bordered composition matrix for 1950–51:

	Semi-durables	Durables	Leisure	Total
T_1	0.082	0.117	0.795	0.994
T_2	0.018	0.016	−0.028	0.006
T_3	0.004	−0.005	0.002	0.000
Total	0.104	0.127	0.769	1

A comparison with the composition matrices for meats (table 1 in section 11.1) reveals a similar but more extreme pattern. More than 99 percent of the expenditure on the three-good group is allocated to T_1 and virtually nothing to T_3. All three observed goods contribute positively to T_1, while T_2 is a contrast between the two durables categories and leisure. Hence, when the household buys T_2, it gives up leisure so that at least some of the household members supply more labor. The income elasticity (the elasticity with respect to full income) of T_2 is about six times as large as that of T_1; see Flinn [138] for further details.

15.4   The Demand for Durable Goods

In section 15.2 we mentioned the Houthakker-Taylor approach, which involves a consideration of inventories of durable goods. Such goods have several other special features; they include the possibility that purchasing decisions are advanced or postponed, and the fact that these decisions often are yes-or-no (to buy or not to buy) decisions, which is in contrast to the assumption of continuous variation of the quantities of other goods. It should therefore come as no surprise that the treatment of durables in systems of consumer demand equations is relatively primitive in the present state of the art.

Durable goods are frequently introduced in terms of a flow of services rather than annual expenditures on these goods. Barten [27] followed the latter procedure for the Dutch data which were used by Paulus [304] for his

14-commodity system. However, it is unlikely that this made much difference for the model as a whole, since durable goods play a minor role in the data. (Expenditures on automobiles were included only toward the end of the sample period; electrical applicances were also of minor importance.) It is worthwhile to add that the problems caused by durable goods are another reason why it is attractive to work with conditional demand equations of a group. If such a group consists of nondurables which are separated from all other goods, the conditional equations of this group are not affected by the presence of durable goods in other groups.[2]

The picture of durables in demand equation systems is not entirely negative. We mentioned in the discussion following the matrix (15.9) that many durables are time-saving goods, yielding a specific substitution relation with leisure. This has interesting implications for the consumption of durable goods. During a depression, households have an excess supply of free time which they would be glad to sell in the labor market if they could. This excess includes the time from involuntarily unemployed household members as well as time from employed members who work a shorter workweek. The availability of this free time for menial household tasks implies that there is little incentive to economize on the use of time by buying time-saving durable goods. But when the economy recovers and more jobs become available and workweeks become longer, free household time becomes scarce and households buy durables in order to economize on the use of time. Ignoring the specific substitution between leisure and durables will then underestimate the demand for durables during economic expansions. For further details see Barnett [23].

15.5   The Effect of Household Composition

Demand equation systems are usually implemented by means of data on per capita consumption. This procedure ignores the effect of changes in the population composition. Since these changes are presently rather substantial due to declining birth rates and increased longevity, it is appropriate to discuss this subject here.

Equivalent adult scales have been used for a long time in the analysis of household budget data. For example, let an adult man count as 1, an adult woman as 0.9, a teenager as 0.7, a child below 13 years as 0.4, and a baby as 0.2, so that a family consisting of two parents, one teenager, and a baby has

---

2. Two other advantages of conditional demand models were mentioned at the end of section 14.2. Note that the separation argument is similar to that which was used for the conditional equations for q_2 and q_3 in the discussion following equation (15.8).

$1 + 0.9 + 0.7 + 0.2 = 2.8$ equivalent adults. If this family spends \$14,000 in a particular year, its expenditure per equivalent adult is thus \$5000.

The equivalent adult scale discussed above refers to the household's budget as a whole. When we consider the consumption of individual goods such as diapers and wine, we must recognize the fact that the age-specific effects on the consumption of such goods are quite different. This leads to different equivalent adult scales for different goods. If the family of the previous paragraph buys q_i units of the ith good, the quantity purchased per equivalent adult is q_i/a_i units, where a_i need not be 2.8 and will in general depend on i. Barten [25] postulated that the household maximizes a utility function whose arguments are quantities per equivalent adult,

$$(15.10) \qquad u\left(\frac{q_1}{a_1}, \ldots, \frac{q_n}{a_n}\right),$$

subject to the budget constraint $\sum_i p_i q_i = M$, where M is the household's income. Note that $\sum_i p_i q_i$ equals $\sum_i a_i p_i (q_i/a_i)$. On comparing this with (15.10) we conclude that traditional consumption theory is applicable to this situation when p_i and q_i are interpreted as $a_i p_i$ and q_i/a_i, respectively. It is then easy to formulate differential demand equations in which changes in the a_i's play a role. See also Bojer [63], Gorman [161], Kapteyn and Van Praag [210], Muellbauer [276, 277, 280, 283], Parks and Barten [303], Ray [337], and Singh and Nagar [362].

15.6   Uniform Substitutes

We know that under preference independence the change in the demand for each good depends only on the change in its own Frisch-deflated price. However, a weaker condition is sufficient for this result. Since this weaker condition has a better chance of being realistic for a group of goods than for the set of all n goods, we shall discuss it for a group S_g consisting of n_g goods in a block independent framework.

For this group, consider the $n_g \times n_g$ submatrix of the Hessian matrix of the utility function in expenditure terms, multiplied by the scalar $\phi M/\lambda$. We write this matrix in the form

$$(15.11) \qquad \frac{\phi M}{\lambda}\left[\frac{\partial^2 u}{\partial(p_i q_i)\partial(p_j q_j)}\right] = \begin{bmatrix} \times & k & \ldots & k \\ k & \times & \ldots & k \\ \vdots & \vdots & & \vdots \\ k & k & \ldots & \times \end{bmatrix},$$

where all off-diagonal elements are equal to a positive value k, while the diagonal elements (indicated by crosses) take positive values which are irrelevant for our purpose. Since the scalar $\phi M/\lambda$ is negative, (15.11) implies that the marginal utility of a dollar spent on each good of S_g declines by the same amount (equal to $k\lambda/\phi M$) when an additional dollar is spent on any other good of that group. We shall refer to such goods as *uniform substitutes*. This concept could be useful for the market analysis of different brands of the same commodity.

It is shown in Appendix B that (15.11) implies, for $i \in S_g$,

$$(15.12) \qquad \sum_{j \in S_g} \theta_{ij} d\left(\log \frac{p_j}{P_g'}\right) = \frac{\theta_i}{1 - k\Theta_g} d\left(\log \frac{p_i}{P_g'}\right),$$

where Θ_g is the marginal share of S_g (equal to the sum of θ_i over $i \in S_g$). On comparing (15.12) with (13.18) and (13.27), we conclude that the conditional demand equations of uniform substitutes can be written so that the substitution term contains the change in just one Frisch-deflated price. As (15.12) shows, the only difference from the case $k = 0$ is an increase in price sensitivity, θ_i being divided by a positive number which is smaller than 1.

Remarks

1. We mentioned in the discussion following equation (15.11) that the uniform-substitute concept may be useful for the market analysis of different brands of a commodity. Applications of this kind would probably also require consideration of the effects of advertising. One way of doing this is by means of the preference shift analysis in Theil [397, section 2.7], which can be used to express advertising effects in terms of price effects under appropriate conditions. A dynamic extension of the approach would be in order in this case. See also Bultez and Naert [71] and Lambin [230].

2. Since the matrix on the left in (15.11) is symmetric positive definite, it can be viewed as the covariance matrix of a vector of random variables. The right-hand side of (15.11) implies that all pairs of these random variables have the same covariance. An alternative approach is to postulate that the left-hand matrix in (15.11) is the covariance matrix of a random vector whose elements are equicorrelated. This amounts to a different preference structure; it does not yield conditional demand equations that contain only one relative price change (compare eq. [15.12]), but it is nevertheless worth pursuing. We should add that several decades ago Hotelling [190] proposed correlation-type measures of this kind for the definition of substitutes and complements.

15.7 Further Extensions of the Theory of the Firm

We have assumed throughout that the firm operates under competitive conditions, which implies that it takes the prices of its products as given. The following extension was obtained by Theil [398] for a single-product firm which operates under monopolistic conditions on the supply side. We write η for the absolute value of the price elasticity of the demand for the product,

$$(15.13) \qquad \eta = -\frac{d \log z}{d \log y},$$

which must satisfy $\eta > 1$ in order that marginal revenue be positive. The supply equation no longer takes the form (4.31), which contains the product price y on the right. Instead, the logarithmic change in supply becomes negatively proportional to the Frisch price index of the inputs,

$$(15.14) \qquad d(\log z) = -\delta d(\log P'),$$

where $\delta > 0$ is a sufficient condition for maximum profit. This δ is defined as

$$(15.15) \qquad \delta = \frac{\gamma - \psi}{\psi} + \frac{\chi}{\eta},$$

where γ, ψ, and η are defined in equations (4.8), (4.12), and (15.13), respectively, while χ is defined as

$$(15.16) \qquad \chi = 1 - \frac{1}{\eta(\eta - 1)} \frac{d^2 \log z}{d(\log y)^2},$$

which gives $\chi = 1$ when the demand for the product is a constant-elasticity function of its price. Note that η and χ in equations (15.13) and (15.16) involve first and second derivatives of $\log z$ in the same way that γ and ψ involve first and second derivatives of $\log C$.

Jovanovic [208] extended these results by applying the theory of rational random behavior. The result is that a disturbance is added to the right-hand side of (15.14) whose distribution is normal with zero mean and variance $\sigma^2\delta/\gamma\psi$, where σ^2 is the same coefficient as that which occurs in (8.14) and (8.24). Note that this variance is a multiple $-\sigma^2/\gamma\psi$ of the coefficient of $d(\log P')$ in the supply equation (15.14), and that the covariance (8.24) equals the same multiple of the coefficient of $d(\log P'^s)$ in (8.23).

The results described in the two previous paragraphs refer to the single-product firm. When the firm makes several products, some of these may be sold under competitive conditions and others under monopolistic conditions. The extension of (15.14) to the multiproduct firm has not yet been performed. Some further extensions and possible extensions are listed below.

1. In section 12.2 we introduced the quality index for the consumer. The quality concept is not so obvious for the firm's inputs. However, the extension of (12.9) for the firm (with w_i replaced by f_i) can be viewed as a sensitivity index in the sense that this index increases when the firm's input mix shifts toward inputs that are more sensitive to price changes and to a change in their Divisia volume index. This follows from (10.25) and the fact that an increased sensitivity index amounts to a shift toward transformed inputs with higher Divisia elasticities. The matter of sensitivity was pursued by Evans [127] and can be extended to the supply side of a profit-maximizing multiproduct firm.

2. In the examples of the input and output independence transformations given in sections 10.5 and 11.3, the composition matrices (T and T^*) depend only on the factor and revenue shares of the observed inputs and outputs. (The Divisia elasticities λ_i and λ_i^* are not determined by these shares.) Therefore, the composition matrices are observable, at least in these examples. To what extent does this hold generally? Also, can the independence transformation be used for statistical estimation with fewer parameters? Is the output independence transformation of the multiproduct firm an appropriate tool for breaking up conglomerates? We know from section 5.8 that under output independence the multiproduct firm can be broken up into independently operating single-product firms, but note that the independence transformation of the multiproduct firm does not specify the inputs of each of the independent single-product firms.

3. In remark (4) at the end of section 14.5 we mentioned the conjugate supply model which permits estimation of the demand equations of the Rotterdam model when both price changes and quantity changes are endogenous. It would be desirable to provide a link between this supply model and the differential approach to the theory of the firm, which would probably involve matters of aggregation over firms as well as partial and general equilibrium.

Appendix A

Alternative Functional Forms

Below is a summary of parametrizations of the firm and the consumer in addition to those discussed in the text. The list is far from exhaustive; its main objective is to provide a picture of the variety of the proposals made.

The translog specification was mentioned in section 13.3 as an example of a "flexible functional form." The price to be paid for this flexibility is usually a large number of parameters. For example, Hall [169] proposed a multiproduct cost function of the form

$$
\text{(A1)} \qquad C(\mathbf{z}, \mathbf{p}) = \sum_{r=1}^{m} \sum_{s=1}^{m} \sum_{i=1}^{n} \sum_{j=1}^{n} \alpha_{rsij} (z_r z_s p_i p_j)^{1/2},
$$

where α_{rsij} is a constant. The occurrence of four subscripts attached to each coefficient implies that equation (A1) is a practical specification only when there are very few inputs and very few outputs.

Quadratic functions of square roots of variables figure prominently among flexible functional forms, particularly those proposed by Diewert [113, 115, 117]. For example, he considers the case in which the consumer's utility is a quadratic function of the square roots of the quantities,

$$
\text{(A2)} \qquad u(\mathbf{q}) = \sum_{i=1}^{n} a_i q_i^{1/2} + \tfrac{1}{2} \sum_{i=1}^{n} \sum_{j=1}^{n} a_{ij} (q_i q_j)^{1/2},
$$

where the a_i's and a_{ij}'s are constants. The corresponding extension for the firm's cost function involves the square roots of the input prices, while that of the consumer's indirect utility function expresses utility as a quadratic function of the square roots of the price-income ratios. An extension of the linear expenditure system which involves a quadratic term in the square roots of the prices was proposed by Nasse [290] and is described in section 14.4.

Johansen [202] proposed a class of additive utility functions. He also considered the Fourgeaud-Nataf formulation, which expresses the demand for each consumer good as a function of the relative price of that good and real income, with the same price index used for both deflations (see also Carlevaro [78]). Barten [35] considered Johansen's class further, as well as corresponding indirect utility functions. He noted that by adding quadratic terms the translog and Diewert's specifications appear as special cases. Of course, the addition of such terms yields a large number of parameters.

Numerous proposals have been made to generalize the Cobb-Douglass production function. The CES and translog specifications in section 4.1 are two examples. A spline extension was formulated by Poirier [318]. Another generalization, from Diewert, is

$$\text{(A3)} \qquad \log z = a + \sum_{i=1}^{n} \sum_{j=1}^{n} b_{ij} \log \frac{q_i + q_j}{2},$$

which reduces to (4.2) when $[b_{ij}]$ is a diagonal matrix. This generalization requires that the q_i's all have the same dimension.

An interesting specification of the block independent utility structure (2.33) is

$$\text{(A4)} \qquad u_g(\mathbf{q}_g) = \alpha_g \left[\sum_{i \in S_g} \beta_i (q_i - \gamma_i)^{k_g} \right]^{k/k_g} \qquad g = 1, \ldots, G,$$

where the α's, β's, γ's, and k's are all constant. This specification is known as the S-branch utility tree and was proposed by Brown and Heien [70]; it amounts to a generalization of the linear expenditure system. Barnett [20] formulated a generalized hypocycloidal demand model, which is blockwise dependent and contains (A4) as a special case.

Theil [384, section 6.9] noted that cumulated distribution functions can be used as utility functions under weak conditions. The logarithm of such a distribution function is additive in its arguments under stochastic independence, which should be compared with preference independence; the extension of this analogy to block independence is the stochastic independence of subvectors of random variables. Van Praag [419] considered in particular the case of lognormal utility functions.

Appendix B

Derivations for Consumption Theory

This appendix consists of four subsections. The first concerns Barten's fundamental matrix equation, its solution, and the derivatives of the indirect utility function. The second deals with the consumer as a profit-maximizing seller of utility (section 6.1). The third provides the second differentials of the volume indexes of section 6.4, which involve a curvature measure of the consumer's distance function. The fourth concerns the uniform substitutes of section 15.6.

Barten's Matrix Equation and Related Matters

Differentiation of $\mathbf{p'q} = M$ (the budget constraint) with respect to M and $\mathbf{p}'$ gives

$$(B1) \qquad \mathbf{p}' \frac{\partial \mathbf{q}}{\partial M} = 1, \qquad \mathbf{p}' \frac{\partial \mathbf{q}}{\partial \mathbf{p}'} = -\mathbf{q}',$$

where $\partial \mathbf{q}/\partial \mathbf{p}'$ is the $n \times n$ matrix with $\partial q_i/\partial p_j$ as (i, j)th element. We also differentiate (2.2) with respect to M and $\mathbf{p}'$, applying the chain rule on the left. This yields

$$(B2) \qquad \mathbf{U} \frac{\partial \mathbf{q}}{\partial M} = \frac{\partial \lambda}{\partial M} \mathbf{p}, \qquad \mathbf{U} \frac{\partial \mathbf{q}}{\partial \mathbf{p}'} = \lambda \mathbf{I} + \mathbf{p} \frac{\partial \lambda}{\partial \mathbf{p}'},$$

after which (2.21) is obtained by arranging the four equations of (B1) and (B2) in partitioned matrix form.

If $\mathbf{U}$ is negative definite, the inverse of the bordered Hessian on the far left in (2.21) can be written as

$$(B3) \qquad \frac{1}{\mathbf{p'U}^{-1}\mathbf{p}} \begin{bmatrix} (\mathbf{p'U}^{-1}\mathbf{p})\mathbf{U}^{-1} - \mathbf{U}^{-1}\mathbf{p}(\mathbf{U}^{-1}\mathbf{p})' & \mathbf{U}^{-1}\mathbf{p} \\ (\mathbf{U}^{-1}\mathbf{p})' & -1 \end{bmatrix}.$$

Premultiplication of (2.21) by the matrix (B3) gives

(B4) $$\frac{\partial \lambda}{\partial M} = \frac{1}{\mathbf{p}'\mathbf{U}^{-1}\mathbf{p}}, \qquad \frac{\partial \mathbf{q}}{\partial M} = \frac{1}{\mathbf{p}'\mathbf{U}^{-1}\mathbf{p}}\,\mathbf{U}^{-1}\mathbf{p},$$

(B5) $$\frac{\partial \mathbf{q}}{\partial \mathbf{p}'} = \lambda \mathbf{U}^{-1} - \frac{\lambda}{\mathbf{p}'\mathbf{U}^{-1}\mathbf{p}}\,\mathbf{U}^{-1}\mathbf{p}(\mathbf{U}^{-1}\mathbf{p})' - \frac{1}{\mathbf{p}'\mathbf{U}^{-1}\mathbf{p}}\,\mathbf{U}^{-1}\mathbf{p}\mathbf{q}',$$

after which (2.22) is obtained from (B5) and some minor rearrangements based on (B4).

Next we take the differential of the ith equation of the demand system (2.1), $dq_i = (\partial q_i/\partial M)dM + \sum_j (\partial q_i/\partial p_j)dp_j$, which we multiply by p_i/M:

$$\frac{p_i}{M}\,dq_i = p_i\frac{\partial q_i}{\partial M}\,d(\log M) + \sum_{j=1}^{n}\frac{p_i p_j}{M}\frac{\partial q_i}{\partial p_j}\,d(\log p_j).$$

It follows from (2.7) and (2.17) that this can be written as

(B6) $$w_i d(\log q_i) = \theta_i d(\log M) + \sum_{j=1}^{n}\frac{p_i p_j}{M}\frac{\partial q_i}{\partial p_j}\,d(\log p_j).$$

Using (2.22) also, we write the last term of (B6) as

(B7) $$\sum_{j=1}^{n}\left(\frac{\lambda p_i p_j u^{ij}}{M} - \frac{\lambda/M}{\partial\lambda/\partial M}\,\theta_i\theta_j - \theta_i\frac{p_j q_j}{M}\right)d(\log p_j)$$

$$= \phi\sum_{j=1}^{n}\theta_{ij}d(\log p_j) - \phi\theta_i\sum_{j=1}^{n}\theta_j d(\log p_j) - \theta_i\sum_{j=1}^{n}w_j d(\log p_j),$$

where the equal sign is based on (2.24) and (2.19). The last term in (B7) is $-\theta_i$ multiplied by the Divisia price index, which is used to deflate the income term in (B6). The second-last term is $-\phi\theta_i$ multiplied by the Frisch price index, which is used to deflate the first term on the right in (B7). The proof of the equivalence of (B6) and (2.23) is completed when we succeed in showing that $\sum_j \theta_{ij} = \theta_i$, which is equation (2.25). For this purpose we note from (2.24) that $\sum_j \theta_{ij}$ equals a multiple $\lambda p_i/\phi M$ of $\sum_j u^{ij}p_j$, which is equal to the product of $\lambda p_i/\phi M$ and the ratio of $\partial q_i/\partial M$ to $\partial\lambda/\partial M$ in view of (B4). It follows from (2.17) and (2.19) that this product is equal to θ_i.

To prove (3.3) we apply the chain rule to (3.1):

$$\frac{\partial u_I}{\partial M} = \sum_{i=1}^{n}\frac{\partial u}{\partial q_i}\frac{\partial q_i}{\partial M}, \qquad \frac{\partial u_I}{\partial p_j} = \sum_{i=1}^{n}\frac{\partial u}{\partial q_i}\frac{\partial q_i}{\partial p_j}.$$

The proof of (3.3) is then completed by means of (2.2) and (B1).

The Consumer as a Profit-Maximizer

The differential of $q_i = -\partial\pi/\partial p_i$ (see eq. [6.5]) is

$$dq_i = -\frac{\partial^2\pi}{\partial p_i \partial y}\,dy - \sum_{j=1}^{n}\frac{\partial^2\pi}{\partial p_i \partial p_j}\,dp_j,$$

which we write, using $w_i d(\log q_i) = (p_i/M)dq_i$, as

(B8) $$w_i d(\log q_i) = -\frac{p_i y}{M}\frac{\partial^2\pi}{\partial p_i \partial y}\,d(\log y) - \sum_{j=1}^{n}\frac{p_i p_j}{M}\frac{\partial^2\pi}{\partial p_i \partial p_j}\,d(\log p_j).$$

In the next paragraph we shall prove

(B9) $$d(\log y) = \frac{M/y^2}{\partial^2\pi/\partial y^2}\,d(\log Q) - \frac{1/y}{\partial^2\pi/\partial y^2}\sum_{j=1}^{n}p_j\frac{\partial^2\pi}{\partial p_j \partial y}\,d(\log p_j),$$

which we substitute in (B8):

(B10) $$w_i d(\log q_i) = -\frac{p_i}{y}\frac{\partial^2\pi/\partial p_i \partial y}{\partial^2\pi/\partial y^2}\,d(\log Q) - \sum_{j=1}^{n}\frac{p_i p_j}{M}\frac{\partial^2\pi}{\partial p_i \partial p_j}\,d(\log p_j)$$

$$+ \frac{1/M}{\partial^2\pi/\partial y^2}\sum_{j=1}^{n}p_i p_j\frac{\partial^2\pi}{\partial p_i \partial y}\frac{\partial^2\pi}{\partial p_j \partial y}\,d(\log p_j).$$

We define

(B11) $$\theta_i = -\frac{p_i}{y}\frac{\partial^2\pi/\partial p_i \partial y}{\partial^2\pi/\partial y^2}, \qquad \phi = -\frac{y^2}{M}\frac{\partial^2\pi}{\partial y^2},$$

so that the first term on the right in (B10) becomes $\theta_i d(\log Q)$, which agrees with the real-income term in (2.23). The last term in (B10) can be written in the form $-\phi\theta_i \sum_j \theta_j d(\log p_j) = -\phi\theta_i d(\log P')$. This agrees with the price deflator term of (2.23), which is shown (apart from sign) in (2.27). Finally, with θ_{ij} defined in (6.7), the second term in (B10) takes the form $\phi \sum_j \theta_{ij}d(\log p_j)$, which completes the proof of the equivalence of (B10) and (2.23) under the specification (B11) and (6.7).[1]

---

1. Note that $\sum_j \theta_{ij} = \theta_i$ follows from (6.6), (6.7), and (B11). Similarly, $\sum_i \theta_i = 1$ follows from (B11) and the homogeneity implication of $\pi(\ )$ which is obtained by replacing p_i by y in (6.6).

To prove (B9) we write (6.3) as $\pi = yu - M$, so that

$$dM = -d\pi + udy + ydu$$

$$= -\left(\frac{\partial\pi}{\partial y}dy + \sum_{j=1}^{n}\frac{\partial\pi}{\partial p_j}dp_j\right) + \frac{\partial\pi}{\partial y}dy + y\frac{\partial^2\pi}{\partial y^2}dy + y\sum_{j=1}^{n}\frac{\partial^2\pi}{\partial y\partial p_j}dp_j,$$

where use is made of $\partial\pi/\partial y = u$ (see eq. [6.5]) for the terms after the parentheses. Using $\partial\pi/\partial p_j = -q_j$ also, we can write this result as

$$dM - \sum_{j=1}^{n}q_j dp_j = y^2\frac{\partial^2\pi}{\partial y^2}d(\log y) + y\sum_{j=1}^{n}p_j\frac{\partial^2\pi}{\partial y\partial p_j}d(\log p_j).$$

By dividing this by M we obtain $d(\log Q)$ on the left, after which (B9) is obtained by solving the equation for $d(\log y)$.

Two Volume Indexes and the Curvature of the Distance Function

The following results were proved by Laitinen [228] for the volume indexes defined in (6.29) and (6.30):

(B12) $\log Q_A(\mathbf{q} + \Delta\mathbf{q}, \mathbf{q}|u(\mathbf{q})) \approx d(\log Q) - \frac{1}{2}(\Pi + \phi\Pi') - \frac{1}{2}\tau[d(\log Q)]^2,$

(B13) $\log Q_B(u(\mathbf{q} + \Delta\mathbf{q}), u(\mathbf{q})|\mathbf{q})$

$$\approx d(\log Q) - \frac{1}{2}(\Pi + \phi\Pi') + d(\log Q)d\left(\log\frac{P}{P'}\right) + \frac{1}{2}\tau[d(\log Q)]^2.$$

The leading term is in both cases the Divisia volume index, which is similar to (6.36). The term $-\frac{1}{2}(\Pi + \phi\Pi')$ also occurs in all three equations, while the last term of (6.36) occurs in (B13) but not in (B12). In addition, (B12) and (B13) contain the square of the Divisia volume index multiplied by $\pm\frac{1}{2}\tau$, where τ is defined as

(B14) $$\tau = -M^2\sum_{i=1}^{n}\sum_{j=1}^{n}\frac{\partial^2 t}{\partial(p_iq_i)\partial(p_jq_j)}\theta_i\theta_j.$$

This τ is a curvature measure of the distance function $t(\ )$, to be compared with the role of ψ with respect to the cost function in (4.12) and (5.10).

An alternative expression is

(B15) $$\tau = -\frac{1}{\phi}\sum_{i=1}^{n}\sum_{j=1}^{n}\theta^{ij}(\theta_i - w_i)(\theta_j - w_j),$$

where θ^{ij} is the (i, j)th element of $[\theta_{ij}]^{-1}$. Thus, τ is a positive multiple $(-1/\phi)$ of a positive definite quadratic form in $\theta_1 - w_1, \ldots, \theta_n - w_n$, so that it is positive except when all goods have unitary income elasticities. Hence τ may be viewed as a measure of the degree to which the consumer's preferences are nonhomothetic. Under preference independence we can simplify (B15) to

$$(B16) \qquad \tau = -\frac{1}{\phi} \sum_{i=1}^{n} \theta_i \left(\frac{w_i}{\theta_i} - 1\right)^2,$$

which amounts to a multiple $-1/\phi$ of the Frisch variance of the reciprocal income elasticities (see the last paragraph of section 12.4).

Uniform Substitutes

We write equation (15.11) in the form

$$(B17) \qquad \frac{\phi M}{\lambda} \left[\frac{\partial^2 u}{\partial(p_i q_i)\partial(p_j q_j)} \right] = \mathbf{D}^{-1} + k\iota\iota',$$

where $\mathbf{D}$ is a diagonal matrix whose diagonal elements (d_i for $i \in S_g$) are all positive. It follows from (2.28) that the left-hand side of (B17) is the gth principal submatrix of the $n \times n$ matrix $[\theta^{ij}]$. Thus, by inverting (B17) we obtain

$$(B18) \qquad [\theta_{ij}] = \mathbf{D} - \frac{k}{1 + k\iota'\mathbf{D}\iota} \mathbf{D}\iota\iota'\mathbf{D},$$

where $[\theta_{ij}]$ is here the $n_g \times n_g$ matrix of the θ_{ij}'s whose subscripts both fall under S_g. We conclude from (B18) that, for $i \neq j$, θ_{ij} equals a negative multiple of $d_i d_j$, which means that uniform substitutes are specific substitutes.

We obtain $\theta_i = d_i - (k\iota'\mathbf{D}\iota)d_i/(1 + k\iota'\mathbf{D}\iota)$ by postmultiplying (B18) by ι and using (2.35). We write this in the simpler form

$$(B19) \qquad d_i = (1 + k\iota'\mathbf{D}\iota)\theta_i,$$

and note that this implies $\theta_i > 0$; hence, uniform substitutes cannot be inferior goods. Summation of (B19) over $i \in S_g$ yields $\iota'\mathbf{D}\iota = (1 + k\iota'\mathbf{D}\iota)\Theta_g$. We solve this equation for $\iota'\mathbf{D}\iota$, which yields the result that $1 + k\iota'\mathbf{D}\iota$ equals the reciprocal of $1 - k\Theta_g$. On combining this with (B18) and (B19), we find that θ_{ii} and θ_{ij} for $i \neq j$ are equal to the ratios of $\theta_i(1 - k\theta_i)$ and $-k\theta_i\theta_j$, respectively, to $1 - k\Theta_g$. Therefore,

$$\sum_{j \in S_g} \theta_{ij} d(\log p_j) = \frac{\theta_i}{1 - k\Theta_g} \left[d(\log p_i) - k \sum_{j \in S_g} \theta_j d(\log p_j) \right]$$

$$= \frac{\theta_i}{1 - k\Theta_g} [d(\log p_i) - k\Theta_g d(\log P'_g)],$$

after which (15.12) is obtained by subtracting $d(\log P'_g)$ multiplied by $\sum_j \theta_{ij} = \theta_i$.

Appendix C

Derivations for the Cost-minimizing Firm

This appendix consists of five subsections. The first two deal with the firm's matrix equation and its solution, which yields the input demand equations. The third develops several properties of the cost function. In the fourth we derive the output supply equations which emerge when the cost-minimizing firm adjusts its outputs so as to maximize profit. At the end we consider the case of input-output separability.

The Matrix Equation of the Firm

We construct the Lagrangean function

(C1) $$L(\mathbf{q}, \rho) = \sum_{i=1}^{n} p_i q_i - \rho h(\mathbf{q}, \mathbf{z}).$$

We obtain (5.12) by differentiating (C1) with respect to $\log q_i$ and equating the derivative to zero. For the second-order condition we differentiate (C1) with respect to $\log q_i$ and $\log q_j$,

(C2) $$\frac{\partial^2 L}{\partial(\log q_i)\partial(\log q_j)} = \delta_{ij} p_i q_i - \rho \frac{\partial^2 h}{\partial(\log q_i)\partial(\log q_j)},$$

where δ_{ij} is the Kronecker delta. For a cost minimum it is sufficient that the $n \times n$ matrix with (C2) as (i, j)th element is symmetric positive definite. This matrix is a (positive) multiple $1/C$ of the matrix $\mathbf{F} - \gamma\mathbf{H}$ because $f_i = p_i q_i/C$ and $\gamma = \rho/C$.[1] Accordingly, we assume that $\mathbf{F} - \gamma\mathbf{H}$ is a symmetric positive definite matrix.

1. Note that $f_i = p_i q_i/C$ is simply a definition and that $\gamma = \rho/C$ is obtained by combining the definition (5.9) with the first-order condition (5.12) under the output-homogeneous condition (5.4) on $h(\ )$; see the first paragraph of section 5.4.

We proceed to differentiate (5.12) with respect to $\log z_r$:

(C3) $\quad p_i q_i \dfrac{\partial \log q_i}{\partial \log z_r} - \rho \dfrac{\partial \log \rho}{\partial \log z_r} \dfrac{\partial h}{\partial \log q_i}$

$$- \rho \sum_{j=1}^{n} \frac{\partial^2 h}{\partial(\log q_i)\partial(\log q_j)} \frac{\partial \log q_j}{\partial \log z_r} - \rho \frac{\partial^2 h}{\partial(\log q_i)\partial(\log z_r)} = 0.$$

The second term equals $-p_i q_i \partial(\log \rho)/\partial(\log z_r)$ in view of (5.12). So, again using $f_i = p_i q_i / C$ and $\gamma = \rho / C$, we can write (C3) after dividing by C for all pairs (i, r) in the form

(C4) $$\qquad (\mathbf{F} - \gamma \mathbf{H}) \frac{\partial \log \mathbf{q}}{\partial \log \mathbf{z}'} - \mathbf{F}\iota \frac{\partial \log \rho}{\partial \log \mathbf{z}'} = \gamma \mathbf{H}^*,$$

where $\mathbf{H}^*$ is defined in (5.14).

Next we differentiate (5.12) with respect to $\log p_j$ for $j \neq i$, and we divide by C. This yields, after rearrangements,

$$f_i \frac{\partial \log q_i}{\partial \log p_j} - f_i \frac{\partial \log \rho}{\partial \log p_j} - \gamma \sum_{k=1}^{n} \frac{\partial^2 h}{\partial(\log q_i)\partial(\log q_k)} \frac{\partial \log q_k}{\partial \log p_j} = 0.$$

Differentiation of (5.12) with respect to $\log p_i$ followed by division by C gives a similar result except for an extra term f_i on the left. Hence,

(C5) $$\qquad (\mathbf{F} - \gamma \mathbf{H}) \frac{\partial \log \mathbf{q}}{\partial \log \mathbf{p}'} - \mathbf{F}\iota \frac{\partial \log \rho}{\partial \log \mathbf{p}'} = -\mathbf{F}.$$

It is shown below that the derivatives of (5.2) can be written as

(C6) $$\qquad \iota' \mathbf{F} \frac{\partial \log \mathbf{q}}{\partial \log \mathbf{z}'} = \gamma \mathbf{g}', \qquad \iota' \mathbf{F} \frac{\partial \log \mathbf{q}}{\partial \log \mathbf{p}'} = \mathbf{0}.$$

The matrix equation (5.13) is then obtained by combining equations (C4), (C5), and (C6).

To verify (C6) we consider the marginal cost of the rth product,

(C7) $$\qquad \frac{\partial C}{\partial z_r} = \sum_{i=1}^{n} p_i \frac{\partial q_i}{\partial z_r} = \frac{C}{z_r} \sum_{i=1}^{n} f_i \frac{\partial \log q_i}{\partial \log z_r},$$

and we differentiate (5.2) with respect to $\log z_r$:

$$\sum_{i=1}^{n} \frac{\partial h}{\partial \log q_i} \frac{\partial \log q_i}{\partial \log z_r} + \frac{\partial h}{\partial \log z_r} = 0.$$

It follows from (5.12) that this is equivalent to

(C8)
$$\frac{C}{\rho} \sum_{i=1}^{n} f_i \frac{\partial \log q_i}{\partial \log z_r} + \frac{\partial h}{\partial \log z_r} = 0,$$

and from (C7) that it is also equivalent to

(C9)
$$\frac{z_r}{\rho} \frac{\partial C}{\partial z_r} + \frac{\partial h}{\partial \log z_r} = 0.$$

We obtain $\rho = \sum_r z_r(\partial C/\partial z_r)$, confirming (5.15), by summing (C9) over r and using (5.4). On combining this result for ρ with (5.6) and (C9), we obtain

(C10)
$$g_r = \frac{z_r}{\rho} \frac{\partial C}{\partial z_r} = -\frac{\partial h}{\partial \log z_r},$$

after which the proof of the first equation in (C6) is completed by substituting (C10) in (C8) and using $\gamma = \rho/C$. The verification of the second equation in (C6) is analogous; it involves differentiation of (5.2) with respect to $\log p_i$ as well as

(C11)
$$\frac{\partial h}{\partial \log q_i} = \frac{f_i}{\gamma},$$

which is obtained from (5.12) and $\gamma = \rho/C$. Note that (C11) is the extension of (4.6) for the multiproduct firm.

The Input Demand Equations

It is a matter of straightforward algebra to verify that

(C12)
$$\begin{bmatrix} \mathbf{F}^{-1}(\mathbf{F} - \gamma\mathbf{H})\mathbf{F}^{-1} & \iota \\ \iota' & 0 \end{bmatrix}^{-1} = \begin{bmatrix} \psi(\Theta - \theta\theta') & \theta \\ \theta' & -1/\psi \end{bmatrix},$$

where

(C13)
$$\psi = \iota'\mathbf{F}(\mathbf{F} - \gamma\mathbf{H})^{-1}\mathbf{F}\iota > 0,$$

(C14)
$$\Theta = \frac{1}{\psi} \mathbf{F}(\mathbf{F} - \gamma\mathbf{H})^{-1}\mathbf{F},$$

(C15)
$$\theta = \Theta\iota = \frac{1}{\psi} \mathbf{F}(\mathbf{F} - \gamma\mathbf{H})^{-1}\mathbf{F}\iota.$$

Premultiplication of equation (5.13) by (C12) yields the following solutions:

(C16)
$$\frac{\partial \log \rho}{\partial \log \mathbf{p}'} = \boldsymbol{\theta}',$$

(C17)
$$\mathbf{F}\frac{\partial \log \mathbf{q}}{\partial \log \mathbf{p}'} = -\psi(\boldsymbol{\Theta} - \boldsymbol{\theta\theta}'),$$

(C18)
$$\frac{\partial \log \rho}{\partial \log \mathbf{z}'} = \frac{\gamma}{\psi}\mathbf{g}' - \gamma\boldsymbol{\theta}'\mathbf{F}^{-1}\mathbf{H}^*,$$

(C19)
$$\mathbf{F}\frac{\partial \log \mathbf{q}}{\partial \log \mathbf{z}'} = \gamma\boldsymbol{\theta}\mathbf{g}' + \gamma\psi(\boldsymbol{\Theta} - \boldsymbol{\theta\theta}')\mathbf{F}^{-1}\mathbf{H}^*.$$

The differential demand equation (5.8) is directly obtained from (C17) and (C19), with θ_i^r defined as the (i, r)th element of the $n \times m$ matrix

(C20)
$$\mathbf{K} = [\theta_i^r] = \boldsymbol{\theta\iota}^{*\prime} + \psi(\boldsymbol{\Theta} - \boldsymbol{\theta\theta}')\mathbf{F}^{-1}\mathbf{H}^*\mathbf{G}^{-1},$$

where $\boldsymbol{\iota}^*$ is a column vector of m unit elements and $\mathbf{G}$ is a diagonal $m \times m$ matrix whose rth diagonal element is g_r. Postmultiplication of (C20) by $\mathbf{g}$ gives

(C21)
$$\mathbf{Kg} = \boldsymbol{\theta},$$

which confirms (5.16). To verify (C21) we note that postmultiplication of (C20) by $\mathbf{g}$ yields $\boldsymbol{\theta}$ for the first term in the third member (because $\boldsymbol{\iota}^{*\prime}\mathbf{g} = 1$); hence we must prove that this multiplication yields zero for the last term. This follows from $\mathbf{G}^{-1}\mathbf{g} = \boldsymbol{\iota}^*$ and

(C22)
$$\mathbf{H}^*\boldsymbol{\iota}^* = \mathbf{0},$$

which is obtained by differentiating (5.4) with respect to $\log q_1, \ldots, \log q_n$.

Properties of the Cost Function

It follows from equations (C16), (C18), and (5.11) that

(C23) $$d(\log \rho) = \frac{1}{\psi}d(\log Q) + \boldsymbol{\theta}'[d(\log \mathbf{p}) - \gamma\mathbf{F}^{-1}\mathbf{H}^*d(\log \mathbf{z})],$$

which shows that ψ can be interpreted as the reciprocal of the Divisia elasticity of total marginal cost (or of the marginal cost of a proportionate output increase). This may be viewed as the firm's version of the consumer's income flexibility, which is the reciprocal of the income elasticity of the marginal utility of income (see eq. [2.19]).

In the next paragraph we shall prove

(C24) $\qquad \dfrac{\partial^2 \log C}{\partial(\log \mathbf{z})\partial(\log \mathbf{z}')} = \gamma^2\left(\dfrac{1}{\psi} - 1\right)\mathbf{g}\mathbf{g}' - \gamma^2(\mathbf{g}\mathbf{\theta}'\mathbf{F}^{-1}\mathbf{H}^* + \mathbf{H}^{*\prime}\mathbf{F}^{-1}\mathbf{\theta}\mathbf{g}')$

$$- \gamma^2\psi\mathbf{H}^{*\prime}\mathbf{F}^{-1}(\mathbf{\Theta} - \mathbf{\theta}\mathbf{\theta}')\mathbf{F}^{-1}\mathbf{H}^* - \gamma\mathbf{H}^{**},$$

where $\mathbf{H}^{**} = \partial^2 h/\partial(\log \mathbf{z})\partial(\log \mathbf{z}')$. This matrix satisfies $\mathbf{H}^{**}\mathbf{\iota}^* = \mathbf{0}$, which follows from differentiation of (5.4) with respect to $\log z_1, \ldots, \log z_m$ (compare eq. [C22]). It is then readily verified, by premultiplying (C24) by $\mathbf{\iota}^{*\prime}$ and postmultiplying by $\mathbf{\iota}^*$ and using $\mathbf{g}'\mathbf{\iota}^* = 1$, that the sum of all m^2 elements of the left-hand matrix in (C24) is equal to $\gamma^2(1/\psi - 1)$, which confirms (5.10).

To verify (C24) we use

(C25) $\qquad \dfrac{\partial \log C}{\partial \log z_r} = \gamma g_r = -\gamma \dfrac{\partial h}{\partial \log z_r},$

which follows from (C10) and $\gamma = \rho/C$. We differentiate the first and last members of (C25) with respect to $\log z_s$. This yields, after rearrangements,

$$\dfrac{\partial^2 \log C}{\partial(\log \mathbf{z})\partial(\log \mathbf{z}')} = \gamma\mathbf{g}\,\dfrac{\partial \log \gamma}{\partial \log \mathbf{z}'} - \gamma\mathbf{H}^{**} - \gamma\mathbf{H}^{*\prime}\,\dfrac{\partial \log \mathbf{q}}{\partial \log \mathbf{z}'},$$

after which (C24) is confirmed by (C19) and

(C26) $\qquad \dfrac{\partial \log \gamma}{\partial \log \mathbf{z}'} = \gamma\left(\dfrac{1}{\psi} - 1\right)\mathbf{g}' - \gamma\mathbf{\theta}'\mathbf{F}^{-1}\mathbf{H}^*,$

which follows from $\gamma = \rho/C$, (C18), and (C25).

We shall need two other properties of the cost function for the supply equations in the next subsection. Let $\mathbf{P}$ be the $n \times n$ diagonal matrix with the input price p_i as ith diagonal element; let $\mathbf{Y}$ be the $m \times m$ diagonal matrix with $\partial C/\partial z_r$ as rth diagonal element. (Hence $\mathbf{Y}$ has the output prices $y_1, \ldots, y_m$ on the diagonal under profit-maximization.) The two properties are

(C27) $\qquad \dfrac{\partial^2 C}{\partial \mathbf{p}\partial \mathbf{z}'} = \mathbf{P}^{-1}\mathbf{K}\mathbf{Y},$

(C28) $\quad \dfrac{\partial^2 C}{\partial \mathbf{z}\partial \mathbf{z}'} = \dfrac{1}{\gamma\rho}\,\mathbf{Y}\mathbf{G}^{-1}\left[\dfrac{\partial^2 \log C}{\partial(\log \mathbf{z})\partial(\log \mathbf{z}')} + \gamma^2\mathbf{g}\mathbf{g}' - \gamma\mathbf{G}\right]\mathbf{G}^{-1}\mathbf{Y}.$

To verify these results we use Shephard's lemma ($\partial C/\partial \mathbf{p} = \mathbf{q}$), which shows that the left-hand side of (C27) equals $\partial \mathbf{q}/\partial \mathbf{z}'$. We also use (C20) and $\iota^{*\prime}\mathbf{G} = \mathbf{g}'$ to write (C19) as

$$(\text{C29}) \qquad \mathbf{F}\frac{\partial \log \mathbf{q}}{\partial \log \mathbf{z}'} = \gamma \mathbf{KG},$$

after which (C27) is confirmed by pre- and postmultiplication of (C29) by $\mathbf{P}^{-1}$ and $\mathbf{G}^{-1}\mathbf{Y}$, respectively, and using (C10) and $\gamma = \rho/C$. To prove (C28), we differentiate

$$\frac{\partial C}{\partial z_r} = \frac{C}{z_r}\frac{\partial \log C}{\partial \log z_r}$$

with respect to z_s, so that $\partial^2 C/\partial z_r \partial z_s$ becomes

$$\frac{C}{z_r z_s}\left[\frac{\partial^2 \log C}{\partial(\log z_r)\partial(\log z_s)} + \frac{\partial \log C}{\partial \log z_r}\frac{\partial \log C}{\partial \log z_s} - \delta_{rs}\frac{\partial \log C}{\partial \log z_r}\right],$$

after which (C28) follows from (C25).

The Output Supply Equations

The first-order condition for maximum profit is $\partial C/\partial z_r = y_r$ for $r = 1, \ldots, m$, which yields $\sum_t (\partial^2 C/\partial z_r \partial z_t)(\partial z_t/\partial y_s) = \delta_{rs}$ when differentiated with respect to y_s. We write this in the form

$$(\text{C30}) \qquad \sum_{t=1}^{m} \frac{\partial^2 C}{\partial z_r \partial z_t} z_t \frac{\partial \log z_t}{\partial \log y_s} = \delta_{rs} y_s.$$

We have $z_t = R g_t/y_t$ from (5.28), so that (C30) for all pairs (r, s) can be written as

$$(\text{C31}) \qquad R\frac{\partial^2 C}{\partial \mathbf{z}\partial \mathbf{z}'}\mathbf{Y}^{-1}\mathbf{G}\frac{\partial \log \mathbf{z}}{\partial \log \mathbf{y}'} = \mathbf{Y},$$

where $\mathbf{Y}$ is the diagonal matrix which was defined in the discussion preceding equation (C27).

We define $\mathbf{y} = \mathbf{Y}\iota^*$ and solve (C31),

$$(\text{C32}) \qquad \mathbf{G}\frac{\partial \log \mathbf{z}}{\partial \log \mathbf{y}'} = \frac{1}{R}\mathbf{Y}\left(\frac{\partial^2 C}{\partial \mathbf{z}\partial \mathbf{z}'}\right)^{-1}\mathbf{Y} = \psi^*\mathbf{\Theta}^*,$$

where

(C33)
$$\psi^* = \frac{1}{R} \mathbf{y}' \left(\frac{\partial^2 C}{\partial \mathbf{z} \partial \mathbf{z}'} \right)^{-1} \mathbf{y},$$

(C34)
$$\mathbf{\Theta}^* = \frac{1}{\psi^* R} \mathbf{Y} \left(\frac{\partial^2 C}{\partial \mathbf{z} \partial \mathbf{z}'} \right)^{-1} \mathbf{Y}.$$

These results confirm (5.34) and (5.35).

Next we differentiate $\partial C / \partial z_r = y_r$ with respect to p_i,

$$\frac{\partial^2 C}{\partial z_r \partial p_i} + \sum_{s=1}^{m} \frac{\partial^2 C}{\partial z_r \partial z_s} \frac{\partial z_s}{\partial p_i} = 0,$$

which implies $\partial \mathbf{z} / \partial \mathbf{p}' = -(\partial^2 C / \partial \mathbf{z} \partial \mathbf{z}')^{-1} (\partial^2 C / \partial \mathbf{z} \partial \mathbf{p}')$ and hence, in view of (C27) and (C32),

(C35)
$$\mathbf{G} \frac{\partial \log \mathbf{z}}{\partial \log \mathbf{p}'} = -\psi^* \mathbf{\Theta}^* \mathbf{K}'.$$

Given the interpretation of $\mathbf{K}'$ as the $m \times n$ matrix of the marginal shares of the inputs, (C35) and (C32) complete the proof of (5.33).

We invert the last two members of (C32) and use (C28) and (5.27):

(C36) $$(\psi^* \mathbf{\Theta}^*)^{-1} = \frac{1}{\gamma} \mathbf{G}^{-1} \left[\frac{\partial^2 \log C}{\partial (\log \mathbf{z}) \partial (\log \mathbf{z}')} + \gamma^2 \mathbf{gg}' - \gamma \mathbf{G} \right] \mathbf{G}^{-1}.$$

We obtain (5.43) by pre- and postmultiplying (C36) by $\mathbf{g}'$ and $\mathbf{g}$, respectively, and using $\mathbf{G}^{-1} \mathbf{g} = \boldsymbol{\iota}^*$ and (5.10).

Input-Output Separability

A firm is said to be input-output separable when its technology can be represented by an equation of the form $h_q(\mathbf{q}) - h_z(\mathbf{z}) = 0$. One possibility is that $h(\ )$ of (5.2) can be separated additively in this way, $h(\mathbf{q}, \mathbf{z}) \equiv h_q(\mathbf{q}) - h_z(\mathbf{z})$, where $h(\mathbf{q}, \mathbf{z})$ is the function which satisfies the output-homogeneous property (5.4). However, this is stronger than is required for input-output separability. For this separability it is (by definition) necessary and sufficient that the firm's technology can be represented by $h_0(\mathbf{q}, \mathbf{z}) = 0$, where $h_0(\ )$ is additively separable,

(C37)
$$h_0(\mathbf{q}, \mathbf{z}) \equiv h_q(\mathbf{q}) - h_z(\mathbf{z}),$$

and this $h_0(\ )$ need not satisfy the output-homogeneous property (5.4).

The matrices $\mathbf{H}$, $\mathbf{H}^*$, and $\mathbf{H}^{**}$ on the previous pages are all submatrices of the logarithmic Hessian matrix of $h(\ )$ which satisfies (5.4). The question arises as to how these matrices can be expressed in terms of the corresponding matrices of $h_0(\ )$ which does not satisfy (5.4). This matter was pursued by Laitinen and Theil [229, Appendix A], and the relevant result for input-output separability can be summarized as follows: We indicate the submatrices of the logarithmic Hessian matrix of $h_0(\ )$ by adding a zero subscript: $\mathbf{H}_0$, $\mathbf{H}_0^*$, $\mathbf{H}_0^{**}$. Then $\mathbf{H}^*$ of the $h(\ )$ which satisfies (5.4) can be written as

(C38)

$$\mathbf{H}^* = \alpha \mathbf{H}_0^* + \alpha \mathbf{H}_0^* \boldsymbol{\iota}^* \frac{\partial h}{\partial \log \mathbf{z}'} + \alpha \frac{\partial h}{\partial \log \mathbf{q}} \boldsymbol{\iota}^{*'} \mathbf{H}_0^{**} + \beta \frac{\partial h}{\partial \log \mathbf{q}} \frac{\partial h}{\partial \log \mathbf{z}'},$$

where α and β are scalars. If (C37) holds, $\mathbf{H}_0^*$ is a zero matrix and (C38) can be simplified to

(C39) $$\mathbf{H}^* = \frac{\partial h}{\partial \log \mathbf{q}} \left(\alpha \boldsymbol{\iota}^{*'} \mathbf{H}_0^{**} + \beta \frac{\partial h}{\partial \log \mathbf{z}'} \right).$$

On combining this with (C11) we find that $\mathbf{F}^{-1}\mathbf{H}^*$ consists of identical rows under input-output separability. Hence $\mathbf{F}^{-1}\mathbf{H}^* = \boldsymbol{\iota}\mathbf{v}'$, where $\mathbf{v}'$ is some row vector consisting of m elements. This $\mathbf{F}^{-1}\mathbf{H}^*$ is premultiplied by $\boldsymbol{\Theta} - \boldsymbol{\theta}\boldsymbol{\theta}'$ in (C20), so that $[\theta_i^r] = \boldsymbol{\theta}\boldsymbol{\iota}^{*'}$ because $(\boldsymbol{\Theta} - \boldsymbol{\theta}\boldsymbol{\theta}')\boldsymbol{\iota} = \mathbf{0}$. This confirms that (5.21) is true under input-output separability.

Appendix D

The Revenue-maximizing Firm

In this appendix we consider a firm which maximizes gross output revenue, $R = \sum_r y_r z_r$, by adjusting outputs subject to the production function constraint for given inputs and output prices. This yields supply equations which describe output changes in terms of input changes and output price changes. This approach is appropriate in wartime situations when inputs are rationed; profit-maximization degenerates to revenue-maximization when inputs, input prices, and output prices are all given. It is also appropriate when the firm faces monopsonistic conditions on the demand side and competitive conditions on the supply side, because the supply equations mentioned above remain valid under competitive supply conditions even when inputs are bought under noncompetitive conditions.

The theory of the revenue-maximizing firm is presented below in outline form. At the end we discuss a measure of the degree to which the inputs and outputs of a multiproduct firm are inseparable (the degree of input-output specificity). This measure involves a simultaneous consideration of the cost-minimizing and revenue-maximizing firms.

The Revenue Function and the Supply Equations under Revenue Maximization

When the firm maximizes revenue, the role of the cost function $C(\mathbf{z}, \mathbf{p})$ is taken over by the revenue function $R(\mathbf{q}, \mathbf{y})$, which specifies the maximum dollar amount obtainable from the outputs when the input vector is $\mathbf{q}$ and the output price vector is $\mathbf{y}$. This revenue function can be used to obtain price and volume indexes for the firm's outputs in the same way that the cost function yields such indexes for inputs (see section 6.2).

We write $\partial R / \partial q_i$ for the marginal revenue of the ith input: the increase in the maximum amount of output revenue which results from a small increase in the ith input. We write $\bar{\theta}_r^i$ for the share of the rth product in this marginal revenue,

$$\text{(D1)} \qquad \bar{\theta}_r^i = \frac{\partial(y_r z_r)/\partial q_i}{\partial R/\partial q_i} \qquad \begin{array}{l} i = 1, \ldots, n \\ r = 1, \ldots, m, \end{array}$$

and note that

$$\text{(D2)} \qquad d(\log Y'^i) = \sum_{r=1}^{m} \bar{\theta}_r^i d(\log y_r) \qquad i = 1, \ldots, n$$

is a Frisch output price index which is comparable to the input price index (5.31). Also note that when the revenue-maximizing firm adjusts its inputs so as to maximize profit, the marginal revenue of the ith input equals its price: $\partial R/\partial q_i = p_i$. This means that (D1) can then be simplified to $\bar{\theta}_r^i = \partial(y_r z_r)/\partial(p_i q_i)$, which should be compared with (4.32) and the multiproduct extension of (4.32) stated in the discussion following equation (5.30).

It is possible to formulate the supply equations of the revenue-maximizing firm so that they contain the same normalized price coefficients θ_{rs}^* as those of the cost-minimizing firm which adjusts its outputs so as to maximize profit. This matter is pursued in the next subsection, which shows that the supply equation for the rth product takes the form

$$\text{(D3)} \quad g_r d(\log z_r) = \frac{1}{\gamma} \sum_{i=1}^{n} \bar{\theta}_r^i f_i d(\log q_i) + \psi^* \sum_{s=1}^{m} \theta_{rs}^* d\left(\log \frac{y_s}{Y''_s}\right) + \omega_r^*,$$

where ω_r^* is a disturbance caused by rational random behavior and $d(\log Y''^1), \ldots, d(\log Y''^m)$ are deflators of the form

$$\text{(D4)} \qquad d(\log Y''^r) = \sum_{i=1}^{n} \theta_i^r d(\log Y'^i) \qquad r = 1, \ldots, m.$$

Note that the input term of (D3) is analogous to the output term of the input demand equation (8.22) of the cost-minimizing firm, with γ in reciprocal form and θ_i^r replaced by $\bar{\theta}_r^i$ of (D1), while the price term of (D3) is identical to that of (8.23) except for the deflator. Double primes are used for the deflator in (D3) in order to indicate that Frisch weights have been applied twice (see eqs. [D2] and [D4]); this double-prime notation is similar to $d(\log P'')$ in (5.39).

Summation of (D3) over r yields the total-output decision of the revenue-maximizing firm. We shall prove in the next subsection that this decision takes the form

$$\text{(D5)} \qquad d(\log Z) = \frac{1}{\gamma} d(\log Q),$$

which is equivalent to the total-input decision (8.25) of the cost-minimizing firm.

Input Demand and Output Supply
Systems in Matrix Form

The result (D3) can be derived from a matrix equation for the revenue-maximizing firm in the same way that (5.8) is derived from the matrix equation (5.13). However, in order to save space we shall derive (D3) from results previously developed under the assumption that profit-maximization is the ultimate goal. It should be obvious that profit-maximizing behavior must be the same regardless of whether it is achieved via cost-minimization or revenue-maximization. We assume that the firm operates under competitive conditions on both the demand and the supply side.

It will be convenient to use the matrix notation of chapter 10 and to extend this to outputs also. We write equation (8.22) for $i = 1, \ldots, n$ as

(D6) $$\mathbf{F\varkappa} = \gamma \mathbf{KG\zeta} - \psi(\mathbf{\Theta} - \mathbf{\theta\theta'})\pi + \mathbf{\varepsilon},$$

where $\mathbf{F}$ and $\mathbf{G}$ are diagonal matrices with $f_1, \ldots, f_n$ and $g_1, \ldots, g_m$, respectively, on the diagonal; $\varkappa$, π, and ε are n-element vectors whose ith elements are $d(\log q_i)$, $d(\log p_i)$, and ε_i, respectively; $\mathbf{K}$ is defined in (C20); and ζ is an m-element vector whose rth element is $d(\log z_r)$. Similarly, we write equation (8.23) for $r = 1, \ldots, m$ as

(D7) $$\mathbf{G\zeta} = \psi^* \mathbf{\Theta}^* (\eta - \mathbf{K'}\pi) + \mathbf{\varepsilon}^*,$$

where η and ε^* are m-element vectors with $d(\log y_r)$ and ε_r^*, respectively, as rth elements. The result (D7) may be clarified by means of (C32) and (C35).

Substitution of (D7) in (D6) gives

(D8) $$\mathbf{F\varkappa} = \gamma\psi^*\mathbf{K\Theta}^*\eta - [\gamma\psi^*\mathbf{K\Theta}^*\mathbf{K'} + \psi(\mathbf{\Theta} - \mathbf{\theta\theta'})]\pi + \mathbf{\varepsilon} + \gamma\mathbf{K\varepsilon}^*,$$

which expresses the change in the demand for the inputs in terms of the input and output price changes. We shall write the expression in brackets in (D8) as $\gamma\psi^*\mathbf{A}^{-1}$, which is equivalent to

(D9) $$\mathbf{A}^{-1} = \mathbf{K\Theta}^*\mathbf{K'} + \frac{\psi}{\gamma\psi^*}(\mathbf{\Theta} - \mathbf{\theta\theta'}).$$

The expression on the right is symmetric positive definite, so that $\mathbf{A}$ is also symmetric positive definite. To prove this proposition we note that γ, ψ, and ψ^* are all positive, that $\mathbf{\Theta} - \mathbf{\theta\theta'}$ is positive semidefinite with rank $n - 1$, and that $\mathbf{K\Theta}^*\mathbf{K'}$ is also positive semidefinite. Since $(\mathbf{\Theta} - \mathbf{\theta\theta'})\iota = \mathbf{0}$, the proposition is verified when we prove that $\iota'\mathbf{K\Theta}^*\mathbf{K'}\iota$ is positive. This is indeed true because $\mathbf{K'}\iota = \iota^*$ and $\iota^{*'}\mathbf{\Theta}^*\iota^* = 1$. Note that $\mathbf{K'}\iota = \iota^*$ is equivalent to $\sum_i \theta_i^r = 1$ for each r (see eq. [C20]).

We proceed to solve (D8) for π, using (D9):

$$\pi = \mathbf{AK\Theta^*}\eta - \frac{1}{\gamma\psi^*}\mathbf{AF}\varkappa + \frac{1}{\gamma\psi^*}\mathbf{A}(\varepsilon + \gamma\mathbf{K}\varepsilon^*).$$

When we combine this with (D7), we obtain

(D10) $\mathbf{G}\zeta = \dfrac{1}{\gamma}\mathbf{\Theta^*K'AF}\varkappa + \psi^*\mathbf{\Theta^*(I - K'AK\Theta^*)}\eta - \dfrac{1}{\gamma}\mathbf{\Theta^*K'A}\varepsilon$

$$+ \mathbf{(I - \Theta^*K'AK)}\varepsilon^*,$$

which is the output supply system of the revenue-maximizing firm. To verify that (D10) is equivalent to (D3) we use (D1),

(D11) $\bar{\theta}_r^i = \dfrac{y_r z_r}{\partial R/\partial q_i}\dfrac{\partial \log z_r}{\partial \log q_i}\dfrac{1}{q_i} = \dfrac{R g_r}{C f_i}\dfrac{\partial \log z_r}{\partial \log q_i} = \dfrac{\gamma g_r}{f_i}\dfrac{\partial \log z_r}{\partial \log q_i},$

where the second equal sign is based on (5.28) and $\partial R/\partial q_i = p_i$ (which holds under profit-maximization) and the third on (5.30). The last member of (D11) is the (r, i)th element of the matrix

$$\gamma\mathbf{G}\frac{\partial \log \mathbf{z}}{\partial \log \mathbf{q}'}\mathbf{F}^{-1} = \mathbf{\Theta^*K'A},$$

where the equal sign is based on (D10). Therefore, the $m \times n$ matrix of the marginal shares of (D1) can be written as

(D12) $\mathbf{\bar{K}} = [\bar{\theta}_r^i] = \mathbf{\Theta^*K'A},$

and (D10) can be simplified to

(D13) $\mathbf{G}\zeta = \dfrac{1}{\gamma}\mathbf{\bar{K}F}\varkappa + \psi^*\mathbf{\Theta^*(I - \bar{K}K)'}\eta + \omega^*,$

where

(D14) $\omega^* = [\omega_1^*, \ldots, \omega_m^*]' = -\dfrac{1}{\gamma}\mathbf{\bar{K}}\varepsilon + \mathbf{(I - \bar{K}K)}\varepsilon^*,$

which confirms (D3) when combined with (D2) and (D4).

Since $\sum_r \bar{\theta}_r^i = 1$ holds for each r, we have

(D15) $\mathbf{\bar{K}'\iota^*} = \iota.$

Hence premultiplication of the third member of (D14) by $\iota^{*\prime}$ gives zero because $\iota'\varepsilon = 0$ and $\iota^{*\prime}(I - \bar{K}K) = \iota^{*\prime} - \iota'K = \iota^{*\prime} - \iota^{*\prime} = 0$. Therefore,

(D16) $\iota^{*\prime}\omega^* = 0.$

It is then readily verified that premultiplication of (D13) by $\iota^{*\prime}$ yields (D5) if it is true that

(D17) $\iota^{*\prime}\Theta^*(I - \bar{K}K)' = 0.$

To prove that (D17) holds we postmultiply (D9) by $\bar{K}'$ and use (D12) in the form $\bar{K}A^{-1} = \Theta^*K'$, which gives

(D18) $K\Theta^*(I - \bar{K}K)' = \dfrac{\psi}{\gamma\psi^*}(\Theta - \theta\theta')\bar{K}',$

after which $\iota'K = \iota^{*\prime}$ and $\iota'(\Theta - \theta\theta') = 0$ complete the proof of (D17).

The Input Demand System of the Revenue-Maximizing Firm

Equation (D8) constitutes the input demand system of the revenue-maximizing firm when it adjusts its inputs so as to maximize profit. We can write (D8) in the form

(D19) $F\varkappa = \gamma\psi^*K\Theta^*(\eta - K'\pi) - \psi(\Theta - \theta\theta')\pi + \omega,$

where

(D20) $\omega = \varepsilon + \gamma K\varepsilon^*.$

Since ω and ω^* are defined in (D20) and (D14) as linear combinations of ε and ε^*, they are normally distributed with zero means under rational random behavior. Using (8.14) and (8.24), we find that the matrix $\omega\omega^{*\prime}$ has the following expectation:

$$-\frac{\sigma^2}{\gamma}(\Theta - \theta\theta')\bar{K}' + \frac{\sigma^2\psi^*}{\psi}K\Theta^*(I - \bar{K}K)'.$$

It follows from (D18) that this is a zero matrix, so that each element of ω is uncorrelated with each element of ω^*. Given the normality, this means that ω and ω^* are independently distributed and hence that the supply system (D13) and the demand system (D19) constitute a two-stage block-recursive system. This is analogous to the corresponding result for the cost-minimizing firm, and it enables the firm to design a decision hierarchy of its input and output management. Note that this hierarchy differs from that described in section 8.6 for the cost-minimizing firm in that the input manager is the superior of the output manager. This follows from (D13), which shows that the output decision is conditional on $\varkappa$, that is, on the decision on the input changes made by the input manager.

The output supply equation (D3) contains the same normalized price coefficients θ_{rs}^* as the corresponding equation for the cost-minimizing firm. It is possible to proceed similarly on the demand side by formulating an input allocation decision with the θ_{ij}'s as normalized price coefficients. For this purpose we consider first the total-input decision of the revenue-maximizing firm by premultiplying (D19) by ι'. Using (D20), $\iota'\varepsilon = 0$, and $\iota'K = \iota^{*'}$, we obtain

$$d(\log Q) = \gamma\psi^*\iota^{*'}\Theta^*(\eta - K'\pi) + \gamma\iota^{*'}\varepsilon^*.$$

It is readily verified from (5.38) and (5.39) that this is equivalent to

(D21) $$d(\log Q) = \gamma\psi^* d\left(\log \frac{Y'}{P''}\right) + \gamma E^*,$$

and that this total-input decision of the revenue-maximizing firm is equivalent to (D5) combined with the total-output decision (8.27) of the cost-minimizing firm.

Next we subtract (D21), multiplied by θ_i, from the ith equation of (D19). The result can be written as

(D22) $$f_i d(\log q_i) = \theta_i d(\log Q) + \gamma\psi^*\bar{\Gamma}_i - \psi \sum_{j=1}^{n} \theta_{ij} d\left(\log \frac{p_j}{P'}\right) + \omega_i',$$

where ω_i' equals the ith element of $\boldsymbol{\omega}$ minus $\gamma\theta_i E^*$ and

(D23) $$\bar{\Gamma}_i = \sum_{r=1}^{m} \sum_{s=1}^{m} \theta_{rs}^*(\theta_i^r - \theta_i) d\left(\log \frac{y_s}{P'^s}\right).$$

The input allocation decision (D22) should be compared with the corresponding decision (8.26) for the cost-minimizing firm. In (D22) we have $\bar{\Gamma}_i$, which is defined in (D23) as a bilinear form that also occurs in (8.28) for Γ_i of (8.26). This form vanishes when the m deflated output prices are constant and also under input-output separability (see eq. [5.21]).

Special Cases

The price terms in equations (D22) and (D3) are simplified to

$$-\psi \theta_i d \left(\log \frac{p_i}{P'}\right) \quad \text{and} \quad \psi^* \theta_r^* d \left(\log \frac{y_r}{Y''_r}\right)$$

when the firm is input independent and output independent, respectively. In both cases we have the change in only one relative price, which indicates that the independence transformation is also applicable to the revenue-maximizing firm. In addition, under output independence we can simplify (D23) to

$$(D24) \qquad \bar{\Gamma}_i = \sum_{r=1}^{m} \theta_r^* (\theta_i^r - \theta_i) d \left(\log \frac{y_r}{P'_r}\right),$$

which is a Frisch-weighted cross-moment of the marginal shares of the ith input and the deflated output price changes.

Under input-output separability the marginal shares (D1) are the same across inputs and equal to θ_r^* defined in (5.37),

$$(D25) \qquad \bar{\theta}_r^i = \theta_r^* \qquad i = 1, \ldots, n$$

$$r = 1, \ldots, m,$$

which should be compared with the analogous result (5.21) for the cost-minimizing firm. To prove that (D25) holds under input-output separability, we postmultiply (D12) by $\mathbf{A}^{-1}$:

$$(D26) \qquad \bar{\mathbf{K}} \mathbf{A}^{-1} = \mathbf{\Theta}^* \mathbf{K}'.$$

We have $\mathbf{K} = \theta \iota^{*\prime}$ under input-output separability (see eq. [C20]), so that (D26) then becomes $\bar{\mathbf{K}} \mathbf{A}^{-1} = \mathbf{\Theta}^* \iota^* \theta'$, which we premultiply by $\iota^{*\prime}$. This gives $\iota' \mathbf{A}^{-1}$ on the left (see eq. [D15]) and θ' on the right, so that $\bar{\mathbf{K}} \mathbf{A}^{-1} = \mathbf{\Theta}^* \iota^* \theta'$ can be written as $\bar{\mathbf{K}} \mathbf{A}^{-1} = \mathbf{\Theta}^* \iota^* \iota' \mathbf{A}^{-1}$, which yields $\bar{\mathbf{K}} = \mathbf{\Theta}^* \iota^* \iota'$ after postmultiplication by $\mathbf{A}$. This shows that under input-output separability all columns of $\bar{\mathbf{K}}$ are equal to $\mathbf{\Theta}^* \iota^*$, which confirms (D25).

Recall from section 5.5 (see the discussion preceding eq. [5.23]) that the input allocation decision takes the single-product form (4.23) under input-output separability. This is also true for the revenue-maximizing firm because $\bar{\Gamma}_i = 0$ and $\omega'_i = \varepsilon_i$ hold in (D22) under this separability; the reader may verify $\omega'_i = \varepsilon_i$ using (D20), $\mathbf{K} = \theta \iota^{*\prime}$, and the ω'_i definition given between

(D22) and (D23). The supply equation (D3) is under input-output separability simplified to

$$(D27) \quad g_r d(\log z_r) = \frac{\theta_r^*}{\gamma} d(\log Q) + \psi^* \sum_{s=1}^{m} \theta_{rs}^* d\left(\log \frac{y_s}{Y'}\right) + \varepsilon_r^{**},$$

where $d(\log Y')$ is defined in (5.38) and ε_r^{**} in (8.30). The verification of (D27) is a matter of using (D25) in (D2) as well as $\mathbf{K} = \boldsymbol{\theta}\boldsymbol{\iota}^{*\prime}$ and $\bar{\mathbf{K}} = \boldsymbol{\Theta}^*\boldsymbol{\iota}^*\boldsymbol{\iota}'$ in (D14).

The Input-Output Specificity of a Multiproduct Firm

We define

$$(D28) \qquad\qquad S = \sum_{i=1}^{n} \sum_{r=1}^{m} \theta_i^r \bar{\theta}_r^i,$$

which can be written in the equivalent form

$$(D29) \qquad\qquad S = 1 + \sum_{i=1}^{n} \sum_{r=1}^{m} (\theta_i^r - \theta_i)(\bar{\theta}_r^i - \theta_r^*)$$

because $\sum_i \theta_i^r = \sum_i \theta_i = \sum_r \bar{\theta}_r^i = \sum_r \theta_r^* = 1$.

The sum on the right in (D29) vanishes under input-output separability; we shall prove below that it is positive when the firm is not input-output separable, and also that it is invariant under the independence transformation. We refer to S as the *input-output specificity* of the multiproduct firm, which may be justified intuitively as follows: Let the ith input be of little use for the rth product relative to the other products in the sense that $\theta_i^r < \theta_i$; that is, if the firm engages in cost-minimization, an increase in the output rate of the rth product implies comparatively little change in the demand for the ith input. We should expect that under revenue-maximization an increased availability of this input will then normally have little impact on the supply of the rth product and hence that $\bar{\theta}_r^i < \theta_r^*$. These two inequalities, $\theta_i^r < \theta_i$ and $\bar{\theta}_r^i < \theta_r^*$, imply that the expressions in parentheses in (D29) are both negative, so that their product yields a positive contribution to the firm's input-output specificity. These two expressions will both tend to be positive, and hence also yield a positive contribution to the input-output specificity, when the ith input is of comparatively great use for the rth product. Therefore, the excess of S over 1 will increase when the importance of the n inputs with respect to the m outputs is more diverse.

To prove that S is invariant under the independence transformation, we write (D28) in the form

(D30) $S = \text{tr } \mathbf{K}\overline{\mathbf{K}},$

where tr $\mathbf{K}\overline{\mathbf{K}}$ (the trace of $\mathbf{K}\overline{\mathbf{K}}$) stands for the sum of the diagonal elements of the square matrix $\mathbf{K}\overline{\mathbf{K}}$. The independence transformation premultiplies (D19) by $\mathbf{R}$ and (D13) by $\mathbf{R}^*$, where $\mathbf{R} = (\mathbf{X}^{-1}\iota)_\Delta \mathbf{X}'$ (see eq. [10.21]) and $\mathbf{R}^* = (\mathbf{X}^{*-1}\iota^*)_\Delta \mathbf{X}^{*\prime}$. The result is that $\mathbf{K}$ is transformed into $\mathbf{R}\mathbf{K}\mathbf{R}^{*-1}$ and $\overline{\mathbf{K}}$ into $\mathbf{R}^*\overline{\mathbf{K}}\mathbf{R}^{-1}$, and hence tr $\mathbf{K}\overline{\mathbf{K}}$ into tr $\mathbf{R}\mathbf{K}\overline{\mathbf{K}}\mathbf{R}^{-1} = \text{tr } \mathbf{K}\overline{\mathbf{K}}$, which proves the invariance of S. The case in which $\mathbf{R}$ or $\mathbf{R}^*$ is singular can be handled by means of a perturbation of the firm's technology (see section 11.5).

We proceed to prove that

(D31) $1 \leq \text{tr } \mathbf{K}\overline{\mathbf{K}} \leq \text{r } (\mathbf{K}\overline{\mathbf{K}}) \leq \min (m, n),$

and that the first two "$\leq$" signs both become equal signs if and only if the firm is input-output separable. The symbol in the third member of (D31) stands for the rank of the matrix $\mathbf{K}\overline{\mathbf{K}}$.

To prove (D31) we use (D12) and (D9),

(D32) $\mathbf{K}\overline{\mathbf{K}} = \mathbf{K}\boldsymbol{\Theta}^*\mathbf{K}'\left[\mathbf{K}\boldsymbol{\Theta}^*\mathbf{K}' + \dfrac{\psi}{\gamma\psi^*}(\boldsymbol{\Theta} - \boldsymbol{\theta}\boldsymbol{\theta}')\right]^{-1},$

so that

(D33) $\text{tr } \mathbf{K}\overline{\mathbf{K}} = \text{tr } [\mathbf{Z}_1(\mathbf{Z}_1 + \mathbf{Z}_2)^{-1}],$

where $\mathbf{Z}_1 = \mathbf{K}\boldsymbol{\Theta}^*\mathbf{K}'$ and $\mathbf{Z}_2 = (\psi/\gamma\psi^*)(\boldsymbol{\Theta} - \boldsymbol{\theta}\boldsymbol{\theta}')$. Note that $\mathbf{Z}_1$ is symmetric positive semidefinite and satisfies $\iota'\mathbf{Z}_1\iota = 1$; that $\mathbf{Z}_2$ is symmetric positive semidefinite of rank $n - 1$ and satisfies $\mathbf{Z}_2\iota = \mathbf{0}$; and that $\mathbf{Z}_1 + \mathbf{Z}_2 = \mathbf{A}^{-1}$ is positive definite.

Next we consider

(D34) $[\mathbf{Z}_1 - \mu_i(\mathbf{Z}_1 + \mathbf{Z}_2)]\mathbf{v}_i = \mathbf{0} \qquad i = 1, \ldots, n,$

where μ_i is a latent root of $\mathbf{Z}_1$ relative to $\mathbf{Z}_1 + \mathbf{Z}_2$ and $\mathbf{v}_i$ is a characteristic vector associated with μ_i. One solution is $\mu_i = 1$, $\mathbf{v}_i = \iota$ because $\mathbf{Z}_2\iota = \mathbf{0}$. The other μ_i's are nonnegative and less than 1 because (D34) implies

$$(1 - \mu_i)\mathbf{v}_i'\mathbf{Z}_1\mathbf{v}_i = \mu_i\mathbf{v}_i'\mathbf{Z}_2\mathbf{v}_i,$$

and $\mathbf{Z}_1$ and $\mathbf{Z}_2$ are positive semidefinite, $\mathbf{Z}_2$ being of rank $n - 1$. The proof of (D31) is completed by noting that the μ_i's and $\mathbf{v}_i$'s are also solutions to

$$[(\mathbf{Z}_1 + \mathbf{Z}_2)^{-1}\mathbf{Z}_1 - \mu_i\mathbf{I}]\mathbf{v}_i = \mathbf{0},$$

so that $\mathbf{K}\overline{\mathbf{K}}$ has a trace equal to the sum of the μ_i's and a rank equal to the number of positive μ_i's. Both this trace and this rank are 1 if and only if the unit root is the only nonzero root, that is, if and only if the firm is input-output separable.

Glossary of Symbols

The most widely used symbols are listed below in alphabetical order. The section in which each symbol is first introduced is indicated in parentheses.

Greek Symbols

γ Elasticity of cost and reciprocal of the elasticity of scale (section 4.3 for the single-product firm, section 5.2 for the multiproduct firm).

Γ_i Covariance of the marginal shares of the ith input and the logarithmic output changes (section 5.5).

ε_i Random disturbance of the ith consumer demand equation (section 8.3) or the ith input demand equation (section 8.4).

$\bar{\varepsilon}_i$ Specific component of ε_i (section 8.3).

ε_r^* Random disturbance of the rth supply equation (section 8.5).

θ_i Marginal share of the ith consumer good (section 2.4) or of the ith input (section 4.4 for the single-product firm, section 5.3 for the multiproduct firm).

θ_i^r Share of the ith input in the marginal cost of the rth product (section 5.2).

θ_{ij} Normalized price coefficient in the ith consumer demand equation (section 2.5) or the ith input demand equation (section 4.5 for the single-product firm, section 5.2 for the multiproduct firm).

θ_i' Conditional marginal share of the ith consumer good within its group (section 9.3) or of the ith input within its group (section 9.5).

θ_r^* Marginal share of the rth product (section 5.7).

θ_{rs}^* Normalized price coefficient in the rth supply equation (section 5.7).

ι Column vector consisting of unit elements.

λ Marginal utility of income (section 2.1).

Λ Diagonal matrix with $\lambda_1, \ldots, \lambda_n$ on the diagonal.

λ_i Divisia elasticity of the ith transformed input (section 10.4) or income elasticity of the ith transformed consumer good (section 11.1).

Π' Quadratic form in Frisch-deflated price changes of consumer goods or inputs (section 6.5).

Π^* Quadratic form in deflated output price changes (section 6.7).

ρ Total marginal cost and the marginal cost of a proportionate output increase (section 5.3).

σ^2 Coefficient in the disturbance covariance specification of consumer demand equations (section 8.3) or input demand equations (section 8.4).

ϕ Income flexibility (section 2.4).

ψ Curvature measure of the logarithmic cost function (section 4.4 for the single-product firm, section 5.2 for the multiproduct firm).

ψ^* Price elasticity of the supply of total output of a multiproduct firm (section 5.7).

Latin Symbols

C The cost of utility for a consumer (section 3.2) or the cost of production for a firm (section 4.2).

c' Marginal cost of information (section 7.3).

F Diagonal matrix with $f_1, \ldots, f_n$ on the diagonal.

f_i Factor share of ith input (section 4.3)

F_T Diagonal matrix with $f_{T1}, \ldots, f_{Tn}$ on the diagonal.

f_{Ti} Factor share of ith transformed input (section 10.2).

G Diagonal matrix with $g_1, \ldots, g_m$ on the diagonal.

g_r The share of the rth product in total marginal cost (section 5.2) or in total revenue (section 5.6).

H $n \times n$ matrix with $\partial^2 h / \partial(\log q_i)\partial(\log q_j)$ as (i, j)th element (section 4.4).

H* $n \times m$ matrix with $\partial^2 h / \partial(\log q_i)\partial(\log z_r)$ as (i, r)th element (section 5.3).

$h(\mathbf{q})$ Logarithmic production function of a single-product firm (opening paragraph of chapter 4).

$h(\mathbf{q}, \mathbf{z})$ Output-homogeneous production function of a multiproduct firm (section 5.1).

M Income of a consumer (section 2.1).

m Number of products of a multiproduct firm (section 5.1).

n Number of consumer goods (section 2.1) or of a firm's inputs (opening paragraph of chapter 4).

$\mathbf{p}$ n-element vector with p_i as ith element.

p_i Price of the ith consumer good (section 2.1) or of the ith input of a firm (opening paragraph of chapter 4).

$d(\log P)$ Divisia price index of consumer goods (section 2.3) or of a firm's inputs (section 4.5).

$d(\log P')$ Frisch price index of consumer goods (section 2.4) or of a firm's inputs (section 4.4).

$d(\log P'')$ Frisch-weighted index of $d(\log P'^1)$, $\ldots, d(\log P'^m)$ (section 5.7).

$d(\log P'^r)$ Frisch input price index for the rth product (section 5.6).

$d(\log P'_g)$ Frisch price index of the consumer goods of group S_g (sections 9.1 and 9.3) or of the input group S_g (section 9.5).

$\mathbf{q}$ n-element vector with q_i as ith element.

q_i Quantity of the ith consumer good (section 2.1) or of the ith input of a firm (opening paragraph of chapter 4).

$d(\log Q)$ Divisia volume index of consumer goods (section 2.3) or of a firm's inputs (section 4.5).

$d(\log Q')$ Frisch-weighted volume index of consumer goods (section 12.2).

$d(\log Q_g)$ Divisia volume index of the consumer goods of group S_g (section 9.1) or of the input group S_g (section 9.5).

R Total revenue of a multiproduct firm (section 5.6).

R, S Transformation matrices of the input independence transformation (section 10.2) or of the preference independence transformation (section 11.1).

S_g Group of consumer goods (section 2.7) or of inputs (section 9.5).

T Composition matrix of the input independence transformation (section 10.4) or the preference independence transformation (section 11.1).

$t(U, \mathbf{q})$ Distance function in consumption theory (section 6.3).

U Utility as an independent variable (section 3.2).

U Hessian matrix of $u(\mathbf{q})$.

u^{ij} (i, j)th element of $\mathbf{U}^{-1}$.

$u(\mathbf{q})$ Utility function of a consumer (section 2.1).

$u_I(M, \mathbf{p})$ Indirect utility function of a consumer (section 3.1).

w_i Budget share of ith consumer good (section 2.2).

y Product price of a single-product firm (section 4.7).

$\mathbf{y}$ m-element vector with y_r as rth element.

y_r Price of the rth product (section 5.6).

$d(\log Y')$ Frisch price index of a firm's products (section 5.7).

z Output of a single-product firm (opening paragraph of chapter 4).

$\mathbf{z}$ m-element vector with z_r as rth element.

z_r Output of the rth product (section 5.1).

$d(\log Z)$ Divisia volume index of a firm's products (section 5.2).

Bibliography

The publications listed below are those referred to in the text, supplemented by some other publications which are directly related to the topics discussed. The list which follows is not exhaustive in spite of its length.

1. Abbott, M., and Ashenfelter, O. Labour supply, commodity demand and the allocation of time. *Review of Economic Studies* 43 (1976): 389–411.

2. Afriat, S. N. The cost of living index. In *Essays in mathematical economics in honor of Oskar Morgenstern*, ed. M. Shubik, pp. 335–65. Princeton: Princeton University Press, 1967.

3. Afriat, S. N. The theory of international comparisons of real income and prices. In *International comparisons of prices and output*, ed. D. J. Daly, pp. 13–69. New York: National Bureau of Economic Research, 1972.

4. Afriat, S. N. *The price index*. Cambridge: Cambridge University Press, 1977.

5. Aigner, D. J. On estimation of an econometric model of short-run bank behaviour. *Journal of Econometrics* 1 (1973): 201–28.

6. Allen, R. G. D. *Mathematical analysis for economists*. London: Macmillan and Co., 1938.

7. Allen, R. G. D. Price index numbers. *Review of the International Statistical Institute* 31 (1963): 281–301.

8. Allen, R. G. D. *Index numbers in theory and practice*. London: The Macmillan Press, 1975.

9. Allen, R. G. D., and Bowley, A. L. *Family expenditure*. London: P. S. King and Son, 1935.

10. Armington, P. S. A theory of demand for products distinguished by place of production. *International Monetary Fund Staff Papers* 16 (1969): 159–78.

11. Arrow, K. J. The measurement of real value added. In *Nations and households in economic growth*, ed. P. A. David and M. W. Reder, pp. 3–19. New York: Academic Press, 1974.

12. Arrow, K. J., Chenery, H. B., Minhas, B. S., and Solow, R. M. Capital-labor substitution and economic efficiency. *Review of Economics and Statistics* 43 (1961): 225–50.

13. Ashenfelter, O., and Heckman, J. The estimation of income and substitution effects in a model of family labor supply. *Econometrica* 42 (1974): 73–85.

14. Ball, R., Lev, B., and Watts, R. Income variation and balance sheet compositions. *Journal of Accounting Research* 14 (1976): 1–9.

15. Ball, R. J., ed. *The international linkage of national economic models.* Amsterdam: North-Holland Publishing Company, 1973.

16. Banerjee, K. S. *Cost of living index numbers.* New York: Marcel Dekker, 1975.

17. Barbosa, F. de H. Rational random behavior: extensions and applications. Ph.D. dissertation, The University of Chicago, 1975.

18. Barbosa, F. de H. Bayesian analysis of the Rotterdam and linear expenditure systems. Discussion paper 7721 of the Center for Operations Research and Econometrics, Catholic University of Louvain, 1977.

19. Barnett, W. A. Maximum likelihood and iterated Aitken estimation of nonlinear systems of equations. *Journal of the American Statistical Association* 71 (1976): 354–60.

20. Barnett, W. A. Recursive subaggregation and a generalized hypocycloidal demand model. *Econometrica* 45 (1977): 1117–36.

21. Barnett, W. A. Theoretical foundations for the Rotterdam model. *Review of Economic Studies,* forthcoming.

22. Barnett, W. A. The joint allocation of leisure and goods expenditure. *Econometrica,* forthcoming.

23. Barnett, W. A. *Consumer demand and labor supply.* Amsterdam: North-Holland Publishing Company, forthcoming.

24. Barten, A. P. Consumer demand functions under conditions of almost additive preferences. *Econometrica* 32 (1964): 1–38.

25. Barten, A. P. Family composition, prices and expenditure patterns. In *Econometric analysis for national economic planning*, ed. P. E. Hart, G. Mills, and J. K. Whitaker, pp. 277–92. London: Butterworths, 1964.

26. Barten, A. P. Theorie en empirie van een volledig stelsel van vraagvergelijkingen. Ph.D. dissertation, Netherlands School of Economics, 1966.

27. Barten, A. P. Het verbruik door gezinshuishoudingen in Nederland, 1921–1939 en 1948–1962. Report 6604 of the Econometric Institute of the Netherlands School of Economics, 1966.

28. Barten, A. P. Evidence on the Slutsky conditions for demand equations. *Review of Economics and Statistics* 49 (1967): 77–84.

29. Barten, A. P. Estimating demand equations. *Econometrica* 36 (1968): 213–51.

30. Barten, A. P. Maximum likelihood estimation of a complete system of demand equations. *European Economic Review* 1 (1969): 7–73.

31. Barten, A. P. Réflexions sur la construction d'un système empirique des fonctions de demande. *Cahiers du séminaire d'économétrie* 12 (1970): 67–80.

32. Barten, A. P. Preference and demand interactions between commodities. In *Schaarste en welvaart*, pp. 1–18. Leiden: H. E. Stenfert Kroese, 1971.

33. Barten, A. P. An import allocation model for the Common Market. *Cahiers économiques de Bruxelles* 50 (1971): 3–14.

34. Barten, A. P. Complete systems of demand equations: some thoughts about aggregation and functional form. *Recherches économiques de Louvain* 40 (1974): 3–18.

35. Barten, A. P. The systems of consumer demand functions approach: a review. *Econometrica* 45 (1977): 23–51.

36. Barten, A. P., d'Alcantara, G., and Carrin, G. J. COMET: a medium-term macroeconomic model for the European Economic Community. *European Economic Review* 7 (1976): 63–115.

37. Barten, A. P., and Geyskens, E. The negativity condition in consumer demand. *European Economic Review* 6 (1975): 227–60.

38. Barten, A. P., Kloek, T., and Lempers, F. B. A note on a class of utility and production functions yielding everywhere differentiable demand functions. *Review of Economic Studies* 36 (1969): 109–11.

39. Barten, A. P., and Turnovsky, S. J. Some aspects of the aggregation problem for composite demand equations. *International Economic Review* 7 (1966): 231–59.

40. Baschet, J., and Debreu, P. Systèmes de lois de demande: une comparaison internationale. *Annales de l'Insée* (Institut National de la Statistique et des Etudes Economiques) 6 (1971): 3–39.

41. Becker, G. S. A theory of the allocation of time. *Economic Journal* 75 (1965): 493–517.

42. Bergson (Burk), A. Real income, expenditure proportionality, and Frisch's "New methods of measuring marginal utility." *Review of Economic Studies* 4 (1936): 33–52.

43. Berndt, E. K., Hall, B. H., Hall, R. E., and Hausman, J. A. Estimation and inference in nonlinear structural models. *Annals of Economic and Social Measurement* 3 (1974): 653–65.

44. Berndt, E. R. Reconciling alternative estimates of the elasticity of substitution. *Review of Economics and Statistics* 58 (1976): 59–68.

45. Berndt, E. R., and Christensen, L. R. The translog function and the substitution of equipment, structures, and labor in U.S. manufacturing 1929–68. *Journal of Econometrics* 1 (1973): 81–113.

46. Berndt, E. R., and Christensen, L. R. The internal structure of functional relationships: separability, substitution, and aggregation. *Review of Economic Studies* 40 (1973): 403–10.

47. Berndt, E. R., Darrough, M. N., and Diewert, W. E. Flexible functional forms and expenditure distributions: an application to Canadian

consumer demand functions. *International Economic Review* 18 (1977): 651–75.

48. Berndt, E. R., and Savin, N. E. Estimation and hypothesis testing in singular equation systems with autoregressive disturbances. *Econometrica* 43 (1975): 937–57.

49. Berndt, E. R., and Savin, N. E. Conflict among criteria for testing hypotheses in the multivariate linear regression model. *Econometrica* 45 (1977): 1263–77.

50. Betancourt, R. R. The estimation of price elasticities from cross-section data under additive preferences. *International Economic Review* 12 (1971): 283–92.

51. Biørn, E. Estimating the flexibility of the marginal utility of income. *European Economic Review* 5 (1974): 177–85.

52. Blackorby, C., Boyce, R., and Russell, R. R. Estimation of demand systems generated by the Gorman polar form: a generalization of the S-branch utility tree. *Econometrica* 46 (1978): 345–63.

53. Blackorby, C., Lady, G., Nissen, D., and Russell, R. R. Homothetic separability and consumer budgeting. *Econometrica* 38 (1970): 468–72.

54. Blackorby, C., Nissen, D., Primont, D., and Russell, R. R. Consistent intertemporal decision making. *Review of Economic Studies* 40 (1973): 239–48.

55. Blackorby, C., Nissen, D., Primont, D., and Russell, R. R. Recursively decentralized decision making. *Econometrica* 42 (1974): 487–96.

56. Blackorby, C., Primont, D., and Russell, R. R. Budgeting, decentralization, and aggregation. *Annals of Economic and Social Measurement* 4 (1975): 23–44.

57. Blackorby, C., Primont, D., and Russell, R. R. Some simple remarks on duality and the structure of utility functions. *Journal of Economic Theory* 11 (1975): 155–60.

58. Blackorby, C., Primont, D., and Russell, R. R. Dual price and quantity aggregation. *Journal of Economic Theory* 14 (1977): 130–48.

59. Blackorby, C., Primont, D., and Russell, R. R. Separability vs. functional structure: a characterization of their differences. *Journal of Economic Theory* 15 (1977): 135–44.

60. Blackorby, C., Primont, D., and Russell, R. R. On testing separability restrictions with flexible functional forms. *Journal of Econometrics* 5 (1977): 195–209.

61. Blackorby, C., Primont, D., and Russell, R. R. *Duality, separability, and functional structure.* New York: Elsevier North-Holland, 1978.

62. Bodkin, R. G. Additively consistent relationships for personal savings and the categories of consumption expenditures, U.S.A., 1949–1963. *Eastern Economic Journal* 1 (1974): 20–51.

63. Bojer, H. The effect on consumption of household size and composition. *European Economic Review* 9 (1977): 169–93.

64. Bowden, R. J. Note on coefficient restrictions in estimating sets of demand relations. *Econometrica* 41 (1973): 575–79.

65. Boyce, R. Estimation of dynamic Gorman polar form utility functions. *Annals of Economic and Social Measurement* 4 (1975): 103–16.

66. Boyle, J. R., Gorman, W. M., and Pudney, S. E. Demand for related goods: a progress report. In *Frontiers of quantitative economics,* vol. 3A, ed. M. D. Intriligator, pp. 87–101. Amsterdam: North-Holland Publishing Company, 1977.

67. Bridge, J. L. *Applied econometrics.* Amsterdam: North-Holland Publishing Company, 1971.

68. Brooks, R. B. Diagonalizing the Hessian matrix of the consumer's utility function. Ph.D. dissertation, The University of Chicago, 1970.

69. Brown, A., and Deaton, A. Surveys in applied economics: models of consumer behaviour. *Economic Journal* 82 (1972): 1145–1236.

70. Brown, M., and Heien, D. The S-branch utility tree: a generalization of the linear expenditure system. *Econometrica* 40 (1972): 737–47.

71. Bultez, A. V., and Naert, P. A. Consistent sum-constrained models. *Journal of the American Statistical Association* 70 (1975): 529–35.

72. Burgess, D. F. Duality theory and pitfalls in the specification of technologies. *Journal of Econometrics* 3 (1975): 105–21.

73. Burmeister, E., and Turnovsky, S. J. The degree of joint production. *International Economic Review* 12 (1971): 99–105.

74. Byron, R. P. Methods for estimating demand equations using prior information: a series of experiments with Australian data. *Australian Economic Papers* 7 (1968): 227–48.

75. Byron, R. P. The restricted Aitken estimation of sets of demand relations. *Econometrica* 38 (1970): 816–30.

76. Carlevaro, F. Formulation et estimation des fonctions de consommation semi-agrégées. *Canadian Journal of Economics* 4 (1971): 441–70.

77. Carlevaro, F. A generalization of the linear expenditure system. In *Private and enlarged consumption,* ed. L. Solari and J.-N. Du Pasquier, pp. 73–92. Amsterdam: North-Holland Publishing Company, 1976.

78. Carlevaro, F. Note sur les fonctions de consommation en prix et revenu réels de Fourgeaud et Nataf. *Econometrica* 45 (1977): 1639–50.

79. Cassel, G. *The theory of social economy,* rev. ed. trans. from the fifth German edition by S. L. Barrow. New York: Harcourt, Brace, 1932.

80. Charette, L., and Bronsard, C. Antonelli-Hicks-Allen et Antonelli-Allais-Barten. *Recherches économiques de Louvain* 41 (1975): 25–34.

81. Chipman, J. S., Hurwicz, L., Richter, M. K., and Sonnenschein, H. F. eds. *Preferences, utility, and demand.* New York: Harcourt Brace Jovanovich, 1971.

82. Christensen, L. R., Jorgenson, D. W., and Lau, L. J. Transcendental logarithmic production frontiers. *Review of Economics and Statistics* 55 (1973): 28–45.

83. Christensen, L. R., Jorgenson, D. W., and Lau, L. J. Transcendental logarithmic utility functions. *American Economic Review* 65 (1975): 367–83.

84. Christensen, L. R., and Manser, M. E. Cost-of-living indexes and price indexes for U.S. meat and produce, 1947–1971. In *Household*

production and consumption, ed. N. E. Terleckyj, pp. 399–446. New York: National Bureau of Economic Research, 1975.

85. Christensen, L. R., and Manser, M. E. Estimating U.S. consumer preferences for meat with a flexible utility function. *Journal of Econometrics* 5 (1977): 37–53.

86. Chu, F. S., Aigner, D. J., and Frankel, M. On the log-quadratic law of production. *Southern Economic Journal* 37 (1970): 32–39.

87. Clements, K. W. A linear allocation of spending-power system: a consumer demand and portfolio model. *Economic Record* 52 (1976): 182–98.

88. Clements, K. W. The trade balance in monetary general equilibrium. Ph.D. dissertation, The University of Chicago, 1977.

89. Clements, K. W. The theory of the firm and multisectoral supply analysis. Report 7818 of the Center for Mathematical Studies in Business and Economics, The University of Chicago, 1978.

90. Clements, K. W., Evans, M., Ironmonger, D. S., and Powell, A. A. A linear expenditure system with adjustment costs. *Economic Record*, forthcoming.

91. Cobb, C. W., and Douglas, P. H. A theory of production. *American Economic Review* 18 (1928): Supplement, 139–65.

92. Cournot, A. *Recherches sur les principes mathématiques de la théorie des richesses.* Paris: L. Hachette, 1838.

93. Court, R. H. Utility maximization and the demand for New Zealand meats. *Econometrica* 35 (1967): 424–46.

94. Cox, D. R. Tests of separate families of hypotheses. In *Proceedings of the fourth Berkeley symposium on mathematical statistics and probability*, ed. J. Neyman, 1: 105–23. Berkeley: University of California Press, 1961.

95. Cox, D. R. Further results on tests of separate families of hypotheses. *Journal of the Royal Statistical Society*, ser. B, 24 (1962): 406–24.

96. Cramer, J. S. Interaction of income and price in consumer demand. *International Economic Review* 14 (1973): 351–63.

97. De Janvry, A., Biery, J., and Nuñez, A. Estimation of demand parameters under consumer budgeting: an application to Argentina. *American Journal of Agricultural Economics* 54 (1972): 422–30.

98. Deaton, A. S. The estimation and testing of systems of demand equations: a note. *European Economic Review* 3 (1972): 399–411.

99. Deaton, A. S. The analysis of consumer demand in the United Kingdom, 1900–1970. *Econometrica* 42 (1974): 341–67.

100. Deaton, A. S. A reconsideration of the empirical implications of additive preferences. *Economic Journal* 84 (1974): 338–48.

101. Deaton, A. S. *Models and projections of demand in post-war Britain.* London: Chapman and Hall, 1975.

102. Deaton, A. S. A simple nonadditive model of demand. In *Private and enlarged consumption*, ed. L. Solari and J.-N. Du Pasquier, pp. 55–72. Amsterdam: North-Holland Publishing Company, 1976.

103. Deaton, A. S. Involuntary saving through unanticipated inflation. *American Economic Review* 67 (1977): 899–910.

104. Deaton, A. S. Specification and testing in applied demand analysis. University of Bristol discussion paper, 1977.

105. Deaton, A. S. The distance function and consumer behaviour with applications to index numbers and optimal taxation. *Review of Economic Studies*, forthcoming.

106. Denny, M. The relationship between functional forms for the production system. *Canadian Journal of Economics* 7 (1974): 21–31.

107. Denny, M., and Fuss, M. The use of approximation analysis to test for separability and the existence of consistent aggregates. *American Economic Review* 67 (1977): 404–18.

108. Desai, M. *Applied econometrics*. New York: McGraw-Hill, 1976.

109. Deschamps, R. Risk aversion and demand functions. *Econometrica* 41 (1973): 455–65.

110. Dhrymes, P. J. On a class of utility and production functions yielding everywhere differentiable demand functions. *Review of Economic Studies* 34 (1967): 399–408.

111. Dickinson, H. D. A note on dynamic economics. *Review of Economic Studies* 22 (1955): 169–79.

112. Diewert, W. E. An application of the Shephard duality theorem: a generalized Leontief production function. *Journal of Political Economy* 79 (1971): 481–507.

113. Diewert, W. E. Functional forms for profit and transformation functions. *Journal of Economic Theory* 6 (1973): 284–316.

114. Diewert, W. E. A note on aggregation and elasticities of substitution. *Canadian Journal of Economics* 7 (1974): 12–20.

115. Diewert, W. E. Functional forms for revenue and factor requirements functions. *International Economic Review* 15 (1974): 119–30.

116. Diewert, W. E. Intertemporal consumer theory and the demand for durables. *Econometrica* 42 (1974): 497–516.

117. Diewert, W. E. Applications of duality theory. In *Frontiers of Quantitative Economics*, vol. 2, ed. M. D. Intriligator and D. A. Kendrick, pp. 106–71. Amsterdam: North-Holland Publishing Company, 1974.

118. Diewert, W. E. Exact and superlative index numbers. *Journal of Econometrics* 4 (1976): 115–45.

119. Diewert, W. E. Superlative index numbers and consistency in aggregation. *Econometrica* 46 (1978): 883–900.

120. Divisia, F. L'indice monétaire et la théorie de la monnaie. *Revue d'Economie Politique* 39 (1925): 980–1008.

121. Dixon, P. B., Vincent, D. P., and Powell, A. A. Factor demand and product supply relations in Australian agriculture: the CRESH/CRETH production system. Working paper of IMPACT project, Melbourne, 1976.

122. Dupuit, J. *De l'utilité et de sa mesure*. Turin: La Riforma Sociale, 1934 (reprint).

123. Eads, G., Nerlove, M., and Raduchel, W. A long-run cost function for the local service airline industry: an experiment in non-linear estimation. *Review of Economics and Statistics* 51 (1969): 258–70.

124. Edgeworth, F. Y. *Mathematical psychics*. London: C. Kegan Paul, 1881.

125. Eichhorn, W., and Voeller, J. *Theory of the price index*. Berlin: Springer-Verlag, 1976.

126. Engel, E. Die Productions- und Consumtionsverhältnisse des Könichreichs Sachsen. *Zeitschrift des Statistischen Büreaus des Königlich Sächsischen Ministeriums des Innern*, 8–9 (1857): 1–54. Reprinted in the *Bulletin de l'Institut International de Statistique*, 9 (1895).

127. Evans, D. The price-quantity covariance and the sensitivity index of the firm. Report 7537 of the Center for Mathematical Studies in Business and Economics, The University of Chicago, 1975.

128. Fane, G. Education and the managerial efficiency of farmers. *Review of Economics and Statistics* 57 (1975): 452–61.

129. Fellner, W. Operational utility: the theoretical background and a measurement. In *Ten economic studies in the tradition of Irving Fisher*, pp. 39–74. New York: John Wiley and Sons, 1967.

130. Ferber, R. Consumer economics, a survey. *Journal of Economic Literature* 11 (1973): 1303–42.

131. Ferguson, C. E. *The neoclassical theory of production and distribution*. Cambridge: Cambridge University Press, 1969.

132. Finizza, A. J. Estimation of demand equations for a subgroup of meat commodities. Ph.D. dissertation, The University of Chicago, 1971.

133. Fisher, F. M., and Shell, K. *The economic theory of price indexes*. New York: Academic Press, 1972.

134. Fisher, I. Mathematical investigations in the theory of value and prices. *Transactions of the Connecticut Academy* 9 (1892): 1–124.

135. Fisher, I. *The making of index numbers*. 3d ed. Boston: Houghton Mifflin Company, 1927.

136. Fisher, I. A statistical method for measuring "marginal utility" and testing the justice of a progressive income tax. In *Economic essays contributed in honor of John Bates Clark*, ed. J. H. Hollander, pp. 157–93. Freeport, N.Y.: Books for Libraries Press, 1967 (first published 1927).

137. Fisk, P. R. Some approximations to an "ideal" index number. *Journal of the Royal Statistical Society*, ser. A, 140 (1977): 217–31.

138. Flinn, C. J. A preference independence transformation involving leisure. Report 7847 of the Center for Mathematical Studies in Business and Economics, The University of Chicago, 1978.

139. Fourgeaud, C., and Nataf, A. Consommation en prix et revenu réels et théorie des choix. *Econometrica* 27 (1959): 329–54.

140. Fox, K. A. *Econometric analysis for public policy*. Ames, Iowa: Iowa State College Press, 1958.

141. Friedman, M. The methodology of positive economics. In *Essays in positive economics*, pp. 3–43. Chicago: University of Chicago Press, 1953.

142. Frisch, R. *New methods of measuring marginal utility*. Tübingen: J. C. B. Mohr, 1932.

143. Frisch, R. Annual survey of general economic theory: the problem of index numbers. *Econometrica* 4 (1936): 1–38.

144. Frisch, R. A complete scheme for computing all direct and cross demand elasticities in a model with many sectors. *Econometrica* 27 (1959): 177–96.

145. Frisch, R. *Theory of production*. Dordrecht: D. Reidel Publishing Company, 1965.

146. Fuss, M. A. The demand for energy in Canadian manufacturing. *Journal of Econometrics* 5 (1977): 89–116.

147. Fuss, M. A., and McFadden, D., eds. *Production economics: a dual approach to theory and applications*. Amsterdam: North-Holland Publishing Company, 1978.

148. Galametsos, T. Further analysis of cross-country comparison of consumer expenditure patterns. *European Economic Review* 4 (1973): 1–20.

149. Geary, P. T., and Morishima, M. Demand and supply under separability. In *Theory of demand, real and monetary*, ed. M. Morishima, pp. 87–147. Oxford: Oxford University Press, 1973.

150. Geary, R. C. A note on "A constant utility index of the cost of living." *Review of Economic Studies* 18 (1950): 65–66.

151. Goldberger, A. S. Directly additive utility and constant marginal budget shares. *Review of Economic Studies* 36 (1969): 251–54.

152. Goldberger, A. S., and Galametsos, T. A cross-country comparison of consumer expenditure patterns. *European Economic Review* 1 (1970): 357–400.

153. Goldman, S. An empirical comparison of alternative functional forms of demand systems. Ph.D. dissertation, The University of Chicago, 1971.

154. Goldman, S. M., and Uzawa, H. A note on separability in demand analysis. *Econometrica*, 32 (1964): 387–98.

155. Gorman, W. M. Community preference fields. *Econometrica* 21 (1953): 63–80.

156. Gorman, W. M. Demand for related goods. Journal paper J3129, Iowa Agricultural Experiment Station, 1956.

157. Gorman, W. M. Demand for fish: an application of factor analysis. Birmingham discussion paper A6, 1959.

158. Gorman, W. M. Separable utility and aggregation. *Econometrica* 27 (1959): 469–81.

159. Gorman, W. M. On a class of preference fields. *Metroeconomica* 13 (1961): 53–56.

160. Gorman, W. M. Conditions for additive separability. *Econometrica* 36 (1968): pp. 605–09.

161. Gorman, W. M. Tricks with utility functions. In *Essays in economic analysis*, ed. M. J. Artis and A. R. Nobay, pp. 211–43. Cambridge: Cambridge University Press, 1976.

162. Gorman, W. M. A possible procedure for analysing quality differentials in the egg market. Discussion paper no. B4 of the London School of Economics and Political Science, 1976.

163. Gossen, H. H. *Entwicklung der Gesetze des menschlichen Verkehrs und der daraus fliessenden Regeln für menschliches Handeln*. 3d ed. (1st ed. 1854). Berlin: R. L. Prager, 1927.

164. Green, H. A. J. *Aggregation in economic analysis.* Princeton: Princeton University Press, 1964.

165. Green, H. A. J. *Consumer theory.* Baltimore: Penguin Books, 1971.

166. Griffin, J. M. Joint production technology: the case of petrochemicals. *Econometrica* 46 (1978): 379–96.

167. Griffin, J. M., and Gregory, P. R. An intercountry translog model of energy substitution responses. *American Economic Review* 66 (1976): 845–57.

168. Griliches, Z., and Ringstad, V. *Economies of scale and the form of the production function.* Amsterdam: North-Holland Publishing Company, 1971.

169. Hall, R. E. The specification of technology with several kinds of output. *Journal of Political Economy* 81 (1973): 878–92.

170. Ham, J. C. A note on the efficient estimation of the linear expenditure system. *Journal of the American Statistical Association* 73 (1978): 208–10.

171. Hanoch, G. CRESH production functions. *Econometrica* 39 (1971): 695–712.

172. Hanoch, G. Production and demand models with direct or indirect implicit additivity. *Econometrica* 43 (1975): 395–419.

173. Hanoch, G. Risk aversion and consumer preferences. *Econometrica* 45 (1977): 413–26.

174. Hanoch, G., and Rothschild, M. Testing the assumptions of production theory: a nonparametric approach. *Journal of Political Economy* 80 (1972): 256–75.

175. Haque, W. Samuelson's self-dual preferences. *Econometrica* 43 (1975): 31–39.

176. Hasenkamp, G. A study of multiple-output production functions: Klein's railroad study revisited. *Journal of Econometrics* 4 (1976): 253–62.

177. Hasenkamp, G. *Specification and estimation of multiple-output production functions.* Berlin: Springer-Verlag, 1976.

178. Hassan, Z. A., and Johnson, S. R. Consumer demand parameters for the U.S.: a comparison of linear expenditure, Rotterdam, and double-log estimates. *Quarterly Review of Economics and Business* 16 (1976): 77–92.

179. Hassan, Z. A., Johnson, S. R. and Finley, R. M. Further evidence on the structure of consumer demand in the U.S.: an application of the separability hypothesis. *Southern Economic Journal* 41 (1974): 244–57.

180. Hickman, B. G., and Lau, L. J. Elasticities of substitution and export demands in a world trade model. *European Economic Review* 4 (1973): 347–80.

181. Hicks, J. R. *Value and capital.* 2d ed. (1st ed. 1939). Oxford: Oxford University Press, 1946.

182. Hicks, J. R. *A revision of demand theory.* Oxford: Oxford University Press, 1956.

183. Hicks, J. R. Direct and indirect additivity. *Econometrica* 37 (1969): 353–54.

184. Hicks, J. R., and Allen, R. G. D. A Reconsideration of the theory of value. *Economica*, n.s., 1 (1934): 52–76, 196–219.

185. Hirota, M., and Kuga, K. On an intrinsic joint production. *International Economic Review* 12 (1971): 87–98.

186. Hirsch, S., and Lev, B. Sales stabilization through export diversification. *Review of Economics and Statistics* 53 (1971): 270–77.

187. Hoa, T. V. Interregional elasticities and aggregation bias: a study of consumer demand in Australia. *Australian Economic Papers* 7 (1968): 206–26.

188. Hoa, T. V. Additive preferences and cost of living indexes: an empirical study of the Australian consumer's welfare. *Economic Record* 45 (1969): 432–40.

189. Hoel, M. A note on the estimation of the elasticity of the marginal utility of consumption. *European Economic Review* 6 (1975): 411–15.

190. Hotelling, H. Edgeworth's taxation paradox and the nature of demand and supply functions. *Journal of Political Economy* 40 (1932): 577–616.

191. Houthakker, H. S. The econometrics of family budgets. *Journal of the Royal Statistical Society*, ser. A, 115 (1952): 1–21.

192. Houthakker, H. S. Compensated changes in quantities and qualities consumed. *Review of Economic Studies* 19 (1953): 155–64.

193. Houthakker, H. S. An international comparison of household expenditure patterns, commemorating the centenary of Engel's Law. *Econometrica* 25 (1957): 532–51.

194. Houthakker, H. S. Additive preferences. *Econometrica* 28 (1960): 244–57; errata, 30 (1962): 633.

195. Houthakker, H. S. New evidence on demand elasticities. *Econometrica* 33 (1965): 277–88.

196. Houthakker, H. S. A note on self-dual preferences. *Econometrica*, 33 (1965): 797–801.

197. Houthakker, H. S., and Taylor, L. D. *Consumer demand in the United States, 1929–1970*. 2d ed. (1st ed. 1966). Cambridge: Harvard University Press, 1970.

198. Howe, H. Development of the extended linear expenditure system from simple saving assumptions. *European Economic Review* 6 (1975): 305–10.

199. Intriligator, M. D. *Econometric models, techniques, and applications*. Englewood Cliffs, N.J.: Prentice-Hall, 1978.

200. Ironmonger, D. S. *New commodities and economic behaviour*. Cambridge: Cambridge University Press, 1972.

201. Jevons, W. S. *The theory of political economy*. 4th ed. (1st ed. 1871). London: Macmillan and Co., 1931.

202. Johansen, L. On the relationships between some systems of demand functions. *Liiketaloudellinen Aikakauskirja* 1 (1969): 30–41.

203. Johansen, L. *Production functions*. Amsterdam: North-Holland Publishing Company, 1972.

204. Johnston, J. *Statistical cost analysis*. New York: McGraw-Hill Book Company, 1960.

205. Jorgenson, D. W., and Griliches, Z. The explanation of productivity change. *Review of Economic Studies* 34 (1967): 249–83.

206. Jorgenson, D. W., and Lau, L. J. The duality of technology and economic behaviour. *Review of Economic Studies* 41 (1974): 181–200.

207. Jorgenson, D. W., and Lau, L. J. The structure of consumer preferences. *Annals of Economic and Social Measurement* 4 (1975): 49–101.

208. Jovanovic, B. Rational random behavior of the firm. Report 7538 of the Center for Mathematical Studies in Business and Economics, The University of Chicago, 1975.

209. Kadane, J. B. Comparison of k-class estimators when the disturbances are small. *Econometrica* 39 (1971): 723–37.

210. Kapteyn, A., and van Praag, B. A new approach to the construction of family equivalence scales. *European Economic Review* 7 (1976): 313–35.

211. Katzner, D. W. *Static demand theory*. London: The Macmillan Company, 1970.

212. Keller, W. J. Savings, leisure, consumption, and taxes. *European Economic Review* 9 (1977): 151–67.

213. Kiefer, N. M. A Bayesian analysis of commodity demand and labor supply. *International Economic Review* 18 (1977): 209–18.

214. Kiefer, N. M., and MacKinnon, J. G. Small sample properties of demand system estimates. In *Studies in nonlinear estimation*, ed. S. M. Goldfeld and R. E. Quandt, pp. 181–210. Cambridge: Ballinger, 1976.

215. Klein, L. R. The use of cross-section data in econometrics with application to a study of production of railroad services in the United States. Mimeographed report of the National Bureau of Economic Research, 1947.

216. Klein, L. R. *A textbook of econometrics*. 2d ed. (1st ed. 1952). Englewood Cliffs, N.J.: Prentice-Hall, 1974.

217. Klein, L. R., and Rubin, H. A constant-utility index of the cost of living. *Review of Economic Studies* 15 (1948): 84–87.

218. Klijn, N. Expenditures, savings and habit formation: a comment. *International Economic Review* 18 (1977): 771–78.

219. Kloek, T. Indexcijfers: enige methodologische aspecten. Ph.D. dissertation, Netherlands School of Economics, 1966.

220. Kloek, T., and Theil, H. International comparisons of prices and quantities consumed. *Econometrica* 33 (1965): 535–56.

221. Kmenta, J. On estimation of the CES production function. *International Economic Review* 8 (1967): 180–89.

222. Konüs, A. A. The problem of the true index of the cost of living. *Econometrica* 7 (1939): 10–29.

223. Koopmans, T. C. Stationary ordinal utility and impatience. *Econometrica* 28 (1960): 287–309.

224. Koopmans, T. C. Representation of preference orderings with independent components of consumption. In *Decision and organization*, ed. C. B. McGuire and R. Radner, pp. 57–78. Amsterdam: North-Holland Publishing Company, 1972.

225. Koopmans, T. C. Representation of preference orderings over time. In *Decision and organization*, ed. C. B. McGuire and R. Radner, pp. 79–100. Amsterdam: North-Holland Publishing Company, 1972.

226. Koopmans, T. C., Diamond, P. A., and Williamson, R. E. Stationary utility and time perspective. *Econometrica* 32 (1964): 82–100.

227. Kuga, K. More about joint production. *International Economic Review* 14 (1973): 196–210.

228. Laitinen, K. Measurement of real income. Report 7846 of the Center for Mathematical Studies in Business and Economics, The University of Chicago, 1978.

229. Laitinen, K., and Theil, H. Supply and demand of the multiproduct firm. *European Economic Review* 11 (1978): 107–54.

230. Lambin, J. J. *Advertising, competition and market conduct in oligopoly over time*. Amsterdam: North-Holland Publishing Company, 1976.

231. Lancaster, K. J. A new approach to consumer theory. *Journal of Political Economy* 74 (1966): 132–57.

232. Lancaster, K. J. *Consumer demand: a new approach*. New York: Columbia University Press, 1971.

233. Lau, L. J. Duality and the structure of utility functions. *Journal of Economic Theory* 1 (1970): 374–96.

234. Lau, L. J. Profit functions of technologies with multiple inputs and outputs. *Review of Economics and Statistics* 54 (1972): 281–89.

235. Lau, L. J. Complete systems of consumer demand functions through duality. In *Frontiers of quantitative economics*, vol. 3A, ed. M. D. Intriligator, pp. 59–85. Amsterdam: North-Holland Publishing Company, 1977.

236. Lee, F. Y. Estimation of dynamic demand relations from a time series of family budget data. *Journal of the American Statistical Association* 65 (1970): 586–97.

237. Leontief, W. W. A note on the interrelation of subsets of independent variables of a continuous function with continuous first derivatives. *Bulletin of the American Mathematical Society* 53 (1947): 343–50.

238. Leontief, W. W. Introduction to a theory of the internal structure of functional relationships. *Econometrica* 15 (1947): 361–73.

239. Leser, C. E. V. Family budget data and price-elasticities of demand. *Review of Economic Studies* 9 (1941): 40–57.

240. Leser, C. E. V. The pattern of Australian demand. *Economic Record* 34 (1958): 212–22.

241. Leser, C. E. V. Demand functions for nine commodity groups in Australia. *Australian Journal of Statistics* 2 (1960): 102–13.

242. Leser, C. E. V. Commodity group expenditure functions for the United Kingdom, 1948–1957. *Econometrica* 29 (1961): 24–32.

243. Leser, C. E. V. Income, household size and price changes, 1953–1973. *Oxford Bulletin of Economics and Statistics* 38 (1976): 1–10.

244. Lev, B. The aggregation problem in financial statements: an informational approach. *Journal of Accounting Research* 6 (1968): 247–61.

245. Lev, B. *Accounting and information theory.* Evanston, Ill.: American Accounting Association, 1969.

246. Lev, B. An information theory analysis of budget variances. *Accounting Review* 44 (1969): 704–10.

247. Lev, B. Testing a prediction method for multivariate budgets. *Empirical research in accounting, selected studies 1969. Journal of Accounting Research* 7 (1969), suppl.: 182–97.

248. Lev, B. The informational approach to aggregation in financial statements: extensions. *Journal of Accounting Research* 8 (1970): 78–94.

249. Lev, B. Financial failure and informational decomposition measures. In *Accounting in perspective: contributions to accounting thought by other disciplines,* ed. R. R. Sterling and W. F. Bentz, pp. 102–11. Cincinnati: Southwestern Publishing Company, 1971.

250. Lev, B. The RAS method for two-dimensional forecasts. *Journal of Marketing Research* 10 (1973): 153–59.

251. Lev, B. Decomposition measures for financial analysis. *Financial Management* 2 (1973): 56–63.

252. Lev, B., and Theil, H. A maximum entropy approach to the choice of asset depreciation. *Journal of Accounting Research* 16 (1978): 286–93.

253. Lloyd, P. J. Substitution effects and biases in nontrue price indices. *American Economic Review* 65 (1975): 301–13.

254. Lluch, C. Consumer demand functions, Spain, 1958–1964. *European Economic Review* 2 (1971): 277–302.

255. Lluch, C. The extended linear expenditure system. *European Economic Review* 4 (1973): 21–32.

256. Lluch, C. Functional form of utility, demand systems, and the aggregate consumption function. *IEEE Transactions on Automatic Control* 18 (1973): 385–87.

257. Lluch, C. Expenditure, savings and habit formation. *International Economic Review* 15 (1974): 786–97.

258. Lluch, C., and Powell, A. A. International comparisons of expenditure patterns. *European Economic Review* 5 (1975): 275–303.

259. Lluch, C., Powell, A. A., and Williams, R. A. *Patterns in household demand and saving.* Oxford: Oxford University Press, 1977.

260. Lluch, C., and Williams, R. A. Consumer demand systems and aggregate consumption in the USA: an application of the extended linear expenditure system. *Canadian Journal of Economics* 8 (1975): 49–66.

261. Lluch, C., and Williams, R. A. Cross country demand and savings patterns: an application of the extended linear expenditure system. *Review of Economics and Statistics* 57 (1975): 320–28.

262. MaCurdy, T. The firm's demand for inputs when these inputs are blockwise dependent. Report 7539 of the Center for Mathematical Studies in Business and Economics, The University of Chicago, 1975.

263. Maks, J. A. H., and Muysken, J. Development and testing of a dynamic demand theory. *De Economist,* 125 (1977): 174–210.

264. Malmquist, S. Index numbers and indifference surfaces. *Trabajos de Estadistica* 4 (1953): 209–42.

265. Marschak, J. Rational behavior, uncertain prospects, and measurable utility. *Econometrica* 18 (1950): 111–41.

266. Marschak, J., and Andrews, W. H., Jr. Random simultaneous equations and the theory of production. *Econometrica* 12 (1944): 143–205.

267. Marshall, A. *Principles of economics.* 4th ed. (1st ed. 1890). London: Macmillan and Co., 1898.

268. Marwah, K. A world model of international trade: forecasting market shares and trade flows. *Empirical Economics* 1 (1976): 1–39.

269. Mattei, A. A complete system of dynamic demand functions. *European Economic Review* 2 (1971): 251–76.

270. McElroy, M. B. Goodness of fit for seemingly unrelated regressions. *Journal of Econometrics* 6 (1977): 381–87.

271. McFadden, D. Constant elasticity of substitution production functions. *Review of Economic Studies* 30 (1963): 73–83.

272. McFadden, D. Quantal choice analysis: a survey. *Annals of Economic and Social Measurement* 5 (1976): 363–90.

273. McFadden, D. Cost, revenue, and profit functions. In *Production economics: a dual approach to theory and applications,* vol. 1, ed. M. Fuss and D. McFadden, pp. 3–109. Amsterdam: North-Holland Publishing Company, 1978.

274. Menger, C. *Grundsätze der Volkswirthschaftslehre.* Vienna: Wilhelm Braumüller, 1871.

275. Morishima, M., ed. *Theory of demand, real and monetary.* Oxford: Oxford University Press, 1973.

276. Muellbauer, J. Household composition, Engel curves and welfare comparisons between households. *European Economic Review* 5 (1974): 103–22.

277. Muellbauer, J. Inequality measures, prices and household composition. *Review of Economic Studies* 41 (1974): 493–504.

278. Muellbauer, J. The cost of living and taste and quality change. *Journal of Economic Theory* 10 (1975): 269–83.

279. Muellbauer, J. Aggregation, income distribution and consumer demand. *Review of Economic Studies* 42 (1975): 525–43.

280. Muellbauer, J. Identification and consumer unit scales. *Econometrica* 43 (1975): 807–09.

281. Muellbauer, J. Economics and the representative consumer. In *Private and enlarged consumption,* ed. L. Solari and J.-N. Du Pasquier, pp. 29–53. Amsterdam: North-Holland Publishing Company, 1976.

282. Muellbauer, J. Community preferences and the representative consumer. *Econometrica* 44 (1976): 979–99.

283. Muellbauer, J. Testing the Barten model of household composition effects and the cost of children. *Economic Journal* 87 (1977): 460–87.

284. Mundlak, Y. Specification and estimation of multiproduct production functions. *Journal of Farm Economics* 45 (1963): 433–43.

285. Mundlak, Y. Transcendental multiproduct production functions. *International Economic Review* 5 (1964): 273–84.

286. Mundlak, Y. Elasticities of substitution and the theory of derived demand. *Review of Economic Studies* 35 (1968): 225–36.

287. Mundlak, Y., and Hoch, I. Consequences of alternative specifications in estimation of Cobb-Douglas production functions. *Econometrica* 33 (1965): 814–28.

288. Mundlak, Y., and Razin, A. Aggregation, index numbers and the measurement of technical change. *Review of Economics and Statistics* 51 (1969): 166–75.

289. Mundlak, Y., and Razin, A. On multistage multiproduct production functions. *American Journal of Agricultural Economics* 53 (1971): 491–99.

290. Nasse, P. Analyse des effets de substitution dans un système complet de fonctions de demande. *Annales de l'Inséé* (Institut National de la Statistique et des Etudes Economiques) 5 (1970): 81–110.

291. Nasse, P. Un système complet de fonctions de demande: les équations de Fourgeaud et Nataf. *Econometrica* 41 (1973): 1137–58.

292. Nerlove, M. *Estimation and identification of Cobb-Douglas production functions.* Amsterdam: North-Holland Publishing Company, 1965.

293. Nerlove, M. Recent empirical studies of the CES and related production functions. In *The theory and empirical analysis of production,* ed. M. Brown, pp. 55–122. New York: National Bureau of Economic Research, 1967.

294. Neumann, J. von, and Morgenstern, O. *Theory of games and economic behavior.* 2d ed. (1st ed. 1944). Princeton: Princeton University Press, 1947.

295. Nicholson, J. L. Appraisal of different methods of estimating equivalence scales and their results. *Review of Income and Wealth* 22 (1976): 1–11.

296. O'Brien, J. M. The covariance measure of substitution: an application to financial assets. *Review of Economics and Statistics* 56 (1974): 456–67.

297. O'Riordan, W. K. An application of the Rotterdam demand system to Irish data. *Economic and Social Review* 6 (1975): 511–29.

298. Owen, J. D. The demand for leisure. *Journal of Political Economy* 79 (1971): 56–76.

299. Pareto, V. *Manuel d'économie politique.* Paris: V. Giard et E. Brière, 1909.

300. Parks, R. W. Systems of demand equations: an empirical comparison of alternative functional forms. *Econometrica* 37 (1969): 629–50.

301. Parks, R. W. Maximum likelihood estimation of the linear expenditure system. *Journal of the American Statistical Association* 66 (1971): 900–03.

302. Parks, R. W. Inflation and relative price variability. *Journal of Political Economy* 86 (1978): 79–95.

303. Parks, R. W., and Barten, A. P. A cross-country comparison of the effects of prices, income and population composition on consumption patterns. *Economic Journal* 83 (1973): 834–52.

304. Paulus, J. D. The estimation of large systems of consumer demand equations using stochastic prior information. Ph.D. dissertation, The University of Chicago, 1972.

305. Paulus, J. D. Mixed estimation of a complete system of consumer demand equations. *Annals of Economic and Social Measurement* 4 (1975): 117–31.

306. Pearce, I. F. An exact method of consumer demand analysis. *Econometrica* 29 (1961): 499–516.

307. Pearce, I. F. *A contribution to demand analysis.* Oxford: Oxford University Press, 1964.

308. Pesaran, M. H. On the general problem of model selection. *Review of Economic Studies* 41 (1974): 153–71.

309. Pesaran, M. H., and Deaton, A. S. Testing non-nested nonlinear regression models. *Econometrica* 46 (1978): 677–94.

310. Pessemier, E. A. Stochastic properties of changing preferences. *American Economic Review* 68 (1978): 380–85.

311. Pfouts, R. W. An axiomatic approach to index numbers. *Review of the International Statistical Institute* 34 (1966): 174–85.

312. Phlips, L. Substitution, complementarity, and the residual variation around dynamic demand equations. *American Economic Review* 61 (1971): 586–97.

313. Phlips, L. A dynamic version of the linear expenditure system. *Review of Economics and Statistics* 54 (1972): 450–58.

314. Phlips, L. *Applied consumption analysis.* Amsterdam: North-Holland Publishing Company, 1974.

315. Phlips, L. Transactions demand for money and consumer behaviour. In *Private and enlarged consumption,* ed. L. Solari and J.-N. Du Pasquier, pp. 15–27. Amsterdam: North-Holland Publishing Company, 1976.

316. Phlips, L., and Rouzier, P. Substitution, complementarity, and the residual variation: some further results. *American Economic Review* 62 (1972): 747–51.

317. Phlips, L., and Sanz-Ferrer, R. A taste-dependent true index of the cost of living. *Review of Economics and Statistics* 57 (1975): 495–501.

318. Poirier, D. J. On the use of Cobb-Douglas splines. *International Economic Review* 16 (1975): 733–44.

319. Pollak, R. A. Additive utility functions and linear Engel curves. *Review of Economic Studies* 38 (1971): 401–14.

320. Pollak, R. A. Conditional demand functions and the implications of separable utility. *Southern Economic Journal* 37 (1971): 423–33.

321. Pollak, R. A. The theory of the cost of living index. Research paper no. 11, Research Division, Office of Prices and Living Conditions, U.S. Bureau of Labor Statistics, 1971.

322. Pollak, R. A. Generalized separability. *Econometrica* 40 (1972): 431–53.

323. Pollak, R. A. Subindexes in the cost of living index. *International Economic Review* 16 (1975): 135–50.

324. Pollak, R. A. The intertemporal cost of living index. *Annals of Economic and Social Measurement* 4 (1975): 179–95.

325. Pollak, R. A. Habit formation and long-run utility functions. *Journal of Economic Theory* 13 (1976): 272–97.

326. Pollak, R. A., and Wales, T. J. Estimation of the linear expenditure system. *Econometrica* 37 (1969): 611–28.

327. Pollak, R. A., and Wales, T. J. Estimation of complete demand systems from household budget data: the linear and quadratic expenditure systems. *American Economic Review* 68 (1978): 348–59.

328. Powell, A. A. A complete system of consumer demand equations for the Australian economy fitted by a model of additive preferences. *Econometrica* 34 (1966): 661–75.

329. Powell, A. A. Aitken estimators as a tool in allocating predetermined aggregates. *Journal of the American Statistical Association* 64 (1969): 913–22.

330. Powell, A. A. Estimation of Lluch's extended linear expenditure system from cross-sectional data. *Australian Journal of Statistics* 15 (1973): 111–17.

331. Powell, A. A. An ELES consumption function for the United States. *Economic Record* 49 (1973): 337–57.

332. Powell, A. A. *Empirical analytics of demand systems*. Lexington, Mass.: D. C. Heath and Company, 1974.

333. Powell, A. A., and Gruen, F. H. G. The constant elasticity of transformation production frontier and linear supply system. *International Economic Review* 9 (1968): 315–28.

334. Powell, A. A., Hoa, T. V., and Wilson, R. H. A multi-sectoral analysis of consumer demand in the post-war period. *Southern Economic Journal* 35 (1968): 109–20.

335. Prais, S. J., and Houthakker, H. S. *The analysis of family budgets*. Cambridge: Cambridge University Press, 1955.

336. Rajaoja, V. *A study in the theory of demand functions and price indexes*. Helsinki: Societas Scientiarum Fennica, 1958.

337. Ray, R. The household Rotterdam model: an application to U.K. consumer demand, 1900–1970. Hull economic research paper no. 28, University of Hull, 1977.

338. Roy, R. *De l'utilité*. Paris: Hermann et Cie, 1942.

339. Russell, R. R. Functional separability and partial elasticities of substitution. *Review of Economic Studies* 42 (1975): 79–85.

340. Salvas-Bronsard, L., Leblanc, D., and Bronsard, C. Estimating demand equations: the converse approach. *European Economic Review* 9 (1977): 301–21.

341. Samuelson, P. A. *Foundations of economic analysis*. Cambridge: Harvard University Press, 1947.

342. Samuelson, P. A. Some implications of "linearity." *Review of Economic Studies* 15 (1948): 88–90.

343. Samuelson, P. A. Using full duality to show that simultaneously additive direct and indirect utilities implies unitary price elasticity of demand. *Econometrica* 33 (1965): 781–96.

344. Samuelson, P. A. The fundamental singularity theorem for non-joint production. *International Economic Review* 7 (1966): 34–41.

345. Samuelson, P. A. Corrected formulation of direct and indirect additivity. *Econometrica* 37 (1969): 355–59.

346. Samuelson, P. A. Complementarity: an essay on the 40th anniversary of the Hicks-Allen revolution in demand theory. *Journal of Economic Literature* 12 (1974): 1255–89.

347. Samuelson, P. A., and Swamy, S. Invariant economic index numbers and canonical duality: survey and synthesis. *American Economic Review* 64 (1974): 566–93.

348. Sato, K. A two-level constant-elasticity-of-substitution production function. *Review of Economic Studies* 34 (1967): 201–18.

349. Sato, K. Additive utility functions with double-log consumer demand functions. *Journal of Political Economy* 80 (1972): 102–24.

350. Sato, K. Ideal index numbers that almost satisfy the factor reversal test. *Review of Economics and Statistics* 56 (1974): 549–52.

351. Sato, K. *Production functions and aggregation.* Amsterdam: North-Holland Publishing Company, 1975.

352. Sato, K. The ideal log-change index number. *Review of Economics and Statistics* 58 (1976): 223–28.

353. Sato, K. The meaning and measurement of the real value added index. *Review of Economics and Statistics* 58 (1976): 434–42.

354. Sato, R. Self-dual preferences. *Econometrica* 44 (1976): 1017–32.

355. Sato, R. Homothetic and non-homothetic CES production functions. *American Economic Review* 67 (1977): 559–69.

356. Sato, R., and Koizumi, T. On the elasticities of substitution and complementarity. *Oxford Economic Papers* 25 (1973): 44–56.

357. Schultz, H. *The theory and measurement of demand.* Chicago: University of Chicago Press, 1938.

358. Shephard, R. W. *Cost and production functions.* Princeton: Princeton University Press, 1953.

359. Shephard, R. W. *Theory of cost and production functions.* Princeton: Princeton University Press, 1970.

360. Simmons, P. A note on budgeting, separability, and generalized separability. *Econometrica* 46 (1978): 455–58.

361. Sims, C. Theoretical basis for a double deflated index of real value added. *Review of Economics and Statistics* 51 (1969): 470–71.

362. Singh, B., and Nagar, A. L. Determination of consumer unit scales. *Econometrica* 41 (1973): 347–55.

363. Slutsky, E. Sulla teoria del bilancio del consumatore. *Giornale degli Economisti* 51 (1915): 1–26; translation, On the theory of the budget of the consumer, chap. 2 of *Readings in price theory*, ed. G. J. Stigler and K. E. Boulding. Chicago: Richard D. Irwin, 1952.

364. Solari, L. *Théorie des choix et fonctions de consommation semi-agrégées.* Geneva: Librairie Droz, 1971.

365. Solari, L., and Du Pasquier, J.-N. eds. *Private and enlarged consumption.* Amsterdam: North-Holland Publishing Company, 1976.

366. Somermeyer, W. H. Een "verdeel"-model. Mimeographed memorandum of the Central Bureau of Statistics (The Hague), 1956.

367. Somermeyer, W. H., Hilhorst, J. G. M., and Wit, J. W. W. A. A method for estimating price and income elasticities from time series and

its application to consumers' expenditures in the Netherlands, 1949–1959. *Statistical Studies* (Central Bureau of Statistics, The Hague) 13 (1962): 30–53.

368. Somermeyer, W. H., and Langhout, A. Shapes of Engel curves and demand curves: implications of the expenditure allocation model, applied to Dutch data. *European Economic Review* 3 (1972): 351–86.

369. Sonnenschein, H. Do Walras' identity and continuity characterize the class of community excess demand functions? *Journal of Economic Theory* 6 (1973): 345–54.

370. Sonnenschein, H. The utility hypothesis and market demand theory. *Western Economic Journal* 11 (1973): 404–10.

371. Sono, M. The effect of price changes on the demand and supply of separable goods. *International Economic Review* 2 (1961): 239–71.

372. Stigler, G. J. The development of utility theory. *Journal of Political Economy* 58 (1950): 307–27, 373–96.

373. Stigler, G. J. The early history of empirical studies of consumer behavior. *Journal of Political Economy* 62 (1954): 95–113.

374. Stigler, G. J. The economics of information. *Journal of Political Economy* 69 (1961): 213–25.

375. Stone, R. *The measurement of consumers' expenditure and behaviour in the United Kingdom, 1920–1938.* Vol. 1. Cambridge: Cambridge University Press, 1954.

376. Stone, R. Linear expenditure systems and demand analysis: an application to the pattern of British demand. *Economic Journal* 64 (1954): 511–27.

377. Stone, R., Brown, A., and Rowe, D. A. Demand analysis and projections for Britain: 1900–1970. In *Europe's future consumption*, ed. J. Sandee, pp. 200–25. Amsterdam: North-Holland Publishing Company, 1964.

378. Strotz, R. H. The empirical implications of a utility tree. *Econometrica* 25 (1957): 269–80.

379. Strotz, R. H. The utility tree—a correction and further appraisal. *Econometrica* 27 (1959): 482–88.

380. Taylor, L. D., and Weiserbs, D. On the estimation of dynamic demand functions. *Review of Economics and Statistics* 54 (1972): 459–65.

381. Theil, H. Qualities, prices and budget enquiries. *Review of Economic Studies* 19 (1953): 129–47.

382. Theil, H. On the use of incomplete prior information in regression analysis. *Journal of the American Statistical Association* 58 (1963): 401–14.

383. Theil, H. The information approach to demand analysis. *Econometrica* 33 (1965): 67–87.

384. Theil, H. *Economics and information theory.* Amsterdam: North-Holland Publishing Company, 1967.

385. Theil, H. On the geometry and the numerical approximation of cost of living and real income indices. *De Economist* 116 (1968): 677–89.

386. Theil, H. Value share transitions in consumer demand theory. *Econometrica* 38 (1970): 118–27.

387. Theil, H. *Principles of econometrics.* New York: John Wiley and Sons, 1971.

388. Theil, H. An economic theory of the second moments of disturbances of behavioral equations. *American Economic Review* 61 (1971): 190–94.

389. Theil, H. *Statistical decomposition analysis with applications in the social and administrative sciences.* Amsterdam: North-Holland Publishing Company, 1972.

390. Theil, H. Some recent developments in consumer demand analysis. In *Economic structure and development: essays in honour of Jan Tinbergen,* ed. H. C. Bos, H. Linnemann, and P. de Wolff, pp. 41–73. Amsterdam: North-Holland Publishing Company, 1973.

391. Theil, H. Measuring the quality of the consumer's basket. *De Economist* 121 (1973): 333–46.

392. Theil, H. A new index number formula. *Review of Economics and Statistics* 55 (1973): 498–502.

393. Theil, H. Mixed estimation based on quasi-prior judgments. *European Economic Review* 5 (1974): 33–40.

394. Theil, H. A theory of rational random behavior. *Journal of the American Statistical Association* 69 (1974): 310–14.

395. Theil, H. More on log-change index numbers. *Review of Economics and Statistics* 56 (1974): 552–54.

396. Theil, H. The theory of rational random behavior and its application to demand analysis. *European Economic Review* 6 (1975): 217–26.

397. Theil, H. *Theory and measurement of consumer demand.* 2 vols. Amsterdam: North-Holland Publishing Company, 1975–1976.

398. Theil, H. The independent inputs of production. *Econometrica* 45 (1977): 1303–27.

399. Theil, H. *Introduction to econometrics.* Englewood Cliffs, N.J.: Prentice-Hall, 1978.

400. Theil, H., and Brooks, R. B. How does the marginal utility of income change when real income changes? *European Economic Review* 2 (1970–71): 218–40.

401. Theil, H., and Gabrielsen, A. A critique of the translog consumption model. Report 7635 of the Center for Mathematical Studies in Business and Economics, The University of Chicago, 1976.

402. Theil, H., and Goldberger, A. S. On pure and mixed statistical estimation in economics. *International Economic Review* 2 (1961): 65–78.

403. Theil, H., and Laitinen, K. A parametrization of the multiproduct firm. Report 7803 of the Center for Mathematical Studies in Business and Economics, The University of Chicago, 1978.

404. Theil, H., and Laitinen, K. Singular moment matrices in applied econometrics. In *Multivariate Analysis-V,* ed. P. R. Krishnaiah. Amsterdam: North-Holland Publishing Company, forthcoming.

405. Theil, H., and Laitinen, K. The independence transformation: a review and some further explorations. In *Essays in the Theory and Measurement of Consumer Behaviour,* ed. A. S. Deaton. Cambridge: Cambridge University Press, forthcoming.

406. Theil, H., and Mnookin, R. H. The information value of demand equations and predictions. *Journal of Political Economy* 74 (1966): 34–45.

407. Theil, H., and Neudecker, H. Substitution, complementarity, and the residual variation around Engel curves. *Review of Economic Studies* 25 (1957): 114–23.

408. Theil, H., and Stambaugh, R. Input independence with respect to a function of output. Report 7541 of the Center for Mathematical Studies in Business and Economics, The University of Chicago, 1975.

409. Theil, H., and Tilanus, C. B. The demand for production factors and the price sensitivity of input-output predictions. *International Economic Review* 5 (1964): 258–72.

410. Tintner, G. The maximization of utility over time. *Econometrica* 6 (1938): 154–58.

411. Tintner, G. The theoretical derivation of dynamic demand curves. *Econometrica* 6 (1938): 375–80.

412. Törnqvist, L. The Bank of Finland's consumption price index. *Bank of Finland Monthly Bulletin* 10 (1936): 27–34.

413. Tribus, M. *Rational descriptions, decisions and design.* New York: Pergamon Press, 1969.

414. Triplett, J. E. The measurement of inflation: a survey of research on the accuracy of price indexes. In *Analysis of inflation*, ed. P. H. Earl, pp. 19–82. Lexington, Mass.: D. C. Heath and Company, 1975.

415. Uebe, G. *Produktionstheorie.* Berlin: Springer-Verlag, 1976.

416. Usher, D. The suitability of the Divisia index for the measurement of economic aggregates. *Review of Income and Wealth* 20 (1974): 273–88.

417. Uzawa, H. Production functions with constant elasticities of substitution. *Review of Economic Studies* 29 (1962): 291–99.

418. Uzawa, H. Duality principles in the theory of cost and production. *International Economic Review* 5 (1964): 216–20.

419. Van Praag, B. *Individual welfare functions and consumer behavior.* Amsterdam: North-Holland Publishing Company, 1968.

420. Van Praag, B. The welfare function of income in Belgium: an empirical investigation. *European Economic Review* 2 (1971): 337–69.

421. Vartia, Y. O. Ideal log-change index numbers. *Scandinavian Journal of Statistics* 3 (1976): 121–26.

422. Verma, V. K. The degree of production interaction among the inputs of a firm. Report 7540 of the Center for Mathematical Studies in Business and Economics, The University of Chicago, 1975.

423. Vincent, D. B., Dixon, P. B., and Powell, A. A. Estimates of the CRETH supply system in Australian agriculture. Working paper of IMPACT project, Melbourne, 1977.

424. Wales, T. J. A generalized linear expenditure model of the demand for non-durable goods in Canada. *Canadian Journal of Economics* 4 (1971): 471–84.

425. Wales, T. J. On the flexibility of flexible functional forms. *Journal of Econometrics* 5 (1977): 183–93.

426. Walras, L. *Eléments d'économie politique pure.* 3d ed. Lausanne: F. Rouge, 1896.

427. Walsh, C. M. *The measurement of general exchange-value.* New York: The Macmillan Company, 1901.

428. Walters, A. A. Production and cost functions: an econometric survey. *Econometrica* 31 (1963): 1–66.

429. Weiss, R. D. Elasticities of substitution among capital and occupations in U.S. manufacturing. *Journal of the American Statistical Association* 72 (1977): 764–71.

430. Wold, H. A synthesis of pure demand analysis. *Skandinavisk Aktuarietidskrift* 26 (1943): 85–118, 220–63; 27 (1944): 69–120.

431. Wold, H., in association with L. Juréen. *Demand analysis.* New York: John Wiley and Sons, 1953.

432. Yoshihara, K. Demand functions: an application to the Japanese expenditure pattern. *Econometrica* 37 (1969): 257–74.

433. Yoshihara, K. The application of alternative demand models to the Japanese expenditure pattern. In *Econometric Studies of Japan*, ed. R. Kosobud and R. Minami, pp. 3–48. Urbana, Ill.: University of Illinois Press, 1977.

Index

Addilog indirect utility function, 27–28, 87, 172–75

Aggregation: over consumers, 176–78; over goods (*see* Block independent preferences; composite demand equation for a group of goods; Blockwise dependent preferences; composite demand equation for a group of goods)

Allocation model: in consumption theory, 13 n, 18, 35, 89, 104; general, 5–6, 153; measure of fit, 170; in production theory, 35, 90, 93 n. *See also* Input allocation decision; Output allocation decision

Almost additive preferences, 109

Antonelli matrix, 185

Barten's matrix equation: in consumption theory, 15, 205–6; extension to production theory, 33, 44, 211–13

Bayesian inference, comparison with rational random behavior, 76, 85 n

Block independent inputs, 37, 106–8

Block independent outputs, 108–9

Block independent preferences, 12 n, 18–19, 58, 98–100; composite demand equation for a group of goods, 100. *See also* Blockwise dependent preferences

Block-recursive decision system, 93, 104

Blockwise dependent inputs, 106–8

Blockwise dependent outputs, 109

Blockwise dependent preferences, 12 n, 100–106; composite demand equation for a group of goods, 101–2; conditional demand equation, 103–6

Budget constraint, 1, 8

Budget share, 10; of a group of goods, 99

Cardinal utility. *See* Ordinal utility

CES production function, 30; homothetic property, 37, 130–32; input independence transformation, 119–20, 130–32; normalized price coefficients, 37; self-dual property, 31; two-level CES function, 107

Cobb-Douglas production function, 29–30; generalizations, 204; input independent form, 36; self-dual property, 31

Complements in Hicks's sense. *See* Substitutes in Hicks's sense

Composite demand equation: for a group of consumer goods, 100–102; for a group of inputs, 106–8

Composition matrix. *See* Input independence transformation; Output independence transformation; Preference independence transformation

Conditional budget share, 166